4. Palace of the Cancelleria.
5. Church of Spirito Santo dei Napoletani.
6. Church of San Girolamo della Carità.
7. Church of Santa Maria dell'Orazione e Morte.

A History of the Oratorio

A History of the Oratorio

VOLUME I

THE ORATORIO IN THE BAROQUE ERA

Italy   Vienna   Paris

---

by Howard E. Smither

THE UNIVERSITY OF NORTH CAROLINA PRESS · CHAPEL HILL

Music Examples by Helen Jenner

Copyright © 1977 by
The University of North Carolina Press
All rights reserved
Manufactured in the United States of America
ISBN 0–8078–1274–9
Library of Congress Catalog Card Number 76–43980

Library of Congress Cataloging in Publication Data

Smither, Howard E
  A history of the oratorio.

  Bibliography: v.1, p.
  CONTENTS: *v. 1. The oratorio in the baroque era:*
Italy, Vienna, Paris.
  1. Oratorio—History and criticism.   I. Title.
ML 3201.S6   782.8' 2'09   76–43980
ISBN 0–8078–1274–9

To my father
and the memory of
my mother

✎ Contents

❦Illustrations

§♪Music Examples

Examples covered by copyright are printed with the permission of
the publishers cited below and with modifications as indicated:

⧉ *Preface*

Sixty-five years have passed since Arnold Schering published his *Geschichte des Oratoriums* (Leipzig, 1911), a book that has served several generations as the "standard work" on the history of the oratorio and that has been reprinted as recently as 1966. Although Schering's is the most detailed and extensive history of the oratorio published heretofore, contributions to the history of the genre by three of his contemporaries shortly preceded it: Guido Pasquetti's *L'oratorio musicale in Italia* (Florence, 1906), José Rafael Carreras y Bulbena's *El oratorio musical desde su origin hasta nuestros días* (Barcelona, 1906), and Domenico Alaleona's *Studi su la storia dell'oratorio musicale in Italia* (Turin, 1908; reprinted as *Storia dell'oratorio musicale in Italia*, Milan, 1945). Only the second of these three deals with the oratorio in general; the other two are restricted to Italy. Since the publication of Schering's work, no history of the oratorio comparable to it in scope and treatment has appeared. Research in this field has continued, however, and has resulted in the appearance of significant books, articles, and doctoral dissertations on the oratorios of individual composers or on particular works.[1] Two books that are especially noteworthy examples are Winton Dean's *Handel's Dramatic Oratorios and Masques* (London, 1959) and Ursula Kirkendale's *Antonio Caldara: Sein Leben und seine venezianisch-römischen Oratorien* (Graz, 1966). Many modern editions of oratorios previously available only in their early manuscript sources have also been published. Thus, as valuable as Schering's work was in its time, it has been made obsolete by new contributions to the history of oratorio as well as by changing views of the history of music in general.

The Oratorio in the Baroque Era: Italy, Vienna, Paris con-

---

1. For a bibliographical summary of research since 1945 on the Baroque oratorio, see Smither, "Report."

stitutes the first volume of a planned three-volume *History of the Oratorio*, the purpose of which is to report on the present state of knowledge in this field. Volume 1 treats the oratorio in the Baroque era in Italy and in two centers outside Italy—Vienna and Paris—where the genre was essentially an Italian importation. Volume 2 will discuss the oratorio in the Baroque era in Protestant Germany and England, and volume 3 will follow the history of the oratorio from the Baroque era to the present. For this first volume, I have synthesized and summarized information in secondary sources and have verified these sources whenever possible by reference to the music or documents treated. Further, in areas where no secondary sources exist or where such sources prove inadequate, I have investigated primary sources in manuscript and printed form—music, librettos, and documents about the history of the oratorio—in an effort to contribute to our knowledge of these areas. The number of primary sources in this field is vast, and many lacunae remain in our understanding of the history of the Baroque oratorio; they will remain until additional specialized research is undertaken to fill them. If the present volume succeeds in stimulating research in the history of the oratorio, it will have performed one of its most important functions. The bibliographical material in the volume, while not exhaustive, is intended to be full enough to provide a point of departure for further research projects in a variety of areas related to the genre. Although this book is intended for the student of music—I have assumed that the reader will have at the very least a basic knowledge of music history and theory—I hope that the student of cultural history with little technical knowledge of music will find parts of the book useful for his purpose.

This volume is necessarily selective. The oratorios by composers and librettists who at present seem to be the most significant ones are either treated at some length or at least mentioned, and many minor figures are mentioned as well. No attempt has been made, however, to offer complete statistics—such as lists of composers' oratorios, of composers working in a given area at a given time, or of oratorio performances; such statistics fall within the province of more specialized studies. The selection of music treated has been made on the basis of previous research in the field, historical significance, inherent musical significance, usefulness in showing the principal tendencies of the Baroque oratorio, and—in some instances—the importance of the music in today's performing repertoire. Also affecting the selection of composers and works for the first two volumes of this study is the waning of the Baroque era at different times in different geographical areas. For instance, volume 2 will close with the English oratorios of Handel, which extend to the mid-eighteenth century, but volume 1 will consider oratorios from the second decade of that century as the latest oratorios of the Italian Baroque. So many oratorios that were composed after that decade by Italian or Italian-trained composers are imbued with strongly pre-Classical tendencies that it has seemed appropriate to reserve the major treatment of the Italian oratorio from about 1720 on for the projected third volume of this history.

It is a pleasure to acknowledge the generous help given me by many persons during the writing of this volume. Many of them are mentioned in the body of the book for their specific contributions, but here I should like to call attention collectively to those and others who have helped. For their valued advice and encouragement I am grateful to my former teacher Donald Jay Grout and to my colleagues in the Music Department at the University of North Carolina at Chapel Hill—particularly to Calvin Bower, William S. Newman, James W. Pruett, and Thomas Warburton. Among those who have contributed by sharing the results of their unpublished research, by providing me with photographic copies of source material, by reading portions of the manuscript and offering useful criticism, or by assisting me in various aspects of my research are Louis E. Auld of Duke University; David Burrows of New York University; Beekman C. Cannon of Yale University; Albert Cohen of Stanford University; Carolyn Gianturco of the University of Pisa; Michael Grace of Colorado College; Julia Ann Griffin of the University of Kentucky; John Hill of the University of Pennsylvania; H. Wiley Hitchcock of Brooklyn College, City University of New York; James Igoe of Chapel Hill; Warren Kirkendale of Duke University; Eleanor McCrickard of the University of North Carolina at Greensboro; Margaret Murata of the University of California at Irvine; Paolo Pancino of Venice; William F. Prizer of the University of Kentucky; the late Gloria Rose; Rudolf Schnitzler of Queen's University, Kingston, Ontario; Kerala Snyder of Yale University; Mary Vinquist of West Chester State College and Chapel Hill; Mark

Weil of Washington University, St. Louis; and Wolfgang Witzen-mann of Rome.

To the graduate assistants who helped me during the late stages of the manuscript preparation, Martha Freitag, Frank Glass, and Mary Kolb, I owe a debt of gratitude for their patient work with bibliography, typing, and proofreading. To my graduate students over the past several years, particularly those in my courses in the history of the oratorio, I wish to express my thanks for participating in lively discussions on many points in this book and for being responsible for my introducing a number of revisions. And to Helen Jenner of Chapel Hill, I am indebted for the autography of the music examples. Staff members at virtually every one of the libraries included below in the list of library abbreviations have helped me either in person or by correspondence; I am deeply indebted to them. I especially wish to express my appreciation to the following persons, however, for their particularly extensive and cordial help in making library and archival materials available to me: Kathryn Logan, James W. Pruett, and the other members of the staff of the Music Library of the University of North Carolina at Chapel Hill; Claudio Sartori of the Ufficio Ricerca Fonti Musicali in Milan; Sergio Paganelli of the Civico Museo Bibliografico Musicale in Bologna; Friedrich Lippmann and Wolfgang Witzenmann of the Musikgeschichtliche Abteilung des Deutschen Historischen Instituts in Rome; Emilia Zanetti of the Biblioteca Musicale "S. Cecilia" in Rome; the Reverend Carlo Gasbarri, Argia Bertini, and Giovanni Incisa della Rocchetta of the Archivio dell'Oratorio (Chiesa Nuova) in Rome. For their sacrifices for this book I owe a special debt of thanks to Doris, Ann, and Tom.

Although my decision to write this book dates from 1970, much of the research for parts 1 and 2 of this volume date from 1965–66, a year that I spent in Rome and for which I gratefully acknowledge the assistance of a Fulbright Senior Research Grant. I am also indebted to the National Endowment for the Humanities for a Senior Fellowship that allowed me to spend the year 1972–73 in Rome for research and writing. For several other grants that provided free time for travel, research, and writing or that defrayed some of the other costs associated with the book, I acknowledge the generosity of the University Research Council of the University of North Carolina at Chapel Hill and the Cooperative Program in the Humanities of that institution and Duke University. A portion of the cost of publication was defrayed by a grant from The Andrew W. Mellon Foundation.

In the text of this volume, references to biblical passages follow the Vulgate, and translations follow the Douay Version. Except in quotations from the Vulgate, which follow modern Vulgate style, the original spelling of quoted titles and texts of musical compositions is retained, but punctuation and capitalization are edited. Spellings of personal names have been standardized. The names of composers usually conform to the usage in *MGG*; an exception is the name George Frideric Handel, which conforms to an English spelling used by the composer.

In the music examples all editorial accidentals are placed either in square brackets or over the note affected; all other added material—such as editorial time signatures, names of personages, and corrections of the original—are placed in square brackets. The bar lines in the music examples of chapter 2 are editorial; all other bar lines follow the source of the example. (N.B.: In the primary sources for most of the examples of chapter 3, the bar lines appear only in the basso continuo part and sometimes at irregular intervals.) The names of personages and a few explanatory words that are in Latin, Italian, or French in the sources are translated into English without comment. In designating sources for music examples, if the primary source and a modern edition are both cited, I have relied on the primary source and have provided the page numbers in the modern edition for the reader's convenience. Thus, the music example may not correspond exactly with the modern edition cited.

Chapel Hill, N.C.　　　　　　　　　　HOWARD E. SMITHER
August 1976

❧Abbreviations

Libraries

A/Wn	Austria/Vienna, Österreichische Nationalbibliothek, Musiksammlung
D-brd/	West Germany: Bundesrepublik Deutschland/
Hs	Hamburg, Staats- und Universitätsbibliothek, Musikabteilung
MÜs	Münster, Santini-Bibliothek
Rp	Regensburg, Proskesche Musikbibliothek
D-ddr/Bds	East Germany: Deutsche Demokratische Republik/ Berlin, Staatsbibliothek, Musikabteilung
F/	France
LY	Lyon, Bibliothèque municipale
Pn	Paris, Bibliothèque nationale
V	Versailles, Bibliothèque municipale
GB/	Great Britain
Lbm	London, British Museum
Lcm	_____, Royal College of Music
I/	Italy
Bc	Bologna, Civico Museo Bibliografico Musicale
Bu	_____, Biblioteca universitaria
Fas	Florence, Archivio di Stato
Fn	_____, Biblioteca nazionale centrale
Fo	_____, Archivo della Congregazione dell'Oratorio
Fr	_____, Biblioteca Riccardiana
Ls	Lucca, Biblioteca del Seminario

MOe	Modena, Biblioteca Estense
Nf	Naples, Archivio musicale della Communità Oratoriana dei Padri Filippini (Girolamini)
Rc	Rome, Biblioteca Casanatense
Rf	_____, Archivio della Congregazione dell'Oratorio dei Padri Filippini
Rli	_____, Biblioteca dell'Accademia nazionale dei Lincei e Corsiniana
Rn	_____, Biblioteca nazionale centrale "Vittorio Emanuele II°"
Rsc	_____, Biblioteca musicale governativa del Conservatorio di Santa Cecilia
Rv	_____, Biblioteca Vallicelliana
Rvat	_____, Biblioteca Apostolica Vaticana
Tn	Turin, Biblioteca nazionale universitaria
Vas	Venice, Archivio di Stato
Vnm	_____, Biblioteca nazionale Marciana
Vsmc	_____, Archivio di S. Maria della Consolazione detta "della Fava"

PL/WRu	Poland, Wroclaw (Breslau), Biblioteka Uniwersytecka
S/Uu	Sweden/Uppsala, Universitetsbiblioteket
US/	United States/
NYp	New York, New York Public Library
Wc	Washington, D.C., Library of Congress

Other Abbreviations

(For bibliographical abbreviations, see the Bibliography.)

A*	alto
Apoc.	Apocalypse
B*	bass
b. c.	basso continuo
C	cantus
Cant.	Canticle of Canticles
Dan.	Daniel
Ecclus.	Ecclesiasticus

Eph.	Ephesians
Exod.	Exodus
Gen.	Genesis
Hag.	Haggai
Isa.	Isaiah, Isaias
Jer.	Jeremiah, Jeremias
Jon.	Jonah, Jonas
Judg.	Judges
Mal.	Malachi
Matt.	Matthew
m(m)	measure(s)
MS(S)	manuscripts(s)
Ms	mezzo soprano
Ps. (Pss.)	Psalm, (Psalms)
S*	soprano
Sam.	Samuel
T*	tenor
Tob.	Tobit, Tobias
trans.	translated, translation, translator
Wisd.	Wisdom

Note: With reference to the above designations of voices that are marked by asterisks, when two or more voices sing together, as in an ensemble, this is indicated by an absence of spacing or punctuation. (For example, SS indicates a duet for two sopranos, and SATB could indicate either a quartet or a four-part chorus, depending on context.)

A History of the Oratorio

CHAPTER I *Introduction*

ʒ❧This chapter introduces in broad and general terms some basic concepts about the oratorio and its history in various subperiods of the Baroque era and in various geographical areas. These concepts—relating to the genre's terminology, social context, antecedents and related genres, and libretto and music—are treated in greater detail in the subsequent chapters of this volume and in volume 2.

Terminology

What is an oratorio? Is it simply any work that is called an oratorio by its composer? Or can a composition be reasonably classified as an oratorio even though the composer has given it some other designation—such as spiritual madrigal, motet, dialogue, cantata, *historia, actus musicus, dramma sacro, componimento sacro,* or *azione sacra*? If this last question be answered in the affirmative, what criteria should be used for selecting the works to be classified as oratorios?

In the present study the general approach to answering the kinds of questions raised above is to accept the Baroque period's concepts of the musical genre called oratorio. These concepts are derived from Baroque writings about music and from a study of the compositions called oratorios in their primary sources. The concepts differ from one subperiod of the Baroque to another, and to some extent from one geographical area to another, but they tend to have certain basic elements in common: the oratorio is nearly always a sacred, unstaged work with a text that is either dramatic or narrative-dramatic. In the dramatic type of text, the plot unfolds entirely through dialogue among the personages; in the narrative-dramatic type the plot is revealed partially by a narrator (designated variously as the *Testo*, *Historicus*, or Evangelist) and partially through dramatic dialogue. In this study, compositions that conform to an approximately contemporary concept of the genre called oratorio are treated as oratorios, regardless of the designations in their primary sources. The following paragraphs illustrate this principle by briefly discussing the basis for certain terminological distinctions that are made in later chapters of this volume and in volume 2.

By the 1660s in Italy, the word *oratorio* had become firmly established as a term for a musical genre. From then to about the 1680s, the word was applied with considerable consistency to a musical setting of a sacred, narrative-dramatic text based on a biblical story, a saint's life, or some other spiritual subject; the text is usually in Italian but may be in Latin; written in poetry throughout, the text is stylistically similar to that of an opera. The oratorio is normally in two large structural parts, although some oratorios are in one part and others, in three. The musical style of an oratorio in Italy of this period is essentially the same as that of an opera in the same time and place, and the duration of an oratorio ranges from about one to two hours. The oratorio functioned as an edifying entertainment performed in an oratory (or prayer hall, the Italian term for which is *oratorio*) or in a private palace but rarely in a church. Although the word *oratorio* was indeed a firmly established term for the genre just described, it was by no means the only one used for it. In Italy of this period, the terms applied to this genre include *cantata*, *dialogus*, *dialogo*, *dramma sacro*, *drama tragicum*, and *componimento sacro*. Provided they conform to the concept of the oratorio just described, works from this period designated by these or any other terms are treated as oratorios in this study.

In mid-seventeenth-century Italy, from approximately 1640 through the 1650s, the problems of oratorio terminology are more complex. In this period the oratorio as a musical genre appears not to have been widely recognized. Only in Rome does the word *oratorio* seem to have been used in relation to musical compositions, and its use was less consistent than it became later in the century. Although the word certainly meant that the work it designated was intended for performance in an oratory, it may also have been used to identify a genre. The earliest documented use of *oratorio* to identify a musical composition is found in a letter written in 1640 by the Roman musical amateur Pietro Della Valle in which he calls one of his brief, unstaged, sacred dialogues an oratorio (see below, p. 174). This work, with a narrative-dramatic text, was intended for the Roman oratory of the Chiesa Nuova (the church of Santa Maria in Vallicella); it is labeled *dialogo* in its manuscript source, and its duration is about twelve minutes. A survey of all known musical compositions that are designated *oratorio* in sources of Italian provenance from the mid-century[1] shows that all could be termed dialogues in a broad musical sense, since they feature varying successions of solo passages, ensembles, and choruses. All the works labeled *oratorio* are unstaged, and their musical styles are similar to those of operas and secular cantatas in the period. Yet these dialogues may be classified by their texts into two groups: (1) those with dramatic or narrative-dramatic texts and thus with dialogue among personages and (2) those with essentially reflective texts without personages. The works in group 1 are much like oratorios dating from the 1660s on, but they tend to be much shorter: those in one structural part range from about eight to twenty-six minutes, and those in two parts range from about seventeen to sixty-four minutes. Since the term *oratorio* was inconsistently used in the mid-century period, one cannot be certain whether the works in group 1 were designated *oratorio* because they were recognized as a genre or only because they were intended to be performed in an oratory. Nevertheless, in most respects they are so much like examples of the genre known as oratorio from the 1660s on—they differ from the later works mainly in their brevity and earlier musical language—that it would seem reasonable to classify these works, too, as examples of the same genre. Therefore, any works of the mid-century that are like those of group 1, even though not labeled *oratorio* in their sources, are treated as oratorios in this study. Among the works to which this generalization applies are the Latin dramatic works of Carissimi—including his *Jephte*, a landmark in the history of the oratorio yet one not known to have been called an oratorio in its time.

1. For reports on this survey, see Smither, "Carissimi," and Smither, "Oratorio."

With regard to the works in group 2, the same kind of uncertainty exists: were they called oratorios because they were considered to have the characteristics of a distinct musical genre, or were they so called because of their intended function in an oratory? The latter reason seems the more probable, since their reflective texts make them quite unlike the oratorio in its next stage of development in the same geographical area. If it be true, however, that mid-century Romans did indeed consider the reflective oratorio as a genre, one existing side by side with the dramatic and narrative-dramatic oratorio, then it would seem that one criterion for distinguishing a reflective oratorio from other reflective, spiritual, dialogue cantatas or reflective dialogue motets would be the intended function of the work. Therefore, if a reflective sacred work of the mid-century were not designated *oratorio* in its source, one would need to know that it was intended for an oratory in order to identify it as an oratorio.

The term *oratorio* may or may not have been used before 1640 to designate a musical composition—if it was, there is no known documentation to that effect. Nevertheless, there are compositions from earlier in the century that were unstaged dramatic dialogues of the type described above as examples of group 1, that were performed in oratories, and that would seem to be accurately described as oratorios in the sense of a distinct dramatic or narrative-dramatic genre. Of special importance among these works are some of the compositions in Giovanni Francesco Anerio's *Teatro armonico spirituale di madrigali* ("Harmonic Spiritual Theater of Madrigals," Rome, 1619), composed specifically for use in oratories. The works in this book are spiritual madrigals, as one knows from the book's title page; a number of them also bear the heading *dialogo*, for they utilize dialogue procedures in both text and music; and some of the dialogues are clearly oratorios and are treated as such in this study, despite the absence of that term in their sources. Emilio de' Cavalieri's *Rappresentatione di Anima et di Corpo* ("Representation of the Body and the Soul," Rome, 1600), a staged work that has occasionally been called an oratorio by modern historians, is not considered in this study to be an oratorio. The work plays a role in the history of the oratorio because it was performed in a Roman oratory and because it no doubt exerted an influence on other works performed in oratories; yet as a staged work it is closer to opera than to oratorio. The latter, as mentioned above, is essentially an unstaged genre through-out the Baroque era.

The principal question of terminology concerning sacred dra-matic music of seventeenth-century France is that of the classifica-tion of such music composed in Paris by Marc-Antoine Charpentier. He labeled none of his sacred dramatic works with the term *oratorio*—a term that is not known to have been used at all in seventeenth-century France—but rather he called them *historia, motet, canticum, dialogus,* and *méditation.* Nevertheless, some of his works designated by these terms are closely modeled on the Latin oratorios of Carissimi, with whom Charpentier studied in Rome. Since it is clear that these works by Charpentier follow an Italian oratorio tradition and since they are obviously analogous to the oratorio in Italy, they are classified in this study as oratorios. Thus in their texts and music Charpentier's sacred dramatic works are to sacred music in seventeenth-century France what the oratorio is to sacred music in seventeenth-century Italy. The analogy does not, however, include the function of the Charpentier works: there were no oratories in Paris, and some of these sacred dramatic works by Charpentier functioned as motets sung during Mass.

In Protestant Germany the term *oratorio,* or *Oratorium* (the Latin equivalent that the Germans adopted), was virtually never used to designate a composition with a German text until the first decade of the eighteenth century. Indeed, the only known seven-teenth-century use of *Oratorium* for a piece with a German text occurs in a late seventeenth-century Dresden chronicle; there the term refers to a lost composition by Nicolaus Adam Strungk on the subject of the Resurrection—it was performed in Dresden in 1686 and 1690.[2] In the virtual absence of works called oratorios in seventeenth-century Protestant Germany, there arises the ques-tion of whether any works from that time and place might be called oratorios today. To be sure, some compositions by Heinrich Schütz have often been so called; the best known of them are his Easter and Christmas "oratorios." Since both of these have some similarities to the oratorio as the Italians conceived of it in Schütz's time, they are discussed in volume 2 of the present study. Never-theless, these works differ from the oratorio in certain prominent features—most notably in the strict quotation of a biblical story,

2. Cf. Steude, "Markuspassion," pp. 102–3.

which constitutes the text of each work. No compositions known to have been called oratorios in Schütz's time have texts drawn entirely from the Bible, as these two works have; but compositions called *historiae*, composed in Protestant Germany from the time of Luther until well into the eighteenth century, do indeed have such texts. Unlike composers in France, who used the term *historia* in a rather general way for any sacred, dramatic, or narrative-dramatic work, those in Lutheran Germany used it for a clearly defined genre. Schütz called these two works *historiae*, and in them he followed the tradition of the Lutheran *historia*, not that of the oratorio. Therefore to use the term *oratorio* rather than *historia* for Schütz's works can lead to a misunderstanding of the meanings of both terms. In this study the same principle stated above concerning Charpentier's music is applied to that of Lutheran Germany of the seventeenth century: only if a work seems clearly analogous in text and music to compositions called oratorios in Italy, where *oratorio* had a well-defined meaning, is that term applied to it. For example, the term is used for Andreas Fromm's *Actus musicus de Divite et Lazaro* (Stettin, 1649) and for Dietrich Buxtehude's *Die Hochzeit des Lammes* (1678), since both works are textually and musically analogous to the oratorio in Italy.[3] The analogy does not extend to their functions, however, since neither of them was intended to function in the same way as an oratorio did in Italy.

By the early eighteenth century throughout the European continent, the term *oratorio*, or *Oratorium*, had become the generally recognized one for unstaged, sacred dramatic compositions of large scale, normally ranging from one to three hours in duration. Terminological problems relating to sacred dramatic music of this period are by no means as complex as are those relating to that of the seventeenth century. Although Mattheson, writing in the early eighteenth century, mentions the possibility of applying the term *oratorio*, not only to unstaged sacred, but also to unstaged secular dramatic works, the latter application of the term would be highly exceptional—in fact, the present author knows of no such application by any composer in the entire Baroque era. In 1732 Handel, who was generally consistent in restricting the term *oratorio* works that are dramatic and sacred, began to emphasize

---

3. Although the music of the Buxtehude work is lost, much about it can be inferred from its extant printed libretto.

oratorio performances in England. Among the few exceptions to his normal terminological practice are his use of the term *oratorio* for *Israel in Egypt*, *Messiah*, and the *Occasional Oratorio*—all of which have nondramatic librettos. The first two are closer to the traditional oratorio, since they have texts based on biblical narrative, but the *Occasional Oratorio* is an oratorio only in the vague sense that it is a large-scale, sacred composition. Such secular works by Handel as *Semele* and *Hercules* have at times been called oratorios in the Handel literature; nevertheless, they were not originally called oratorios by their composer, they do not conform to a Baroque concept of the oratorio (except for Mattheson's hypothetical suggestion mentioned above), and thus they are not treated as oratorios in this study.

Social Context

The present study is concerned primarily with the development of the musical genre described above. Nevertheless, that development cannot be fully explained apart from its social context, since its various phases emerged as responses to social demands. The immediate social context within which the oratorio originated, the religious community called the Congregation of the Oratory, was itself one of many responses to the demands of Roman Catholic reform in the sixteenth century. Without some knowledge of that reform movement in general, of the Congregation of the Oratory in particular, and even of the personality of its founder, St. Philip Neri (for the Congregation was a projection of his personality), the origin of the oratorio as a musical genre cannot be fully understood. There is ample evidence that in sixteenth-century Rome Neri used music as a means to draw into his oratory large numbers of souls from all walks of life so that he might then lead them on a path to salvation; and there is equal evidence that long after his death the earliest oratorios, among them those in G. F. Anerio's *Teatro* mentioned above, fulfilled a similar function. In the course of the seventeenth century, opera increased in popularity, and music in the oratories acceded to the demands of an opera-loving society. Oratorio style became increasingly operatic, and in the oratories the means became an end. The emphasis on musical performance began to make of the oratory a virtual concert hall—despite the struggles to the contrary of some pious and conscientious clergy—for that emphasis was a response to a demand made by both the public and the wealthy patrons of the oratories. Among the most fascinating aspects of oratorio history in the Italian Baroque is the change of the genre's social context from that of a spiritual exercise in an oratory to that of an essentially secular concert.

North of the Alps, the oratorio may be conveniently classified according to three areas with differing religious viewpoints—the Roman Catholic, the Lutheran, and the Anglican. The Roman Catholic areas, in which Vienna and Paris are of special importance for the oratorio, tended to import the genre from Italy. The social context of the oratorio in Vienna was not a public place— as were the oratories of Rome, which anyone could attend—but rather the private chapel of the Hapsburg imperial court. Thus the language of the Viennese oratorio was not German, the language of the people, but rather Italian, the dominant language of the highly sophisticated and thoroughly Italianate court. Throughout the Baroque era oratorio flourished most luxuriantly in an opera-loving society, and the Viennese court was among Europe's most munificent patrons of Italian opera. In Paris, French opera began its history in 1671; it was also in the 1670s that Charpentier returned from Rome to Paris and composed his earliest oratorios. Like those by composers at the Viennese court, Charpentier's oratorios represent the importation of an Italian genre into a foreign culture. Unlike the Viennese oratorios, however, Charpentier's are in the Latin language; they were thus useful for performance as large motets during Mass, for in the Parisian society of his time there seems to have been no demand for oratorios in either Italian or French.

Seventeenth-century Protestant Germany, unlike the Roman Catholic south, made no strong demands for either opera or oratorio. Sacred dramatic and narrative-dramatic works were indeed performed in Lutheran churches in the seventeenth century, and—as pointed out above—some of these works were analogous to the oratorio of Italy. Nevertheless, in Protestant Germany the oratorio did not become a recognized genre until the early eighteenth century, and the recognition first came in Hamburg. The explanation for the genre's development in that city and at that time is to be found in Hamburg's social climate. A rich seaport and a highly cosmopolitan city, Hamburg could boast the first public opera house outside of Italy. Established in 1678, the Hamburg opera performed works in German, many of which used biblical subjects. Thus the opera prepared a social climate that would accept oratorio and created a demand for the genre. Despite that demand, Hamburg's church and city officials reacted negatively to the earliest oratorio performances in the city, only to give way in a few years to the pressures of the opera-loving public and to permit the oratorio, not only in concerts, but also in the Hamburg cathedral. The oratorio was the principal composition on the most important days of the church year, and even female opera singers were allowed to participate in its performance.

England was the last of the geographical areas mentioned above to cultivate the oratorio, which was introduced there only in the early eighteenth century. English oratorio was essentially the creation of Handel, whose concentration on that genre can be explained largely by social and economic factors. Throughout the 1720s and 1730s Handel's reputation in London as a dramatic composer was based primarily on his serious Italian operas; but public interest in such operas began to shift, from the late 1720s on, in favor of more popular entertainment—as represented by *The Beggar's Opera*, first performed in 1728. Ten years later Handel was forced by economic pressure virtually to abandon Italian opera, and remembering the successes of his earliest English oratorios of 1732–33, he turned again to oratorio as both an economically sound and artistically viable genre. The economic success of his oratorios is not fully explained by his consummate skill in musical invention, for such skill is exhibited also in some of his operas that were box-office failures. That the audience could understand the librettos' language is an important factor in the success of the oratorios, but of perhaps equal importance is a factor of social psychology. The London society of Handel's time was familiar with the Old Testament stories that formed the basis of most of the librettos, and the audiences could identify with the Israelites as a highly nationalistic people led by heroic figures and given special protection by God, who was worshiped with magnificent ceremony.

Antecedents and Related Genres

An understanding of the history of the Baroque oratorio depends in part upon a knowledge of the genre's relationship to other dramatic music, and particularly to that with a sacred text. Long before the origin of the oratorio, throughout the Middle Ages and Renaissance, sacred dramatic music was cultivated both within and outside the church. The most important of these sacred dramatic genres are briefly treated in chapter 2. Some of the genres were staged and others, unstaged; in at least a general sense, however, all are antecedents of the oratorio. The medieval liturgical drama, for instance, is a distant antecedent, related to the oratorio only by its sacred dramatic text; the late-Renaissance Gospel motet and *lauda*, on the other hand, are among the oratorio's immediate antecedents—they influenced its origin.

Among the most important immediate antecedents of the oratorio in early Baroque Italy are the earliest operas and the dramatic dialogues, with texts in either Latin or Italian, that appeared in books of motets or spiritual madrigals. The brief secular cantata for one or more solo voices, which was beginning to emerge at about the same time as the oratorio, forms a part of the oratorio's musical context. Musically similar to the secular cantatas but more closely related to the oratorio are the relatively few cantatas with spiritual texts, works that would seem appropriate to be sung in oratories; in fact, some of these would qualify as oratorios in the sense of a distinct musical genre.

Outside of Italy, the *sepolcro* of Vienna is of special relevance to the oratorio, though not as an antecedent but as a parallel development and a closely related genre, one similar to the oratorio in virtually every respect but its staging. In Germany and France sacred dramatic dialogues are among the most important antecedents of the oratorio. The repertoire of such dialogues was particularly large in seventeenth-century Protestant Germany. Other sacred dramatic genres of importance in that time and place were the *historia*, *actus musicus*, and oratorio Passion, as well as certain large works performed at the Lübeck *Abendmusiken*. Only a few examples from the rich development of sacred dramatic music in seventeenth-century Protestant Germany are oratorios in the sense indicated in the section on terminology; yet all the types basic to that development are treated in volume 2, for all are relevant to an understanding of oratorio history. In England the sacred dramatic dialogue of the seventeenth century is only a distant antecedent of the oratorio; it appears not to have had a direct effect on the origin of the English oratorio, which must be credited to Handel.

Libretto and Music

The origin of the oratorio was, in a general sense, the result of a complex web of interacting social and musical tendencies, some of which have been mentioned above and others of which will be treated in the chapters that follow. Yet in a more restricted sense, in both their librettos and music the earliest oratorios stem directly from the sacred dramatic dialogues mentioned above and from opera. The librettos of the earliest Latin oratorios are largely in prose, and they derive from the dramatic dialogue motet; on the other hand, the librettos of the earliest Italian oratorios are in poetry, and they derive from the dramatic dialogue-madrigal and from opera. The musical styles of Latin and Italian oratorios are similar and are strongly influenced by opera, as are dialogue motets and madrigals of the time. After the mid-seventeenth century oratorio librettos in both languages tend to be in poetry throughout; both the texts and the music are modeled on those of contemporary opera. Thus oratorio and opera tend to exhibit the same kinds of stylization of "affections," or emotional states, in their poetry and music and the same kinds of structural and stylistic changes during the course of the Baroque period. As opera changes from the flexible combination of recitative and aria of the mid-seventeenth century toward the more highly stylized and rationalistic structures of the eighteenth century, oratorio changes with it—or in some respects a bit behind it; as opera abandons the strophic and other procedures identified with the aria of the mid-seventeenth century in favor of the da capo aria, oratorio does so as well; as opera minimizes the use of the chorus, so does oratorio; indeed, as Zeno and Metastasio introduce changes in the Italian opera libretto, they do likewise in the Italian oratoro libretto, and thus they change certain aspects of the oratorio's general structure.

In eighteenth-century Protestant Germany and England, however, the oratorio departs significantly in libretto and music from the operatic trends of the time. In Germany the departures are influenced by the Lutheran tradition, particularly by that of the chorale and the Passion. In German oratorios chorale texts and tunes are included to reflect the feelings of a Christian congregation; the chorus becomes more important than in the Italian oratorio. Furthermore, in Protestant Germany oratorios based on Gospel stories often continue to use the narrator in the person of the Evangelist, as the Passion had traditionally done, even though the narrator's part was abandoned in oratorio texts throughout most of Europe. In Handel's English oratorios the considerably greater emphasis on the chorus than is found in contemporary opera reflects the influence of French classical tragedy, English choral music, and the German oratorio; and the de-emphasis of the da capo aria is only one of several aspects of Handel's growing rejection in his oratorios of certain conventions of Italian serious opera.

At the beginning of this chapter, oratorio texts are referred to as either dramatic or narrative-dramatic, depending upon the absence or presence of a narrator's role in the libretto. Although this is a useful means of classifying librettos in a general way, it can be misleading unless one bears in mind two important points. First, in both types the dramatic element tends to be more important than the narrative. Even in the narrative-dramatic libretto, the most prominent type in the seventeenth century, the narrative passages are usually less extensive and important than either the dramatic dialogue among the personages or the reflective portions in which the personages express their feelings in arias, ensembles, or choruses. In fact after the mid-century, in many librettos of the narrative-dramatic type, the narrator is used only once or twice within each part of a two-part oratorio, to introduce new phases of the dramatic action. The second point to bear in mind is that in both types of libretto the narrative element tends to be present. Even in the dramatic libretto, characteristic of the eighteenth century, at least a modicum of narration and description is usually included in the recitatives of the personages so that the audience may be able to imagine the scenery and physical acts of the drama; in some dramatic works the listeners are given the additional aid of brief descriptions of the scene, which they may read in the printed libretto. It is curious that among the exceptions to the first generalization stated above—the predominance of the dramatic element—are two of the greatest works called oratorios in the late Baroque, Handel's *Messiah* and J. S. Bach's Christmas Oratorio, both of which are essentially narrative and reflective rather than dramatic.

PART I   *The Antecedents and Origins of the Oratorio*

CHAPTER II   *The Middle Ages,*
Renaissance, and
Roman Catholic Reform

֍ Some Antecedents of the Oratorio

The impulse to express religious feelings and concepts by means of narrative, drama, and music—the elements common to most oratorios—is revealed in several forms of Christian worship in the Middle Ages and Renaissance. Since these forms spring from the same basic impulse as the oratorio and use similar means, they may be considered the oratorio's antecedents. Some are its immediate antecedents, exerting a direct influence on its origin; others are more remote, and they influence it indirectly or not at all.

The essential elements of the oratorio are present in the Mass, particularly in the chanted Gospel passages and the reenactment of the Last Supper. The most important antecedent of the oratorio in the Mass is the musical recitation of the Gospel story of the Passion during Holy Week. The medieval Divine Office, too, included extended narratives, called *historiae*, that are antecedents of the oratorio; like the recitation of the Passion in the Mass, these were unstaged, as were oratorios in the Baroque era. Other unstaged antecedents of the oratorio are found among the *laude* of the Middle Ages and Renaissance and among the narrative-dramatic motets and the Lutheran chorales and *historiae* of the sixteenth and seventeenth centuries. Staged drama is closer to opera than to oratorio; yet opera and oratorio have much in common, and sacred dramas with music, including Latin liturgical dramas and works in the vernacular, are all within the broad stream of development that gave rise to both opera and oratorio.

Unstaged Sacred Dramatic Genres

An extremely important antecedent of the oratorio is the Passion, for its texts, as found in the four Gospels, include the same kinds of narrative and dramatic elements as are characteristic of most oratorio texts from the genre's origin to the present, and the musical presentation of that text has an unbroken history beginning in the early Middle Ages. Furthermore, from the early Baroque on, the relationship between the Passion and the oratorio grew ever closer. The foreshadowing of the oratorio in the musical renditions of the Passion dates from at least the ninth century, when the three "roles" in the Passion story—the Evangelist, Jesus, and the other characters—were distinguished from one another by differing pitch or manner of performance. By the thirteenth century the roles had begun to be divided among several singers,[1] and by the mid-fifteenth century the words of the *turbae* were at times set polyphonically; both of these developments increased the dramatic realism of the performance. Of the various ways of setting the text of the Passion to music in the sixteenth and seventeenth centuries,[2] the one that is most realistically dramatic and that most clearly anticipates the oratorio is the responsorial Passion, in which the parts of individual personages are set for soloists and those of the *turbae*, for chorus. This type is represented, for example, in the Passions according to Mark and Luke set by Orlando di Lasso[3] and in those according to Matthew and John set by Tomás Luis de Victoria.[4]

Another genre that originated in the Middle Ages, the *historia* of the Divine Office, may be considered a distant antecedent of the oratorio.[5] The principle of the Divine Office, or the prayer of the canonical hours, can be traced back to the apostolic period of Christianity; it has roots reaching far into pre-Christian Jewish

1. B. Stäblein, "Die einstimige lateinische Passion," in *MGG*, 10:col. 897, pl. 61/2.
2. For more details about Passion settings, see the consideration of the Lutheran *historia* in vol. 2.
3. Printed in Lasso, *Werke–N*, 2:27–43.
4. Described in Kade, *Passionskomposition*, pp. 150–52.
5. Attention was first called to the relationship between the Divine Office and the oratorio in Meyer, "Offizium"; the thesis of that article is restated in Meyer-Baer, "Office."

practices.[6] During the fourth- and fifth-century rise of monasticism in the Western church, the previously flexible practice of private prayer at certain hours of the day became increasingly organized into a liturgical structure for group prayer. Of primary importance for the liturgical development of the Divine Office was the sixth-century Rule of St. Benedict, a powerful influence on monastic practices throughout the Western church. This rule clearly organized the prayers of eight canonical hours: matins, lauds, prime, terce, sext, none, vespers, and compline. The elements of the Divine Office were the psalms, canticles, hymns, antiphons, responsories, and prayers, as well as various readings from the Bible, the writings of the church fathers, and the lives of saints. Of these elements the antiphons and responsories, sung to introduce and separate the psalms and various readings of the Divine Office, are antecedents of the oratorio. By at least the tenth century the texts of the antiphons and responsories distributed throughout the canonic hours of the day were often written as the constituent parts of a large composite unit that narrated the story of the feast being celebrated; such a composite unit was called a *historia*.[7] Although the earliest *historiae* are in prose, the rhymed *historia* became increasingly prominent from the tenth through the twelfth centuries. It reached the peak of its development in the thirteenth century and declined in the fourteenth and fifteenth centuries; the Council of Trent rejected it in the sixteenth century. The majority of the medieval *historiae* are rhymed, and most are hagiographical, although some are biblical.[8] Examples of hagiographical *historiae* are the eleventh-century *Historia de Sancta Afra martyre*, by Hermannus Contractus;[9] a twelfth-century anonymous *historia* for the feast of St. Arnulf;[10] and the thirteenth-century *historiae* for the feasts of St. Francis and St. Anthony by Julian von Speier.[11]

6. For historical surveys of the origin and medieval development of the Divine Office, see Apel, *Chant*, pp. 19–23; Batiffol, *Bréviaire*, pp. 1–267; Pascher, *Stundengebet*, pp. 16–59; Wagner, *Einführung*, 1:123–31; and W. Irtenkauf, "Offizium," in *MGG*, 9:cols. 1907–10.

7. Regarding this use of the term *historia*, see *Analecta hymnica*, 5:6; W. Blankenburg, "Historia," in *MGG*, 6:col. 466; and Wagner, *Einführung*, 1:301.

8. For surveys of the rhymed office (also called *historia rhythmata* or *rimata*), see Wagner, *Einführung*, 1:300–318, 3:315–19, 3:349–51; and W. Irtenkauf, "Reimoffizium," in *MGG*, 11:cols. 172–73. The texts of well over seven hundred rhymed *historiae* are printed in *Analecta hymnica*, vols. 5, 13, 17, 18, 24–26, 28, 41a, and 45.

9. Music and text printed in Brambach, *Historia*.

10. Text printed in Wagner, *Einführung*, 1:308–11.

11. Music and text of both printed in Felder, *Reimofficien*.

Unlike the Passion, the *historia* of the Divine Office did not maintain a tradition up to the time of the oratorio's origin; thus it did not exert a direct formative influence on the oratorio.

The oratorio's most significant medieval forerunners in the vernacular of Italy are the *laude*,[12] with narrative and dramatic texts. The *laude* were simple expressions of popular religion sung in meetings of confraternities, or religious brotherhoods of laymen. Although confraternities date from the early Middle Ages, the period of their greatest growth was the twelfth and thirteenth centuries.[13] Of particular importance for the development of narrative and dramatic *laude* are the Umbrian confraternities that originated about 1260; the members of these brotherhoods were called *flagellanti, battuti,* and *disciplinati* because of their practice of public self-flagellation.[14] Private self-flagellation had long been practiced as a means of penance in monasteries, but in 1259–60 the practice suddenly became public. First in Perugia and then throughout Umbria, large numbers joined these confraternities, which held services in churches and oratories and conducted public penitential processions during which the members flogged themselves while stripped to the waist. The outward cause of the flagellant movement was the fanatical example and preaching of the Franciscan hermit Ranier Fasani, who came out of seclusion and appeared in Perugia in 1259. Deeper causes were the social disorganization of the time, the influence of the extremely austere Franciscan Spirituals, and the apocalyptic prophesies of Joachim of Fiore. The flagellant movement spread from Umbria throughout Italy and even to northern Europe—particularly to Germany and the Low Countries—and it became one of the period's chief currents of popular religion.

The poetic-musical structure of the majority of the medieval *laude* sung in the meetings of confraternities is similar to that of

12. Both of the Italian forms *lauda* (pl. *laude*) and *laude* (pl. *laudi*) were used in the Middle Ages and Renaissance and are still used today; I have adopted the former spelling. For discussions of the medieval *lauda* from the standpoints of poetry and function, see Bartholomaeis, *Origini*, pp. 206–45, and D'Ancona, *Origini*, 1:112–62. For modern editions of medieval *lauda* texts, see Jacopone, *Laudi*, and Bartholomaeis, *Laude*, 1:1–27. On the *lauda* in the history of music, see K. Jeppesen, "Laude," in *MGG*, 8:cols. 313–23. For extensive bibliographical studies of the *lauda* and its history, see Tenneroni, *Inizii*; Frati, "Giunte"; and Monti, "Bibliografia."

13. For a history of medieval confraternities, see Monti, *Confraternite*.

14. For the origin and development of the flagellant movement, see Monti, *Confraternite*, 1:197–285; Bartholomaeis, *Origini*, pp. 195–206; and D'Ancona, *Origini*, 1:106–112.

the *ballata*; most of the texts are in a lyrical, reflective style, of which St. Francis of Assisi's *lauda* called *Canticle of the Sun* is an early example. Yet a significant number of the poems, particularly those of the Umbrian confraternities of flagellants, include narrative and dramatic elements. These are the kinds of poems that foreshadow the oratorio text of the seventeenth century. Although most *lauda* texts were written by anonymous and relatively unskilled poets, those by Jacopone da Todi are significant literary works. Characteristic of his narrative and/or dramatic *laude* are a dialogue between the Body and Soul ("Audite una 'ntenzione ch'è 'nfra l'anema e 'l corpo"), a narrative and dialogue on the life and achievements of St. Francis of Assisi ("O Francesco, da Deo amato"), and—his most famous—a dialogue based on the Passion story that emphasizes the lament of the Virgin ("Donna de paradiso").[15] The chief musical sources of medieval *laude* are the manuscripts of Cortona and Florence that have been transcribed by Fernando Liuzzi;[16] the manuscript of Cortona dates from the late thirteenth century and that of Florence, from the early fourteenth. Together these manuscripts contain 135 *lauda* texts, most of which have musical settings, all monophonic; approximately one-fourth of the texts include narrative and/or dramatic elements. Characteristic of such *laude* are those based on the stories of the Annunciation ("Da ciel venne messo novello," "Salutiam divotamente"), the Nativity ("Nova stella apparita"), the Passion ("De la crudel morte de cristo," "Iesu Cristo redemptore"), the Virgin's lament ("Salve, virgo pretiosa," "Ogne pia amica," "Piange Maria cum dolore," "Voi ch'amate lo criatore," "Or piangiamo, che piange Maria," "Davanti a una colonna"), the Resurrection ("Iesu Cristo glorioso," "Laudamo la resurrectione," "Co la madre del beato"), and saints' lives (St. Francis of Assisi: "Laudar vollio per amore"; St. Anthony of Padua: "Ciascon ke fede sente"; St. Lawrence: "Martyr glorioso, aulente flore"; St. George: "Sancto Giorgio, martyr amoroso"; St. Paul: "Con divota mente pura ed agechita"; and St. Alexis: "Sancto Allexio stella resplendente"). Although the above-mentioned examples would not seem to lend themselves to staging,[17] more fully developed

15. Approximately one-fourth of the ninety-two items in Jacopone, *Laudi* are narrative and/or dramatic works.

16. Liuzzi, *Lauda*.

17. A possible exception—according to Bartholomaeis, *Origini*, p. 219—is Jacopone's "Donna de paradiso."

dramas, or *sacre rappresentazioni*—essentially extended *laude* on some of the same subjects—were staged by the Umbrian confraternities beginning in the late thirteenth century.

The tradition of the singing of *laude* continued throughout the Renaissance and much beyond; and although the tradition grew steadily weaker after the Renaissance, some vestiges of it survived until the late nineteenth century.[18] The *lauda* was particularly popular in fifteenth- and sixteenth-century Florence, where confraternities known as *laudesi*, consisting mostly of artisans, preserved a long-established tradition of singing *laude* in their devotional meetings.[19] As a literary genre, too, the *lauda* attracted considerable attention in Florence; the first of several Renaissance printed editions of Jacopone da Todi's *laude* appeared there in 1490, and some of Florence's best authors (including Feo Belcari, Castellano Castellani, Lorenzo de' Medici, and Girolamo Savonarola) wrote *laude*.[20] The first polyphonic settings of *lauda* texts date from the late fourteenth century, and the first musical print of *laude*, all of which are polyphonic, is the collection *Laude, libro secondo* (Venice: Petrucci, 1507; Petrucci's *Laude, libro primo* appeared in 1508).[21] Although none of the *laude* in the *libro secondo* have narrative or dramatic texts, musical settings with such texts appear later in the sixteenth century in the books printed for use by the Roman Oratory of Philip Neri. Those sung in Neri's oratory are among the immediate antecedents of the oratorio; they will be treated below in connection with music in that oratory.

A Renaissance and early Baroque antecedent of the oratorio is the motet that uses a Gospel narrative as its text. Among the numerous sixteenth-century motets of this type are those by Or-

18. For a chronological list of ninety-four books of printed *laude* dating from the late fourteenth to the late nineteenth centuries, see Frati, "Giunte," 1:443–50.

19. Cf. the brief description of Florentine *lauda* singing quoted from Crescimbeni, *Historia*, in *Laude spirituali*, pp. vi–vii, and also quoted in Jeppesen, *Laude*, p. xv, n. 1. For archival documentation of the continuing performance of *laude* in the first half of the sixteenth century at Florence, see D'Accone, "Chapels," pp. 3, 11, 12, 23. The Florentine Filippo Giunti, in the dedication of his print of Serafino Razzi's *Libro primo delle laudi spirituali* (Venice, 1563; for a facsimile reprint, see Razzi, *Laude*), attests to a decline in the singing of *laude* in the gatherings of confraternities and in private homes, but he indicates that *laude* were still sung in convents.

20. For a collection of 507 *laude* printed in Florence between 1480 and 1510, see *Laude spirituali*; and for a thorough literary study of the fifteenth-century *lauda*, see Coppola, *Poesia*.

21. Jeppesen, *Laude*, includes a modern edition of Petrucci's *Laude, libro secondo*, part of his *libro primo*, and other *laude* from the period ca. 1500.

lando di Lasso on the Gospel stories of Jesus and two disciples on the road to Emmaus, the finding of Jesus in the temple, the Annunciation to the Virgin Mary, the raising of Lazarus, and the marriage feast at Cana.[22] In these works by Lasso there is little distinction between the musical settings of the narrative passages and the lines of the various personages in the story. In some sixteenth-century works, however, the dialogue between personages is set antiphonally to provide a more realistic effect. Particularly striking in this respect is the Lutheran composer Leonhard Päminger's Easter responsory "Maria Magdalena et altera Maria"; its text combines a Gospel passage with the Easter sequence, and its music is antiphonal, with various vocal groupings alternating to represent the dramatic dialogue among the personages.[23] In early seventeenth-century motets with similar texts, the role of each personage is often set for a different soloist, accompanied by the basso continuo; this type of setting adds an element of dramatic realism not possible before the development of monody and leads directly to the origin of the Latin oratorio. The Latin dialogues of the early seventeenth century are treated in chapter 3.

In addition to the medieval use of the term *historia* that was mentioned above, there is a sixteenth- and seventeenth-century use that also designates an antecedent of the oratorio. In Lutheran Germany that term or its German equivalent, *Historie*, was often applied to a biblical narrative either to be read or to be sung. The Passion was the principal type of *historia* set to music, but other stories, including those of the Resurrection and the Nativity, were also set to music in a similar manner. As pointed out above in relation to the Passion, the responsorial type of text setting is the one most relevant to the history of the oratorio. The sixteenth- and seventeenth-century Lutheran *historia* appears to have had little influence on the origin and earliest development of the oratorio, since such *historiae* were geographically and ideologically far removed from Rome, where the oratorio began. In the course of the seventeenth century, however, the Lutheran *historia* became one of the strongest roots of the oratorio in the German language.

22. Printed in Lasso, *Werke*, 7:9–13, 14–15, 16–24; 15:23–29, 30–40. For references to numerous sixteenth-century motets with Gospel-narrative texts, see Moser, *Evangelium*, pp. 19–54.
23. For a description of this work, see Moser, *Evangelium*, p. 53; Moser considers the work a "motetlike Easter oratorio." The relationship of this type of antiphonal motet to the oratorio is also mentioned in Kroyer, "Dialog," p. 15.

The *historia* is treated in greater detail in connection with the German oratorio in volume 2.

Staged Sacred Dramatic Genres

The Latin drama that grew from accretions to the liturgy, usually referred to as liturgical drama, achieved its essential development between the tenth and thirteenth centuries. Because it is a sacred dramatic genre normally sung in its entirety, the liturgical drama may be regarded among the oratorio's forerunners. The earliest type of liturgical drama was the *visitatio sepulchri,* based on the visit of the three Marys to the holy sepulchre after Christ's Resurrection. The germ from which the *visitatio sepulchri* dramas grew was the "Quem quaeritis," a brief dialogue that first appears in manuscripts of the early tenth century. Often classified today as a trope, this dialogue was performed before the mass of Easter morning.[24] A gradual process of elaborating the "Quem quaeritis" resulted in a group of extended *visitatio sepulchri* dramas for Easter, as well as dramas modeled on them for the feasts of Christmas, Epiphany, and the Ascension. Other subjects used as the basis for liturgical dramas were various New Testament stories —including the Passion, the raising of Lazarus, the conversion of St. Paul, the Annunciation, and the Purification—as well as stories from the Old Testament—including those of Isaac and Rebecca, Joseph and his brethren, and Daniel. All of these and other subjects used for liturgical dramas later provided the basis of oratorios. Liturgical dramas sometimes include quotations from, or paraphrases of, biblical passages, as do Latin sacred dialogues and oratorios in the first half of the seventeenth century. These quotations and paraphrases result in certain similarities between passages of liturgical dramas and seventeenth-century Latin dialogues and oratorios, as comparisons by Arnold Schering have shown.[25] Nevertheless, the latest significant period of the liturgical drama is separated from the beginning of the oratorio by more than three

24. The commonly accepted theory that the "Quem quaeritis" dialogue was originally a trope of the antiphon for the introit of the Easter mass and was later detached from that position is set forth in Young, *Drama,* 1: chaps. 7–14. That theory has recently been questioned in McGhee, "*Quem quaeritis.*" For general surveys of the liturgical drama's history, see Smolden, "Drama," and Young, *Drama.* For a survey of Latin liturgical drama and sacred drama in the vernacular, see W. Lipphardt, "Liturgische Dramen," in *MGG,* 8: cols. 1010–51.

25. Schering, *Oratorium,* pp. 13–15.

centuries. Although the liturgical drama is a distant forerunner of the oratorio, there appears to be no continuous development from the former to the latter.[26]

Sacred plays in the vernacular existed as early as the eleventh century in Spain and France and somewhat later in other areas. When music played only a subsidiary role in such plays, as was usually the case, they had little in common with the oratorio. The *sacra rappresentazione*[27] of Italy is exceptional, however, because of the prominence of music in its performance; for that reason, and because of its geographical proximity to the area of the oratorio's origin, it is a closer relative of the oratorio than are other sacred plays in the vernacular. Having originated by extension of the thirteenth-century dialogue *lauda* of Umbria, the *sacra rappresentazione* became a significant genre in central and northern Italy in the fourteenth century and reached the peak of its development in fifteenth- and sixteenth-century Florence. The Florentine *sacre rappresentazioni* were written primarily in *ottava rima*, and most of the poetic lines were intoned to melodic formulas;[28] the principal musical numbers, however, were *laude, frottole, canzone*, and (in the sixteenth century) madrigals. Most of the musical numbers in the sixteenth-century *sacre rappresentazioni* are found in the *intermedi*, musical-dramatic interludes used between the scenes of a play to add variety and enlarge upon the events of the drama. Among the most important Florentine authors of *sacre rappresentazioni* are Belcari, Castellani, and Lorenzo de' Medici —all mentioned above in connection with the Florentine *lauda*. The subjects treated include Abraham and Isaac, the Annunciation, the Passion, the prodigal son, and numerous saints' lives. In Rome, the birthplace of the oratorio, *sacre rappresentazioni* were performed primarily by the Archiconfraternita di Santa Lucia del

26. This conclusion is contrary to that expressed by Schering, ibid., p. 16: "From the liturgical drama of the Middle Ages grew the Latin oratorio." There he seems to imply that the Latin dramatic dialogue of the early seventeenth century was a continuation of the liturgical drama; on pp. 11 and 18, however, he speaks of it as a rebirth of the liturgical drama. He does not mention its relationship to the sixteenth-century motet with narrative and dramatic text.

27. For histories of the origin and development of the *sacra rappresentazione*, see: D'Ancona, *Origini*, and Bartholomaeis, *Origini*. For modern editions of selected *sacre rappresentazioni*, see Bartholomaeis, *Laude*; Belcari, *Rappresentazioni*; and Coppola, *Rappresentazioni*. For an extensive bibliography of *sacre rappresentazioni* see Cioni, *Bibliografia*; and for a discussion of music in Florentine *sacre rappresentazioni*, see Becherini, "Rappresentazioni."

28. Becherini, "Rappresentazioni," p. 193.

Gonfalone. This society was particularly well known in the fifteenth and early sixteenth centuries for its elaborate Passion plays performed annually on Good Friday in the Colosseum.[29] In the early sixteenth century these performances became increasingly spectacular and expensive, and their audiences grew disruptive and endangered the public safety; after the 1539 performance the Passion plays in the Colosseum were discontinued by order of Pope Paul III. Later in the century, when the archconfraternity requested permission of the pope to reinstitute them, permission was denied. By the end of the sixteenth century, the *sacra rappresentazione* was outmoded; yet occasional performances continued to be given in the seventeenth century. This genre has a direct connection with the history of the oratorio, for Emilio de' Cavalieri appears to have intended his opera *Rappresentatione di Anima et di Corpo* (1600) as a renewal of the *sacra rappresentazione*. This work, an important antecedent of the oratorio, is treated below.

The Society of Jesus, established as an order in 1540, began early in its history to foster dramatic productions in its schools. Except for a few early dramas performed in the Mamertine College at Messina, Jesuit school drama was a Roman creation.[30] The first Jesuit plays in Rome, performed in the mid-1560s at the German College and the Roman College, were intended as a means of competing with other entertainments that the city offered to students during carnival time; soon, however, the plays developed into a means of instruction in rhetoric and religion. The earliest noteworthy author of Jesuit dramas was Stefano Tucci, whose works were particularly important in Rome during the period 1547–97; they were permitted to be performed in the Jesuit colleges while all the other theaters of Rome were closed by order of Pope Gregory XIII, an order prompted by the immorality of the plays that were attended by ecclesiastical dignitaries during the carnival season of 1537.[31] Jesuit dramas were usually based on biblical stories or hagiography; normally in Latin, they employed elaborate stage sets and machines.[32] Although the dramas were largely spoken, inserted musical numbers were essential to the

29. D'Ancona, *Origini*, 1:354–56; Alaleona, *Oratorio*, pp. 9–11; Vattasso, "Rappresentazioni."

30. For the history of the sixteenth-century Jesuit school drama in Messina, see Soldati, *Mamertino*; for the development in Rome, see Gnerghi, *Teatro*.

31. For the closing of the theaters, see Pastor, *Popes*, 20:547–48.

32. For the visual elaboration of the Jesuit school dramas, see Bjurström, "Theater."

genre. The influence of Jesuit drama on the formation of oratorio is more a matter of function than of style or structure. It seems likely that the success of the Jesuits in combining religious education with dramatic entertainment exerted a significant influence on the Oratorians in Rome, who first began to use the oratorio as edifying entertainment in their spiritual exercises.

The Oratorians and Their Social Context

The immediate context within which the oratorio originated was formed by the Congregation of the Oratory, founded in sixteenth-century Rome by Philip Neri. The "Apostle of Rome," as Neri was called, and his Oratorians exerted a powerful reforming influence on Roman society in the second half of the sixteenth century, a period in which Catholic reform was the most prominent feature of cultural life in this city and, indeed, in all of Italy. Concomitant with the reform was the domination of Spain in Italian political life; Spanish influence was also prominent in the reform movement, most notably in the Inquisition and the work of Ignatius of Loyola's Society of Jesus. The Oratorian movement emerged from a complex interaction of social forces at work in the political and religious life of sixteenth-century Italy, and particularly of Rome. Some of them are outlined below.

Italian Politics, the Papacy, and Roman Catholic Reform[33]

At the beginning of the sixteenth century, the Italian peninsula was politically divided among numerous small states and five major ones: Naples, the Papal States, Florence, Venice, and Milan. Often at war with one another, the Italian states were prevented by their jealousies and rivalries from uniting for their mutual protection against common enemies. Thus in the first third of the century, the peninsula was subject to frequent invasions by French, Spanish, and German armies. The Italian states vacillated in their alliances

33. For surveys of Italian political and cultural history that include useful sections on the sixteenth century, see *Cambridge*, vols. 1–2; Jamison, *Italy*; Procacci, *History*; Spitz, *Renaissance*; Trevelyan, *History*; and Visconti, *Controriforma*. For papal history in the sixteenth century—as well as for much other religious, political, and cultural history—see Pastor, *Popes*, vols. 6–24. For the Catholic reform in Italy, see the works listed above as well as Daniel-Rops, *Catholic*; Dickens, *Counter Reformation*; Janelle, *Catholic Reformation*; Kidd, *Counter-Reformation*; Symonds, *Reaction*; and Willaert, *Concile*.

with one another and with the invading powers. The papacy constantly sought alliances that appeared to be the most profitable for the Papal States and the reigning pope's family. For instance, the alliance of Pope Alexander VI (Rodrigo Borgia, 1492–1503) with the French king, Louis XII, gave the pope's favorite son, the brutal and notorious Cesare Borgia (an archbishop and cardinal), the support he needed to conquer Romagna and terrorize the rest of Italy between 1499 and the pope's death in 1503. The climax of the turbulent period of invasions was the sack of Rome in 1527, which resulted in part from a confusion of changing alliances by Pope Clement VII (Giulio de' Medici, 1523–34). Having wavered between an alliance with the Hapsburg emperor-elect, Charles V (who was also the king of Spain), and the French king, Francis I, Clement concluded a treaty of alliance with Francis in 1525 on the assumption that the latter would be victorious in the crucial battle of Pavia. Francis lost, however, and Charles's victory made his empire the chief power in Europe. The pope then changed his alliance to Charles, only to break it, renew it, and break it again—all within a year. Late in 1526 Charles again sent troops into Italy, this time to conquer Milan and to demonstrate his power to the pope; the sack of Rome, however, was unpremeditated. On 6 May 1527, without the knowledge of Charles, the more than twenty thousand Spanish and German troops—by then a mutinous, violent mob—poured into Rome to sack and plunder unmercifully while Clement took refuge in Castel Sant'Angelo, where he was detained for seven months until he could pay his ransom.

The sack of Rome marked the end of a period in Italian political and cultural history. The pope came to terms with Charles, and in 1530 at Bologna, he crowned him Roman emperor. Charles then placed Italy under Spanish domination; he eventually bestowed the Spanish monarchy and all imperial rights in Italy upon his son, Philip II. From the sack of Rome until the end of the century, and to a lesser extent on into the seventeenth century, Spain dominated Italian political life. With a Spanish viceroy in Milan and another in Naples, and with troops stationed in both cities, the Spanish hegemony in sixteenth-century Italy was undisputed. The papacy, controlling the most powerful of the Italian states, was not always subservient to Spain and at times even forcefully opposed her; on the whole, however, Spanish-papal relations tended to be amicable. The papacy needed the Hapsburgs in its Counter-Reformation struggle against Protestantism in the north, and Philip II needed the friendship of the papacy, since religious orthodoxy was important to his political program. Venice remained aloof from Spain but did not quarrel with her. The Florentine rulers were generally submissive to Spanish policy until the reign of Grand Duke Ferdinando I (1587–1609), who pursued a policy of rapprochement with France to counteract Spanish influence in Italy. The smaller states either aligned themselves with Spain or, if they did not, were too weak to threaten her.

The popes who reigned in the first third of the sixteenth century were primarily concerned with politics, military exploits, the advancement of their families, and the patronage and enjoyment of the cultural achievements of the Italian Renaissance. The need for church reform had long been recognized by many clergy, both north of the Alps and in Italy, but the popes, preoccupied with other matters and apparently incapable of understanding the seriousness of the crisis in the church, failed to provide the spiritual and intellectual leadership required for a thorough reform. An exception was the Dutch pope, Adrian VI (Adrian Florisze Boeyens, 1522–23), who was genuinely concerned with church reform but whose reign was too brief to be effective. In Italy the voice of the austere reformer Girolamo Savonarola (1452–98) was only one of many that were raised against abuses in the church; but this prior of the Dominicans at San Marco in Florence and dictator of the city was condemned to death by a mock trial arranged by Pope Alexander VI and was excommunicated, hanged, and burned. Other reformers of the fifteenth and sixteenth centuries were also treated brutally, but some achieved a certain degree of success, even while they remained within the fold of the Roman Catholic church. Especially important in this respect are those mentioned below (see pp. 33–34), who reformed some religious orders and established new ones. Popes Julius II (Giuliano della Rovere, 1503–13) and Leo X (Giovanni de' Medici, 1513–21), who ruled more as secular monarchs than spiritual leaders, were among the greatest patrons of arts and letters in their time. Although church reform was a part of the program of the Fifth Lateran Council, called by Julius and continued by Leo, the council left the church virtually unchanged; meanwhile, under Leo's pontificate the Lutheran Reformation began. Clement VII, weak and indecisive in both the temporal and spiritual spheres, urged Charles V to arrest the progress of the Reformation in Germany but did virtually nothing himself to initiate church reforms.

Throughout this period in Rome, until the devastation of the sack, Renaissance cultural life, unbounded in its enthusiasm for classical antiquity, thrived. Bramante, Michelangelo, and Raphael were among the artists in the service of the popes; Pietro Bembo, Jacopo Sadoleto, and Bernardo Accolti, among the scholars and poets. The musicians in the papal chapel were mostly Franco-Netherlandish, but two Italian composers were Costanzo Festa and Bernardo Pisano. Julius II showed a special interest in music by his bull of 1512 in which he reorganized the chapel of St. Peter's, subsequently called the Cappella Giulia. Secular music was intensively cultivated, not only at the papal court, but at the courts of the numerous cardinals and noblemen in Rome, who vied with one another for excellence in their musical entertainments. In this period the private and public lives of the popes and princes of the church were often licentious and more pagan than Christian; equally licentious were the festivities and entertainments of the populace, for the hierarchy set the standards of morality of the Roman people. The sack of Rome was widely regarded by both the educated and the populace as a punishment from God for the sins of Rome and its church. Bishop Giovanni Staffileo, for example, in a speech on the reassembling of the Rota in 1528, reflected the feeling of many when he said that the city had been visited by this catastrophe "because all flesh has become corrupt, because we are not citizens of the holy city of Rome, but of Babylon, the city of corruption. . . . We have all sinned grievously . . . let us reform, turn to the Lord, and He will have pity upon us."[34] Roman Catholic reform was slow to come, however, since the abuses were too deeply entrenched in the political, economic, and moral life of the church for immediate remedy and Clement VII was too thoroughly conditioned by his past to change his ways.

Official church reform began during the reigns of the popes from Paul III (Alessandro Farnese, 1534–39) to Pius IV (Giovanni Angelo de' Medici, 1559–65), and it reached its sixteenth-century peak under the popes from Pius V (Michele Ghislieri, 1566–72) to Sixtus V (Felice Peretti, 1585–90). Both Paul III and his successor Julius III (Giovanni Maria del Monte, 1550–55) were men of the

34. Quoted in Pastor, *Popes*, 10:446.

Renaissance who retained many of the attitudes toward politics, nepotism, and pleasurable pursuits held by their sixteenth-century predecessors. Nevertheless, Paul III initiated positive measures for reform by bringing into existence the Council of Trent (1545) and appointing to the College of Cardinals some sincere reformers, including Giovanni Pietro Carafa, Gaspero Contarini, Jacopo Sadoleto, and Reginald Pole—all of whom served on a reform commission. As a measure to combat Protestantism in Italy, Paul III established the Congregation of the Inquisition (1542), modeled generally upon the Spanish Inquisition. The period of Paul IV (Giovanni Pietro Carafa, 1555–59), who had been the prime mover in the establishment of the Inquisition under Paul III, was a holy reign of terror. Morally austere in his personal life, Paul IV set himself the task of reforming the church and Roman society by decree. His chief tools were the Inquisition and the censorship of publication; the first published *Index of Prohibited Books* appeared during his reign. By no means hypocritical himself, he nevertheless engendered hypocrisy in the Roman people, who would find it expedient to appear to conform to the moral standards and religious doctrines imposed by such harsh means. During the reign of Paul IV's successor, Pius IV, the Council of Trent was reconvened; completing its work in 1563, it provided the Roman Catholic church with a foundation for reform and a much-needed clarification of its position in matters of faith and morals. For the remainder of the century, the chief tasks of the papacy were the implementation of the reforms recommended by the Council of Trent and the work of the Counter-Reformation in northern Europe, in which the Jesuits played a prominent role. The oppressive measures of the Inquisition continued to be used; they were applied with particular zeal by Pius V, who had been the grand inquisitor under the reign of Paul IV. Yet there were also positive steps toward reform, including the cleansing of the formerly corrupt Curia by intelligent appointments and the founding of numerous new educational institutions.

Simultaneously with the Roman Catholic reform at the highest levels of church administration, a reform in progress among the religious orders resulted in either the modification of existing orders or the establishment of new ones. Among the new and reformed orders or congregations were the Oratory of Divine Love, a reform society founded around 1517 in Rome by Gaetano di Thiene and Giovanni Pietro Carafa, which developed into the Theatine order; the Capuchins, a reform movement of Franciscans initiated by Matteo Bassi around 1520, which became an independent order in 1619; the Barnabites, founded by Antonio Maria Zaccaria in 1530; the Society of Jesus, founded by Ignatius of Loyola in 1539 and confirmed as an order in 1540; the Discalced Carmelites, a reform of the Carmelite order initiated by Theresa of Jesus (Theresa of Avila) in 1562; and the Congregation of the Oratory, begun informally by Philip Neri in the 1550s and approved as a congregation in 1575. Most of the modified and new orders were essentially contemplative; the members sought to help the church by prayer and by sanctifying themselves through mortification of the flesh and control of the spirit. If they were at times in charge of hospitals, schools, or missions, such activity was secondary to their essential purpose. In striking contrast to this view was that held by the Society of Jesus and the Congregation of the Oratory. Although these two organizations would not deny the value of the contemplative life, they were more practical in their approach; they sought to reform the church by direct social action, and to do so they rejected the traditional monastic framework and obligations. The Jesuits and Oratorians were the primary forces in the spiritual revival of the Roman people during the reform period of the sixteenth century. Despite their similarity of basic outlook, however, they were quite different from each other in their organizational structure and their mode of social action.

The founder of the Jesuits, Ignatius of Loyola (1491–1556), arrived in Rome to begin his work in 1537.[35] Formerly a Spanish soldier, who had been lamed by a battle wound, Ignatius had undergone an intense mystical experience and had resolved to enter a spiritual knighthood in the service of the church. After a pilgrimage to the Holy Land, he had decided to improve himself for his work by further education, first in his native Spain and then in Paris. While studying in Paris, he gathered around him the nine men—four of whom were Spaniards and the others Portuguese, French, and Savoyards—who were to be the first members of the Society of Jesus. By 1538 all nine of Ignatius's followers had joined

35. The literature on the history of the Jesuits is enormous. Among the more useful general surveys are Bangert, *Society*; Broderick, *Jesuits*; Campbell, *Jesuits*; Guibert, *Jesuits*; and Harney, *Jesuits*. A detailed study of the earliest period of the Jesuits in Italy is Tacchi-Venturi, *Compagnia*.

S.IGNATII LOIOLAE SOC:IESU FUND. EFFIGIES EX TYPO GYPSEO QUI APUD PP.
EJUSDEM SOC. PATAVII ASSERVATUR EX DONO P.O.M. CLEMENTIS XIII.

FIGURE II-I. Ignatius of Loyola (1491–1556). From an engraving after
the death mask.
(Reproduced by permission of the Jesuit Archive, Rome.)

The Middle Ages, Renaissance, and Roman Catholic Reform   35 him in Rome; six members of the group, including their leader, had been ordained priests. For the first year of their Roman period, Ignatius and his men attracted considerable attention, some of it unfavorable, for their novel practices and teachings. Sermons were rarely heard in Rome outside the seasons of Advent and Lent, but Ignatius and his companions stressed preaching and continued to preach even after Easter; furthermore, since Ignatius considered weekly communion to be a sign of a good Catholic, they urged frequent confession and communion, a virtually obsolete custom in their period. Their popularity rapidly grew, despite false charges about them made by members of a Protestant faction in Rome; they were eventually exonerated by an official church inquiry instigated by Ignatius himself. Having already taken vows of poverty and chastity before coming to Rome, they decided in 1539 to become a religious order; conceiving their order as a militant body, they took vows of complete submission to the pope and of obedience to their superior, who was to be called a general. Ignatius drew up a constitution in which absolute, unquestioning obedience to superiors was of primary importance. In 1540 Pope Paul III confirmed the Society of Jesus as an order.

The Jesuits exerted a powerful influence, not only in Rome, where their role in the increase in church attendance and reception of the sacraments was clearly evident, but also north of the Alps and in the Far East and the New World. The Society of Jesus was more important than any other institution in the Counter-Reformation process of reclaiming areas that had been lost to Lutheranism. The reasons for the dramatically rapid development and remarkable success of the Society are to be found not only in the dedication of Ignatius and his associates but also in the system that they established: Jesuits were required to be well educated and rigorously trained in self-discipline through the use of Ignatius's *Spiritual Exercises*, first published in 1548 but conceived about twenty-five years earlier; they were not restricted by the usual monastic obligation of reciting Divine Office together but could do so privately, a novelty that allowed them the freedom to organize their time according to the ever-changing requirements of their social ministry; and they received the full support of the papacy plus special privileges, such as that of preaching and administering the sacraments anywhere, without the permission of the local bishop or parish priest. Education was an important feature of the Jesuits' program, and their educational institutions were highly effective. The first Jesuit college was founded at Gandía, Spain, in 1546. At Rome, Ignatius established the Roman College in 1551; one year later the German College was founded —also in Rome—and was administered by the Jesuits for the training of missionaries to Protestant Germany. Meanwhile other colleges were established within and outside Italy; by the time of Ignatius's death in 1556, Jesuits had established provinces with numerous colleges in Italy, Spain, and Portugal and had made a tentative beginning in Germany. The significance of Ignatius's life and work was recognized by his canonization in 1622.

The visual arts and music continued to flourish but changed their character in Rome under the reform popes. Nudity was no longer permitted in sacred art—this proscription created a clear distinction between sacred and secular works—and the artist was warned not to represent anything in his sacred art that was contrary to church dogma; his works were subject to examination by the Inquisition on these points.[36] Important for the architecture of the Catholic reform was the mother church of the Jesuit order—the Giesù in Rome (see Figure II–2, no. 6), which was begun in 1568 and consecrated in 1584; its design was widely copied elsewhere by the Jesuits and other orders, for it perfectly fulfilled the needs of the Catholic reform. In keeping with the new emphases of the Jesuits, it was designed to include a spacious nave (ideal for preaching to a large congregation), numerous confessionals, and many altars for masses said simultaneously. As pointed out above, the Jesuit schools used drama with music as an important part of their educational program. On the whole, until the seventeenth century Jesuits were little interested in the cultivation of music. The German College was a significant exception: its reputation for fine music was well established before 1600.[37] The Council of Trent's recommendations concerning music opposed secular elements in church works and stressed the importance of making the words intelligible.[38] Giovanni Animuccia and Giovanni Pierluigi da Palestrina are among the composers who served the papal

36. Mâle, *L'Art*, p. 1; and Weisbach, *Kunst*, p. 8.

37. For useful studies of the Jesuit contribution to the visual arts and music in the sixteenth and seventeenth centuries, see Wittkower, *Baroque*; for music in the German College in the same period, see Culley, *German*.

38. For the Council of Trent's position on church music, see Weinmann, *Konzil*; Fellerer, "Council"; and Lockwood, *Counter-Reformation*, pp. 74–79.

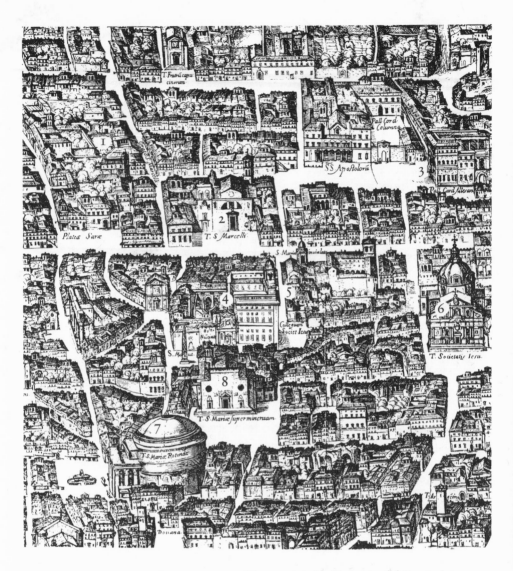

FIGURE II-2. Section of a 1593 map of Rome: (1) the Oratorio del Santissimo Crocifisso, or the Oratorio di San Marcello; (2) the church of San Marcello; (3) the Palazzo Bonelli, where Handel's oratorio *La Resurrezione* was first performed in 1708 under the patronage of Francesco Maria Ruspoli; (4) the Collegio Romano; (5) the Palazzo Pamphilj; (6) the Giesù; (7) the church of Santa Maria della Rotonda (the Pantheon); (8) the church of Santa Maria sopra Minerva. (Tempesta, *Roma*.)

chapel during this period, and the later sacred works of both reflect the influence of the reform. Animuccia was also important in the musical development of Philip Neri's Oratory; music by Palestrina was no doubt performed there as well. A leading figure in the commission on church music that was established to implement the recommendations of the Council of Trent was Cardinal Carlo Borromeo, the archbishop of Milan; the later sacred works of his maestro di cappella at the Milan cathedral in 1563–72, Vincenzo Ruffo, are particularly clear examples of the practical application of certain of the reform ideals.[39] The Spanish element among musicians in the reform period is reflected in the presence in Rome of a number of Spanish composers and performers—among them Cristóbal de Morales, Bartolome Escobedo, Tomás Luis de Victoria, and Francesco Soto de Langa. The last named, a singer and composer, made a significant contribution to the musical life of Philip Neri's Oratory, and Victoria may have done so as well, as indicated below.

Philip Neri and His Oratory

Philip Neri (1515–95)[40] was born in Florence of middle-class parents who were from noble, but no longer affluent, families. Francesco Neri, Philip's father, was a notary, an alchemy enthusiast, and a great admirer of Girolamo Savonarola, whom he remembered well: he had been about twenty-two years old when the Dominican reformer was burned. Philip was sent to the Dominican friary of San Marco for at least part of his education; later in his life he was known as an admirer of Savonarola and of the Dominicans at San Marco. One of his favorite teachers there, Servatio Mini, was a poet of *laude*, as were Savonarola and other Dominicans;[41] Philip undoubtedly became acquainted with *laude* at San Marco and elsewhere in Florence, a city important for the cultivation of this genre by the *laudesi*.

39. Lockwood, "Ruffo," and Lockwood, *Counter-Reformation*.
40. The most recent detailed study of Neri's life and work is Ponnelle, *Néri* (Ponnelle, *Neri*-Eng.; Ponnelle, *Neri*-It.); a more recent popular biography, which is generally reliable, is Trevor, *Neri*. Both include bibliographies of previous biographies and other sources. An invaluable source of information about Neri by those who knew him is *Processo*, carefully edited and copiously annotated with historical commentary.
41. Regarding Philip's association with Mini, see *Processo*, 3:177–78. The Dominicans of San Marco seem to have been of special importance for the cultivation of the *lauda*; Serafino Razzi, whose large collection of *laude* was published in 1663 (cf. the facsimile, Razzi, *Laudi*), was a Dominican of that friary.

B·P·PHILIPPVS·NERVS·EL·
CONGREG·ORATORII·FVNDATOR.

FIGURE II-3. St. Philip Neri (1515–95). The earliest known portrait.
(Reproduced by permission of I/Rf.)

In about 1533 Philip was sent to live with a relative at San Germano, near Montecassino, to learn his relative's business. Philip rejected the commercial life, however, and soon went to Rome, probably at first as a pilgrim. Little is known of his life in Rome from the mid-1530s to the late 1540s. He lived in the house of a Florentine customs officer, functioned as a tutor for the gentleman's children, and at the same time studied philosophy at the Sapienza (the University of Rome) and theology with the Augustinians. His period of study probably lasted no more than a year, after which he decided to devote his life to prayer and charitable works. He gave much practical assistance in the hospitals of Rome, which were in a deplorable state. He also spent many hours praying in the churches of Rome and in the catacombs of San Sebastiano on the ancient Via Appia. Of a mystical nature, he was particularly drawn to the catacombs as a place for prayer. There on Pentecost in about 1544 he experienced the mystical ecstacy that he interpreted as the love of God filling his heart and that confirmed his religious commitment. Despite his life of prayer and charitable work, Philip never joined a religious order, nor did he intend to establish one. After he had become a priest, however, he sent many of those who confessed to him to religious orders, particularly to the Dominicans and the Jesuits—Ignatius of Loyola is said to have compared Philip to a bell calling men into the Society of Jesus yet remaining outside.[42]

In the late 1540s Philip's confessor was Persiano Rosa, a priest at the church of San Girolamo della Carità. In 1548, with Rosa's assistance, Philip founded the Confraternita della Santissima Trinità dei Pellegrini (Confraternity of the Most Holy Trinity for the Pilgrims). The purpose of the confraternity was to aid the poor pilgrims who would be in Rome during the coming Holy Year of 1550. Until the arrival of the pilgrims, the members of the confraternity, laymen from all walks of life, performed various charitable works and met to pray together. A service for which they became well known was the Forty Hours devotion, in which a consecrated Host was exposed in a monstrance for forty hours to commemorate the period of Christ's entombment.[43] This service, which had become popular in Milan earlier in the century

42. *Processo*, 1:180.

43. Regarding Philip Neri and the Forty Hours service, see Santi, *Quarant'ore*, pp. 181–82; *Processo*, 1:71–72, n. 235; and Tacchi-Venturi, *Compagnia*, 1:229–37.

and had medieval antecedents, was soon adopted and strongly promoted by the Jesuits. The service forms a part of the complex background of the seventeenth-century *sepolcro*, discussed in chapter 8. Like Ignatius of Loyola, Philip favored frequent communion; the Forty Hours service was used as a means of fostering devotion to Christ in the Eucharist. After the Holy Year had passed, Rosa urged Philip to become a priest. Thus in 1551 the latter entered the priesthood and moved to San Girolamo della Carità (see the end papers, no. 6). Although he left the confraternity at this time, he had established it with strong roots; it operated a charitable hospice and convalescent home for over three centuries.[44]

Within a year after his move to San Girolamo, Philip began to attract a small group of six to eight laymen who came to his living quarters in the early afternoons to participate in informal religious discussions and to pray together. By 1554 attendance at these gatherings had grown considerably; since Philip needed larger quarters for the group, he was permitted to use a loft, previously a granary, over a side aisle of the church.[45] This loft was remodeled as an *oratorio*, an oratory or prayer hall. It is difficult to estimate the hall's seating capacity, since the church was drastically remodeled in the second half of the seventeenth century, but it would appear to have accommodated 150 to 200 persons.[46] In the spiritual exercises in this hall, Philip first introduced the practice of singing *laude*, a custom he no doubt remembered from his Florentine boyhood. From at least 1554 on, one may speak of the Oratory as an institution. Philip and his followers came to use the Italian word *oratorio* to refer to the institution as well as to their prayer hall and to the meetings, or "spiritual exercises" as they were also called, that took place in the hall. Thus they would commonly speak of "holding the oratory" on a certain day or at a certain time, of holding spiritual exercises "in the oratory," and of the association of priests and brothers who constituted "the Oratory." The large organization that eventually developed (discussed

44. For the history of this organization from its origin to the nineteenth century, see Morichini, *Istituti*, pp. 169–79.

45. Regarding the date 1554 as that of the move to the loft, see Gasbarri, *Oratorio fil.*, p. 17.

46. The area that is today regarded as Philip's oratory at San Girolamo is much smaller than in his time because of added walls and a basic change in the interior structure of the church.

FIGURE II-4. San Girolamo della Carità (left), after the seventeenth-
century renovation.
(Vasi, *Magnificenze*, pt. 7, no. 111.)

below) was officially called the Congregation of the Oratory, since
the oratory, in every sense, was their chief work, their way of
effecting church reform. The members of the organization, mostly
priests, were called Oratorians or Fathers of the Oratory.

A practice that Philip instituted as early as 1552 was that of
taking his followers on an all-day walk to visit the seven principal
churches of Rome: San Pietro in Vaticano, San Giovanni in Laterano, Santa Maria Maggiore, San Paolo fuori le mura, San Lorenzo
fuori le mura, Santa Croce in Gerusalemme, and San Sebastiano.[47]
These visits were occasions for a mixture of devotion and recreation. Devotions were held in the churches, and food and wine were
provided for the midday meal, usually in the garden of the Villa
Mattei (today a public park called the Villa Celimontana). After
the meal an "outdoor oratory," which included all elements of the
feast-day spiritual exercises conducted during the summer on the
Janiculum hill (discussed below), was held. An early seventeenth-

47. For a description and history of the visits to the seven churches, see Gasbarri, *La
visita.*

century list of the Oratorians' expenses for such a visit included, in addition to expenses for the food, those for the transportation of an organ and for singers; lutes and wind instruments were also used.[48] The visits normally took place several times each year, and one of them was always scheduled on *giovedì grasso* (Fat Thursday), the last Thursday of the carnival season; it was intended to offer a spiritual alternative to the licentious entertainments of the season. In the earliest period the visit to the seven churches was made by about twenty-five to thirty men; by the end of Philip's life, it had become so popular that as many as 2,000 persons, including high-ranking ecclesiastics, participated.

The history of the Oratory for more than two centuries is one of constant expansion, first in Rome, then throughout Italy and in other countries. An important early event in the expansion took place about 1564, when Philip was asked to become the rector of the large church of the Florentines in Rome, San Giovanni dei Fiorentini (see the end papers, no. 1). He accepted the position on the order of Pius IV. This position indirectly benefited the Oratory, since it offered Philip the opportunity to send six of his most faithful followers to San Giovanni to live as a religious community; they formed the nucleus of what later became the Congregation of the Oratory. Philip did not move to San Giovanni, however, as San Girolamo is nearby, and he continued the oratory there; in addition to their duties at San Giovanni, his six disciples assisted Philip daily with the oratory. By 1574 the oratory had become so popular that it overflowed the hall at San Girolamo. Philip found larger quarters, a hall near San Giovanni dei Fiorentini that was called by various names, including Sant'Orsola della Pietà, Oratorio dei Fiorentini, and Oratorio della Pietà (see Figure II–5 and the end papers, no. 2).[49] In 1526 Clement VII had given the old church of Sant'Orsola to the Arciconfraternita della Pietà dei Fiorentini, and the archconfraternity had demolished it to build their oratory on the same site. This oratory is also of interest in the seventeenth century, for it was the location of performances of oratorios by Stradella and his contemporaries (see below, p. 260). Although this building provided more space than San Girolamo for the

48. Ibid., pp. 36, 60–62.
49. For references to the history of this oratory, which was destroyed in 1888 to make way for an extension of Corso Vittorio Emanuele II, see Armellini, *Chiese*, 1:433, and Huelsen, *Chiese*, pp. 111, 501–2. The oratory is mentioned as a location for the Oratorians' spiritual exercises in *Processo*, 4:116.

FIGURE II-5. The courtyard and entrance to Sant'Orsola della Pietà—
also called the Oratorio dei Fiorentini and the Oratorio
della Pietà, among other names. The building was demolished in 1888 to make way for an extension of a
street, the present Corso Vittorio Emanuele II.
(Courtesy of the Museo di Roma.)

Oratorians' spiritual exercises, the arrangement soon proved unsatisfactory because of difficulties with the Florentines who owned
it. Thus Philip and his followers began to investigate the possibilities of obtaining a church exclusively for their own use. In 1575
Gregory XIII granted them the old church of Santa Maria in
Vallicella and at the same time formally recognized them as a
religious community. Rather than having the old church restored,
Philip had it demolished and in its place had a new one constructed;
officially it retained the old name, but informally it was called the
Chiesa Nuova, the name by which it is best known today (see the
end papers, no. 3). The size and sumptuousness of the Chiesa
Nuova testify to the popularity of Philip and his work. Since he
was loved and supported by those from the most humble to the
most exalted of Rome's social strata, obtaining the funds for
building his new church was not a problem. In 1577 the central

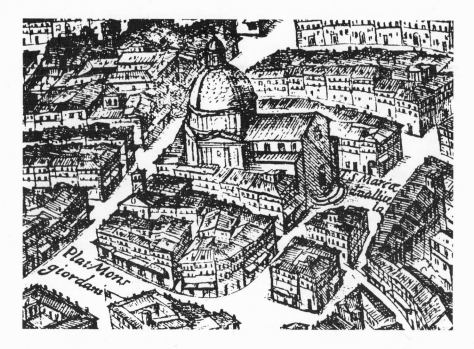

FIGURE II-6. The Chiesa Nuova (Santa Maria in Vallicella) in 1593, before the construction of the oratory that now stands beside it.

(Tempesta, *Roma*.)

part of the Chiesa Nuova was completed and dedicated; the Oratorians may have moved into quarters nearby as early as 1576.[50] By 1578 the community had increased from the six who first moved into San Giovanni to thirty-eight;[51] hundred of Romans were attending the daily oratory. The Oratorians were not to have an entirely suitable hall at the Chiesa Nuova until 1640, when the one designed by Francesco Borromini, which stands next to the church, was completed. Meanwhile they used various halls that they were able to acquire near or adjoining the church,[52] and they used the church itself for those spiritual exercises that attracted the largest attendance.[53] The move to the Chiesa Nuova was the last

50. It is uncertain whether the date was 1576 or 1578. (*Processo*, 3:141, n. 1962.)

51. Pastor, *Popes*, 19:180, 584.

52. For the exact locations of four halls used for the spiritual exercises at the Chiesa Nuova in the sixteenth and early seventeenth centuries, see Gasbarri, *Oratorio fil.*, p. 50.

53. Alaleona, *Oratorio*, p. 27.

one; that church is still the home of the Fathers of the Oratory in Rome. Philip did not move there when his congregation did, however, as he preferred not to leave his old quarters at San Girolamo. He moved to the Chiesa Nuova only when ordered to do so by the pope in 1583, and he selected the smallest and worst room in the Oratorians' living quarters. It was after he had moved to the Chiesa Nuova, during the last period of his life, that he became widely regarded as a living saint; it was also then that Gregory XIII offered him a cardinalate, which he refused.[54] Immediately after his death in 1595, his followers began to press for his canonization. In 1622—together with Ignatius of Loyola, Francis Xavier, Theresa of Jesus, and Isidore the Husbandman (Isidore of Madrid)—he was canonized. It is indicative of the continuing Spanish political and cultural influence that all but Philip were Spaniards.

The Congregation of the Oratory and the Spiritual Exercises

The institution that Philip founded is clearly a projection of his personality. Only in terms of that personality, which has often been compared to that of St. Francis of Assisi, can one understand the character of the Congregation of the Oratory and the spiritual exercises that formed the immediate social context within which the oratorio developed. Philip was a mystic, and he saw himself as a kind of hermit, detached from the values of the world. Yet he worked in the world, with unswerving dedication, to lead those around him to sanctification. He had no desire to seek ecclesiastical titles or honors. His success seems to have depended upon his extraordinarily attractive and cheerful personality and his wisdom in estimating the spiritual needs of those who came to him for guidance. A fun-loving and sometimes whimsical man, he was particularly well known for his unusual sense of humor. His pranks and practical jokes, about which there are numerous stories, were often intended to counteract tendencies of pride and foster humility in himself and his associates. He was especially interested in working with young people and was highly successful in involving them in a combination of recreational and spiritual experiences. Utterly unlike his older contemporary, Ignatius of Loyola, he was casual and informal in method and wished to avoid consistency of rule,

54. *Processo*, 1:287.

structure, and discipline in favor of ad hoc decisions and procedures motivated by his love of God and fellow man. It is not surprising that a person of such independence, such nonconformity, was uninterested in joining an existing religious order or in founding a new one.

When it became clear to Philip and his associates that the Oratory would benefit if they were recognized as an official community within the church, he agreed. Nevertheless, he did not permit the Congregation of the Oratory to become a religious order, as a few of his disciples would have preferred. His refusal to move to San Giovanni dei Fiorentini to join his disciples in a common life and his reluctance to move to the Chiesa Nuova are only two among many indications of his unwillingness to serve as the superior of a religious order. He insisted that the congregation be a democratic organization. Although he was elected its prefect, he tried not to become involved in its deliberations; he was always consulted on important matters, however, and his opinions were respected. Unlike a religious order, the members of the Congregation of the Oratory, reflecting Philip's independent spirit, take no vows of poverty or obedience. They are either secular priests or brothers, working together in free association, bound together only by Christian charity, and free to leave the congregation whenever they wish. Although Philip did not oppose the formation of oratories modeled on his in other cities, he insisted that they be organizationally independent. During his lifetime oratories like the one in Rome were begun in three other cities of the Papal State (San Severino, Fermo, and Camerino) as well as in Naples, Palermo, and Cotignac, France. Within a century after his death, approximately one hundred oratories were functioning throughout Europe —two thirds of them were outside Italy—and a few were active in the Far East and the New World.[55] (English-speaking oratories did not begin until 1848, when John Henry Newman, as a new convert to the Roman Catholic church, joined the congregation and founded oratories at Birmingham and London.)

The earliest of Philip's spiritual exercises, the afternoon meetings for discussion and prayer that began in his living quarters at San Girolamo, were nothing more than informal continuations of his contacts with his penitents—those who frequently confessed to

55. For a list of oratories with the dates of their foundation, see Capecelatro, *Neri*, 2:701–4.

him. The meetings were held daily and were intended to reinforce the experience of the confessional. By the time increased attendance had forced the meetings to move into the first oratory, they had developed a certain structure; yet they retained the casual manner that was so much a part of Philip's personality. One of his disciples, Cesare Baronio, later a cardinal and the author of a monumental history of the church, described the spiritual exercises of around 1557–58 in the first volume of his history, since it seemed to him that they must have been much like meetings of early Christians:

There was first a little silent prayer, and then a brother would read some spiritual book. During that reading usually the same father [Philip Neri], who supervised everything, would discuss what was read, explaining it, amplifying it, and impressing it into the hearts of the listeners. And sometimes he would ask others about it, proceeding almost in the manner of a dialogue; and this exercise would last perhaps an hour, to the very great enjoyment of all. After that a brother would go up, in turn, to a chair that was raised by a few steps, and without any ornament of language he would preach a sermon woven from the approved lives of the saints, from some place in the Scriptures, and from some place in the writings of the Fathers. After him would follow a second [brother], and he would preach another sermon in the same style, but on a different subject. Finally came the third, who would tell of the history of the church, according to the order of the time. Each [sermon] lasted one-half hour. When that was done, to the marvelous utility and consolation of the listeners, a spiritual *lauda* was sung. And after a few more prayers, the exercise concluded. When things were organized in this manner and established with the authority of the pope, it seemed that, as much as the present times allow, the ancient apostolic manner had been renewed.[56]

The role of the laymen, or brothers, in these early services at San Girolamo is of special interest. They not only functioned as readers, but they commented on the reading when Philip asked them, and they also preached sermons in simple, conversational language. When their participation as preachers involved Philip in an investigation by the Inquisition in 1568 under Pius V, the Oratory was saved by the intervention of Philip's powerful friend, Carlo Borromeo. Those who attended the oratory in this early period were men from all strata of society—but more from the artisan class than the aristocracy. (Women were not admitted to

56. Translated from the Italian: Baronio, *Annali*, 1:160; for Baronio's Latin version, which differs slightly but not in essentials, see Baronio, *Annales*, 1:473.

the oratory in the sixteenth century.) The music in the spiritual exercises described by Baronio plays only a small role: one brief composition performed near the end of a service lasting slightly more than two and one-half hours.

By the 1570s the Oratorians had developed several clearly distinguished types of spiritual exercises for different times of the day and different seasons, and for different sizes and types of groups. The tentative beginnings of all these date back to the 1550s.[57] On ferial days—except Saturdays—an exercise began in the early afternoon, after the midday meal;[58] this was, and is still, a period of relaxation for Romans, and the Oratorians intended to make good use of the time. This service lasted about two and one-half hours and included all the elements of that of the late 1550s described above by Baronio. The type of person who attended these exercises had changed by 1570, for in that year the composer Giovanni Animuccia mentioned an increase in the attendance at the Oratory of "prelates and the most important gentlemen";[59] in 1576 the poet, musician, and future Oratorian Giovenale Ancina wrote in a letter that those present at the daily afternoon spiritual exercises that he had been attending in the oratory at San Giovanni dei Fiorentini included "honorable persons: bishops and prelates."[60] There had also been a change in those selected to

57. In the index of *Processo*, vol. 4, under the entry "Oratorio," the references to the times and types of meetings in the 1550s tend to be brief and inconsistent but generally include the essentials discussed here. For descriptions of the spiritual exercises, see Gasbarri, *Oratorio rom.*, pp. 276–79; Gasbarri, *Oratorio fil.*, pp. 31–34; Damilano, *Ancina*, pp. 32–35; Alaleona, *Oratorio*, pp. 22–28; and Ponnelle, *Neri*-Eng., pp. 202–3, 263–65, 389–402.

58. Contemporary documents indicating the time of day for such services usually state that they begin at "nineteen hours" or "twenty hours." (Cf. the documents quoted in *Processo*, 2:309 and Pastor, *Popes*, 19:585.) These times must be interpreted in terms of a manner of measuring time, common in sixteenth-century Italy, according to which the numbering of the hours begins at sunset or slightly after, at the time of the "Angelus," signaled by the ringing of church bells. Thus the documents indicate that the services begin about four to five hours before sunset; in addition, they sometimes indicate that the services begin after a meal—the midday meal. This system of numbering the hours of the day was still in use in late eighteenth-century Italy, when Wolfgang Goethe explained it thoroughly in his *Italienische Reise*. See Goethe's explanation and diagram, comparing German and Italian systems of time measurement, in his *Reise*, at the entry dated Verona, 17 September 1786, in *Goethes Werke*, published under the auspices of Sophie of Saxony, ed. Gustav von Loeper, et al. 133 vols. in 143 (Weimar: Hermann Böhlau, 1887–1919), Abteilung 3, vol. 1, p. 209. See also the references to the Italian system of time measurement in Hale, *Renaissance*, p. 13, and Ward, *Time*, 1:16.

59. Animuccia, *Il secondo libro delle laudi* (Rome, 1570), dedication.

60. Ancina to Matteo Ancina, 28 May 1576, in *Processo*, 2:309; part of the letter is quoted in Damilano, *Ancina*, p. 15.

preach, for Ancina stated that the sermons were given by four or five highly qualified persons; one whom he heard was a distinguished Jesuit.[61] Ancina does not mention the participation of laymen. Those who had previously preached the sermons had become observers—they would evidently not presume to preach before bishops and prelates. Yet Philip's tradition of making the sermons informal, of avoiding a rhetorical style, was retained in this period, as it has been throughout the history of the Oratorians in Rome. According to the same letter by Ancina, "At the end [of the spiritual exercise] they perform a little music to console and restore the spirits torn by the preceding discourses." Thus the role of the music in the afternoon service was still limited to that described above by Baronio. It is not clear from Ancina's and other contemporary descriptions of the afternoon service whether the music consisted of congregational singing or performances by professional musicians, but it was probably the former. In 1577 it is certain that congregational singing was used, for the dedication of *Il terzo libro delle laudi spirituali* (Rome, 1577), published for the Oratorians' exercises, states that the *laude* have been kept simple so that they "can be sung by all." In addition to the afternoon service, another one took place on ferial days in the evening, at the time of the "Angelus" or an hour before it. This exercise was only about one hour long, was attended primarily by the Fathers of the Oratory, and included the penitential practice of self-flagellation three days each week; normally the only music sung was a Marian antiphon. In the mornings on Sundays and other feast days, exercises slightly longer but that included approximately the same amount of music were held, also mainly for the Fathers of the Oratory.[62]

More important for music than the exercises discussed above was the one, open to the public, held on Sundays and other feast days after vespers; this service came to be known as the *oratorio vespertino*. On these days during the period from Easter to All Saints Day, vespers would be followed by a sermon in the church. After the sermon the Oratorians and those who wished to attend

61. About 1578 the Oratorian Francesco Maria Tarugi also stated that the sermons in the oratory were given by priests. (*Processo*, 2:33, n. 1084.)

62. A *lauda* might have been sung at the morning and evening services in the early seventeenth century, if Agostino Manni's *Essercizi spirituali* (Brescia, 1609) reflects Roman Oratorian practice at that time.

the service would take a pleasant walk to a high point on the Janiculum hill, across the Tiber, near the monastery of Sant'Onofrio. In this beautiful spot with a marvelous view of the city, they would hold spiritual exercises consisting of a *lauda*, a brief sermon recited from memory by a boy, another *lauda*, and one or two sermons by Oratorians, each sermon preceded and followed by a *lauda*. The place on the Janiculum hill where these exercises were held is clearly evident today, for the Oratorians had an outdoor theater constructed there in the first quarter of the seventeenth century for the spiritual exercises; the theater is now used for summer dramatic performances.[63] During the warmest part of the summer, the Oratorians did not take the walk to the Janiculum; instead they conducted the service in the central part of Rome—often in a courtyard, garden, or *piazza* by a church. Philip described these summer services in a report that he submitted to the pope:

Our Congregation, other than [holding] the daily spiritual discussions which take place in our Oratory, has been accustomed on feast days to holding the same exercises as a kind of recreation in various parts of Rome; and the more to allure every sort of person, between the discussions of the priests we are accustomed to have some boys recite some edifying sermons, and it is seen that our Lord is served with each of these nets for fishing souls. Last year these exercises were continued in the courtyard of the Minerva [the church of the Dominicans, Santa Maria sopra Minerva, see Figure II–2, no. 8] with a much greater crowd than usual all summer, and this year the same thing was done continually, as long as good weather lasted, in the vineyard of the Compagnia de' Napoletani, with a crowd of perhaps three or four thousand persons; and now with the same attendance it has been transferred to the church of the Brescians in Giulia street. Practice has shown that by inserting the pleasure of spiritual music and the simplicity and purity of boys into the serious exercises done by serious persons one draws many more people of every sort.[64]

Philip's emphasis in this report upon a mixture of recreation and devotion is characteristic of his religious attitude in general. The function of the music, as of the sermons recited by boys, is to attract more people of all classes to the exercises; that it achieved

63. For historical comments on the theater of the Oratorians on the Janiculum hill, see Gasbarri, *Oratorio rom.*, pp. 323–25.

64. Translated from Marciano, *Oratorio*, 1:37. The "vineyard" mentioned is possibly the large courtyard behind the church of Santo Spirito della Compagnia dei Napoletani (see end paper, no. 5).

its purpose is clear from the thousands who attended. Although the date of the above document is uncertain, it was written after 1575, for Philip uses the official term *Congregation* for his organization. Another report—this one sent by the Oratorians to Gregory XIII in 1578—corroborates much of the information in the one previously quoted and adds some further details. After discussing the daily exercises, the report continues:

There is a sermon on feast days after Vespers.
And after the sermon the fathers of the house go to Giulia street to the church of Santo Spirito de la Compagnia de' Napoletani, where more than three thousand persons gather. And there, since it is more comfortable, the people are allured by devotional music and by having boys recite some edifying things written by the fathers of the house. And then [the exercise] concludes with two discussions of compunctious and affective things. Where, through the grace of God, there has been and there is notable fruit. And those from the German College come there to listen, much to their edification.[65]

Since the church mentioned is much too small for 3,000 people, the exercises described must have taken place outdoors, in the same "vineyard" mentioned in the report previously quoted. This report, like the previous one, refers to the use of music to allure the people to the service. During the winter months, from All Saints Day to Easter, the *oratorio vespertino* was held in the oratory, or perhaps in the Chiesa Nuova. The attendance would necessarily be restricted to the capacity of the location used, but otherwise the service appears to have been essentially the same as that held in the summer.

Few details are known about the music at the *oratorio vespertino*, but general indications show that this service included more music (before and after each sermon) and more elaborate compositions than the services on ferial days; yet it might also have included congregational singing. The dedication of the third book of *laude* (1577), cited above, states that the reason the two previous books (by Animuccia, 1563 and 1570) were more elaborate is that they were intended for the *oratorio vespertino*: they were meant "to hold the people" at "those extraordinary exercises, which are conducted publicly on feast days, now in one, now in another part of Rome." Despite these remarks, the first of Ani-

65. Translated from Pastor, *Popes*, 19:585–86.

FIGURE II-7. Giovanni Animuccia (d. 1571).
(Reproduced by permission of I/Bc.)

IESVS. MARIA.

CANTO.

IL PRIMO LIBRO
DELLE LAVDI DI GIO: ANIMVCCIA,
COMPOSTE PER CONSOLATIONE, ET A
REQVISITIONE DI MOLTE PERSONE,
SPIRITVALI, ET DEVOTE,
TANTO RELIGIOSI, QVANTO SECOLARI.

In Roma per Valerio Dorico, l'Anno 1563.   A

FIGURE II-8. Title page of Giovanni Animuccia's first book of *laude*, written for Philip Neri's Oratory at San Girolamo della Carità.
(Courtesy of GB/Lcm.)

muccia's *lauda* books contains simple music; the second book, however, is indeed more elaborate. Animuccia's reason for the change in style in the second book, as mentioned above, is that the oratory had begun to be frequented by more distinguished persons, whom he evidently wished to please. The *oratorio vespertino* would clearly require trained musicians for the performance of the type of music found in Animuccia's second *lauda* book. It is for this service that some of the finest musicians of Rome are said to have performed gratis for many years.[66] Animuccia, the first maestro di cappella of the oratory, was a compatriot of Philip Neri; he was in Rome by at least 1551 and succeeded Palestrina in 1555 as maestro of the Cappella Giulia. It is not certain when he began to

66. Alaleona, *Oratorio*, p. 29.

direct the music in the oratory, but it may have been in the 1550s, since that is when his close association with Philip began. He continued in his position at the oratory until his death in 1571.[67] Palestrina was probably among the performers in the oratory at times, but he appears never to have been the maestro di cappella at the oratory, as Baini assumed.[68] The noted Spanish composer Tomás Luis de Victoria was a chaplain at San Girolamo della Carità from 1578 to 1585. He lived in the same house as Philip Neri for five years and probably participated in the music of the oratory, but no documentation of such participation is known.[69] Francesco Soto de Langa (1534 or 1538–1619), another Spaniard and a soprano in the papal chapel, lived with the Oratorians from 1566 and became an Oratorian in 1571. He contributed to the music in the oratory as the maestro di cappella (1571–96), a singer, a composer, and a compiler of *laude* for publication.[70] Soto was particularly well known for drawing large crowds to the oratory to hear his solo performances of *laude*;[71] one would assume that he sang these simple pieces in ornamented versions, but no documentation has come to light regarding his performance practice. The *oratorio vespertino* in the winter period is the one that eventually grew to be the most important for its music.[72] This was particularly the case near the end of the sixteenth century when the number of sermons was reduced to one[73]—a measure allowing more time for the music before and after the sermon and

67. For Animuccia's connection with the Oratory, see Casimiri, "Òasi," pp. 121–22; and K. Fellerer, "Animuccia," in *MGG*, 1:col. 483.

68. In Baini, *Palestrina*, 2:5, Palestrina is assumed to have taken the place of Animuccia at the oratory in 1571, when the latter died; yet Soto appears to have become the maestro di cappella in that year. Regarding Palestrina's connections with the Oratorians, see Alaleona, *Oratorio*, pp. 76–78, and Casimiri, "Òasi," pp. 123–25.

69. Casimiri, "Vittoria," pp. 148–53.

70. J. Llorens, "Soto de Langa," in *MGG*, 12:cols. 939–40; Casimiri, "Òasi," pp. 122–23; Gasbarri, *Oratorio rom.*, pp. 146–45 [sic].

71. Alaleona, *Oratorio*, pp. 40–41.

72. According to Ponnelle, *Neri*-Eng., pp. 398–99, the increasing emphasis on music in the *oratorio vespertino* in the winter months resulted from the influence of the Naples Oratory, founded in 1586. More research on the role of music in the Naples Oratory would be necessary to verify this hypothesis. Research on music in the Naples Oratory is in progress by Mario Borrelli of Naples. A summary of the development of the Naples Oratory from 1586 to 1615, written in 1651 by Antonio Talpa (one of the founders of the Naples Oratory), indicates, contrary to Ponnelle's assertion, that the Neapolitan *oratorio vespertino* was quite close to that of Rome and that the service was introduced "by the Fathers of Naples in imitation of the Fathers of Rome." (Borrelli, *Costituzioni*, p. 364.) For a survey of the late sixteenth- and early seventeenth-century music owned by the Naples Oratory, with editions of some of the music, see *IMAMI*, vol. 5.

73. Alaleona, *Oratorio*, p. 28; Damilano, *Ancina*, p. 35.

contributing to the general format of the seventeenth-century oratorio as a musical genre: a composition in two structural parts, with a pause between them for a sermon. The earliest compositions known that could be termed oratorios, some of the works in Giovanni Francesco Anerio's *Teatro armonico spirituale di madrigali* (Rome, 1619), were composed for the *oratorio vespertino*.

Antecedents of the Oratorio in Neri's Oratory

At the beginning of this chapter, a number of antecedents of the oratorio, both distant and immediate, were discussed. Of those genres only the *lauda* was characteristically fostered in Philip Neri's oratory. His Florentine background is no doubt responsible for his introduction of *laude* into the spiritual exercises. As mentioned above, the tradition of singing *laude* at devotional exercises was strong in Florence and was cultivated by the Dominicans at San Marco, where he received part of his education; furthermore, some of the *lauda* texts set by Animuccia for Philip's oratory were of Florentine origin. Philip was familiar, not only with the Renaissance *lauda*, but with that of the Middle Ages as well. He owned a copy of the *Laude di Frate Jacopone da Todi*,[74] and he included that book among the spiritual writings that were read and commented upon in the daily exercises in the oratory.[75] Thus it is not surprising that Philip and the Oratorians turned to *laude* for their music and that *laude* constitute most of the music printed in the sixteenth century especially for his oratory.

Books of Laude *Printed for the Oratory*

Between 1563 and 1600 three series of *lauda* books were printed for use in Philip Neri's oratory; these are noted in the following list:[76]

74. Pastor, *Popes*, 19:176, n. 2; Ponnelle, *Neri*-Eng., p. 204.

75. Ponnelle, *Neri*-Eng., pp. 204–5, 207–10.

76. This list is adapted from Smither, "Laude," pp. 192–93. In the list spellings, including endings that do not agree in gender, are those given on the title pages. Capitalization and punctuation have been slightly modified. Library locations for items I/1 and I/2 are found in *RISM*, ser. B II, vol. 1, "Animuccia." For all other items, designations are given for *RISM*, ser. B I, vol. 1. The number of voices used in the book is stated, in brackets, for those books that do not include this information on their title pages.

I/1:1563.   Il primo libro delle laudi di Gio. Animuccia composte per consolazione et a requisitione di molte persone spirituali et devote tanto religiosi quanto secolari. In Roma per Valerio Dorico, l'anno 1563. [4 v.]

I/2:1570.   Di Gio. Animuccia il secondo libro delle laudi. Dove si contengno mottetti, salmi, et alte diverse cose spirituali vulgari, et latine . . . In Roma per gli heredi di Antonio Blado, stampatori camerali, l'anno 1570. [2–8 v.]

I/3:1577.   Il terzo libro delle laudi spirituali stampate ad instantia delli Reverendi Padri della Congregatione dell'Oratorio. Con una istruttione per promuovere e conservare il peccatore convertito. In Roma per gli heredi di Antonio Blado, stampatori camerali, l'anno M.D.LXXVII. [3 v., *RISM* 1577³a.]

SERIES II

II/1:1583.   Il primo libro delle laude spirituali a tre voci stampata ad instanza delli Reverendi Padri della Congregatione dello Oratorio. Con privilegio del Sommo Pontifice. In Roma, per Alessandro Gardano, 1583. [Essentially a reprint of I/3, but with larger format; six *laude* are deleted, and some *laude* are modified. *RISM* 1583³.]

II/2:1583.   Il secondo libro delle laude spirituali a tre et a quattro voci, stampata ad instanza delli Reverendi Padri della Congregatione dello Oratorio. Con privilegio del Sommo Pontifice. In Roma per Alessandro Gardano. 1583. [*RISM* 1583⁴.]

II/1R:1585.   [Reprint of II/1:1583. *RISM* 1585⁹.]
II/2R:1585.   [Reprint of II/2:1583. *RISM* 1585¹⁰.]
II/3:1588.   Il terzo libro delle laudi spirituali a tre e a quattro voci stampata ad instanza delli Reverendi Padri della Congregatione del'Oratorio. Con privilegio del Sommo Pontefice. In Roma per Alessandro Gardano. Ad instantia d'Iacomo Tornieri. 1588. [Dedication by Francesco Soto. *RISM* 1588¹¹.]

II/1–3:1589. Libro delle laudi spirituali dove in uno sono com-
presi i tre libri già stampati. E ridutta la musica à più
brevità e facilità con l'accrescimento delle parole, e
con l'aggiunta de molte laudi nuove, che si can-
teranno nel modo che dentro si mostra. Stampata ad
instanza delli Reverendi Padri della Congregatione
dell'Oratorio. Con privilegio del Sommo Pontefice.
Con licentia de' superiori. In Roma, per Alessandro
Gardano, ad instantia de Iacomo Tornieri. 1589.
[2–4 v. Reprint: II/1, II/2, II/3. RISM 1589.²]

II/4:1591. Il quarto libro delle laudi a tre et quatro voci stampate ad instantia delli Reverendi Padri della Congregatione del'Oratorio. Con licenza d' superiori. In
Roma. Apud Alexandrum Gardanum. Impensis As-
canij & Hieronymi Donangeli. 1591. [Dedication by
Francesco Soto. RISM 1591³.]

II/5:1598. Il quinto libro delle laudi spirituali, a tre, & a quattro voci del Reverendi P. Francesco Soto, sacerdote
della Congregatione dell'Oratorio. In Ferrara, appresso Vittorio Baldini, stampatore camerale, 1598.
Con licenza de' superiori. Ad instanza delli RR. PP.
di detta Congregatione. [RISM 1598⁴.]

SERIES III

III/1:1599. Tempio armonico della Beatissima Vergine N. S. fab-
ricatoli per opra del R. P. Giovenale A.[ncina] P.
della Congreg. del'Oratorio. Prima parte à tre voci
stampata in Roma da Nicolò Mutij 1599. [RISM
1599⁶.]

III/2:1600. Nuove laudi ariose della Beat.ᵐᵃ Vergine scelte da
diversi autori à quattro voci per il rever. D. Giovanni
Arascione piemontese da Cairo prete secolare. In
Roma, per Nicolò Mutij 1600. [Dedication by
Giovenale Ancina, 15 November 1599, states, on f.
3ᵛ, that this is the second part of his *Tempio armonico. RISM* 1600⁵.]

This list represents nine different books and four reprints
(II/1, II/1R, II/2R, II/1–3), and the books include approximately
five hundred different texts and slightly fewer musical composi-

FIGURE II-9. Agostino Manni (1548–1618).
(Reproduced by permission of I/Rf.)

tions. Animuccia, the earliest maestro di cappella of Neri's oratory, was the composer of books I/1 and I/2. Soto is generally considered to be the compiler and/or composer of the *laude* in series II,[77] although his name appears only in II/3, 4, and 5. The entire repertory of *lauda* texts is anonymous in the printed books, but many of the texts were drawn from preexisting *lauda* books and were written by poets whose names are known.[78] Some of the texts in the earlier books are of Florentine origin, but it is probable

77. J. Llorens, "Soto de Langa," in *MGG*, 12:cols. 939–40; *Processo*, 1:34, n. 131; Alaleona, *Oratorio*, p. 52.
78. According to Prizer, "Animuccia," a study in preparation. I gratefully acknowledge the help of Professor William F. Prizer, who kindly made available to me the unpublished results of his research on the *lauda*.

that those in the later books were either written or adapted from existing sources by Agostino Manni (1548–1618.)[79] A well-educated person and poet of some skill, Manni joined the Oratory in 1577, the year in which I/3 was published. In addition to his *lauda* texts, Manni wrote a number of other works, including two books of spiritual exercises reflecting Oratorian practices and possibly the *Rappresentatione di Anima et di Corpo* set to music by Emilio de' Cavalieri and performed at the oratory in 1600; the *Rappresentatione* is discussed in chapter 3. Giovenale Ancina (1545–1604),[80] the author of about one-third of the texts and the compiler and composer of the music in III/1 and 2, became an Oratorian at Rome in 1578. He was a member of the Naples Oratory for the first ten years of that institution's existence (1586–96). After returning to Rome briefly in 1596, he suddenly left to avoid being made a bishop by Clement VIII; he eventually returned, however, at the insistence of the pope. He was consecrated the bishop of Saluzzo in 1602 and was beatified by Leo XIII in 1889.

Like other sixteenth-century *laude* the texts of the *laude* printed for use in Neri's oratory continue a tradition that dates from the Middle Ages. Both the medieval and sixteenth-century *laude* include poems of praise, meditations, invocations, exhortations, descriptions of sacred scenes, narratives, monologues, dialogues, and various mixtures of these types.[81] The Oratorians' *lauda* books consist mostly of pieces with Italian texts. The only exceptions are I/2, which includes twenty-seven Latin motets and only eighteen Italian *laude*; II/3, which includes two pieces with Spanish texts; and II/5, which includes one piece with a Spanish text. The *laude* in these books have three to seventeen strophes sung to the same music. Refrain forms, particularly those popular in Florence in the late fifteenth and early sixteenth centuries and associated with the *frottola* and the *canto carnascialesco*, predominate in the earlier books.[82] There are also nonrefrain forms in the earlier books, and these tend to continue in the later books. The most frequent lengths of poetic lines in the later books are those of seven and eleven syllables, as are all of the lines in

79. Alaleona, *Oratorio*, p. 38.

80. For Ancina's life and works, see Damilano, *Ancina*.

81. For discussions and examples of the texts of Oratorian *laude*, see Alaleona, *Oratorio*, pp. 51–57, 82–88; Pasquetti, *Oratorio*, pp. 95–115; and Damilano, *Ancina*, pp. 42–74.

82. According to Prizer, "Animuccia."

FIGURE II-10. Title page of Giovenale Ancina's *Tempio armonico*
(Rome, 1599).
(Courtesy of I/Bc.)

Examples II–1 through II–4. The texts of Examples II–3 and II–4 (pp. 67–69), which include a mixture of seven- and eleven-syllable lines, are more characteristic of the later *laude* than those of Examples II–1 and II–2, which use only one length of line. Some *laude* of the sixteenth century, including some Oratorian *laude*, are based on secular songs, and others appear to be based on preexisting *laude*.[83]

EXAMPLE II-1. *Lauda*, "Anima mia che pensi"—Anon. (I/3, pp. 39–40).

(C. = Corpo. A. = Anima.)

(B. = Body. S. = Soul.)

C. Anima mia che pensi?
   Perchè dogliosa stai,
   sempre traendo guai?

B. My soul, what are you thinking?
   Why are you so sad,
   always bearing grief?

A. Vorrei riposo, e pace,
   vorrei diletto, e gioia,
   e trovo affanno, e noia.

S. I would have rest, and peace,
   I would have joy, and delight,
   but I find sorrow, and boredom.

C. Ecco i miei sensi prendi,
   qui ti riposa, e godi
   in mille varij modi.

B. Here are my senses, take them;
   rest here, and enjoy yourself
   in thousands of diverse ways.

A. Non vo' più ber queste acque,
   che la mia sete ardente
   infiamman maggiormente.

S. No more will I drink these waters,
   which my burning thirst
   increase with greater flame.

83. For comments on *lauda* text sources, in addition to Prizer, "Animuccia," see Alaleona, *Oratorio*, pp. 57 and 75, n. 1; Alaleona, "Laudi"; and Damilano, *Ancina*, pp. 42–47.

(EXAMPLE II-I, continued)

C. Prendi gl'honor del mondo:
  qui gioir quanto vuoi,
  qui satiar ti poi.

B. Take the worldly honors:
  here rejoice as you wish,
  here you can be satisfied.

A. No, no, ch'io so per prova
  con quanto assentio, e fele,
  copre il suo falso mele.

S. No, for I know from experience
  with how much bitterness and gall
  its false honey is covered.

C. Alma, d'ogni altra cosa
  tu sei più bella, e vaga;
  in te dunque ti appaga.

B. Soul, your beauty is greater
  than any other thing;
  in yourself be satisfied.

A. Già non mi feci io stessa;
  e come in me potrei
  quetar gli affetti miei?

S. But I did not make myself;
  and how would I be able
  to calm my own affections?

C. Lasso, che di noi fia?
  Se ritrosa sei tanto,
  starenci sempre in pianto.

B. Alas, what will happen to us?
  If you are so contrary,
  we shall always be in tears.

A. Questo no, se m'ascolti,
  e se meco rimiri
  a più alti desiri.
  Terra, perchè mi tiri
  pur'alla terra? Hor segui il
   volar mio,
  et ambedue riposarenci in Dio.

S. Not so if you listen to me,
  and if with me you gaze upon
  more noble objects of desire.
  Earth, why do you draw me
  still to the ground? Now follow
   my flight,
  and we shall both repose in God.

EXAMPLE II-2. *Lauda*, "Nell'apparir del sempiterno Sole"—Soto
  (anon. in II/2, fols 8^v–9^r; attrib. to Soto in III/2, p. 19).

Nell' ap-pa-rir del sem-pi-ter-no So-le, ch'a mez-za not-te

più ri-lu-ce in-tor-no che l'al-tro non fa-ria di mez-zo gior-no, -no,

* *The tie is required for some of the stanzas.*

(EXAMPLE II-2, continued)

Nell'apparir del sempiterno Sole,
    ch'a mezza notte più riluce
      intorno
    che l'altro non faria di mezzo giorno,

With the appearance of the eternal Sun,
    which at midnight shines more brightly
      forth
    than the other does in midst of day,

Cantaron gloria gli angioli nel cielo
    et meritaro udir si dolc'accenti
    pastori, che guardavano gli
      armenti.

The angels sang glory in the sky
    and the shepherds watching their flocks
    were worthy of hearing such sweet
      accents.

Onde là verso l'humile Bethlemme
    preson la via dicendo, "Andiamo un
      tratto
    et si vedrem' questo mirabil fatto."

From there toward the humble Bethlehem
    they took the road, saying, "Let us
      go
    and try to see this marvelous event."

Quivi trovarò in villi panni
      advolto
    il fanciul con Gioseffe e con Maria—
    O benedetta e nobil compagnia.

There they found, wrapped in common
      cloth,
    the boy with Joseph and with Mary—
    Oh blessed and noble company.

Giunti i pastori all'humile presepe,
    di stupor pieni e d'alta meraviglia
    l'un verso l'altro fissero le cilia.

The shepherds at the humble manger,
    filled with amazement and great marvel,
    fixed their eyes upon each other.

Poi cominciaro vicendevolmente,
    con boscareccie e semplice parole,
    lieti a cantar fin che nascesi il sole:

Then they began alternately,
    with rustic and simple words,
    joyously to sing until the sun was born:

℣ "Io," dicea l'uno, "alla cappanna mia
    vorrei condurlo, ch'è lontana poco,
    dove ne cibo mancherià ne foco."

"I," said one, "would like to take him
    to my cabin, not far away,
    where neither food nor fire is lacking."

℟ "Io," dicea l'altro, "alla città regale
    con frettolosi passi porterollo,
    stretto alle braccia, e attaccato
      al collo."

"I," said the other, "will take him
    quickly to the royal city,
    holding him close, his arms about
      my neck."

℣ "Io mi vo' por le picciol' mani in seno
    et col fiato scaldar le membra sue,
    me che non scalda l'asinello o 'l bue."

"I want his little hands at my breast
    and to warm his limbs with my breath,
    better than the ass or the ox can do."

℟ "Et io vo' pianger si dirottamente
    ch'empia di calde lachrime un catino
    dove si bagni il tenero bambino."

"And I want to weep so bitterly,
    that I may fill a basin with hot tears
    in which the tender child is bathed."

(EXAMPLE II-2, continued)

℣ "Io vo' tuor meco un poco d'esto fieno
  ch'è qui d'intorno, e non havrò paura
  d'orso, o di lupo, o d'altra ria
  ventura."

"I want [to take] a little of this hay
  that lies about, and I will have no fear
  of bear, or wolf, or other
  misadventure."

℟ "Et io, del latte, ond'è la faccia asperso
  prender vorrei, se non che mi
  pavento,
  vorrei servarlo in un' vasel d'argento."

"And I, if I were not afraid, would like
  to take the milk that sprinkled on
  his face,
  and serve it to him in a silver vessel."

℣ "Io vo' pregarlo con sommessa
  voce:
  'Signor perdona li peccati mei,
  che perciò credo che venuto
  sei.' "

"I want to pray to him with submissive
  voice:
  'Lord, pardon my sins, for I believe
  that this is the reason why you have
  come.' "

℟ "Et io, vo' dirli baldanzosamente:
  'facciamo a cambio: tu mi dona
  il cielo
  et io t'impresto hor questo picciol
  velo.' "

"And I want to say to him with boldness:
  'Let us make a trade: you give me
  heaven
  and I will lend you now this little
  veil.' "

℣ "Io non vo' chieder ne città, ne regni,
  ma sol' vo' dirli con un dolce
  riso,
  ben sia venuto il Re del Paradiso."

"I will not ask in cities or kingdoms,
  but will only tell them with sweet
  laughter
  that he has come, the King of Paradise."

℟ "Et io vo' gir per l'universo mondo
  fin in Turchia gridando sempre mai:
  'Dio s'è fatto huomo, e tu meschin
  nol' sai.' "

"And I want to go throughout the world,
  as far as Turkey, ever crying out:
  'God was made man, and you, poor soul,
  don't know it.' "

Il pietoso Giesù, pendendo in croce,
  a la dolente madre, che piangea,
  così mesto dicea:

"Donna, che piangi la mia dura morte,
  il tuo dolor' molto più grave sento,
  che l'aspro mio tormento."

Ella gemendo fisse i lumi santi
  nel figlio amato, e disse: "O
    dolce vita,
  tu muor, io resta in vita?

"Morir teco vorrei, teco esser
    voglio
  e viva e morta, e con te, caro
    pegno
  pender anch'io sul legno."

Pitiful Jesus, hanging on the cross,
  to his sorrowing, weeping mother
  thus sadly spoke:

"Lady, weeping for my hard death,
  your sorrow I feel much more deeply
  than the harshness of my torment."

She tearfully turned her holy eyes
  to her beloved son, and said: "O
    sweet life,
  you die, I remain in life?

"I would die with you, I want to be
    with you,
  in life and death, and with you,
    dear pledge,
  I too want to hang on the wood."

EXAMPLE II-4. *Lauda*, "Solo e pensoso"—Soto (II/5, final lauda).

(EXAMPLE II-4, continued)

Solo e pensoso in mezzo a' bruti
    immondi,
    già de' suoi danni accorto,
    stava il figlio famelico, dolente,
    e ripetendo i dì lieti e giocondi.

Privo hor d'ogni conforto
    sè stesso accusa e del suo error
        si pente
    et parla e piange inconsolabilmente:

"O del buon padre mio magion felice!
    A quanti servi e quanti
    in te di bianco pane il cibo avanza!
    Io qui di fame, misero,
        infelice,
    perisco in doglia e in pianti:
    nè di satiarmi, in così dura stanza,
    pur di galle e di ghiande ho mai
        speranza."

Indi, come huom che scuote un grave
    sonno,
    "Sorgerò," e ratto, disse,
    "n'anderò al mio padre"; il fare al
        dire aggiunge.
    O lacrime veraci, O quanto ponno!
    Già tien le luci fisse
    ne figlio il padre, benchè sia da lunge.
    Corre e l'abbraccia, e a sè lo
        ricongiunge.

Padre eterno del ciel, pietoso Iddio,
    io son' il figlio ingrato,
    dissipator de' tuoi thesori e doni;
    io, dato in pred'a un giovenil desio,
    tanti anni ho traviato,
    ma la tua gran pietà non
        m'abbandoni,
    et al pentito peccator perdoni.

Alone and pensive in midst of ugly
    filth,
    already aware of his loss,
    stood the famished son, sorrowing
    and recalling the pleasing and
        cheerful days.
Deprived now of every comfort,
    he accuses himself and repents
        his errors,
    and he speaks and weeps inconsolably:

"Oh happy mansion of my good father!
    To how many servants does he give
    so much food, white bread!
    I wretched and miserable, here from
        hunger
    perish in sorrow and weeping:
    nor to satisfy myself, in such hard straits,
    do I even have hope of oak gall
        or acorns."

Then, as a man roused from a deep
    sleep,
    "I shall arise," and rapt, he said,
    "I shall go to my father"; and he joined
        action to words.
    Oh truthful tears, oh how much they say!
    With fixed eyes, even from a distance,
    the father already sees his son.
    He runs to embrace and to rejoin
        him.

Eternal father of heaven, merciful God,
    I am the ungrateful son,
    dissipater of your treasures and gifts;
    I, the prey to a youthful desire,
    for so many years have strayed;
    but let not your great mercy
        abandon me,
    and may you pardon a penitent sinner.

The musical structure of the Oratorians' *laude* is normally binary, with both sections repeated.[84] The musical style of the majority of the pieces—particularly those in I/1, I/3, and most of series II—is closer to that of the light secular forms of the period —such as the *canzonetta*, *balleto*, or *villanella*—than to the madrigal or motet. The melody, in the highest voice, is usually given a chordal or nearly chordal accompaniment by two or three lower voices; such *laude* would be appropriate for congregational singing. Examples II–1 through II–3 are characteristic in their formal structure, melodic style, and texture. Example II–1, originally notated with a C time signature (see Figure II–11), illustrates a dancelike rhythm with hemiola that became popular in the sixteenth and seventeenth centuries. Example II–2 uses the repeated-note dactylic beginning, prominent in *laude* and also in light secular vocal and instrumental music of the time. Example II–4 is one of the relatively few *laude* in series II that use a more polyphonic texture. Because of this trait and its textual repetitions, the work is closer than most *laude* to madrigal style; it would have been appropriate for performance by trained musicians at the *oratorio vespertino*. Although many of the pieces of series III are similar to the majority of the *laude* in their use of chordal texture (some of the chordal pieces are curious for their parallel fifths),[85] there tends to be slightly more emphasis on polyphonic texture than in I/1, I/3, and series II. The most polyphonic *laude* and those stylistically the closest to madrigals are the ones in Animuccia's second book (I/2), intended for the *oratorio vespertino* and calculated to interest the prelates and gentlemen who attended the oratory, as pointed out above; some of these *laude* are double-chorus pieces for eight voices.

The most significant sixteenth-century antecedents of the oratorio performed in the oratory are the *laude* with narrative and dramatic elements in their texts. These are of special importance for their close relationship to the oratorio in both text and function. Such *laude* continue a tradition that dates from the Middle Ages—

84. For modern editions of Oratorian *laude*, see Alaleona, *Oratorio*, pp. 60–74, 82–86, 216–30; Damilano, *Ancina*, pp. 113–45; Schering, *Oratorium*, p. 35, and "Anhang," pp. xiii–xv; Testi, *Seicento*, pp. 181–83; and Dent, "Laudi," pp. 77–80.

85. For a *lauda* by Ancina opening with a series of triads in parallel motion, see Damilano, *Ancina*, p. 124; for a non-Oratorian *lauda* that proceeds in parallel triads throughout until the approach to the final cadence, see Alaleona, *Oratorio*, p. 73; and Dent, "Laudi," pp. 81–82.

FIGURE II-11. The *lauda* "Anima mia, che pensi?" from *Il terzo libro delle laudi spirituali* (Rome, 1577).
(Courtesy of I/Bc.)

one that gave rise to the *sacra rappresentazione*, as pointed out above. In the sixteenth century they are paralleled by Italian secular music, for numerous madrigals and related genres also include narrative and dramatic elements.[86] *Laude* of this type do not represent a large percentage of the Oratorian repertory. Of the approximately five hundred different texts, only thirty-eight (i.e., about 7.6 percent) include narrative and dramatic elements.[87] The book including the largest number of such *laude* is II/4, which appeared in 1591; the succeeding books include progressively fewer *laude* of this type.[88]

The Oratorian *lauda* texts with narrative and dramatic elements may be classified in four groups: dialogues, dialogues combined with narrative, monologues combined with narrative, and narratives. Most of these texts deal with general themes that would be appropriate at any time in the church year, but some, such as those on Passion and Christmas themes, are related to specific periods. Most numerous are the dialogues, which constitute seventeen of the thirty-eight texts. In these works the entire text is like a miniature drama, consisting of a dialogue between characters who are either specified or implied. The dialogue between the Body and the Soul illustrated in Example II–1 is representative. Dialogues between the Body and the Soul date from the period of Jacopone da Todi, as indicated above; this text is particularly significant, for it was later used in Cavalieri's *Rappresentatione di Anima et di Corpo* (see Example III–1, pp. 87–88). The characters of Example II–1, the Body and the Soul, are in conflict over worldly and spiritual values. The Soul has the last word, the final answer to the problem, although the Body never actually agrees with the Soul's viewpoint. Among the other dialogue *laude* in the Oratorian repertory are those between an Angel and a Soul, the Angel Gabriel and the Virgin, a Guide and a Pilgrim, a Questioner

86. For examples of madrigals and related genres that include narrative and dramatic elements in their texts, see Einstein, *Madrigal*, 3:nos. 32–34, 41, 56, 59, 60, 62–64, 69, 74, 75, 84, 86, 88; the texts are translated into English in the 1971 reprint of Einstein, *Madrigal*, 3:xv–lvi.

87. Smither, "Laude," pp. 190–91. All thirty-eight dialogues are listed, with references to sixteenth-century sources and to locations in modern editions, in ibid., pp. 193–98. It is of interest that 7.6 percent is a smaller percentage of narrative and dramatic *laude* than is found in either the works of Jacopone da Todi or the repertory represented in the medieval MSS in Florence and Cortona edited in Liuzzi, *Lauda*.

88. For the number and percentage in each book, see the chart in Smither, "Laude," p. 198.

and his Heart, a Questioner and some Shepherds, a Soul and Jesus, and a Samaritan Woman and Jesus.

Each of the other types of text in the fourfold classification mentioned above is much less numerous than the dialogue. Eight of the texts combine narrative with dialogue, and thus they resemble, on a miniature scale, the text of a seventeenth-century oratorio with a *testo*, or narrator's part. In Example II–2, a Christmas piece, narrative is used almost exclusively to introduce the dialogue, charming for its naive, rustic quality. The dialogue is marked by versicle and response signs in the first printing of the *lauda* (in book II/2), as it is in Example II–2, and thus was probably performed by two alternating groups, or perhaps by two soloists with instrumental accompaniment. In Example II–3, a Passion *lauda*, the narrative portions introduce and connect the lines of dialogue. In the texts combining narrative with monologue, of which there are ten, the narrative functions variously as an introduction, as continuity between the lines of monologue, and as a conclusion. All three narrative functions are found in the first three strophes of Example II–4, which is a *lauda* based on the story of the prodigal son. The beginning of this example, "Solo e pensoso in mezzo a' brutti immondi," is clearly modeled on that of Petrarch's sonnet "Solo e pensoso i più deserti campi"; the final strophe, "Padre eterno del ciel," is reminiscent of another of Petrarch's sonnets, "Padre del ciel, dopo i perduti giorni." Both of the Petrarch sonnets were set as madrigals in the sixteenth century: the former, by Luca Marenzio and the latter, by Cipriano de Rore. In the concluding strophe of Example II–4, the poet meditates on the meaning that the story has for him, and he invokes God's mercy. This conclusion foreshadows the type of text often used for the final choruses of seventeenth-century oratorios. Only three of the texts of the Oratorian *laude* are purely narrative, and all three are in III/1; the subject of two of these is the journey of Clement VIII from Rome to Ferrara in 1598, and the remaining one, by Ancina, appears to be autobiographical.[89]

Other Music in the Oratory

Animuccia's second *lauda* book (I/2) includes more motets than *laude*, as pointed out above. Since this book was printed for

89. Damilano, *Ancina*, p. 63.

use in Neri's oratory and was intended for the *oratorio vespertino*, it is clear that works with both Latin and Italian words were used in that service. Two of the twenty-seven motets in I/2 are Gospel motets: "Venit Iesus in civitatem Samariae," based on John 4:5–14, and "Ascendens Iesus Hierosolymam," based on Matt. 20:17–23. The texts of both works are quite close to the Vulgate, and both include narrative and dramatic elements.

For the music of the *oratorio vespertino*, numerous books of *laude*, spiritual madrigals, motets, and related works would have been available; yet specific information regarding the music actually used is lacking.[90] Among the more likely choices of books containing works with Italian texts are: Serafino Razzi, *Libro primo delle laudi spirituali* (Venice, 1563); Animuccia, *Il primo libro di madrigali con alcuni motetti et madrigali spirituali* (Rome, 1565); the collections of Simone Verovio titled *Diletto spirituale* (Rome, 1586 and 1592; *RISM* 1586², 1586³, and 1592¹⁶); and Palestrina, *Il primo libro de madrigali a cinque voci* (Venice, 1581; this includes settings of strophes from Petrarch's canzona "Vergine bella che di sol vestita") and *Delli madrigali spirituali a cinque voci* (Rome, 1594). Only a few works in the above books are settings of texts that include narrative and dramatic elements. The book including the greatest number of such texts is Razzi's collection, but even there they are no more prevalent than in the repertory of *laude* printed for Neri's oratory.

A Reappraisal of Some Oratorio Antecedents

As stated above, the principal type of music sung in the Oratorians' spiritual exercises was the *lauda*. Of the *laude* printed for use in the oratory, a small percentage include narrative and dramatic elements in their texts. These *laude* are more closely related to the oratorio than any of the other antecedents mentioned above, since they foreshadow it both in text and function. Despite their close relationship to the oratorio, however, their role as roots of the oratorio is less important than it was once thought to be. Previous

90. Reasons for assuming that the following books might have been used in the oratory are presented in Pasquetti, *Oratorio*, pp. 69–71.

historians of the oratorio have tended to describe the origin of the *oratorio volgare* as a kind of evolutionary process in music performed in the oratory—a process in which the *lauda* with narrative and dramatic elements in its text gradually increased in importance and changed in style. For instance, Pasquetti and Alaleona speak of an increasing tendency to use texts with narrative and dramatic elements in the sixteenth-century Oratorian *laude*.[91] Pasquetti states unequivocally that "the oratorio developed from the *lauda*."[92] Alaleona considers the *lauda* to have continued "tranquilly and slowly its evolution in the midst of the Oratorian exercises, arriving only much later [than 1600] at the degree of the dialogue and the fully developed oratorio."[93] And Schering, considering the Oratorian music after Neri's death, speaks of "the further development of the *lauda* to a new species of art, the oratorio as such."[94] Nevertheless, this evolutionary concept is questionable. The increase in the number of printed *laude* with narrative and dramatic elements stops with book II/4 (1591), and the number decreases in the last three books. Judging from the small number of such *laude* in relation to the total Oratorian repertory, one could conclude that the Oratorians in the sixteenth century were relatively uninterested in music with narrative and dramatic texts. As will be shown below, they became keenly interested in such music only in the seventeenth century, after the significant period of *lauda* composition had passed. Although the *laude* with narrative and dramatic elements in their texts undoubtedly influenced the origin of the oratorio by establishing a precedent for the musical rendition of such texts in the oratory, it is an oversimplification to view the seventeenth-century oratorio as a further development of the *lauda*. The influence of non-Oratorian music—the non-Oratorian genres considered above as well as new ones, such as opera—on the origin of the oratorio was no doubt as strong as that of the *lauda*.

It would seem reasonable to assume that the Latin antecedents of the oratorio, such as the Gospel motet, lead to the *oratorio latino* and that the Italian antecedents lead to the *oratorio vol-*

91. Ibid., pp. 98–99; Alaleona, *Oratorio*, pp. 86, 111–12.
92. Pasquetti, *Oratorio*, p. 195.
93. Alaleona, *Oratorio*, p. 107.
94. Schering, *Oratorium*, p. 37.

gare.[95] Although that interpretation of the antecedents in the two languages seems valid with reference to the texts, it should not be too strictly maintained. The possibility should not be excluded that both the Latin and Italian antecedents exerted an influence on the development of the oratorio in each of the two languages.

The *oratorio volgare* and *oratorio latino* emerged in the seventeenth century from a complex interaction of influences, both social and musical. The musical influences are found both within and outside the oratory; they are liturgical and nonliturgical, Latin and Italian, staged and unstaged, sacred and secular. Some of the social and musical influences were sketched in this chapter; others will be treated below.

95. The notion of two separate lines of oratorio development, one Latin and the other Italian, is basic to Alaleona, *Oratorio*; Pasquetti, *Oratorio*; and Schering, *Oratorium*.

CHAPTER III

The Early Baroque:
Antecedents and
Incunabula of the Oratorio

ᔍ*Antecedents*

The Catholic reform movement, in which the Oratorians were active during the sixteenth-century, was still much in evidence during the Baroque era. The principal popes of the early Baroque— Clement VIII (Ippolito Aldobrandini, 1592–1605), Paul V (Camillio Borghese, 1605–21), Gregory XV (Alessandro Ludovisi, 1621–23), and Urban VIII (Maffeo Barberini, 1623–44)—continued to implement the Tridentine recommendations for reform, to apply the oppressive measures of the Inquisition and the *Index of Prohibited Books*, and to promote the Counter-Reformation efforts in Protestant areas.[1] Likewise the Oratorians continued the same types of activities in which they had engaged during the sixteenth century. Prominent among these were the daily spiritual exercises with several sermons and relatively little music and the more musically elaborate *oratorio vespertino*, held outdoors in the summer and indoors with greater musical emphasis in the winter.

Yet the early Baroque witnessed some changes in the papacy that generally influenced Roman society, including the Oratorians. The papal court increasingly departed from the reform austerity that had characterized it from the 1560s through the 1580s. The renewed tendencies toward a more luxurious life for the popes and

1. For the history of the papacy in this period, see Pastor, *Popes*, vols. 23–29.

their relatives—nepotism was returning—and toward more active patronage of the arts reached a peak during the long reign of Urban VIII.[2] In this atmosphere of increasing luxury and artistic emphasis in Rome, theatrical productions other than Jesuit school dramas were again permitted. Romans began to cultivate the new genre of opera, with oratorio soon to follow.

The musical thought and style that resulted in opera, and consequently in the related genre of oratorio, emanated from Florence. Of particular importance was the Camerata, which met at the home of Giovanni de' Bardi, the count of Vernio, from about 1570 to 1592 but was most active between 1577 and 1582.[3] Music was only one of the many topics treated by this informal group of intellectuals who gathered at Bardi's home, but the musical thought that was developed there, particularly by Vicenzo Galilei and Bardi himself, was to have far-reaching effect. Of primary importance to the Camerata was ancient Greek music theory, especially as revealed in the research of the classicist Girolamo Mei. The most influential musical concept developed in the Camerata was that a compromise between speech and song is necessary for the singing of drama. The thought of the Camerata influenced the discussions of other intellectual groups and academies in Florence (e.g., the Accademia degli Alterati and the group led by the nobleman Jacopo Corsi),[4] and it influenced Florentine musical practice in general.

Examples of music embodying the ideas of the Camerata are found among the works of Bardi and Galilei—works composed in chordal style that followed their composers' conceptions of ancient Greek theory.[5] The earliest dramatic productions reflecting the thought of the Camerata were performed in Florence outside the sphere of the Camerata. These are *Satiro* and *La disperazione di Fileno*, pastorals by Laura Giudiccioni ne' Luchesini set to music by Emilio de' Cavalieri and produced during the carnival season of 1591. Neither the texts nor the music of these works is extant. Jacopo Corsi and Jacopo Peri began in 1594 to set Ottavio Rinuc-

2. Haskell, *Patrons*, p. 3; pp. 3–166, on Roman art patronage in the seventeenth century, constitutes a valuable study of the social context of the arts in this period.

3. For a reappraisal and summary of the activities of the Camerata, see Palisca, "Camerata."

4. For information about the activities of the Alterati, of which Corsi was a member, see Palisca, "Alterati."

5. For music examples, see Palisca, "Camerata," pp. 225–30.

cini's *Dafne*, although the work was not performed until 1598; then Cavalieri's setting of *Giuoco della cieca*, adapted by Laura Giudiccioni from Giovanni Battista Guarini's *Pastor fido*, was performed in 1595; and Rinuccini's *Euridice*, with music by Peri and Caccini, was performed in 1600 under the direction of Cavalieri.

The new tendencies in music fostered in Florence were soon to influence music in the oratory of the Chiesa Nuova in Rome. Cavalieri was the chief agent of this influence.

Music and Musicians in Neri's Oratory

Emilio de' Cavalieri (ca. 1540–1602) was born in Rome of a noble family.[6] His brother, also a musician, was the Mario del Cavalieri who is listed in the records of the Oratorio del Santissimo Crocifisso (The Oratory of the Most Holy Crucifix) as having been paid for Lenten music in 1568 and 1572.[7] Emilio himself was in charge of the Lenten music in the same oratory from 1578 to 1584;[8] he is also listed as having ordered payment in 1597 to Giovanni Maria Nanino and other musicians for their participation in the music at that oratory.[9] Cavalieri moved to Florence in 1588 to become the superintendent of the artists who worked at the court of Ferdinando de' Medici, the grand duke of Tuscany. The terms of his appointment indicate that among his many other duties he was to supervise "all the musicians of the chapel . . . both singers and instrumentalists."[10] In the following year he was the director and one of the composers of the *intermedi*, conceived and staged by Bardi, for the comedy presented to celebrate the marriage of Ferdinando de' Medici and Christine of Lorraine. Cavalieri was well aware of the Camerata's ideas; he may have been among those who attended its meetings, but there is no certain knowledge of this.[11] Despite several extended absences from Florence for activities in Rome during the 1590s, Cavalieri continued in his position at the Tuscan court until 1600. During one of his

6. For a survey of Cavalieri's life and music, see W. Kirkendale, "Cavalieri."

7. See the extracts from the records for those years in Alaleona, *Oratorio*, pp. 330–31. The history and activities of the Oratorio del Santissimo Crocifisso are treated below, in chapter 5.

8. Alaleona, *Oratorio*, p. 332; W. Kirkendale, "Cavalieri," p. 10.

9. Alaleona, *Oratorio*, p. 335.

10. Quoted in Pirrotta, "Camerata," p. 176.

11. Palisca, "Camerata," p. 208.

extended visits to Rome, from September of 1593 until at least late March of 1594, he appears to have gone frequently to the oratory of the Chiesa Nuova, for he states in a letter that "it is filled with prelates every morning."[12] In another letter written during the same visit, his personal contact with Philip Neri is established by an amusing anecdote that is quite consistent with Philip's jovial personality. Cavalieri wrote that he was present when the soprano Vittoria Archilei sang in Philip's room. "She sang a Benedictus, but they wanted to hear *spagnole* and *galanterie* [popular songs]. There were many people there, and in the end Messer Filippo had a priest of the Vallicella dance. He did the *canario* and the *pedrolino*, and Vittoria said to me that he danced stupendously and must practice frequently. Messer Filippo then gave the benediction to several, notably to Vittoria, and so that she would remember him he gave her a good slap and made her promise to come back another time."[13] Late in 1600 Cavalieri left Florence permanently to live in Rome. Prejudice against him as a Roman at the Tuscan court, his frequent absences from Florence, and the conflicts between Peri and Caccini at the performance of *Euridice* in October 1600, which he was unable to resolve satisfactorily, were no doubt factors contributing to his departure.

Cavalieri's influence on the history of the oratorio stems from the two performances in February 1600 (during the carnival season) of his opera *Rappresentatione di Anima et di Corpo* in the oratory of the Chiesa Nuova. He heard this work performed during a visit to Rome that lasted from December 1599 to April 1600.[14] The score of the *Rappresentatione* was edited by Alessandro Guidotti and was printed in the fall of 1600.[15] It has the distinction of being the earliest printed opera, appearing several months before the two different settings of *Euridice* by Caccini and Peri; it is also the first printed score with a figured bass.

12. Cavalieri to Belisario Vinta, 9 December 1593, in Palisca, "Cavalieri," p. 343.
13. Cavalieri to Marcello Accolti, 18 January 1594, ibid., p. 346.
14. Palisca, "Cavalieri," p. 344.
15. *Rappresentatione di Anima et di Corpo. Nuovamente posta in musica del sig. Emilio del Cavalliere, per recitatar cantando. Data in luce da Alessandro Guidotti, Bolognese. Con licenza de' superiori. In Roma, appresso Nicolò Mutij l'Anno del Jubileo. M.DC.* (Copies in I/Rv and I/Rsc.) Guidotti's dedication was signed on 3 September 1600. The dedication and prefatory remarks printed at the front of the score are reprinted in Solerti, *Origini*, pp. 1–12. For a facsimile reprint of the score, see Cavalieri, *Rappresentatione*-Facs. A critical edition is lacking. For performing editions, see Cavalieri, *Rappresentazione*-G; Cavalieri, *Rappresentazione*-T; and *CDMI*, vol. 10.

RAPPRESENTATIONE
DI ANIMA, ET DI CORPO

Nuouamente poſta in Muſica dal Sig. Emilio del Caualliere,
per recitar Cantando.

Data in luce da Aleſſandro Guidotti Bologneſe.

Con Licenza de' Superiori.

IN ROMA
Appreſſo Nicolò Mutij l'Anno del Iubileo. M. D C.

FIGURE III-1. Title page of Emilio de' Cavalieri's *Rappresentatione di
Anima et di Corpo* (Rome, 1600).
(Cavalieri, *Rappresentatione*-Facs.)

Guidotti's dedication calls attention to Cavalieri's importance for having revived the ancient practice of setting drama to music. The dedication, which names some of Cavalieri's earlier dramatic works, comments on the appropriateness of the style of this work for inciting devotion and on the extremely favorable reception of the *Rappresentatione* in the oratory. The large audiences for the two performances included fifteen and twenty cardinals, respectively.[16] Cavalieri was pleased with the work's reception and wrote in one of his letters that those who had heard both the Peri-Caccini *Euridice* in Florence and his *Rappresentatione* in Rome preferred the latter, "because the music moved them to tears and laughter and pleased them greatly, unlike this music of Florence, which did not move them at all, unless to boredom and irritation."[17]

The text of the *Rappresentatione*, divided into three acts, was printed at the back of the score and was also printed separately in 1600.[18] According to the introductory note in the separate printing, the score had already appeared, "to the great satisfaction of those versed in music." The purpose of printing the libretto separately was to satisfy the desires "of those who do not understand music."[19] Thus the libretto in this form was not intended for another performance but only for reading—there was evidently no libretto available to the audience at the first performance. The libretto printed separately includes two prose additions, as the title page indicates (*con l'aggiunta di due prose*). These additions are brief sermons, following Acts I and II, and are related to the main theme of the *Rappresentatione*. They are to be spoken by two boys called Timoroso and Elevato, allegorical characters not in the play itself. Timoroso's function is to instill in his listeners the fear of the wrath of God and of "Inferno, where the fire burns eternally." Elevato urges man, who has a noble intellect, to turn his thoughts heavenward and to contemplate the "infinite greatness and innumerable treasures of Heaven." The sermons present vivid de-

16. W. Kirkendale, "Cavalieri," p. 16.

17. Cavalieri to Accolti in postscript of letter to Ferdinando I de' Medici, probably 24 November 1600, in Palisca, "Cavalieri," p. 352.

18. The libretto as printed at the back of the score is reprinted, with modified spelling and punctuation, in Solerti, *Origini*, pp. 13–39. The title page of the libretto printed separately reads as follows: *Rappresentatione di Anima et di Corpo, con l'aggiunta di due prose. Data in luce da Alessandro Guidotti, Bolognese* (Rome, 1600; copy in I/Rv: S. Borr. R. III. 18).

19. *Rappresentatione* (Rome, 1600; separate printing of libretto), p. 2.

scriptions of hell and heaven, perhaps reflecting the manner in which they were represented by the staging in the performance. These insertions relate to the practice of the *oratorio vespertino* in which sermons were recited from memory by boys and were preceded and followed by music. These or similar sermons may well have been recited between the acts at the performances of the *Rappresentatione*, but there is no certain information that they were, nor is it known whether the *Rappresentatione* performance functioned as an *oratorio vespertino*. A prefatory note in the printed score mentions the possibility of using four *intermedi*, one before the prologue and one after each act. Nevertheless, no poetry or music of *intermedi* for this work is known to exist; it is doubtful that *intermedi* were actually included in the performances. When the libretto of the *Rappresentatione* was reprinted at Siena in 1607 under Guidotti's name, it did not mention Cavalieri.[20] This version seems to have been taken from the back of the printed score; it includes neither the prose insertions nor any type of prefatory material. The Siena print was apparently intended purely as reading matter, for no Siena performance of the work is known.

The text is anonymous in the first two sources of the *Rappresentatione*, and the publisher of the Siena print apparently assumed that Guidotti was its author, not its editor. In twentieth-century literature the text has been variously attributed to Laura Giudiccioni, with whom Cavalieri had previously collaborated; to Alessandro Guidotti, whose name is on the title page of all sources; and to Agostino Manni, who was the Oratorians' chief poet in this period and who seems the most likely one to have written the work.[21] Paolo Aringhi (1600–76)—the biographer of numerous Oratorians, including Manni—attributes the libretto to him. Aringhi joined the Oratory in 1622 and therefore knew some of those who remembered and perhaps even participated in the per-

20. Alessandro Guidotti, *Rappresentatione di Anima e di Corpo* (Siena, 1607). (Two copies in I/Rvat: Capponi, VI, 169/3; and Dramm. Allacci, 274/13.) According to Cioni, *Bibliografia*, p. 308, the libretto of the *Rappresentatione* was also reprinted in Rome under the name of Pellegrino Romito and in Venice, anonymously. Nevertheless, both of these texts, as well as others with the same title that were printed in the early seventeenth century at Treviso and Viterbo, are totally different from the one set by Cavalieri. (Copies of the Rome, Venice, Treviso, and Viterbo prints, respectively, are located as follows: I/Rc: Comm 221/3; I/Rvat: Capponi V, 855/12, 855/14, and 865/78.)

21. Alaleona, *Oratorio*, p. 39, n. 1.

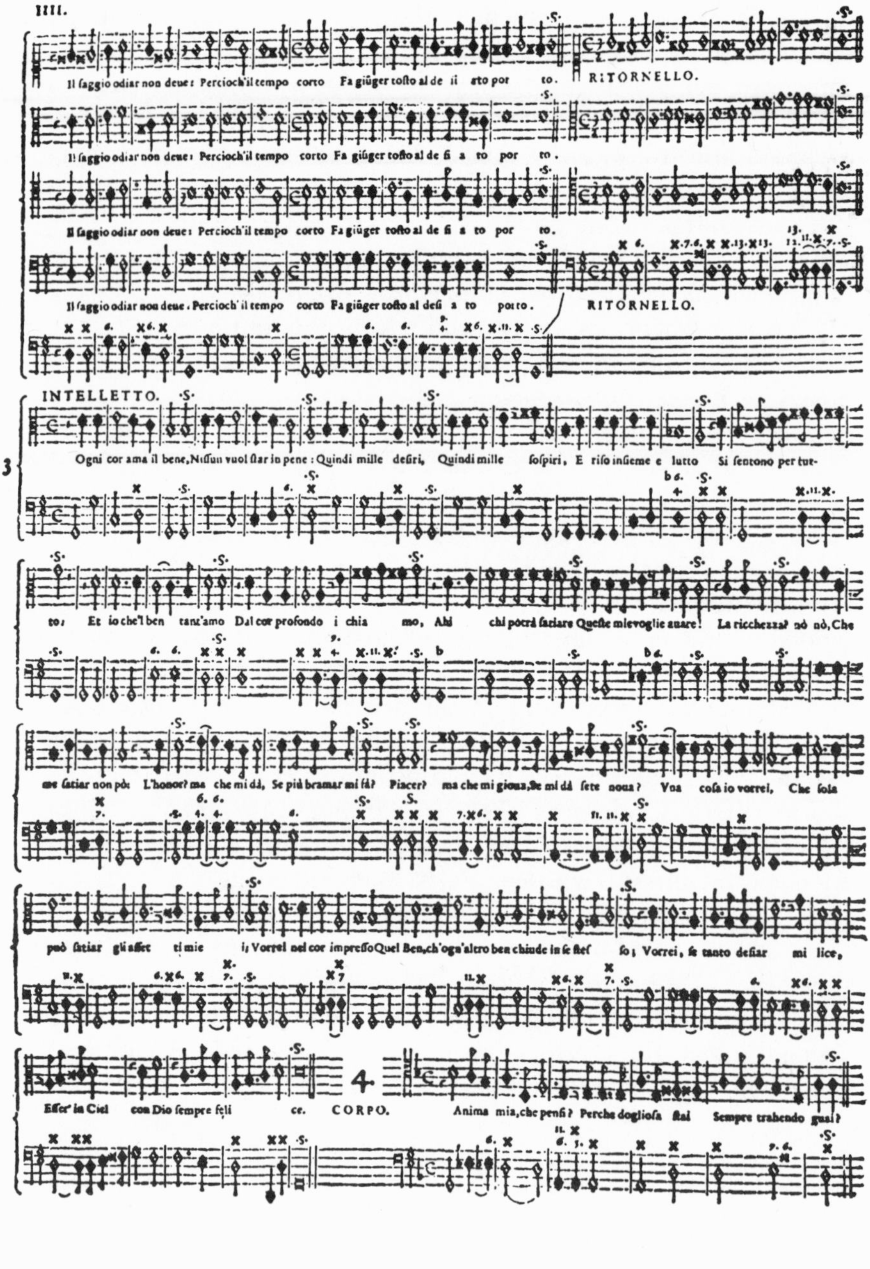
IIII.
Il saggio odiar non deue: Perciochè'l tempo corto Fa giûger tosto al de fi a to por to.
RITORNELLO.
Il saggio odiar non deue: Perciochè'l tempo corto Fa giûger tosto al de fi a to por to.
Il saggio odiar non deue: Perciochè'l tempo corto Fa giûger tosto al de fi a to por to.
Il saggio odiar non deue. Perciochè'l tempo corto Fa giûger tosto al desi a to porto.
RITORNELLO.
3
INTELLETTO.
Ogni cor ama il bene, Nissun vuol star in pene: Quindi mille desiri, Quindi mille sospiri, E riso insieme e lutto Si sentono per tut-
to; Et io che'l ben tant'amo Dal cor profondo i chia mo, Ahi chi potrà satiare Queste mie voglie auare! La ricchezza? nò nò, Che
me satiar non pò: L'honor? ma che mi dà, Se più bramar mi fà? Piacer? ma che mi gioua, Se mi dà sete noua? Vna cosa io vorrei, Che sola
può satiar gli affet ti mie i; Vorrei nel cor impresso Quel Ben, ch'ogn'altro ben chiude in se stes so; Vorrei, se tanto desiar mi lice,
Esser' in Ciel con Dio sempre feli ce.
4
CORPO.
Anima mia, che pensi? Perche dogliosa stai Sempre trahendo guai?

FIGURE III-2. Two pages from Cavalieri's *Rappresentatione*. The dialogue between the Body and the Soul ("Anima mia, che pensi?") begins at no. 4, at the bottom of the facing page.

(Cavalieri, *Rappresentatione*-Facs., pp. iv–v.)

For the text set to music in a book of *laude*, see Figure II-11 (p. 71) and Example II-1 (p. 63).

formances of the *Rappresentatione*.[22] Aringhi's attribution is corroborated in a publication of 1648 by Erythraeus.[23]

The text of the dialogue *lauda* between the Body and the Soul, which was first printed in 1577 in *lauda* book I/3 (Example II–1, pp. 63–64), forms nearly all of act I, scene 4. In fact, it has been suggested that the idea for the entire *Rappresentatione* developed from the conflict between the Body and the Soul in this *lauda*.[24] The *Rappresentatione* included fourteen characters, all allegorical except the Guardian Angel. It also included an unidentified chorus, which comments on the action, plus choruses of Angels in heaven, Damned Souls in inferno, and Blessed Souls in heaven. In act I and most of act II, the conflict develops between the forces of the world and sensual pleasure on the one hand and the forces of heaven on the other. The conflict is finally resolved in act II, scene 7, where the Guardian Angel and the Body strip the beautiful but deceptive clothing from the World and Worldly Life and thus reveal their true ugliness. Finally convinced that the forces of heaven are right, the Body and Soul drive away the World and Worldly Life. Act III reinforces the moral of the play by showing the suffering of the Damned Souls when the mouth of hell opens, and the joy of the Blessed Souls when heaven opens. The finale of act III is written so that the work may conclude either with or without a dance. It is clear from the stage directions that three stage areas were used for the opera—one each for heaven, the world, and hell; it is not clear whether these areas were on three different levels or were side by side on one level.[25] From the use of the word *Rappresentatione* in the title and from the nature of the libretto, it would seem that the librettist, and no doubt the composer as well, considered this work to be in the tradition of the *sacra rappresentazione* that had been so popular in the late fifteenth

22. For a biographical sketch of Aringhi, see Gasbarri, *Oratorio rom.*, p. 172. Aringhi errs in attributing the music to Dorisio Isorelli, however, rather than to Cavalieri. (See the quotation from Aringhi in Alaleona, *Oratorio*, pp. 42–43.) This error necessarily casts some doubt on his accuracy in regard to the *Rappresentatione*.

23. Erythraeus, *Pinacotheca*, pp. 144–45.

24. Alaleona, *Oratorio*, p. 104. This *lauda* is not among those in the MSS of *laude* that are largely by Manni in I/Rv: o, 67–68. Although Manni might have been its author, as Alaleona suggests, there is no definite information to that effect.

25. For an illustration of a sixteenth-century stage set for a Passion play in which paradise and inferno are on the same level—at the extreme left and right, respectively—and various locations on earth are in the center, see G. Cohen, *Mis en scène*, pl. 1.

century but had diminished in popularity during the sixteenth century.[26]

The music of the *Rappresentatione* is clearly the work of a skilled professional musician who is fully conversant with the newest musical styles and structures. If Cavalieri's recitative is less sensitive to the nuances of the Italian language than Peri's in *Euridice*, his mixture of recitative and dancelike aria styles in the solo passages creates an attractively varied impression. Characteristic in this respect is the setting of the *lauda* text "Anima mia che pensi," which is partially quoted in Example III-1. At the opening of this passage (no. 4 in the example—the numbers are those of the original), the Body sings his strophe in recitative, after which the Soul responds (no. 5) in aria style with a melody and bass that are later varied in no. 11; hints of the same bass are also found in no. 9. The Body continues in nos. 6, 8, and 10 to sing in recitative style, and these passages are melodically and harmonically almost the same. Thus the passages of both characters suggest the strophic variation procedure that was to become common in the early seventeenth century. Other solos and ensembles

EXAMPLE III-1. *Rappresentatione di Anima et di Corpo*—Cavalieri (Cavalieri, *Rappresentatione*-Facs., pp. iv–v).

26. Becherini, "Rappresentazioni," pp. 233–35.

(EXAMPLE III-1, continued)

(For a translation see Example II-1.)

of the work are more strictly in either recitative or dance style. A particularly charming dancelike episode is the music of Pleasure and Two Companions in act II, scene 4. The choruses of the *Rappresentatione* are virtually all in a simple, chordal style, and sometimes they approach choral recitative.

Although Cavalieri's *Rappresentatione* is not an oratorio, it is of primary importance to the history of the oratorio. This elaborate work, presented during the carnival season in a Holy Year, marks the beginning of the performance in the oratory of sacred dramatic music using the new recitative style. In the service of sacred dramatic texts, that style was to become an essential element of the oratorio.

Paolo Aringhi calls the *Rappresentatione di Anima et di Corpo* a *dialogo*, and he states that Manni also wrote other spiritual dialogues that were set to music in recitative style and sung by boys in the oratory.[27] Other *rappresentazioni* may well have been performed in the oratory, for there exists in the Biblioteca Vallicelliana (formerly the Oratorians' library) a manuscript text of a *Rappresentatione del figliol prodigo fatta in musica*, possibly written by Manni.[28]

Dorisio Isorelli (1544–1632)—a singer, violist, and composer —joined the Congregation of the Oratory in 1599 as a lay brother and remained an Oratorian until his death. Originally from Parma, he was a protégé of Cavalieri, with whom he had been associated at the Oratorio del Santissimo Crocifisso in Rome.[29] He had also been active at the court of Ferdinando de' Medici in Florence and had taken part in the music of the festivities of 1589 under Cavalieri's direction. He was experienced as a composer and performer of music in the new Florentine style, and he certainly was much involved with the production of Cavalieri's *Rappresentatione*, since he was the oratory's maestro di cappella in the period from 1599 to 1604.[30] Isorelli's presence in the congregation must

27. See the quotations from Aringhi in Alaleona, *Oratorio*, pp. 38, 42. It is of terminological interest that Aringhi was not the only one to have called the *Rappresentatione* a *dialogo*. On the front cover of the copy of this work in I/Rsc, the following is written in what appears to be a seventeenth-century hand: "Dialogo musicale dell'Anima et del Corpo."

28. The manuscript is in I/Rv: o, 68. The entire text is printed in Alaleona, *Oratorio*, pp. 235–43; on p. 235 Alaleona suggests that Manni is the author.

29. Palisca, "Cavalieri," pp. 347–48, n. 39.

30. In Alaleona, *Oratorio*, p. 43, n. 1, it is suggested that Isorelli may even have collaborated with Cavalieri in the composition of the *Rappresentatione*, but there is no documentary evidence that clearly supports this assumption.

have been an influence toward the new musical style in the oratory. His name is found above one of the items in the manuscript of the partly monodic *Lamentationes* for Holy Week, mostly by Cavalieri, that was used at the Chiesa Nuova.[31]

Isorelli's successor, the Flemish composer Francesco Martini (1568–1628), joined the Oratorians in 1602 and held the position of maestro di cappella from 1604 until 1623. He had been trained in the traditional contrapuntal style; the only extant works by him are contrapuntal motets and *laude*, none of which include narrative or dramatic elements or a basso continuo.[32] Little is known of the music performed in the oratory during Martini's period. From his background and style of composition, it would seem doubtful that he actively promoted the newest musical tendencies; but those tendencies were strong and would certainly have found their way into the oratory.

Although there is little direct evidence regarding the kind of music performed in the oratories of Rome during the first two decades of the seventeenth century, an inventory made in 1620 of the music used in the Bologna Oratory can shed some light on the activities in Rome.[33] The Bologna Oratory was founded in 1615; so the music in this inventory represents a collection gathered over a five-year period. In virtually every respect the Roman Oratory provided the models for the activities of the Bologna Oratory:[34] thus the Bolognese Oratorians undoubtedly looked to their Roman counterparts for guidance in purchasing music for their oratory. The Bolognese inventory of 1620 consists of forty-three items, representing more composers active in Rome than in any other area. It includes more works with Italian texts than Latin. First on the list is a new book, Giovanni Francesco Anerio's *Teatro armonico spirituale di madrigali* (Rome, 1619), which is extremely important for the early history of the oratorio. Other items listed are G. F. Anerio's *Ghirlanda di sacre rose* (Rome, 1619), Agostino Agazzari's *Primo libro di madrigaletti a tre voci* (Venice, 1607), Severo Bonini's *Madrigali e canzonette spirituali per cantare a una*

---

31. The *Lamentations* are in I/Rv: o, 31.

32. For a summary of Martini's life and works, see Alaleona, *Oratorio*, pp. 43–46.

33. The inventory is printed in Mischiati, "Bologna," pp. 138–39.

34. For a survey of the history of the Bologna Oratory, see Comelli, *Bologna*. Close contacts with Rome are mentioned throughout this book. For the order of events in the spiritual exercises of the Bologna Oratory in 1621, which were much like those of the Roman Oratory, see Mischiati, "Bologna," pp. 131–32, n. 2.

voce sola (Florence, 1607), one of Pietro Pace's two books called *Scherzi et arie spirituali*, Paolo Quagliati's *Affetti amorosi spirituali* (Rome, 1617), and only one book of Oratorian *laude* (book II/3). Also listed is a text called a *rappresentazione*, by "D. Giulio," which includes the characters Christ, the Magdalene, and some Angels; the inventory calls the work, in its musical setting a *dialogo*. Another Bolognese inventory is dated 1622 and includes the music in the Oratorians' church, the Madonna di Galliera.[35] This inventory lists mostly Latin liturgical music, some from the sixteenth century, but it also includes works with Italian texts. Among the items not mentioned in the previous inventory is G. F. Anerio's *Selva armonica* (Rome, 1617). Taking both inventories into consideration, one finds that the Oratorians at Bologna—and probably those at Rome as well—performed music in a wide variety of styles: sixteenth-century polyphony by Costanzo Porta, Andrea Gabrieli, and Palestrina; simple Oratorian *laude*; relatively conservative music with basso continuo by Ludovico Grossi da Viadana, P. Pace, and G. F. Anerio; music in a less conservative style by Quagliati; and music clearly in the Florentine monodic style by Bonini. The *rappresentazione* mentioned above is not the only dramatic music in the Bolognese repertory, for dramatic dialogues, mostly in Italian but some in Latin, were also performed there. All the publications by Anerio and that by Quagliati include dialogues; some of these are among the examples treated below.

The Dramatic Dialogue

The interest of late sixteenth- and early seventeenth-century composers in setting dramatic texts to music, as evidenced in the birth of opera, extended also to the madrigal and related genres, both secular and spiritual, and to the motet. Although the texts of sixteenth-century madrigals and motets were occasionally dramatic dialogues, as pointed out in chapter 2, the lines of individual characters were set polyphonically. In the early seventeenth century, however, with the advent of the basso continuo, such lines could be set for soloists, and thus the dialogue's dramatic realism could be increased.

It is not uncommon for early seventeenth-century books of

35. The inventory is printed in Mischiati, "Bologna," pp. 139–42.

secular madrigals to include one or more dialogues, either with or without narrative passages. Such dialogues were often placed at the end of the book as its climax. In Monteverdi's *Il sesto libro de madrigali* (Venice, 1614), for example, the final number is a seven-voice pastoral dialogue, "Presso un fiume tranquillo."[36] The narrative passages in that work are sung by SSATB and have introductory and connecting functions; the dialogue, between Eurillo and Filena, is sung by soloists (T and S, respectively); and the conclusion is sung by all (SSSATB). Like this one, the majority of the dialogues in early Baroque collections of madrigals use pastoral texts. Similar dialogues, although often for fewer voices and sometimes for two soloists only, are found in the numerous collections of vocal chamber music with basso continuo published under such general titles as *musiche, varii concenti, arie,* or *affetti.*[37]

The spiritual counterparts of these secular books, with texts in Italian, bear similar titles; common are *madrigali spirituali, affetti spirituali, arie sacre,* and *scherzi sacri.* The books of spiritual music include dialogues that are similar in textual and musical styles to those in the secular books. The texts of spiritual dialogues are not pastoral, of course, but are based on subjects similar to those of the *laude* of the sixteenth century. Despite the similarity of the subject of these dialogues and those of *laude*, these works are not to be confused with *laude*; they were never called *laude* in their sources. There appear to have been no early Baroque books of *laude* that used the basso continuo. The significant period of *lauda* composition had passed, but the term *lauda* continued to be applied to the same type of text and music for which it had been used in the sixteenth century. Because of their language, dialogues with Italian texts would not have been sung in church during Mass, but they were appropriate for informal devotional purposes, such as exercises in oratories. Latin dialogues are found in numerous books of motets, published under a variety of titles, such as *concerti sacri, concerti ecclesiastici, sinfonie sacre, sacrae cantiones,* and *affetti spirituali.* Perhaps the earliest dramatic dialogue of the seventeenth century is a Latin work, Viadana's "Fili

36. Monteverdi, *Opere*, 6:113–30.
37. Examples of such dialogues are found in the following publications: Pietro Benedetti, *Musiche* (Florence, 1611); Francesco Dognazzi, *Il primo libro de' vari concenti* (Venice, 1614); Andrea Falconieri, *Il quinto libro delle musiche* (Florence, 1619); and Giulio S. P. del Negro, *Grazie ed affetti di musica moderna* (Milan, 1613) and *Secondo libro delle grazie ed affetti di musica moderna* (Venice, 1614).

quid fecisti,"[38] from his *Cento concerti ecclesiastici* (Venice, 1602). Although intended to be used as motets, the Latin dialogues were no doubt performed in oratories as well. Arnold Schering uses the term *oratorio dialogue* to refer to the kind of dialogue treated in this section of the present chapter.[39] Although that term points to the historical position of these works as antecedents of the oratorio, it should not be taken to imply that such dialogues were necessarily intended for oratories nor that they are necessarily oratorios.

Texts of the Dialogue. The texts of sacred dialogues of the early Italian Baroque may be classified generally by language (Italian and Latin), source (biblical and nonbiblical), and style. Stylistic distinctions depend upon whether the text is in poetry or prose, whether it employs narrative lines or is strictly a dialogue among personages, whether it develops a plot or is essentially reflective, and—if biblical—whether it treats the biblical passage strictly or freely. The chief characteristics of dialogue texts will be illustrated below by four examples each of Italian and Latin dialogues.

Most Italian dialogues of the early Baroque are nonbiblical. They often use allegorical personages—such as Death, Life, Body, or Soul—who are at times combined with biblical characters— primarily Jesus and the Virgin Mary or one or more Angels. The names of the personages in the dialogues are sometimes given in the headings, but often they must be inferred from the text. The few Italian dialogues that are based on such biblical sources as the stories of the Annunciation, Christmas, or the Passion treat those sources quite freely. Like the secular madrigals and related genres of which they form the spiritual counterparts—and also like late sixteenth-century *laude*—the Italian dialogues have poetic texts, with lines of seven and eleven syllables predominating. Some dialogues are written in rhymed couplets, with the personages alternating at irregular intervals; others have stanzas of three or more lines, with the personages changing at each stanza. Italian dialogues rarely include narrative passages, and their plot development tends to be minimal, although some works of Anerio's *Teatro* are notable exceptions.

38. Printed in Blume, *Monodische*, "Notenbeilagen," pp. 25–27.
39. Schering, *Oratorium*, p. 12.

FIGURE III-3. Title page of Paolo Quagliati's *Affetti amorosi spirituali* (Rome, 1617).
(Courtesy of I/Rsc.)

FIGURE III-4. Beginning of Quagliati's dialogue "Quando sarà quel giorno" from his *Affetti*. (Cf. pp. 96–97 and Example III–4, p. 113.)
(Courtesy of I/Rsc.)

The Early Baroque: Antecedents and Incunabula 95

Among the books of music in the 1620 inventory of the Bologna Oratorians is Paolo Quagliati's *Affetti amorosi spirituali* (Rome, 1617), which includes the dialogue "Quando sarà quel giorno." (The complete text is printed below.) This nonbiblical text is similar to dialogue *laude* of the sixteenth century in that the two personages, the Angel and the Soul, sing alternate stanzas. The dialogue exhibits little plot development. The Angel exhorts the Soul to flee his worldly imprisonment. From the beginning the Soul wishes to do so, yet he is hesitant and questioning. Finally the Soul is convinced ("Questo cred'io"), and the concluding chorus rejoices. Dialogues characteristically conclude with an ensemble, set either for the voices that sing the roles or for added voices.

Dialogue, "Quando sarà quel giorno"—
Quagliati, *Affetti amorosi spirituali*

Personages: Angel (S), Soul (T), Chorus of Angels (SST).

ANGELO
Quando sarà quel giorno, Anima cara,
che fuor ti veggia d'amorosi nodi,
e dolce libertade un giorno godi?

ANGEL
When will be the day, dear Soul,
that I see you loose from amorous knots,
and one day enjoying sweet liberty?

ANIMA
Bramo vedermi fuor di questo laccio,
bramo vedere il mio celeste Sole,
che fa dolce fiorir rose e viole.

SOUL
I desire to be out of this trap,
I desire to see my heavenly Sun,
which makes roses and violets sweetly
    bloom.

ANGELO
Fuggi la prigionia, fuggi il tormento;
se tu ami questo mondo, ancor tu brami
eterno precipizio, e morte chiami.

ANGEL
Flee the imprisonment, flee the torment;
if you love this world, still you desire
eternal ruin, and you summon death.

ANIMA
Amo Giesù ben mio, Giesù mia vita.
E, se mia vita lui è data in sorte,
amo dunque la vita, e non la morte.

SOUL
I love Jesus my treasure, Jesus my life;
and if the destiny of my life to him is given,
then will I love life and not death.

ANGELO
O come saggia sei, come felice.
Lascia, beata te, lascia ogni impresa,
che di sì strano ardor t'ha l'alma
    accessa.

ANGEL
Oh, how wise you are, how happy.
Forsake, blessed one, forsake every deed
which has inflamed your soul by such
    strange passion.

ANIMA	SOUL
Come dall'amor mio poss'io ritrarmi,	How can I withdraw my love
se tanto a me cortese, humile e pio	if so gracious, humble, and loving
si mostra ogn'ora il doce Signor mio?	my sweet Lord is always to me?

ANGELO	ANGEL
Deh vedi che son dolci le lusinghe,	Oh, you will see how sweet are the blandishments,
perchè giunto ti veggia al desir suo,	because you will see yourself joined to his desire,
per far maggiore il beneficio tuo.	to increase the benefit to you.

ANIMA	SOUL
Questo cred'io, e, quando questo fia,	This I believe, and, if this be so,
più mi contento ognor per lui morire,	more content will I ever be to die for him,
che per cosa mortale assai gioire.	than to rejoice for a mortal thing.

ANGELO	ANGEL
Or poi, che di Giesù così gioisci,	Now since for Jesus you rejoice,
cantano a gara i nostri lieti cori:	our joyful choirs will compete in song:

CORO D'ANGELI	CHORUS OF ANGELS
O felici sospir, beati ardori.	O happy sighs, blessed ardor.

The 1622 inventory of the Bologna Oratorians lists G. F. Anerio's *Selva armonica* (Rome, 1617), which includes two dialogues with Italian nonbiblical texts. Unlike the above text set by Quagliati, these both proceed in rhymed couplets with irregular alternations of personages. The first of the two dialogues, "Giesù nel tuo partire" (the text is printed below), begins with a parody of the first two lines of Alfonso d'Avalos's madrigal "Anchor che col partire, / io mi sento morire," one of the most famous texts of the sixteenth century, set by Gioseppe Caimo, among others. The dialogue is written for two personages, the Soul and Christ. There is even less plot development in this dialogue than in the one quoted above; the text merely reflects the sorrow of the Soul upon the departure of her spouse, Christ, and the efforts of the latter to console her. Characteristically, both personages join at the end of the dialogue to form a satisfactory musical conclusion; yet the text of the last three couplets is written from the standpoint of the Soul, who is expressing sorrow at the departure of Christ.

Dialogue, "Giesù nel tuo partire"—
G. F. Anerio, *Selva armonica*

Personages: Soul (S[1]), Christ (S[2] or T).

ANIMA
Giesù, nel tuo partire
io mi sento morire.

SOUL
Jesus, in your parting,
I feel that I am dying.

CHRISTO
Se tu m'amassi, sposa,
tutta lieta e gioiosa
saresti, essendo ch'io
hor vado al Padre mio.

CHRIST
If you loved me, my bride,
all happy and joyful
would you be, since now
I go to my Father.

ANIMA
Del tuo sublime honore
gioisco, almo Signore.
Ma come voi ch'io viva
se di te amor son priva.

SOUL
For your sublime honor
I rejoice, dear Lord.
But how am I to live
if of your love deprived.

CHRISTO
Meco sempre star puoi,
Anima, se tu voi.

CHRIST
You can always be with me,
Soul, if you wish.

ANIMA
Questo pur mi consola
se ben rimangh'hor sola;
ma 'l mondo non intende
come, fia partendo
tu, dolce vita mia,
io teco sempre stia.

SOUL
This indeed consoles me
if now I remain alone;
but the world does not understand
how, if you are leaving,
my sweet life,
I may be ever with you.

CHRISTO
Nella mai bella immago
l'occhio di mirar vago
prenderà tal diletto
qual non cape inteletto.

CHRIST
Your lovely eyes in gazing
upon the ever beautiful image
will take such delight
that the mind will not understand.

ANIMA
Ma quando fia quel giorno
ch'io miri il viso adorno?

SOUL
But when will be the day
that I gaze upon your face adorned?

A 2: ANIMA, CHRISTO
Sposo diletto e caro,
a me par troppo amaro
mancar della tua vista
la cui forza conquista
ogni rubello core;
pur da me fuggi, amore.

A 2: SOUL, CHRIST
O spouse, beloved and dear,
to me it seems too bitter—
the absence of the sight
of you whose power conquers
every rebellious heart;
yet from me you flee, my love.

The other dialogue in Anerio's *Selva armonica*, "O tu che vai per via" (the text is printed below), is written for three personages —the Soul, Death, and Life—and a closing Heavenly Chorus. Unlike the texts treated above, this one has a clearly developed plot and includes some quick exchanges between personages. The Soul feels Death approaching and is willing to give up his life, for he has made provision in heaven through the intercession of the Virgin. Yet when Death asks for the "end," or goal, of the Soul's life, he is denied it. Then Life speaks for the only time in the dialogue; he has been sent by God to give eternal life to the Soul. Life and Death then accompany the Soul to heaven, to the welcoming strains of the Heavenly Chorus.

Dialogue, "O tu che vai"—
G. F. Anerio, *Selva armonica*

Personages: Soul (S), Death (B), Life (T), Heavenly Chorus (SATB)

ANIMA	SOUL
O tu che vai per via,	O you who are on your way,
dimmi, per cortesia,	tell me, if you please,
chi sei? Chi cercar tenti	who are you? Whom do you try to seek,
con tanti tuoi spaventi?	with your many terrors?

MORTE	DEATH
Son Morte.	I am Death.

ANIMA	SOUL
Hor che vuoi di?	Now what do you wish?

MORTE	DEATH
Tua vita.	Your life.

ANIMA	SOUL
Eccola qui.	Here it is, right here.

MORTE	DEATH
Hoggi non la vogl'io.	Today I do not want it.

ANIMA	SOUL
Pigliala a tuo desio.	Take it whenever you wish.
Già fatto ho provisione.	I have now made provision.

MORTE	DEATH
Dove?	Where?

ANIMA	SOUL
Nella maggione del Cielo.	In the mansion of Heaven.
MORTE	DEATH
E chi c'hai tu?	And who gave it to you?
ANIMA	SOUL
La madre di Giesù.	The mother of Jesus.
MORTE	DEATH
E per qual merto l'hai?	And by what merit do you have it?
ANIMA	SOUL
Ho sol lodato i rai di Sua Eccellenza, e poi servito a i voler suoi. Ma tu ch'ogn'hor mi chiami, altro da me più brami?	I only praised the rays of Her Excellency, and then I served at her wishes. But you, constantly calling me, what more do you wish of me?
MORTE	DEATH
Il fin della tua vita.	The end of your life.
ANIMA	SOUL
Il fin della mia vita ottenerlo non puoi.	The end of my life you cannot obtain.
MORTE	DEATH
Ed a chi dar la vuoi?	And to whom will you give it?
ANIMA	SOUL
A quel ch'è vita eterna di gloria sempiterna.	To him who is eternal life of eternal glory.
MORTE	DEATH
Non è commun editto ch'ognun da me fia afflitto?	Is the edict not common that all be afflicted by me?
ANIMA	SOUL
Si, ma non sempre a un modo.	Yes, but not always the same way.
VITA	LIFE
Che sento, vedo, e odo? Morte, non ha condegno quest'alma del tuo regno. E perchè Dio m'addita	What do I feel, see, and hear? Death, this soul does not deserve your kingdom. And because God directed me

ch'io venga a dargli vita	to come and give him life,
meco essergli consorte	be with me his consort
sin a del Ciel le porte.	up to the gates of Heaven.

MORTE	DEATH
Da poi che so interdetta	Since I know this interdict,
faccia quel fin ch'aspetta.	make the end as expected.
Teco al Celeste Choro	With you and the Heavenly
vuò recondurla.	Chorus I shall lead him back.

ANIMA	SOUL
Moro.	I am dying.

CELESTE CHORO	HEAVENLY CHORUS
Vieni, Anima beata,	Come, blessed Soul,
colombella d'amore,	dove of love,
vien, che sei esaltata	come, for you are exalted
dall'eterno Signore.	by the eternal Lord.

The final example of an Italian dialogue is "Dal più sublime regno," from Antonio Cifra's *Scherzi sacri . . . libro primo* (Rome, 1616). This is the only one of the four that is based on a biblical story, that of the Annunciation (Luke 1:26–38), which is among the most frequently used sources of biblical dialogues in both Italian and Latin. In this dialogue the story unfolds through exchanges between its two characters, the Angel and the Virgin Mary, until the final chorus, which adds a brief concluding narrative. Like the two preceding dialogues, this one is written in rhymed couplets.

Dialogue, "Dal più sublime regno" —
Cifra, *Scherzi sacri . . . libro primo*

Personages: Angel (T), Mary (S), Chorus (SSST).

ANGELO	ANGEL
Dal più sublime regno	A heavenly messenger
messaggero celeste a voi ne vegno,	from the sublimest kingdom I come to you,
Vergine al Ciel diletta,	O Virgin, delight to Heaven,
da Dio Madre di Dio fra mille	chosen by God from thousands as Mother
eletta.	of God.

MARIA
Qual alto anuntio, e quale
nuovo titolo io sento. Ohimè mortale
verginella son io,
non s'avanza tant'alto il merto mio.

MARY
What noble news and what
new title do I hear. Alas, a mortal
virgin am I,
my merit is not that high.

ANGELO
Quai segni di timore
manda nel vostro volto il vostro core?
Voi da l'eterno Padre
sete fatta del Figlio e sposa
    e madre.

ANGEL
What signs of fear
does your heart send to your face?
You by the eternal Father
have been made a spouse and mother of
    the Son.

MARIA
Come esser può che sia,
vergine ancora, ohimè, madre Maria?

MARY
Oh how can it happen
that Mary, still virgin, be a mother?

ANGELO
Quel sacro eterno fiato
spirerà nel ben sen frutto beato.

ANGEL
That eternal sacred breath
will inspire in your womb blessed fruit.

MARIA
Eccomi, Angel divino,
umilissima ancella a voi m'inchino.
Deh, riportate a Dio,
sacro nuntio celeste, il voler mio.

MARY
Behold, divine Angel,
a humble handmaid to you I bow.
Oh, relate to God,
sacred heavenly messenger, my will.

CORO
Al sacro nuntio appena
havea la Verginella
risposto "Ecco l'ancella,"
ch'in su le cetre d'oro
ogni celeste coro
fe' rimbombar di questo dì giocondo
le meraviglie eterne. E il nostro mondo
d'ogni intorno s'udia,
fatto quasi ecco, risonar Maria.

CHORUS
To the sacred messenger
the Virgin had scarcely replied,
"Behold the handmaid,"
when, above, the golden lyres
made every heavenly chorus
resound with the eternal marvels
of this joyful day. And in our world
everywhere was heard,
almost as an echo, resounding, Mary.

The texts of Latin dialogues, unlike those in Italian, are written in prose and are nearly all based on biblical sources.[40] The

40. For a study of the texts and music of Latin dramatic dialogues in the period 1600–30, see Smither, "Dialogue." The appendix of that article lists sixty-one Latin dialogues and cites the original sources and the locations of modern editions. For a dialogue in a modern edition that has appeared since that article, see Massenkeil, *Oratorium* (and Massenkeil, *Oratorium*-Eng.), pp. 20–27. Winter, "Studien," is a study of several texts of Latin dialogues of the early seventeenth century.

most frequently used sources are the Canticle of Canticles, from which were drawn love duets between the "bride" and "groom" of that book, and the story of the Annunciation. Gospel stories are far more prominent as dialogue sources than are stories from the Old Testament. This is no doubt because the Latin dialogue was intended to function primarily as a musical elaboration of a scriptural narrative read during Mass on a given day in the church year, and many more narratives from the Gospels than from the Old Testament were included in those readings. The liturgical position of a Latin dialogue sung during Mass appears to have been that of the gradual or offertory, for which it substituted.[41] Although a Gospel dialogue would be particularly appropriate for performance on the day when its biblical source was the Gospel reading, those dialogues with texts that are not clearly associated with a specific season might well have been performed in churches, and oratories too, at virtually any time of the church year. Among the Gospel sources of Latin dialogues, in addition to the Annunciation, are the stories of the Nativity, the Passion, and the Resurrection as well as those of the temptation of Jesus (Matt. 4:1–11), the finding of Jesus in the temple (Luke 2:42–50), the prodigal son (Luke 15:11–32), the Samaritan woman at the well (John 4:7–40), Jesus' feeding of the five thousand (John 6:5–14), the raising of Lazarus (John 11:17–45), and Jesus' discourse on the Eucharist (John 6:32–59). Among the few Old Testament sources are the stories of Cain and Abel (Gen. 4:9–12), Adam and Eve's banishment from Paradise (Gen. 3:1–16), and the sacrifice of Isaac (Gen. 22:1–13). The extremely few nonbiblical dialogues in Latin are based on the lives of saints or, like some of the Italian dialogues quoted above, are made up of a mixture of allegorical and biblical characters.

The degree to which the text of a biblical dialogue depends upon its source varies from a nearly literal quotation of the source to a free text, or one that uses only the subject matter of the source. Commonly, the texts quote parts of the biblical source literally and other parts freely, with word substitutions, changed word order, and deletions. The passages deleted are usually the connecting narratives. Unlike the later Latin oratorios of Carissimi and others, the majority of the biblical dialogues use neither narrative passages nor insertions that are extraneous to the bibli-

41. Schering, "Beiträge," p. 65; Smither, "Dialogue," p. 414; Chauvin, "Ratti."

cal source. Most of the dialogues present the ideas of the text in the order in which they are presented in the Bible, but a few, particularly those from the Canticle of Canticles, use a patchwork procedure, combining ideas consecutively that are not consecutive in the source. Like the Italian dialogues those in Latin normally conclude with an ensemble of the personages who sang the dialogue or with a chorus. The concluding number usually stands outside the drama or narrative and either reflects on it or simply repeats the last line of the last soloist.[42]

The first of the dialogue texts illustrated below, Ignatio Donati's "Domine, si fuisses hic" from his *Motetti concertati* (Venice, 1618), is based on the story of the raising of Lazarus. It is characteristic of the majority of the Latin dialogues in that it is made up of biblical quotations with slight changes and in that all narrative passages, except for the final line, have been deleted.

Dialogue, "Domine, si fuisses hic"—
Donati, *Motetti concertati*

Text source, John 11:21–45.
Personages: Martha (A), Jesus (T), Magdalene (S), Jews (TB), Chorus (SATTB)

MARTA
Domine, si fuisses hic frater meus non fuisset mortuus. Sed et nunc scio quia quaecumque proposceris a Deo dabit tibi Deus.

MARTHA
Lord, if you had been here my brother would not have died. But even now I know that whatever you ask of God, God will give to you.

JESUS
Resurget frater tuus.

JESUS
Your brother will rise.

MARTA
Scio quia resurget in resurrectione in novissimo die.

MARTHA
I know that he will rise at the resurrection, on the last day.

JESUS
Ego sum resurrectio et vita; qui credit in me, etiam mortuus fuerit vivet. Et omnis qui vivit, et credit in me, non morietur in aeternum. Credis hoc?

JESUS
I am the resurrection and the life; he who believes in me, even if he die, shall live. And whoever lives and believes in me, shall never die. Do you believe this?

42. Contrary to Schering's assertion in his *Oratorium*, pp. 15–16, that Latin dialogues often close with a choral setting of a liturgical text such as an antiphon or responsory, I have not found liturgical texts used as conclusions. (Smither, "Dialogue," p. 410.)

MARTA	MARTHA
Utique Domine, ego credidi quia tu es Christus Filius Dei vivi, qui in hunc mundum venisti.	Certainly, Lord, I believe that you are the Christ, the Son of God, who has come into the world.
MAGDALENA	MAGDALENE
Domine, si fuisses hic non esset mortuus frater meus.	Lord, if you had been here my brother would not have died.
JESUS	JESUS
Ubi posuistis eum?	Where have you laid him?
MARTA-MAGDALENA	MARTHA-MAGDALENE
Domine, veni et vide.	Lord, come and see.
JUDAEI	JEWS
Ecce quomodo amabat eum.	See how he loved him.
JESUS	JESUS
Tollite lapidem.	Take away the stone.
MARTA	MARTHA
Domine, jam foetet, quatriduanus enim est.	Lord, he will stink now, for he has been dead four days.
JESUS	JESUS
Nonne dixi tibi quoniam si credideris, videbis gloriam Dei? Lazare veni foras. Solvite eum, et sinite abire.	Have I not told you that if you believe you will behold the glory of God? Lazarus, come forth. Unbind him, and let him go.
CHORUS	CHORUS
Et multi crediderunt in eum.	And many believed in him.

The text of Agostino Agazzari's dialogue "In illo tempore," from his *Dialogici concentus* (Venice, 1613), is based on the story of Jesus' discourse on the Eucharist. Like the previous one this text is made up of quotations from its biblical source. All the connecting narrative in the Bible has been deleted except for an essential narrative line beginning "Murmurabant." Yet this dialogue differs from the one just quoted in that the beginning of its first line is narrative and nonbiblical: it is an introductory formula used for Gospel readings, found in the Missal but not found in the Bible at this point. This beginning is significant, for it shows the dialogue's close connection with the liturgy and points to the work's conception as a musical elaboration of a Gospel reading in the Mass. The final chorus simply repeats Jesus' last line, which expresses the essential idea of the dialogue.

Dialogue, "In illo tempore"—
Agazzari, *Dialogici concentus*

Text source, John 6:32–59.
Personages: Chorus (SSATTB), Jesus (T), Crowd (AAB).

CHORUS
In illo tempore dixit Jesus turbis:

CHORUS
At that time Jesus said to the crowd:

JESUS
Non Moises dedit vobis panem de caelo, sed Pater meus dat vobis panem de caelo verum.

JESUS
Moses did not give you the bread from heaven, but my Father gives you the true bread from heaven.

TURBA
Domine semper da nobis panem hunc.

CROWD
Lord, give us always this bread.

JESUS
Ego sum panis vitae qui de caelo descendit. Qui venit ad me, non esuriet; qui credit in me, non sitiet unquam.

JESUS
I am the bread of life, which has come down from heaven. He who comes to me shall not hunger; he who believes in me shall never thirst.

CHORUS
Murmurabant ergo Judaei de illo, dicentes:

CHORUS
The Jews therefore murmured about him, saying:

TURBA
Nonne hic est filius Joseph, cujus nos novimus patrem et matrem? Quomodo ergo dicit: Quia de caelo descendi?

CROWD
Is this not the son of Joseph, whose father and mother we know? How, then, does he say, "I have come down from heaven"?

JESUS
Nolite murmurare. Ego sum panis vivus. Si manducaverit ex hoc pane, vivet in aeternum; et panis quem ego dabo, caro mea est.

JESUS
Do not murmur. I am the living bread. If anyone eat of this bread, he shall live forever; and the bread that I will give is my flesh.

TURBA
Quomodo potest hic nobis carnem suam dare ad manducandum?

CROWD
How can this man give us his flesh to eat?

JESUS
Caro mea vere est cibus, et sanguis
meus vere est potus. Qui manducat
hunc panem vivet in aeternum.

JESUS
My flesh is food indeed, and my blood
is drink indeed. He who eats this
bread will live forever.

CHORUS
Qui manducat hunc panem vivet in
    aeternum.

CHORUS
He who eats this bread will live
    forever.

The Annunciation dialogue set by Severo Bonini—"Missus est Gabriel Angelus," from his *Primo libro de motetti a tre voci* (Venice, 1609)—is a more nearly complete biblical passage than either of the two quoted above, since it includes not only the dialogue of the personages but the narrative passages as well. The inclusion of narrative makes this text closer in style to the Latin oratorios of Carissimi than are the Latin dialogues quoted above. Yet here, too, biblical lines have been deleted in the interest of economy.[43] This work, as does the previous one, concludes with a repetition of the final idea stated by the last personage of the dialogue.

Dialogue, "Missus est Gabriel Angelus"—
Bonini, *Il primo libro de motetti a tre voci*

Text source, Luke 1:26–38.
Personages: Chorus (SSATB), Angel (A), Mary (S).

CHORUS
Missus est Gabriel Angelus ad Mariam
virginem desponsatam Joseph, et
ingressus ad eam, dixit:

CHORUS
The Angel Gabriel was sent to the Virgin
Mary, the bethrothed of Joseph, and when
he had come to her, he said:

ANGELUS
Ave gratia plena; Dominus tecum;
benedicta tu in mulieribus.

ANGEL
Hail, full of grace, the Lord is with
you; blessed are you among women.

CHORUS
Quae cum audisset, turbata est in
sermone eius, et ait angelus:

CHORUS
When she had heard him she was troubled
at his word, and the angel said:

43. For a comparison of the text of this dialogue with its biblical source, see Smither, "Dialogue," p. 411.

ANGELUS
Ne timeas, Maria, invenisti enim
gratiam apud Dominum; ecce concipies,
et paries Filium, et vocabitur nomen
eius Jesum.

ANGEL
Fear not, Mary, for you have found
grace with the Lord; behold you shall
conceive and bring forth a Son, and
his name shall be called Jesus.

CHORUS
Dixit autem Maria:

CHORUS
But Mary said:

MARIA
Quomodo fiet istud, angele Dei,
quoniam virum non cognosco?

MARY
How shall this happen, angel of God,
since I do not know man?

CHORUS
Et respondens angelus dixit ei:

CHORUS
And the angel answered and said to her:

ANGELUS
Audi Maria, Spiritus Sanctus
superveniet in te, et virtus Altissimi
obumbrabit tibi; quod enim ex
te nascetur vocabitur Filius
  Dei:

ANGEL
Hear, Mary, the Holy Spirit shall come
upon you and the power of the Most High
shall overshadow you; for he who shall
be born of you shall be called the Son of
  God.

MARIA
Ecce ancilla Domini, fiat mihi secundum
verbum tuum.

MARY
Behold the handmaid of the Lord; be it
done to me according to your word.

CHORUS
Fiat mihi secundum verbum tuum.

CHORUS
Be it done to me according to your word.

The final illustration of a dialogue—"Dic mihi sacratissima Virgo," from Giovanni Francesco Capello's *Sacrorum concentum* (Venice, 1610)—is biblical in only the general sense that it refers to the Crucifixion of Jesus. The personages are not named in the source, but one is clearly the Virgin Mary; she answers the questions of an anonymous personage and thus expresses her reaction to the Crucifixion. This is the only Latin dialogue quoted here that approaches the type of expression often found in *laude*, with its question-and-answer procedure and its emphasis upon an individual's emotional response. It is also the least like a Latin oratorio because of the virtual absence of plot development. The concluding duet—like that of the Italian dialogue "Gesù nel tuo partire," quoted above—expresses the idea of only one of the personages, in this case the Virgin Mary.

Dialogue, "Dic mihi sacratissima Virgo"—
Capello, *Sacrorum concentum*

Personages: Anonymous personage (T), Mary (S).

ANONYMOUS
Dic mihi sacratissima Virgo,
quo cruciabaris dolore quando
filium tuum flagellatum ac spinis
  coronatum vidistis?

ANONYMOUS
Tell me, most holy Virgin, by what
grief were you tortured when you saw
your Son flogged and crowned with
  thorns?

MARIA
Heu mi, nimis acerba quaris; tunc
siliens tremula stabam ac nimio
dolore dolorem pene
  sentiebam.

MARY
Alas, what you ask is too bitter;
then silently I stood trembling, and
with exceeding pain, [His] pain I
  almost felt.

ANONYMOUS
Quid filius tuus tibi merenti
dixit?

ANONYMOUS
What did your Son, O worthy one, say
to you?

MARIA
En dulcis mater, en filium tuum,
en quam crudelem mortem patior.

MARY
Behold, sweet mother, behold your Son;
behold how cruel a death I suffer.

ANONYMOUS
Et tu quid illi morienti dixisti
O mestissima mulier?

ANONYMOUS
And you, what did you say to him as he
was dying, O most sorrowful mother?

MARIA
Mi fili, fili mi solus moreris?

MARY
My Son, my Son, you die alone?

A 2: ANONYMOUS, MARIA
Moriar et ipsa tecum. En tecum
morior.

A 2: ANONYMOUS, MARY
I myself would die with you. Behold,
I die with you.

Music of the Dialogue. A number of textual distinctions have been made above between Italian and Latin dialogues, and several distinctions may also be made regarding their music. The organ is virtually always specified for the basso continuo part in the Latin works, but no instrument is specified for most of those in Italian;

the ends of poetic lines in works with Italian texts are often pointed up by cadences in the music, but the Latin texts, being in prose, do not have a like influence on the music; and Italian dialogues tend to show the influence of dance style more frequently than those in Latin. In other respects Italian and Latin dialogues are musically much alike. Choruses and ensembles tend to use mixtures of imitative and chordal style, with more emphasis on the latter; instrumental parts other than the basso continuo are rarely found, although occasionally an instrumental sinfonia or ritornello is used; and solo passages exhibit a considerable stylistic variety.

Any attempt to generalize about musical style in the solo passages of early Baroque dialogues runs the risk of oversimplification, since the works were composed by a rather large number of composers who represent a variety of tendencies. Yet it may be said, in quite broad terms, that the prevailing style is neither highly conservative, as are Viadana's generally contrapuntal motets for solo voice and organ, nor is it quite new, as are the noncontrapuntal Florentine monodies; rather, the dialogues occupy a variety of positions between those extremes.[44] Thus in the majority of the dialogues, the bass is subordinate to the vocal line, the latter having the more interesting rhythmic and melodic designs. The intervals between the two parts are usually those that would be permitted in late Renaissance conservative counterpoint, but imitation is rare. The continuo lines tend to be relatively smooth, often almost vocal in quality. Rarely does one find a solo passage approximating the recitative style identified with the Florentine monodists and Monteverdi, with its rhythms molded to the text, its unprepared dissonances for affective expression of the text, and its static or slowly moving bass line.

Examples III–2 through III–7 (pp. 111–17), selected from the dialogues of which the texts were quoted and translated above, provide a representative sample of the solo styles. Examples III–2 through III–4 are taken from the dialogues with Italian texts; all three reveal the influence of the text's poetic structure, although that influence is not consistently evident. In Example III–2 the

44. The musical styles treated in Smither, "Dialogue," pp. 416–24, are those of Latin dialogues, but most of them are also found in Italian dialogues of the same period. Highly exceptional is Romano Micheli's Latin dialogue on the Annunciation, a twenty-voice canon with thirty *obblighi*, studied and edited in Smither, "Micheli."

EXAMPLE III-2. Dialogue, "Dal più sublime regno"—Cifra (*Scherzi sacri . . . libro primo*, Rome, 1616).

ANGEL—A heavenly messenger from the sublimest kingdom, I come to you, O Virgin, delight of Heaven, chosen by God from thousands as Mother of God. MARY—What noble news and what new title do I hear! Alas, a mortal virgin am I, not deserving of such high honor.

musical setting of the first strophe, sung by the Angel (mm. 1–7), marks the end of every poetic line by a cadence (on the words "regno," "vegno," "diletta," and "eletta"). In the second strophe, sung by Mary, the line endings ("quale," "mortale," "io," and "mio") are not all marked by cadences, since the meaning of the text would not admit of such a procedure; in the remainder of the dialogue (not quoted here), the line endings are so marked. The music of Example III–3 is less strongly influenced by the poetic structure, since this text, with its quick exchanges between the Soul and Death, does not lend itself readily to such treatment. In Example III–4, however, a cadence marks the end of every poetic line ("cara," "nodi," and "godi"), and the same procedure is followed consistently for the remainder of the dialogue.

SOUL—O you who are on your way, tell me, if you please, who are you? Whom do you seek, with your many terrors? DEATH—I am Death. SOUL—Now what do you wish? DEATH—Your life. SOUL—Here it is, take it. DEATH—Today I do not want it. SOUL—Take it whenever you wish.

In all three of these examples with Italian texts, the bass, subordinate to the vocal line, forms a harmonic foundation, and the intervals between the parts are generally consonances or contrapuntally admissible dissonances. The chief differences among the three examples are in their rhythmic-melodic designs. The beginning of Example III–3 conveys an impression approaching light popular music, with its two initial phrases of equal length followed by a longer phrase that concludes the Soul's opening speech of two rhymed couplets (phrase structure: 6+6+9 beats). This tendency toward symmetry is not, of course, as strong as that in dance style, but passages hinting at dance style appear a number of times in the course of the dialogue. Example III–2 is less symmetrical than Example III–3, but the two are similar in the rhythmic relationship between the continuo and vocal line. Example III–4 is remarkably different from the two just discussed in the rhythmic-melodic style of its vocal line and thus in the relationship of that line to the continuo. The highly ornamental vocal style, moving in much shorter time values than the continuo, is used in this dialogue more for the role of the Angel than for that of the Soul (not quoted here), but the latter also includes some ornamental passages. Similar passages are occasionally found in other dialogues, but such profusion of ornamentation is rare.

EXAMPLE III-4. Dialogue, "Quando sarà quel giorno"—Quagliati (*Affetti amorosi spirituali*, Rome, 1617).

When will be the day, dear Soul, that I see you loose from amorous knots, and one day enjoying sweet liberty?

The Latin dialogues illustrated in Examples III–5 through III–7 represent three quite different tendencies. The first example, by Agazzari, is the most conservative of the group. Its continuo line moves in melodic intervals characteristic of the bass in late sixteenth-century polyphony, and the contours of the melody given to Jesus, with word painting on "de caelo descendit" (mm. 14–15), are also reminiscent of sixteenth-century practice. Yet this is a modernized motet style, for the continuo is less active than the voice, imitation is absent, and the vocal line frequently uses the rhythmic pattern ♩♪♪, a declamatory element more common in the early seventeenth-century motets than in those of the sixteenth century. The choral passage of this example, sung by the Crowd, is characteristic for its chordal style, although the six-voice choruses functioning as the *Historicus* of this dialogue (not in the example) are imitative.

EXAMPLE III-5. Dialogue, "In illo tempore"—Agazzari (*Dialogici concentus*, Venice, 1613).

JESUS—Moses did not give you the bread from heaven, but my Father gives you the true bread from heaven. CROWD—Lord, give us always this bread. JESUS—I am the bread of life, which has come down from heaven.

In Example III–6 the style of the vocal line and the relationship between it and the continuo are closer to what appears to be the norm for early Baroque Latin dialogues. The continuo functions essentially as a harmonic support, as does that in the preceding example, but the vocal style is more declamatory. In fact, the declamation in this example clearly foreshadows that used in the next generation by Carissimi and his contemporaries. Noteworthy in this respect are the rhetorical repetitions of text and music, usually by ascending sequence, in the part of Jesus at mm. 1, 9–10 and 13–15, and throughout the passage sung by Martha. Of particular interest in Martha's part is the rhetorical use of chroma-

EXAMPLE III-6. Dialogue, "Domine, si fuisses hic"—Donati (*Motetti concertati*, Venice, 1618).

JESUS—Take away the stone. MARTHA—Lord, he will stink now, for he has been dead four days. JESUS—Have I not told you that if you believe you will behold the glory of God? Lazarus, come forth. Unbind him . . .

ticism in the continuo and in the ascending sequential repetition of the vocal line at the phrase "jam foetet" ("he will stink now"). Chromaticism is common in vocal music throughout the Baroque era to express pathos, and its use here reflects Martha's horror at the thought of what they will find if the tomb of Lazarus is opened.[45] Also of interest in this example is the continuo movement in fourths and fifths, with implications of functional tonality, in mm. 7–9 and mm. 15–16.

The final illustration from a Latin dialogue, Example III–7, is not characteristic of the majority of the dialogues but represents the minority that reflect the influence of late madrigal and early monodic styles. The continuo moves at a slower rate than does that of most dialogues, and the vocal line is closer than most to a Florentine style of recitative. Like the late madrigal and early monody, the example includes numerous points (marked with an asterisk above the vocal line) where dissonances are treated in a rhetorical manner that would not have been admissible according to the rules of late Renaissance counterpoint. The following places are of particular interest from the standpoint of affective text expression by dissonance: m. 3, a dissonance at the highest point of the line on the first syllable of "dolore"; m. 6, the first note, to express the "thorn" of "ac spinis" (note also the diminished chord of the organ for the same expressive purpose); m. 8, on the exclamation "Heu," an odd suspension dissonance (assuming the organist plays a major chord at the beginning of the measure), with upward chromatic resolution (see also m. 13); and m. 14, the repeated dissonance on "dolorem pene." Chromaticism is used rhetorically for the expression of the text in m. 5, where a chord change involving chromaticism introduces the word "flagellatum," and in mm. 8 and 13, which are similar at the beginning but continue differently to express the Virgin's anguish. Traditional word painting is used in mm. 10–12, where a trembling motive is placed on "tremula" and is followed by a cessation of rhythmic and melodic motion on "stabam." This dialogue contains far more instances of text expression, both of the affective and of the traditional late Renaissance types, than do most dialogues of the early Baroque. The new monodic style clearly influences the cadences, particularly that in m. 7, a notated *trillo* of the type

45. For a more extensive treatment of musical-rhetorical figures to which these are related, see pp. 229–33.

EXAMPLE III-7. Dialogue, "Dic mihi sacratissima Virgo"—Capello (*Sacrorum concentum*, Venice, 1610).

ANONYMOUS—Tell me, most holy Virgin, by what grief were you tortured when you saw your Son flogged and crowned with thorns? MARY—Alas, what you ask is too bitter; then silently I stood trembling, and with exceeding pain, [his] pain I almost felt.

illustrated by Giulio Caccini in the foreword of his *Le nuove musiche* (Florence, 1602).

The duration of most dialogues of the early Baroque, including all those mentioned above, is between two and five minutes. For reason of their brevity and the resulting limited dramatic development of their texts, they could scarcely be termed oratorios according to seventeenth-century uses of the term, despite certain textual and musical elements that they have in common with oratorios. Dialogues with somewhat greater length and dramatic development that were contemporary with some of these, found in Anerio's *Teatro*, will be treated below.

Anerio's Teatro *and Some Incunabula of the Oratorio*

Anerio's Life and Work[46]

Giovanni Francesco Anerio (ca. 1567–1630), born in Rome, was the son of a trombonist and singer, Maurizio, and the younger brother of the composer Felice (ca. 1560–1614). The Anerio family was devoted to Philip Neri. He was the confessor of Giovanni Francesco's mother, Fulginia (who also did Philip's laundry), from the 1550s and of his father from the 1560s. Giovanni Francesco occasionally confessed to Neri; it was said to have been through Neri's intercession that he was miraculously healed from a serious illness around 1585.[47] Giovanni Francesco received the first tonsure in 1583, at about sixteen years of age; but he was not ordained a Jesuit priest until 1616. On 7 August of that year, he celebrated his first sung mass in the Giesù. According to a contemporary account, a large crowd came to this event to hear "all the musicians of Rome," who were divided into eight choirs.[48] It is not known whether Neri encouraged Giovanni Francesco to enter the Society of Jesus, as he had done with many others; but since the Oratorians maintained a close relationship with the Jesuits, it is not surprising that Anerio as a Jesuit priest would compose his *Teatro* expressly for use in the Oratory founded by Neri.

As a boy Anerio was a singer under Palestrina in the Cappella Giulia (1575–79). Also a student of the organ, he is listed as an organist in the payment records for the Lenten services of 1595 at the Oratorio del Santissimo Crocifisso. He is said to have been the maestro di cappella at the church of San Giovanni in Laterano from 1600 to 1603, but no documentation has been found to support this report.[49] He held the post of maestro di cappella at the cathedral in Verona from 1609 through part of 1611, but in the latter year he returned to Rome as the prefect of music at the Roman Seminary. By 1613 Anerio had become the maestro di cappella at the church of Santa Maria dei Monti, a position that he

46. For summaries of G. F. Anerio's life and work, see L. Pannella, "Anerio, G. F.," *Dizionario biografico*, 3:175–79; Hobbs, "Anerio," 1:109–53; and Williams, "Anerio," 1:1–9.

47. Numerous details regarding the relationship between the Anerio family and Neri are found in the family's depositions for the process of Neri's canonization in *Processo*, 1:318–21, 338–39, 410–12. On Felice Anerio's relationship to Neri's Oratory, see Dardo, "Felice Anerio."

48. Casimiri, "Disciplina," p. 8.

49. Haberl, "Anerio," p. 61.

held until at least 1620. He was still in Rome in 1621, but at some time thereafter he went to the area of Venice, for he was an organist at a special service in 1624 in a church at nearby Treviso. His next known position is that of maestro di cappella at the Warsaw court of the king of Poland, Sigismund III. In 1628 he was succeeded in that position by his former student, Marco Scacchi. During his return trip from Warsaw to Rome in 1630, Anerio became ill and died in Graz, Austria, where he is buried.

Anerio was primarily a composer of sacred music, with his motets more numerous than his masses. The influence of Palestrina is clearly evident in the masses—particularly in the dissonance practice, certain aspects of melodic style, and parody technique. Virtually all the masses use the basso continuo, however, and for this reason and for their more strongly metrical rhythm, they represent a modernization of the Palestrina style. The motets also show the influence of Palestrina. Yet here, too, the style has been modernized, particularly with regard to the new emphasis on solo passages within motets and on motets for solo voice and continuo. Anerio's settings of both secular and spiritual texts in Italian are less numerous than those in Latin, although he published several books of madrigals and related genres. As with other Roman madrigalists in his period, Anerio seems to have been strongly influenced by the style of Marenzio.[50]

The Teatro

G. F. Anerio's *Teatro armonico spirituale di madrigali a cinque, sei, sette, & otto voci, concertati con il basso per l'organo* ("Harmonic Spiritual Theater of Madrigals for Five, Six, Seven, and Eight Voices, Concerted with the Organ Bass," Rome, 1619) consists of ninety-four spiritual madrigals intended for use in oratory services.[51] The phrase *Teatro armonico* in the title may have been chosen to point up the difference between the contents of this book and that of the large collection of Roman Oratorian music that had preceded it, Ancina's *Tempio armonico* (*lauda* book III/1–2, 1599–1600). The oratory had changed: its music had

50. Einstein, *Madrigal*, 2:855–56.
51. The only detailed study of Anerio's *Teatro* is Hobbs, "Anerio." Much of the following section is based on material presented in that study. For more general treatments of the *Teatro*, see Alaleona, *Oratorio*, pp. 112–25; Pasquetti, *Oratorio*, pp. 148–70; and Schering, *Oratorium*, pp. 42–50, 64.

FIGURE III-5. Title page of Giovanni Francesco Anerio's
Teatro armonico spirituale di madrigali (Rome,
1619).
(Courtesy of I/Rsc.)

begun to reflect the dramatic tendencies of the time; "Harmonic Theater" would seem to be an appropriate substitution for the old "Harmonic Temple." Indeed, most of the madrigals in the *Teatro* include dramatic elements in their texts. Although all the texts are anonymous, there is reason to assume that Agostino Manni, who died the year before the *Teatro* was published, was the author of some of them.[52] The *Teatro* is of primary importance for the history of the oratorio in the early Baroque, for among its madrigals are several works that are sufficiently extended and dramatically developed that they may be termed the earliest oratorios—or better, "incunabula of the oratorio."[53]

The dedication of the *Teatro* was written by Orazio Griffi, a priest at San Girolamo della Carità and a composer. The dedication is important for the light it sheds on the origin and function of the *Teatro* as well as on Oratorian history. Griffi dedicated the work to St. Jerome (San Girolamo), after whom his church was named, and to Philip Neri. The dedication is translated here in its entirety:

To Father St. Jerome, Doctor of the Holy Church, and to Blessed Philip Neri.

It has seemed to me a very reasonable and suitable thing, Glorious Champions of Christ, that the present winter *Theater* of the Gospels, Stories of Sacred Scriptures, and praises of all the Saints, should be issued forth by the press. [The texts were] recently set to music by the Reverend Mr. Giovanni Francesco Anerio, at my urging, for the use of your Oratory under your most felicitous and holy names, in order to render to you in part, my Advocates and Protectors, the proper recognition for the high regard and devotion which I owe you. And it is very suitable [that the dedication be] to you, St. Jerome, for having received and kept the Blessed Philip Neri for a period of thirty-three years in your house, where, with the help of your intercession, he arrived at such an eminent degree of Sanctity that not without marvel and amazement can his works be told. And [it is very suitable that the dedication be] to you, Blessed Philip, for having done works so heroic and distinguished, under his protection in this same house, that the reform of the ways of many of the faithful, it can be said truthfully, has had its beginning in large part from you. Easier and more effective means could not be found for drawing

52. Alaleona, *Oratorio*, p. 114.

53. This term was first used in Schering, *Oratorium*, p. 43, to refer to sixteen of the dialogues in Anerio's *Teatro*; it is used for seven of Anerio's dialogues in Hobbs, "Anerio," 1:174.

souls to the perfect love and fear of God than daily familiar discussions and holy persons making known to them the ugliness of sin, the pains of Hell, the beauty of the blessed souls, and the reward of eternal glory; and in this way brought to penitence, they are introduced to the frequentation of the most holy Sacraments and to the performance of works of mercy. This you accomplished, Blessed Philip, inspired to do so by His Divine Majesty, by beginning the Oratory in this same house; and then you founded that of the Most Reverend Fathers of Vallicella under the name of the Congregation of the Oratory, which today, more than ever, flourishes with most holy progress and universal profit. And also the Most Reverend Fathers of Jerome [M. R. P. Girolamini] of Naples were begun, who from your house, St. Jerome, took their name, and from you, Philip, the Oratory. And to attain the desired aim so much more easily, and to draw, with a sweet deception, the sinners to the holy exercises of the Oratory, you introduced Music there, seeing to it that vernacular and devotional things were sung, so that the people, being allured by song and tender words, would be all the more disposed to spiritual profit; nor was your idea in vain, since some, coming at times to the oratory only to hear the music, and then remaining, moved and captivated by the sermons and the other holy exercises that are done there, have become servants of God. Therefore, having seen great profit proceed thus from music through having frequented successively for a period of forty-five years both of these oratories, I have wanted, in the company of the above-mentioned Reverend Composer, to share the merit by making participants in this practice, by means of prints, those oratories that are erected in a likeness of these [two], both within and outside Rome, and also those persons like the Regular Clergy and others to whom it is not granted because of obedience to be able to go [to the oratories]. Receive, therefore, St. Jerome, the poor affection of an unworthy Priest of your house, and you, Blessed Philip, the heart ready to serve your Holy Oratory, asking in this only by means of that mercy of His Divine Majesty and your intercessions to be able to rejoice eternally in the most beautiful Theater of Paradise.

From your house called St. Jerome of Charity [San Girolamo della Carità] in Rome, on the First of November, 1619.

Your least and most humble servant,

Horatio Griffi.[54]

Among the points in this dedication that are particularly noteworthy is Griffi's mention that he had frequented both ora-

54. The dedication is printed in Alaleona, *Oratorio*, pp. 245–46; for a facsimile of the dedication and a slightly different translation from the one given here, see Hobbs, "Anerio," 2:297–300.

tories, those at San Girolamo and the Chiesa Nuova (Vallicella), for forty-five years. This indicates that the oratory at San Girolamo continued to function, presumably with the kinds of exercises established there by Philip Neri, when the Oratorians moved away. Yet the priests at San Girolamo, though strongly influenced by the Oratorians, were evidently not members of the Congregation of the Oratory.[55] Griffi's hope that the printing of the *Teatro* would promote the use of such music in oratories other than those at San Girolamo and the Chiesa Nuova was realized in at least one city, Bologna, and probably in others as well.[56] Of interest are Griffi's statements that the works were "recently set to music" and that they were composed at his own urging. Although the madrigals of such a large collection might well have been composed over a period of two or more years, Anerio was apparently hard at work on them in the year before their publication. In a letter of 10 March 1618—which he sent to the duke of Modena, together with a composition that he had been asked to write for an oratory that the duke frequented—Anerio mentions that he had recently been quite busy "in various musical occupations, and particularly in an oratory where I must continually write new works."[57] He no doubt refers in this letter to the oratory of San Girolamo della Carità; the new works that kept him so busy were probably some of those published in the following year in the *Teatro*.

Griffi's dedication makes clear the function of music in the oratory and of the *Teatro* in particular. He says that music is intended to be a "sweet deception" to draw sinners into the spiritual exercises, and he calls the *Teatro* a "winter Theater," a work intended for the musically elaborate *Oratorio vespertino* held during the winter months. This point is made even clearer by a table, printed in the organ book of the *Teatro*, that lists the Sundays and other feast days from 1 November through Easter, together with an indication of which madrigals are proper for each day. For most of the days, the table lists two madrigals each; according to established Oratorian practice in the spiritual exer-

55. Alaleona, *Oratorio*, p. 157.

56. The only evidence known thus far of the *Teatro*'s having been used outside of Rome is the 1620 inventory discussed above of the music owned by the Bologna Oratory. It seems reasonable to assume, however, that oratories in other cities, such as the extremely active one at Naples (mentioned in Griffi's dedication), owned the *Teatro* as well.

57. Anerio to the duke of Modena, Cesare d'Este, 10 March 1618, in Roncaglia, *Modena*, pp. 90–91.

cises, one of the two madrigals would precede and one would follow the sermon. The table includes three madrigals each for two of the Sundays (Christmas and Palm Sunday) and only one each for five of the Sundays (including Easter). In addition to the madrigals intended for Sundays and other feasts, there are some called *commune* (Common of the Apostles, Common for a Martyr, Common of Confessors, etc.), and others called *indifferenti*, which could be used at any time of the church year. The *Teatro*, then, with its numerous "proper" and a few "common" and "indifferent" madrigals, provided all the elaborate music necessary for use in an oratory during the winter season; it did not include *laude*, although they were still sung in oratories of this period. It is misleading to apply the term *lauda* to the compositions of the *Teatro*[58] or to consider even the simplest ones to be only slightly different from *laude*.[59] Quite to the contrary, they are clearly madrigals, as their title page indicates; furthermore, some of them are dialogue madrigals that are sufficiently extended to represent the oratorio in its earliest stage of development.

The only complete set of partbooks of the *Teatro*, now in the Biblioteca del Conservatorio di Musica Santa Cecilia at Rome, was originally the property of the Oratorians at the Chiesa Nuova. The flyleaf of each partbook bears an inscription in a seventeenth-century hand, possibly that of Griffi, that this was the copy that he presented to the Oratorians at the Chiesa Nuova. The fact that Anerio's *Teatro* was composed and printed at the instigation of a priest at San Girolamo, rather than at the Chiesa Nuova, would seem to indicate that the oratory at San Girolamo was more interested in fostering the newer musical tendencies than that at the Chiesa Nuova, where the conservative composer Martini was the maestro di cappella from 1604 until 1623. Yet from the physical appearance of the copy of the *Teatro* owned by the Oratorians at the Chiesa Nuova, it is clear that at some time the book was used there for performances.

The texts of the majority of the madrigals in the *Teatro* depend for their subject matter upon the occasion for which they were intended. The readings for the Mass or the Divine Office on a given day or appropriate hagiographical writings would provide the theme for a given day's sermon in an oratory and for the

58. In Pasquetti, *Oratorio*, p. 155, a dialogue in the *Teatro* is referred to as a *lauda*.
59. In Alaleona, *Oratorio*, p. 113, the simplest works in the *Teatro* are so considered.

Teatro madrigals that were performed before and after it. The madrigal texts are rarely allegorical. The relationship between the madrigals designated for a certain day and the theme of the day is not always close. Although some of the madrigals clearly present the scriptural story of the day through narrative and/or dramatic means, others omit details that the listener needs to supply. Within the context of an oratory service, he would be in a position to supply the details from the sermon, which would refresh his memory.[60] The *Teatro*'s poetry is clearly influenced by the sixteenth-century *lauda* in several respects: the subject matter, the use of certain poetic expressions, and the variety of metrical and rhyme schemes. Yet these poems also differ from *laude* in the irregularity of their strophes, which makes a strophic musical setting unsuitable. Although virtually all the texts of the *Teatro* might be considered dramatic in a general sense, more than half of them include narrative and/or dramatic elements comparable to those discussed above in connection with the Oratorian *laude*. Thus the *Teatro* includes dialogues, dialogues combined with narrative, monologues combined with narrative, and narratives. Any of these types might also include passages of commentary or exhortation.

In the music of the dramatic madrigals in the *Teatro*, a solo voice is usually used for the role of an individual personage and an ensemble for that of a group. A passage of narrative, commentary, or exhortation is set for either a soloist or an ensemble. The setting of the narrative passages tends to be quite varied; at times the narratives are distributed among several solo voice parts and ensemble groupings. In setting the parts of individual personages, Anerio adopted certain conventions: the role of Jesus—even the twelve-year-old Jesus—is always a bass, and the bass also sings the roles of the elderly Simeon, Joseph's father, King Nebuchadnezzar, the elderly Isaac, God's voice, Goliath, and the prodigal son's father. The tenor sings Satan, Joseph the husband of Mary, Saul, Ananias, Abraham, Jairus, and Rachael—the last being a curious and exceptional choice of vocal range. The alto sings no solo roles, but the soprano sings those of women, children, young men, and servants.[61]

60. For a quotation from the beginning of a sermon taken from a seventeenth-century MS collection of sermons used in the oratory at San Girolamo, see Pasquetti, *Oratorio*, p. 147.
61. Hobbs, "Anerio," 1:170.

The music of the *Teatro*, some features of which are illustrated in the works to be discussed below, represents the conservative madrigal of its time. The intervals of melody and counterpoint used are essentially those of Palestrina's style. Thus chromaticism and unprepared dissonances are rare. The style of the madrigals is unlike that of Palestrina, however, in its more vigorous rhythmic patterns and greater emphasis on vertical sonority and on chord progressions comparable to those of functional tonality. In their textures the ensemble passages reflect the influence of Marenzio's madrigals; imitation is frequent, but multiple subjects, said to be prominent in Anerio's secular madrigals,[62] seem not to be so in these works. The double choruses tend to be chordal and antiphonal. The solo style is derived more from the type of melodic line used in the polyphonic madrigal than from monody. The continuo is subordinate to the vocal line but is nearly as active as the vocal bass in a polyphonic madrigal. Recitative is not used— that is, one does not find clear instances of Florentine *stile rappresentativo*—but there are occasional moments of a conservative declamatory style that suggest recitative. Only two of the works include instrumental numbers—one each—and these are among the works treated below. In their general structure nearly all the madrigals are sectional, with strong cadences followed by double bars between the sections. Within some of the madrigals, sections begin with similar head motives, as is indicated below. A large chorus nearly always constitutes the final section of a madrigal. Most of the madrigals include four to six sections and are six to eight minutes in duration.[63] Four of them, however, include from fourteen to twenty-four sections and range from about sixteen to twenty minutes in duration. These longer works are discussed below.

Incunabula of the Oratorio

Fourteen of the madrigals in Anerio's *Teatro* are labeled *dialogo*.[64] This term seems to have been inconsistently applied in the print, however, since other works that do not bear this label are clearly

62. Einstein, *Madrigal*, 2:856.
63. Hobbs, "Anerio," 1:173. For a list of all the madrigals, together with the number of sections, the duration, and other information about each, see table 8 in Hobbs, "Anerio," 1:285–88.
64. Those labeled *dialogo* in the print are so labeled in table 8, ibid.

dialogues: they are equally dramatic and as long as some of those so labeled. The *Teatro*'s four longest works, discussed below, have dramatic texts, are termed *dialogo* in the print, and last from sixteen to twenty minutes. Thus they fall within the normal range of duration of compositions in one large structural part designated by the term *oratorio* in Italian sources of the mid-seventeenth century, the period when that term first began to be applied to a musical genre.[65] In their length, dramatic development, and function in an oratory these four dialogues are like oratorios. The phrase *incunabula of the oratorio* seems appropriate to describe them, for they truly represent the oratorio in its infancy. The primary difference between these works and those called oratorios in the mid-century is one of musical style; these are stylistically close to the polyphonic madrigal and lack the operatic element of recitative common in the genre known as oratorio in the mid-century. One might wish to call certain other dramatic dialogues in Anerio's book incunabula of the oratorio, but if so, the term *oratorio* would be used in an exceptional sense for them because of their brevity. Among these are five dialogues ranging from ten to twelve minutes in length: "Deh non vedete voi," "Diteci pastor-elli," "Doppo un lungo diggiuno," "Felice giorno," and "Il vecchio Isach"; still other dramatic dialogues in the *Teatro* range from six to ten minutes, and the term *oratorio* would be even less applicable to them.[66]

Dialogo dell'Anima, [San Michele, e l'Angelo Custode].[67] The subject matter for the text of this work, which begins "Deh pensate o mortali," is in the tradition of those *laude* and *sacre rappresentazioni* that include angelic and allegorical personages; such works had been written ever since the late Middle Ages. In the *Teatro* the work is listed among the *indifferenti*, considered appro-

65. For the durations and some other characteristics of works called oratorios in Italian sources of the mid-seventeenth century, see Smither, "Carissimi," pp. 66–69, and Smither, "Oratorio," pp. 659–63.

66. The following shorter dialogues in the *Teatro*, which range from about eight to eleven minutes long, are available in modern editions of their texts and/or music. In Alaleona, *Oratorio.* pp. 251–59, "Rispondi Abramo" (text and music); pp. 260–69, "Sedea lasso Giesù" (text and music); pp. 116–17, "La Verginella Madre" (text). In Pasquetti, *Oratorio*, pp. 148–49, "Viene al tempio la Donzella" (text); pp. 155–56, "La Verginella Madre" (text); pp. 161–64, "Il vecchio Isach" (text); pp. 164–67, "Sedea lasso Giesù" (text). In Schering, *Oratorium*, p. 44, "Il fanciullo Gioseffo" (text); and "Anhang," pp. ii–iii, "Sedea lasso Giesù" (text).

67. For a modern edition, see Hobbs, "Anerio," 2:175–209.

priate for any time of the church year. The text, without a narrator, includes only a dialogue among personages. Of the work's twenty sections (lasting about sixteen minutes in its musical setting), the first nineteen consist of brief speeches distributed among the three personages; the final section is a chorus of angels. The dramatic development, which is the least extensive found in the works treated here, unfolds in one place. The Guardian Angel (T) has brought the Soul (S), as the latter had wished, to see the powerful St. Michael the Archangel (B). According to the Guardian Angel's description, St. Michael is warlike in appearance and carries the balance by which he weighs souls to determine whether they will go to heaven or hell. Upon seeing St. Michael, the Soul is filled with fear; he is also moved by hearing about the love of God, who died for him. After the Soul confesses that he is a sinner, he is converted. This conversion is the climax of the text; there follows a joyful episode in which the Guardian Angel and St. Michael give the Soul numerous rewards. At the end the chorus of angels (SATB-SATB), singing the praises of the converted Soul, enters for the only time.

The essential aspects of the text's poetic style, which is characteristic of the *Teatro* madrigals in general, may be seen in the following quotation of the first four speeches:

SAN MICHELE
Deh pensate, o mortali,
ale miserie, a i mali
che durano in eterno,
già nel profondo inferno.
Questa bilancia al fine,
o tu che ascolti e senti,
fia che t'apporti un dì gloria o
    tormenti.
Pensa dunque che fai
o gloria eterna o sempiterni guai.

ST. MICHAEL
Ah think, O mortals,
of the misery, of the evils
which endure forever,
in deep hell.
This balance, in the end,
O you who listen and hear,
is what will bring you, one day, glory or
    torments.
Think, then, what it may be,
either eternal glory or eternal trouble.

ANGELO CUSTODE
Alma infelice e da peccati oppressa,
al fin t'ho pur condotta ove
    bramai.
Questi, questi è colui
che pesar debba un giorno i falli tui.
Mira la spada ignuda,
mira quella bilancia,

GUARDIAN ANGEL
Unhappy soul, oppressed by sins,
finally I have led you where you
    desired to go.
This is the one
who one day must weigh your faults.
See the unsheathed sword,
see that balance,

quell'ali sue veloci,	those fast wings of his,
quella sua fronte armata,	that armed brow,
quella veste dorata!	that golden coat!
Esso t'accenda al core	He will light flames of love in your heart
con le parole sue fiamme d'amore.	with his words.

ANIMA	SOUL
Ahi che tremar mi sento!	Ah, how I feel myself tremble!
O che spavento,	Oh what fear,
qual visione è questa,	what a vision is this,
così dura e molesta!	so hard and troubled!

SAN MICHELE	ST. MICHAEL
Alma infelice, ascolta	Unhappy soul, listen,
e l'occhio tuo rivolta	and turn your eyes
a questa spada	to this sword
pria che discenda e cada.	before it descends and falls.

Thus the speeches of the different personages vary in the number of lines; a strophic musical setting, characteristic of sixteenth-century *laude*, would not be possible. Most of the lines have seven or eleven syllables, although there are occasional exceptions. The rhyme schemes are irregular, but rhymed couplets predominate. Rhetorical repetitions for emphasis are used occasionally, as in lines 5–9 of the Guardian Angel's speech quoted above.

The musical setting of the text reveals a number of the *Teatro*'s general characteristics. The work is scored for soloists, chorus, and organ continuo, with no other instruments indicated. The work's solo style, essentially that of the conservative madrigal with continuo, is illustrated in Examples III–8 through III–10 (pp. 130–31). The first number, "Deh pensate o mortali" (Example III–8), characterizes the formidable personage of St. Michael with heroic gestures—the jagged melodic outline at the beginning and the extremely wide range, the lowest note of which paints the word "inferno." In this example the organ bass is a simplified version of the vocal line, a characteristic of most bass solos in the *Teatro*. Example III–9 illustrates a semideclamatory style frequently encountered in the *Teatro*. Yet this type of declamation seems closer to that normal in polyphonic madrigals of the time than to Florentine recitative, particularly after the first two measures, when melodic and contrapuntal considerations become in-

EXAMPLE III-8. *Dialogo dell'Anima, [San Michele, e l'Angelo Custode]*—G. F. Anerio (*Teatro*; Hobbs, "Anerio," 2:175).

Ah think, O mortals, of the misery, of the evils which endure forever, in deep hell.

EXAMPLE III-9. *Dialogo dell'Anima, [San Michele, e l'Angelo Custode]*—G. F. Anerio (*Teatro*; Hobbs, "Anerio," 2:176–77).

Unhappy soul, oppressed by sins, finally I have led you where you desired to go. This is the one who one day must weigh your faults. See the unsheathed sword, see that balance, those fast wings of his . . .

EXAMPLE III-10. *Dialogo dell'Anima*, [*San Michele, e l'Angelo Custode*]—G. F. Anerio (*Teatro*; Hobbs, "Anerio," 2:178–79).

Ah, how I feel myself tremble! O what fear, what a vision is this, so hard and troubled!

creasingly pronounced (see especially mm. 21–22 and 27–30). Characteristic madrigalisms are the militaristic, almost marchlike passage beginning at "Mira la spada ignuda" and the quick notes on "veloci." Even more clearly declamatory and approaching more closely to recitative style is Example III–10. Yet here, too, there are clear indications of Anerio's conservatism. In the opening measure, for instance, the composer consistently uses consonant intervals between the two lines; a true monodist would probably have retained the low G throughout the measure and would have treated the resulting dissonance (G to f'-sharp) as an expression of the affection of fear in the text.[68] Furthermore, despite the declamatory approach in the melodic line, the cadential approaches (mm. 42–43 and 46–47) are not in the new style (as are those in Example III–7, mm. 7 and 15, on p. 117) but are formulas common in the sixteenth century.

68. For a similar melodic line in which such a dissonance is used for affective purposes, see Monteverdi, *Orfeo*, Act II, Orfeo's lament "Tu se' morta," particularly at the text "tu se' da me partita." (Monteverdi, *Opere*, 11:62–63.) See also Examples IV–9 and V–7.

Dialogo del Figliuol Prodigo.[69] This dialogue, which begins "Due figli un padre havea," is based on the story of the prodigal son, found in Luke 15:11–32. It is designated in the *Teatro* as proper to Passion Sunday, and it is also listed among the *indifferenti* as a work appropriate for any time of the year. The text consists of fourteen sections and lasts about sixteen minutes in Anerio's setting, as does the dialogue discussed above. This work includes sections of narrative, which are set for the chorus (SSATTB); the personages are the Son (S), the Father (B), and the Servants (SAT). The dramatic development, somewhat more extensive than in the dialogue treated above, may be divided into three episodes, the last followed by a moralizing conclusion. At the beginning, after the chorus narrates the essential background information, the Son requests his part of his father's wealth so that he may leave, be independent, and lead a happy life. In the second episode the Son, by now impoverished and hungry, laments his misfortune and returns to his father to ask forgiveness. The final episode is one of rejoicing: the Father orders the Servants to bring gifts and prepare a banquet. The chorus concludes the work.

The metrical style of this text is similar to that of the dialogue discussed above except in the sections of excitement, especially of rejoicing, where the poetic lines are unusually short. The Son's first speech begins with an eleven-syllable line, but it then continues with lines of four syllables, in rhymed couplets, to express the joy he anticipates upon leaving his home:

FIGLIUOL	SON
Dammi la parte mia chè più non voglio	Give me my part, for no longer do I want
giovinetto	to be a boy,
star soggetto,	to be subjected,
ma contento	but happy,
pien d'argento.	with plenty of money.
Vo' godere,	I wish to enjoy myself,
vo' tenere	I wish to lead
vita quieta	a tranquil life,
vita lieta;	a joyful life;
nè pensare	do not think
di staccare	of separating
questo affetto	this affection
dal mio petto.	from my breast.

69. Printed in Alaleona, *Oratorio*, pp. 270–88. Text, with omissions, printed in Pasquetti, *Oratorio*, pp. 158–61.

Likewise after the return of the Son, the Father orders that the Son be honored, and the Servants respond in lines of five syllables (with the elision of successive vowels):

PADRE	FATHER
Udite o servi,	Hear, O servants,
la mia parola:	my words:
portate un'ampia	bring an ample
e ricca stola.	and rich robe.

SERVI	SERVANTS
Ecco portata	Here we have brought
un aurea veste	a golden robe,
che sembra in ore	which seems in gold
color celeste.	a heavenly color.

PADRE	FATHER
Porgete al dito	Bring for his finger
aurato anello.	a golden ring.
Presto s'uccida	Quickly kill
anche un vitello.	also a calf.

SERVI	SERVANTS
Ecco l'anello	Here is the ring;
mettilo al dito.	place it on his finger.
Ecco il vitello	Here is the calf
per il convito.	for the banquet.

PADRE	FATHER
Si porta il lutto	Bring the lute
e s'empia tutto	and let it be filled
di simphonie	with symphonies,
di melodie.	with melodies.

The musical styles of this dialogue are comparable to those illustrated in the examples discussed above, except for the greater emphasis on dance rhythm in triple meter for the setting of the short lines, which reflects excitement. In the Son's first number (Example III–11, p. 134), the text of which is quoted above, measures 1–4 employ the solo madrigal style, in C time and with an active bass, that is most common in the *Teatro*; but the passage following the change of meter is in dance style to reflect the happiness that the Son anticipates in his new life. Likewise the setting of the exchange between the Father and the Servants, quoted above, is almost entirely in triple meter.

Give me my part, for no longer do I want to be a boy, to be subjected, but happy, with plenty of money. I wish to enjoy myself, I wish to lead a tranquil life, a joyful life; do not think of separating this affection from my breast.

This dialogue is unusual for the *Teatro* in its requirement of instruments other than the organ. At the end of the episode of rejoicing quoted above, after the Father calls for "simphonie" and "melodie," an instrumental *simphonia* is played by six instruments: violin, cornetto, violin or cornetto, theorbo, lute, and organ. This number is in two sections, the first in C time and the second in triple time. The instruments used for the *simphonia* also double the vocal parts in the final chorus. The chorus enters five times in the dialogue, usually with a mixture of imitative and chordal textures, in the madrigal style characteristic throughout the *Teatro*.

Dialogo di David.[70] This biblical dialogue, which begins "Mentre su l'alto monte," is based on the story of David and Goliath (I Sam. 17:3–18:9) and is listed in the *Teatro* among the *indifferenti*. The work includes seventeen sections and lasts about eighteen minutes. Thus it is slightly longer than the two works treated above, and in this respect it more nearly resembles the oratorio of the mid-century. Like the *Dialogo del Figliuol Prodigo*, this one includes sections of narrative. The first of these, at the beginning, is set for a solo tenor voice; the others are for double chorus (SATB-SATB). The personages in the drama are Goliath (B), David (S), and various groups of Israelites (TT; SSA; AA; BB; SATB-SATB). The text may be divided into two large episodes followed by a moralizing conclusion. The first episode covers the events leading up to the conflict of David and Goliath and including the latter's death. This episode includes narrative background and challenges and threats by David and Goliath. The conflict itself is neither dramatized nor narrated, but the chorus, at one point functioning as both a commentator and a narrator, registers its reaction to the event:

O colpo avventuroso!	Oh fortunate blow!
Ecco il gigante estinto,	Behold the giant dead—
per mano d'un fanciul, deluso e vinto.	by the hand of a boy—deluded and conquered.

Following this chorus David introduces the second episode by encouraging the daughters of Jerusalem to rejoice, and the remainder of the episode consists of ensembles and choruses of praise and joy. The moralizing conclusion begins with a duet (SS) exhorting mortals to arm themselves with humility. This is answered by the full double chorus representing the mortals thus arming themselves for combat against the monster who menaces souls on earth.

Goliath sings twice in this work, and both times his part shows a stylistic relationship to that of St. Michael in the first of the *Teatro* dialogues treated above, for both are powerful, militaristic personages. Like St. Michael, Goliath is a bass, and his part includes a wide range and numerous skips in the melodic line.

70. For a modern edition see Hobbs, "Anerio," 2:135–74.

Example III–12, the beginning of Goliath's first number, illustrates these aspects of his style, as well as his passage work on "hebrea" ("Hebrew") and "crolato" ("shaken"). Here, as usual, the continuo part is a simplified version of the bass solo. David sings four times, and his part, too, includes passage work comparable to Goliath's. Of special interest in the music of David are the melodic similarities among the beginnings of three of his numbers (Example III–13, a-c); also similar to these is the beginning of the rejoicing of the Israelites (Example III–13, d). A detailed study of the beginnings of sections throughout the *Teatro* would be necessary to determine the full significance of such head-motive treatment. It would appear that Anerio was interested in introducing an element of cyclical unification by common head motives occasionally in the *Teatro*, and he may also have intended such melodic similarities to contribute to the characterization of personages.[71]

EXAMPLE III-12. *Dialogo di David*—G. F. Anerio (*Teatro*; Hobbs, "Anerio" 2:136–37).

Hear my words, O Hebrew people. I am that great colossus of the Philistines, who has never yet by human power been shaken.

71. For brief discussions of the head-motive treatment in this work and in "Eccone al gran Damasco," see Hobbs, "Anerio," 1:230–33, and Schering, *Oratorium*, p. 64 (where the term *Leitmotiv* is used).

Example a:

From that grotto of Avernus such a strange monster issued forth . . .

Example b:

Come, come then, behold, I gird myself . . .

Example c:

See the proud leader . . .

Example d:

With gaiety, with sweetness . . .

Solo.

Ccone al grã damafco oue fã ftanza Di nimico   voler di

tè mentita Gente ch'al noftro Dio fuor d'ogn'vfanza manca di legge   e

vuol tener fua vita A più mirabil fede a più poffanza Del noftro grã maeftro

e ciò n'inuita forti guerrier quiui à reftar il piede   per diffender l'honor fal-

uar   la fede   Hor cõ il poter voftro e l'ardir mio   fpero far ftrage

fauguinola e fiera di tutti quelli che credò quel Dio Di vergin dõna nato   e

la più vera legge di moife hanno in olbio   E vogliam con la fua far

ch'el   la pera Ch'in guiderdone il patrimonio efpreffo voftro farà vi

Eccone pronti
tace.

donerò vi donerò me fteffo.

OO 2

FIGURE III-6. Beginning of G. F. Anerio's *Dialogo della conversione di San Paolo* from the *Sesto* and *Organo* books of his *Teatro*.
(Courtesy of I/Rsc.)

Dialogo della Conversione di San Paolo.[72] The closest of all the dialogues in the *Teatro* to the mid-century oratorio, this one, which begins "Eccone al gran Damasco," consists of twenty-four sections, and its music lasts about twenty minutes. The biblical source of its text is the story, from Acts 9:1–22, of St. Paul's conversion. The text begins with a narrative introduction set for tenor solo, but that is its only narrative section. The personages are Saul (T), Saul's Followers (SATB; SATB-SATB; T), Jesus (B), Ananias (T), and a chorus of Israelites (SATB). In addition to functioning as Saul's followers and a group of Israelites, the chorus comments anonymously on the action at one point (SATB) and also sings the final reflection (SATB-SATB). The text may be divided into four episodes and a reflective conclusion. The first episode is that of the persecution of the Christians by Saul and his followers, and it includes warlike solos and choruses, plus an instrumental *combattimento*. The second episode is that of Saul's conversion on the road to Damascus, during which he is over-powered by Jesus' voice. Saul's followers comment on the terror of the scene; one of them (T) states that to him Saul appears dead, for he seems neither to breathe nor to have a pulse. In the third episode, which takes place in Damascus, Jesus appears to Ananias and tells him to go to Saul, who will be one of His followers. The final episode includes Ananias's visit to Saul and the latter's confession of faith in Jesus and exhortation for others to change their lives. The final chorus sings of heaven, hope, and the eternal Lord.

The music of this work differs from that of the dialogues treated above primarily in the greater emphasis on the chorus and instruments. The instrumental *combattimento*—for two violins, cornetto, lute, theorbo, and organ—is used to create the effect of Saul's battle with the Christians. It begins in triple meter then changes to C time and uses the *concitato* rhythmic patterns characteristic of battle chansons and madrigals in the sixteenth and early seventeenth centuries, as illustrated in Example III–14. Like the *Dialogo di David*, this work shows some similarity among the beginnings of three sections, as shown in Example III–15. Although the first few notes of these head motives are reminiscent of those in the *Dialogo di David* (Example III–13), their continuations are different from those and are enough alike to function as elements of unification in this work.

72. For a modern edition see Hobbs, "Anerio," 2:210–64. Text printed in Schering, *Oratorium*, "Anhang," pp. iii–vi.

EXAMPLE III-14. *Dialogo della Conversione di San Paolo*—G. F. Anerio (*Teatro*; Hobbs, "Anerio," 2:230–31).

EXAMPLE III-15. *Dialogo della Conversione di San Paolo*—G. F. Anerio (*Teatro*; Hobbs, "Anerio," 2:210, 251–52, 256).

Example a:

Behold at Great Damascus where people harbor inimical will . . .

Example b:

This Jesus my God? Wounded and crucified? I confess and I believe.

The Early Baroque: Antecedents and Incunabula

(EXAMPLE III-15, continued)

Example c:

Band of elect souls, from the worldly battle to the other life [good Jesus invites you].

PART II *The Oratorio in Italy, Circa 1640–1720*

CHAPTER IV

Mid-Century Rome I:
The Oratorio Volgare

❧ In the approximately thirty years between Anerio's *Teatro* and the mid-century, Romans became aware of a new musical genre, the oratorio, developing in their city's oratories. By the 1660s the genre had become firmly established in Rome and had begun to be cultivated in other cities of Italy, as well as in other countries of Europe. The present chapter treats briefly the Roman social, artistic, literary, and musical backgrounds of the oratorio from the 1620s to the 1660s and then considers some examples of the mid-century *oratorio volgare*.

Social, Artistic, and Literary Background

Rome's Patrons of the Arts and Literature

In the period under consideration in this chapter, the early Baroque tendencies of the papacy (mentioned at the beginning of chapter 3) continued, and the popes and their families remained the leading patrons of the arts and literature in Rome. Certain aspects of Roman Catholic reform were in evidence, and the Counter-Reformation efforts north of the Alps continued; yet life at the papal court was luxurious, and nepotism was rampant. The papacy played only a secondary role in international politics, its chief political concerns being local—the administration of the Papal States and of the city of Rome.

More encouragement was given to the arts and literature during the long pontificate of Pope Urban VIII (Maffeo Barberini,

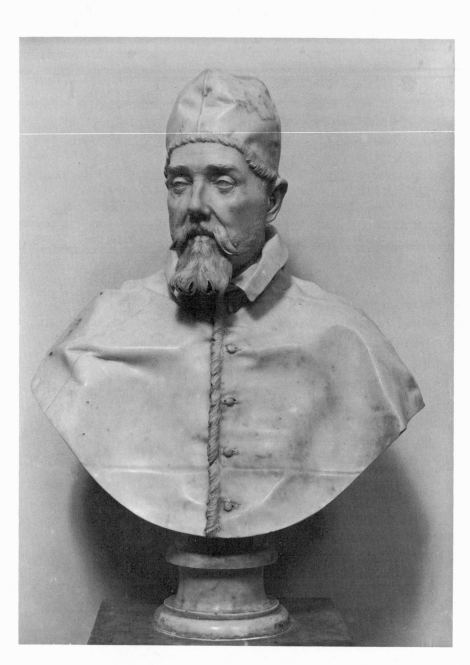

FIGURE IV-I. Pope Urban VIII (Maffeo Barberini, 1623–44). In marble, by
Gian Lorenzo Bernini.
(Reproduced by permission of the Galleria Nazionale d'Arte Antica,
Rome.)

1623–44) than during those of his two successors because of Urban's strong cultural interests and those of his family.[1] As a young man, Maffeo Barberini (b. 1568) had become well versed in Italian, Latin, and Greek literature; he had also begun to write poetry, an activity that he continued throughout his life. After his election to the papacy, his poems, mostly in Latin, were published repeatedly: they were translated into several languages, provided with commentaries, and set to music.[2] His fondness for poetry is reflected in his appointment of the important Florentine poet Giovanni Ciampoli, who figures as a librettist in the early history of the oratorio, to the post of Secretary of Briefs.[3] Urban was a strong advocate of poetry that would foster high Christian ideals, and he considered Ciampoli to be among the authors of such poetry. Urban's taste in sculpture is reflected in his choice of Gian Lorenzo Bernini to create the monuments he desired. Soon after Urban's election as pope, he commissioned Bernini to create a magnificent canopy for the high altar in St. Peter's; this colossal work with twisted columns was begun in 1624 and was completed nine years later. Urban revealed his interest in music by his support of the opera performances at the Barberini Palace and his conferring of benefices and honors on outstanding musicians. For instance, Domenico Mazzocchi, important for the development of the oratorio and other genres in this period, received a benefice in 1637;[4] the singer-composer Loreto Vittori—a virtuoso castrato active in opera, at the oratories, and as a member of the Sistine Chapel—was knighted in 1641.[5]

Following the lead of his three predecessors, Urban placed members of his family in high and enormously lucrative positions, which enabled them to pursue their cultural interests as freely as they wished. His three nephews—Francesco (1597–1679), Taddeo (1603–47), and Antonio (1607–71)—followed Urban's lead in lavishly supporting the arts and literature. Francesco was made a cardinal at twenty-three years of age. Scholarly by nature, he

1. For Urban VIII's patronage of the arts, see Pastor, *Popes*, 29:408–544.

2. Among the musical settings are Johannes Hieronymous Kapsberger, *Poematia et carmina composita à Maffaeo Barberino* (Rome, 1624) and Domenico Mazzocchi, *Maphae I, S. R. E. Card. Barberini nunc Urbani PP. VIII. poemata* (Rome, 1638).

3. For Ciampoli's role in the early history of the oratorio, see the discussion of his *Coro di Profeti*, below, pp. 168–69.

4. Witzenmann, *Mazzocchi*, p. 29.

5. F. Torrefranca, "Barberini," in *MGG*, 1:cols. 1235–38.

was the founder of the extremely rich Barberini Library, and he was also the protector of the confraternity of San Girolamo della Carità, famous for its oratory. In 1625 the pope purchased for Francesco the property on which the Barberini Palace was constructed.[6] Largely completed by 1632 under Bernini and his assistant Francesco Borromini, this imposing structure housed the Barberini Library, was a gathering place for scholars and artists, and was of primary importance for the cultural life of the city. The family began their operatic patronage there with Stefano Landi's *Sant'Alessio* (1632), and the palace became the principal center of Roman opera. Francesco was particularly important as the sponsor of opera performances. Taddeo was the first of the Barberini to live in the new palace, although all three of the brothers lived there at various times. Taddeo was a patron of the arts, but he was less active in this regard than his brothers. The youngest of Urban's nephews, Antonio, was made a cardinal in 1628 at twenty years of age; a recipient of numerous prebends, he was raised in 1638 to the high position of Camerlengo (Treasurer of the Holy See). Antonio was much interested in splendid entertainments and was an avid patron of music, including that performed in oratories. Among the numerous excellent musicians who served Antonio were Marco Marazzoli and Luigi Rossi, both important for the history of the oratorio, opera, and cantata;[7] and among his poets were Francesco Buti and Giovanni Lotti, both authors of texts set to music for the oratories.

After the death of Urban VIII (1644) and the election of Innocent X (Giambatista Pamfilj, 1644–55), the Barberini were forced to flee Rome for political reasons. In 1645 Antonio fled to Paris, where he was welcomed by Cardinal Mazarin; Francesco and Taddeo also fled to France—the former to Paris and the latter to Provence. Thus Barberini patronage ceased for several years, during the family's absence from Rome, but by 1653 political negotiations made possible their return. In that year Antonio was again in Rome, where he began to commission new operas; but Barberini patronage was henceforth reduced in scale.

In taste the antithesis of Urban, his successor Innocent X had little liking for literature and complained that poets and artists were troublesome.[8] Like Urban, Innocent made cardinals of his

6. For a history and description of the palace, see Pastor, *Popes*, 29:498ff.
7. For other musicians in the service of Antonio Barberini, see Prunières, "Barberini."
8. For Innocent X as a patron of the arts, see Pastor, *Popes*, 30:382–411.

ANT·EP̄VS·PRÆNEST.CARD·ANTONIVS·BARBERINVS
S·R·E·CAM·SIG·GRATIAE·ET·BREVIVM·ET·S·CONG·DE
PROPAG·FIDE·PRAEFECT·ARCHP̄BR·BAS·S·MARIAE·MAI·
MAG·FRAN·ELEMOSIN·ROMANVS·
XXX·AVG·M·DC·XXVII·
Obijt die 1 Augusti 1671.

Steph.Picart Sculp· Jo:Iacobus de Rubeis Formis Romæ ad Templ·Pacis Cum Priuil·S·Pontif·

FIGURE IV-2. Cardinal Antonio Barberini (1607–71).
(Rossi, *Effigie*, 1:18.)

nephews, but they were of little importance to the political and cultural life of Rome. Innocent's pontificate tended to be unfavorable to the arts and literature. Although the pope retained the same artists whom Urban had appointed, he made no effort to appoint new ones, perhaps out of disinterest. Nevertheless, he is important for having commissioned a number of architectural projects and monuments, including the famous Fountain of the Four Rivers, designed by Bernini, in the Piazza Navona.

During the pontificate of Alexander VII (Fabio Chigi, 1655–67), the leadership of Rome was once again in the hands of a patron of the arts and literature.[9] Fabio Chigi had written poetry in his youth; he retained his interest in literature throughout his life. During his pontificate he enjoyed surrounding himself with poets and scholars and holding discussions on humanistic topics. Alexander made an effort during the first year of his papacy to abolish the practice of nepotism, but thereafter he yielded to pressures. By then, however, he had appointed his Secretary of State: Cardinal Giulio Rospigliosi (the future Pope Clement IX), a poet and the most important librettist of Roman operas in the second third of the century. One of Alexander's close advisers was an illustrious member of the Congregation of the Oratory: Cardinal Virgilio Spada—a student of the sciences, the author of a theological treatise, and an amateur composer. Certainly the most imposing of Alexander's many commissions in the arts was for Bernini to create the magnificent colonnades in front of St. Peter's. The designs were begun in 1656, and the work was completed in 1667.

Alexander was a reformer of liturgical music. His Apostolic Constitution, *Piae sollicitudinis* of 23 April 1657, is important not only because it initiated a reform but also because it sheds light on practices in the churches and oratories of Rome. The opening of the constitution calls attention to its purpose:

We, occupied in looking after the decorum and reverence of the churches destined for divine praises and prayer, and of the oratories of our gracious city (from which examples of good works go forth into all parts of the world), are compelled, by the desire of pious solicitude, to keep far away from them anything ostentatious, and especially choirs of music and symphonies [*musicos concentus et symphonias*] in which anything indecorous or divorced from ecclesiastical rite is mixed in, with offense of the Divine Majesty, scandal of the faithful, and impediment of the elevation of hearts and devotion to things that are above.[10]

The constitution forbade the use of music suggesting "dance or profane, rather than ecclesiastical melody." During the celebration of the Divine Office or when the Blessed Sacrament was exposed,

9. For Alexander VII as a patron of the arts, see ibid., 31:269–313.

10. Translated in Culley, *German*, pp. 266–67; for the original Latin see Romita, *Ius*, pp. 77–78.

FIGURE IV-3. Pope Alexander VII (Fabio Chigi, 1655–67). In terra-cotta, by
Gian Lorenzo Bernini.
(Reproduced by permission of the Galleria Nazionale d'Arte Antica,
Rome.)

ecclesiastical authorities were "forbidden, under strict penalties, to permit anything to be sung . . . except those words which are prescribed in [either] the Breviary or the Roman Missal, in the Proper or Common Office for the feast or commemoration of the Saint of each day; or which at least are taken from Sacred Scripture or the writings of the Holy Fathers, but which must first be specially approved by the Congregation of Cardinals presiding over sacred rites."[11] A few years later, in 1663, Alexander evidently spoke out again on the subject of texts used in church,[12] and on 30 July 1665 there appeared a detailed instruction, signed by the Secretary of the Apostolic Visitation, on the meaning of the previous constitution. The following item from the instruction is of special interest: "That in the masses, nothing be sung other than the words prescribed by the Roman Missal . . . and especially that, after the epistle nothing be sung except the gradual or tract; and after the Credo, no words be sung other than those of the offertory; and after the Sanctus, the Benedictus or a motet will be sung, but only with the words which the Church puts in the breviary or missal in honor of the saint."[13] Thus Alexander opposed music that was ostentatious, secular in style, and nonliturgical in text in the churches of Rome. These documents imply that in 1665, as earlier in the century, motets with nonliturgical texts were still being substituted for liturgical items of the Mass; some of the motets must have been Latin dialogues of the type discussed in chapter 3 and perhaps were Latin oratorios like Carissimi's shorter ones,[14] treated in chapter 5.

Although the reigning popes and their families tended to set the pattern of artistic life in Rome, numerous other prominent personages also supported the arts and literature. Among these were two nephews of previous popes—Marc'Antonio Borghese, the patron of Luigi Rossi prior to his joining the service of Antonio Barberini, and Ippolito Aldobrandini, the patron of Domenico Mazzocchi. Queen Christina of Sweden—who startled the world by abdicating her throne (1654), becoming a Roman Catholic convert, and establishing her residence in Rome (1656)—became one of the city's most active artistic and literary patrons.[15]

11. Translated in Terry, *Rite*, p. 192; for the original Latin see Romita, *Ius*, p. 78.
12. Culley, *German*, p. 267.
13. Translated ibid., p. 302; for the original Italian see Romita, *Ius*, p. 80.
14. Regarding the possibility of church performances of Carissimi's oratorios, see pp. 217–19.
15. For Queen Christina's patronage of music, see Sandberger, "Christine."

The Visual Arts and Borromini's Oratory

Rome was the center of Baroque activity in the visual arts of this period, as is most clearly revealed in architecture and decoration.[16] Thus the visual surroundings of music, the buildings together with their paintings and sculpture, clearly exhibit the characteristics of the period: restless movement, interest in the illusion of depth and in the organization of colossal space, fluidity among the parts of a structure, and the striving for an immediately striking effect. The three outstanding masters were Pietro da Cortona (1596–1669), Gian Lorenzo Bernini (1598–1680), and Francesco Borromini (1599–1667). Among the important works of painter and architect Cortona are his grandiose fresco, *Glory of the Barberini* (also called *Triumph of Divine Providence*), on the ceiling of the large salon in the Barberini Palace and his fresco decoration of the nave, dome, and apse of the Oratorians' church, the Chiesa Nuova. The works of Bernini, who was both a sculptor and an architect, are more in evidence throughout Rome today than those of the other two. In addition to his works mentioned above, particularly striking are his Altar of the Chair of St. Peter (1657–66) in San Pietro in Vaticano, and his Cornaro Chapel, with its Ecstacy of St. Teresa (ca. 1647–52), in Santa Maria della Vittoria.

Francesco Borromini was the only one of the three men mentioned above who was exclusively an architect. Among his works are the small, elliptical church of San Carlo alle Quattro Fontane and the lovely church of Sant'Ivo, with its lantern crowned by a fantastic spiral. Borromini is of special importance to the history of the oratorio, for he was the architect of the famous oratory of the Chiesa Nuova, where the Congregation of the Oratory sponsored performances of oratorios for more than 250 years and where music is still performed today.[17] Prior to the construction of the Borromini oratory, four different locations in or beside the Chiesa Nuova had served as oratories.[18] In 1637

16. For a survey of Italian Baroque art, see Chastel, *Art*, and Wittkower, *Art*. From the eighteenth to the mid-twentieth century, art and literature of the seicento have suffered the derision of most critics and historians. (For a survey of the chief critical writings, see Grandi, *Croce*, p. 127ff.) The established viewpoint that seicento art and literature are the products of the corrupted taste of a decaying Renaissance has been increasingly modified since the mid-twentieth century. Most of the references in this section and the following one, on poetry, are to works that represent the recent trends of reevaluation.

17. For an exhaustive study of Borromini's style, see Portoghesi, *Borromini*, which includes, on pp. 49–50, several drawings and photographs of Borromini's oratory.

18. Gasbarri, *Oratorio fil.*, p. 50.

FIGURE IV-4. The Chiesa Nuova (right) and its adjoining oratory, the headquarters of the Congregation of the Oratory in Rome.
(Vasi, *Magnificenze*, pt. 7, no. 157.)

Borromini was selected as the architect of the oratory to be erected at the left of the church. The oratory was virtually finished in 1640 and began to be used then, but the three-year period of construction was one of numerous changes in plans by the Fathers of the Oratory and the architect. The deliberations concerning their plans reveal a striving for modesty and restraint, an attitude essential to the lives of the Oratorians that also extends to their music. Although Borromini's style was generally well suited to their attitude, the architect found it necessary to negotiate for numerous compromises: at one point, for instance, the Oratorians decided to use stucco for the principal facade, but Borromini convinced them to adopt a polished brick surface; later they gave him permission to use travertine for the columns of the portal rather than thin bricks, "as long as they are not made of marble, so that in all things befitting modesty be observed."[19] Borromini beautifully fulfilled

19. Portoghesi, *Borromini*, p. 53.

the task that the Oratorians had set for him (see Figure IV–4). The undulating facade, its convex central portion accentuated by a balcony behind which a large niche curves gently inward, is neither extravagant nor ostentatious. The interior of the oratory is a simple rectangular hall; the seating capacity is approximately five hundred, plus ten to fifteen in the loggia intended for cardinals.

Poetic Styles and the Oratorio

Librettos of the *oratorio volgare* in this period were intended to communicate to a wide audience and thereby to assist in attracting people of every station of life into the oratory. Although the librettos are often couched in simple language, they are by no means free from the influence of the chief poetic tendencies of the time, particularly when the librettist was a poet of considerable stature such as Giovanni Ciampoli or Francesco Balducci.

The most influential poetry in the first half of the seventeenth century was that of Giovan Battista Marino (1569–1625); his contemporary Gabriello Chiabrera (1552–1637) represents a different style that became increasingly influential in the second half of the century.[20] Characteristics of both styles are found in oratorio texts.[21] Marino's style represents a reaction against the strong influence of Petrarch, which dominated the poetry of the cinquecento. Abandoning Petrarchan themes and becoming largely concerned with spiritual, moral, and ethical values in the areas of earthly and divine love, Marino concentrates on the exterior world, the world of the senses: the analysis of sensual love and of all that can be seen, heard, tasted, or touched. Marino's reaction against the cinquecento may also be seen in his rhetoric—especially in his use of metaphors that evoke surprise, amazement, or astonishment, which he said was the poet's purpose: "E' del poeta il fin la meravigla" ("The aim of the poet is the marvelous").[22] Marino's style emphasizes the sonority of the word itself and the pleasure

20. For a brief survey in Italian of these two styles, with bibliography, see Elwert, *Poesia*, which is a slightly modified version of the earlier article in German, Elwert, "Barocklyrik." For a comparison of Marino and Chiabrera, see Elwert, *Poesia*, p. 132ff., and Wilkins, *Literature*, pp. 293–97. For a study in English of Marino, see Mirolo, *Marino*.

21. Although the influence of these styles will be mentioned from time to time in the course of this and the following chapters, far more research on oratorio librettos is needed to clarify their relationship to the literary tendencies of the time.

22. Mirolo, *Marino*, p. 118.

derived from the effects of phonic surprise. His poetry ran counter to the Christian poetic ideals of Urban VIII, who ordered that Marino's epic *L'Adone* and other of his works be put on the *Index of Prohibited Books*. The aspects of Marino's style that appear in oratorio texts seem chiefly to be his use of metaphors for surprise and his interest in the sonorous effects of words; but even Marino's sensuality appears in the so-called *oratorio erotico* of the later seicento.

Chiabrera, like Marino, represents a reaction against the Petrarchism of the cinquecento; but Chiabrera's reaction was to the structure of poetry. Although Marino continued to employ traditional forms, Chiabrera rejected the sonnet and madrigal of the cinquecento and the norm of seven- and eleven-syllable lines. Chiabrera's poetry was so much in accord with the ideals of Urban VIII that a few months after Urban's elevation to the papacy he honored the poet by a special brief, drawn up by Ciampoli: Chiabrera had "raised lyric poetry from the baseness of sensuousness to the heights of natural and Christian idealism and had shown the world that poetic genius was able to fulfill itself without being the slave of folly and unclean vices."[23] Chiabrera's dependence upon ancient classical models, Pindar and Anacreon in particular, won him the praise of the Accademia dell'Arcadia, the academy formed in late seicento Rome by poets in the circle of Queen Christina of Sweden.

Musical Background

During the period of the origin and earliest development of the *oratorio volgare*, Roman opera acquired its distinguishing features, the madrigal declined in importance, and the cantata (including the dialogue species) became the most popular type of vocal chamber music. These four genres have many features in common; for this reason terminological ambiguity—particularly among the madrigal, cantata, and oratorio[24]—is frequently encountered.

Roman opera sponsored by the Barberini reflects the influence of the church in its propensity for sacred subjects. Secular opera,

---

23. Pastor, *Popes*, 31:245.
24. Church music, such as the motet and sacred concerto, has less in common with these genres than with the *oratorio latino*, to be treated in the following chapter.

and even comic opera, flourished as well; but in Rome, more than elsewhere, operas were based on subjects that were later to become primarily the province of oratorio. The lives of saints had been the subjects of Jesuit dramas at their colleges in Rome since the sixteenth century; in the seventeenth century the Jesuits showed an interest in opera as well.[25] The canonization of Saints Ignatius of Loyola and Francis Xavier in 1622 was the occasion for the performance of Johannes Hieronymous Kapsberger's elaborate musical pageant, *Apotheosis sive Consecratio SS. Ignatii et Francisci Xaverii* ("Apotheosis, or the Consecration of Saints Ignatius and Francis Xavier") at the Roman College. Other Roman operas on the lives of saints are *Sant'Alessio* (1632), *Santa Teodora* (1635), and *San Bonifazio* (1638)—all staged by the Barberini; these librettos were no doubt influenced by the poetic ideals of Urban VIII, for their author was Giulio Rospigliosi (the future Pope Clement IX), who was Urban's secretary. Operas with sacred subjects were performed not only in colleges, private theaters, and palaces but in monasteries as well. In 1636, according to a contemporary account, "after dinner in the monastery of the Padri Ministri degli Infermi there was represented in music the *Life of Saint Mary Magdalene* in the presence of seven cardinals, the Prince Prefect of Rome [Taddeo Barberini], many prelates, and other gentlemen of the court; for the composition of the work, the ability of the actors, and the beauty of the costumes, the drama was received with much applause."[26] Despite the oratoriolike subject matter of such works, they were clearly operas: they were not called oratorios and were not, so far as is known, performed in the oratories of Rome.[27] Other characteristics that Roman opera had in common with the oratorio are purely musical: various styles of recitative, the momentary use of passages in aria style within a recitative, various types of aria structure, an interest in vocal ensembles and choruses, and the use of instruments for the accompaniment of solo voices.[28]

25. For surveys of Jesuit drama and opera, with bibliographies, see H. Hüschen, "Jesuiten," in *MGG*, 7:col. 27; Sommervogel, *Bibliothèque*, 10:1308ff. (with references to earlier vols.); and E. Purdie, "Jesuit Drama," in *Oxford*, pp. 508–15. Jesuit sponsorship of oratorio performances appears to have begun only in the late seventeenth century.

26. Translated from Ademollo, *Roma*, p. 22.

27. There is some evidence, however, that the Oratorians in Bologna might have performed operatic works. See the *rappresentazione* mentioned on p. 91.

28. For characteristics of Roman opera, see Goldschmidt, *Oper*, 1:5–86; Grout, *Opera*, pp. 61–77; Murata, "Operas"; and Rotondi, "Opera."

Although the cantata was growing in importance in this period, the polyphonic madrigal was in a declining stage—a fact commented upon by a number of composers.[29] Pietro Della Valle, a musical amateur well informed on the tendencies of music in his time, wrote in 1640 that madrigals were not composed much in his day, there being little occasion to sing them.[30] Alfred Einstein refers to Domenico Mazzocchi's *Madrigali a cinque voci et altri varij concerti* (Rome, 1638) as "the last milestone on the road over which the madrigal has traveled."[31] In Mazzocchi's dedication to Cardinal (Antonio) Barberini, he refers to the rare use of madrigals but calls attention to Cardinal Barberini's having heard these works sung with the consort of his viols.

The madrigals of this period use from one to five or more voices and usually employ a basso continuo accompaniment; but the madrigals for few voices are sometimes so much like cantatas that the distinction between the two genres is vague. In general, cantatas are longer than madrigals and include sections for vocal solos, duets, and trios, with the solos in recitative or aria style; madrigals, on the other hand, tend to emphasize imitative counterpoint. However, each genre may include some of the elements that are most characteristic of the other.[32] The vague distinction that exists between madrigal and cantata—partly the result of vague terminology in the time and partly because of a fusion of the genres—may also be seen among madrigal, cantata, oratorio, and opera in at least one famous work: Monteverdi's *Combattimento di Tancredi e Clorinda*, composed in 1624 but published in 1638 in the composer's eighth madrigal book. With this work, however, the terminological ambiguity is the result of more recent attempts to classify a hybrid composition; the composer is said to have "established the secular oratorio"[33] and to have composed a "scenic madrigal,"[34] a "scenic cantata,"[35] and a "dramatic cantata."[36] The text employs a narrator and two personages in the manner of an oratorio, but the performance is intended to be

29. For a fuller treatment of the madrigal in its period of decline, see Rose, "Madrigals."
30. Della Valle, "Musica," p. 171.
31. Einstein, *Madrigal*, 2:867.
32. For a brief comparison of the madrigal and cantata, see Rose, "Madrigals," p. 159.
33. Bukofzer, *Baroque*, p. 138.
34. Schrade, *Monteverdi*, p. 302.
35. Ibid.
36. Abert, *Monteverdi*, p. 37.

semioperatic. For this work the term *oratorio* is the least satisfactory of those cited above. Even in a nonscenic performance the *Combattimento* could not have been called an oratorio (although it could have been called a cantata) simply because its text is so much different in content from those sung in oratorios.

The Oratories and Their Music

The Musical Prominence of the Oratories

The prominence of the oratories as musical centers in Rome may be documented from a variety of sources. Pompilio Totti's *Ritratto di Roma moderna* ("Portrait of Modern Rome"), published in 1638 for the use of visitors to Rome, provides comments on musical and other events, along with information about churches, palaces, and monuments. Totti includes all the prominent oratories and mentions the beauty of their services and music. This was useful information for a visitor to the city who did not have access to the lavish aristocratic entertainments in private palaces, for at the oratories he could hear the best performers and works by the best composers of Rome. According to Totti, at San Girolamo della Carità "in the winter, during the evening, they do very beautiful Oratorios [fanno bellissimi Oratorij]"; at the Chiesa Nuova (where, he says, the new building by Borromini is under construction) every weekday except Saturday "they do four sermons of one-half hour each at the end of which some spiritual motets are sung," and "from the first of November until Easter, in the evening, they do devotional Oratorios [fanno devoti Oratorij] with good sermons and music for a period of an hour and a half"; at the church of Santa Maria dell'Orazione e Morte (St. Mary of Prayer and Death, see end paper, no. 7), "very solemn Oratorios are done, sometimes during Lent [si fanno solennissimi Oratorij. E talvolta nella Quadragesima]"; at the Oratorio del Santissimo Crocifisso (The Oratory of the Most Holy Crucifix, see Figure II–2, no. 1, and Figure V–1) in the evenings during Lent, one of the best preachers of Rome delivers a sermon, "accompanied by exquisite instrumental music and excellent vocal music"; and at Santa Maria della Rotonda (the Pantheon, see Figure II–2, no. 7), there is a congregation that has an "Oratory for singing their offices [Oratorio per cantare il loro offitij]."[37] Thus Totti advertises the oratories and in so doing calls attention, not only to their musical prominence, but also to the meaning of the word *oratorio* in his time: a building or a service, the latter including at least one sermon and music. These were the normal uses of the word, but soon the term for the building and the service became common for the music as well—probably among musicians and poets at first and later in common parlance.

Another writer documenting the musical prominence of the oratories is Pietro Della Valle, a significant figure in the early history of the oratorio. Writing in 1640 of the musical life of Rome, he says, "The oratories are for me a unique delight," and he mentions venturing out on poor streets, even in bad weather, to hear the excellent music at the oratories of Santa Maria dell'Orazione e Morte, San Girolamo della Carità, the Chiesa Nuova, and Santa Maria della Rotonda.[38] Other oratories in Rome sponsored musical performances, but the five mentioned by Della Valle and Totti were the most prominent as musical centers.[39]

That music became increasingly important in the oratory of the Chiesa Nuova in the 1620s and 1630s is revealed by the decrees of the Congregation of the Oratory. Considerable tension was evidently developing between Oratorians interested in elaborate music and those who wished to retain the former modesty in the devotional exercises. In 1625 there is a complaint that "in the past years, on occasion of vocal and instrumental music, there were uproars in the Oratory," so great was the enthusiasm for the music. In 1630 there are further complaints that "on the evening of the Feast of the Annunciation there had occurred scandal and noise" as a result of the music, and there had been such "extraordinary disorders, tumult, impertinences, and scandals as to impede the word of God." All this, they said, was because of the compositions used and because persons from outside the oratory had been invited to sing, which resulted in "rivalry and competition." The Oratorians decided to take measures to ensure the devotional quality of the music and the words sung, and they decided "to remove from the oratory every sort of instrument

37. For the above quotations about the five oratories, see Totti, *Roma*, pp. 201, 228, 193, 291, 223.

38. Della Valle, "Musica," p. 176.

39. For oratories in Rome other than that of the Chiesa Nuova, see Alaleona, *Oratorio*, pp. 155–62.

except organ and cembalo and no longer to permit a sinfonia of any kind, and much less reciting [recitare]."[40] By rejecting elaborate music in favor of a more modest and devotional type, the Oratorians were continuing the tradition of Philip Neri. The removal of most instruments from the oratory in 1630 probably conditioned music there for some time to come, but so many of the early oratorios require violins that they, at least, were probably re-admitted rather soon.

The period of musical expansion at the oratory of the Chiesa Nuova coincides with that of Girolamo Rosini's tenure as prefect of music there from 1623 until his death in 1644. (These are exactly the dates of Urban VIII's pontificate, a period of intense artistic activity throughout Rome.) Rosini's skill as a soprano virtuoso is said by his fellow Oratorian and biographer Paolo Aringhi to have spellbound his audiences—Romans, other Italians, and foreigners from beyond the Alps as well: when he sang, "one saw all the people remain extremely attentive, and afterwards all applauded, some saying 'this one who sings is rather an angel than a man,' and others adding 'there is not, has never been, and never shall be anyone like him in singing.'"[41] Rosini's role in the origin and development of the oratorio as a musical genre cannot be documented in detail, but his influence as prefect of music must have been considerable in this crucial period of oratorio history.

In 1640 an important event in Rome's musical life took place: Borromini's new oratory of the Chiesa Nuova, an excellent hall for musical performance, was opened on 15 August, the Feast of the Assumption. A solemn spiritual exercise was held in the presence of a large gathering that included one of the Barberini cardinals. A more impressive service from the musical standpoint —with a sermon by the Oratorian Cardinal Virgilio Spada—was held there on 22 November, the feast of St. Cecilia, in the presence of an illustrious audience, including Cardinals Francesco and Antonio Barberini.[42] Although the compositions and performers for this service are not known, one may assume that the prefect of music, Girolamo Rosini, took part.

40. For the above quotations, and others, from the decrees of the Congregation of the Oratory, see Gasbarri, *Oratorio rom.*, pp. 285–86. The word *recitare* at the end of the last quotation appears to imply a reaction against dramatic music.
41. Translated from Alaleona, *Oratorio*, p. 47.
42. Gasbarri, *Oratorio rom.*, p. 286.

FIGURE IV-5. Girolamo Rosini (1581–1644).
(Reproduced by permission of I/Rf.)

At the end of the period under consideration, the English traveler Francis Mortoft, in his detailed account of his experiences in Rome early in 1659, pays high tribute to the music performed in the oratories of Crocifisso and the Chiesa Nuova. He reports having heard the music at Crocifisso on two Fridays of Lent[43] and at the oratory of the Chiesa Nuova on eight different occasions.[44] On 2 February, Candlemas day or the feast of the Purification, Mortoft reports, "It beginning to be night, wee went to the [oratory of the] Chiesa Nova, where there is most incomparable

43. Mortoft, *Travels*, pp. 145, 163.
44. Ibid., pp. 118, 140, 144, 146, 155, 158, 161, 168.

Musicke every Sunday and holy day at Night, with Organs and 4 Voyces, and wee heard here such sweete Musicke, that a man could not thinke his paines be il spent, if he should come two thousand mile, if he were sure to be recompensed with nothing else, but to heare such most melodious voyces."[45] Thus from Mortoft's description of the performing forces, it appears that a group of modest proportion was used. Later that month, on Sunday, 23 February, Mortoft mentions more than the music at the oratory of the Chiesa Nuova: "And at the Evening wee went to the Chiesa Nova, where wee heard most sweete Musicke and a sermon. And after, saw a kind of Comody acted by 5 little Boyes against the Maskaradoes, who did every part so prettily, that they could scarcely be excelled by Persons of greater yeares."[46] The "kind of Comody" to which Mortoft refers is apparently a survival of the practice, instituted by Philip Neri, of having boys recite brief spiritual dialogues at oratory services. Of special interest for the mention of musicians' names is Mortoft's report of his experience at the oratory of the Chiesa Nuova two Sundays later, on 9 March. "Wee went to the Chiesa Nova where wee heard that never enough to be praised and delightful Musicke. The subject was Made by A Prince of Rome and Composed by Charissima, who for that is accounted the best in the world, and sung by Bonnaventure, Sinesia and the two Vuulpies, all which made so sweete a harmonye, that never the like must be againe expected, unlesse in heaven and in Rome."[47] Mortoft's "Charissima" is, of course, Giacomo Carissimi, and three of the four singers mentioned are the sopranos Bonaventura Argenti and L. C. Sanese and the alto G. B. Vulpio—all members of the papal chapel.[48] It is impossible to be certain what composition by Carissimi that Mortoft might have heard. It would no doubt have been in the Italian language, for Latin was not favored by this oratory; since the text was by a Roman prince, however, the only extant oratorio by Carissimi that it might have been is his *Daniele*, described below.

It is clear that the Fathers of the Oratory in this period were struggling to retain some semblance of the former simplicity of their exercises. They were interested in proselytizing with up-to-

45. Ibid., pp. 118–19.
46. Ibid., p. 140.
47. Ibid., p. 146.
48. Ibid., p. 146, n. 1; Celani, "Cantori," p. 787.

date methods, as were the Jesuits; but unlike the latter they wanted to avoid lavish display. Stopping short of full-fledged theater, they sponsored neither elaborate drama nor opera. The oratorio as a musical genre was strongly conditioned by the Oratorians' efforts to maintain the same balance of modernity and restraint as they had in choosing the architect, design, and manner of construction of the new oratory itself.

Musical Genres in the Oratories

The extant records of the Oratorians at the Chiesa Nuova do not indicate what music they used in the period considered in this chapter. It would seem a reasonable assumption, however, that during the 1620s, and perhaps later, they continued to perform dialogues like those in Anerio's *Teatro*, described in chapter 3. Probably in the 1630s and certainly before 1638, a large oratorio entitled *Coro di profeti*, with a text by Ciampoli and music probably by D. Mazzocchi, was performed at the oratory of the Chiesa Nuova; in 1640 Pietro Della Valle composed his brief oratorio, intended for the same oratory, for the feast of the Purification. Both works are described below. A further glimpse of musical practice at the Chiesa Nuova is provided by a brief published description of a performance given in 1645 by the famous soprano Loreto Vittori: during a spiritual exercise on a winter evening, Vittori sang a lament of Mary Magdalene that depicts her weeping for her sins and throwing herself at the feet of Christ; the work produced such an overpowering emotional effect on its listeners that it moved them to tears.[49] Laments of Mary Magdalene and also those of the Virgin Mary at the Crucifixion of Jesus had long been set to music as *laude* and madrigals; by the mid-1600s they had become a species of the solo cantata.[50]

The records of the archconfraternity of Santa Maria dell'Orazione e Morte for 1646 that describe their spiritual exercises

49. For the full description see Erythraeus, *Pinacotheca*, p. 217; the description is quoted in Latin in Alaleona, *Oratorio*, p. 139, and in Witzenmann, *Mazzocchi*, p. 254. Regarding the questionable authorship of the lament, previously attributed to D. Mazzocchi, see Witzenmann, *Mazzocchi*, p. 23.

50. For other such laments in Roman MSS of the period, see I/Bc: Q 43, fol. 8off., *Lamento della Madalena*, based on Monteverdi's *Lamento d'Arianna*; and fol. 92ff., *Pianto di Maria Vergine alla croce*. A comparable work, but with a Latin text, is Monteverdi's *Pianto della Madonna a voce sola sopra il Lamento d'Arianna*, beginning "Jam moriar Filli," from his *Selva morale e spirituale* (Venice, 1640), printed in Monteverdi, *Opere*, 15:757–62.

during Lent call attention to the performance of dialogues in a remarkably theatrical setting. Although the archconfraternity had an oratory, these exercises were held in the church itself, perhaps because of its greater size.[51] During March of 1646 the church was draped in black; the tribune of the high altar functioned as a stage. Flat panels depicting clouds and angels extended from the tribune to the vault of the church. Every Monday of the month a different scene, representing a "mystery," was depicted on this stage by two-dimensional figures in perspective. These figures, as well as the clouds and angels, were illuminated by lamps placed behind them. The scenes were visual illustrations of sermons and musical compositions—the latter described as "excellent music representing, each Monday, the mysteries listed below; and dialogues were sung concerning the mystery that was being represented on that day." The mysteries listed as having been represented visually and musically on the four Mondays of the month are "Jesus praying in the garden with the apostles," "Jesus at the column being scourged by two rogues," the " 'Ecce homo' when they show him, crowned with thorns, to the people," and "Jesus crucified between two thieves on Mount Calvary."[52] Other than the subjects of the dialogues, nothing is known of them. Since the stage appears to have been filled with the tableaux representing the mysteries, the dialogues would seem not to have been acted but presented in a concert manner as oratorios. The expenses for these scenes were paid by the governor and four protectors of the archconfraternity, one of the protectors being Pietro Della Valle.

At the end of this period, Mario Savioni published his *Concerti morali e spirituali a tre voci differenti* (Rome, 1660) in which he states that if singers are pleased with these pieces he promises to follow them with "a group of madrigals for five voices, likewise moral, which will serve to be sung at the end of each concerto [of this book], the words being on the same subjects as these; thus cantatas for oratories will be completed."[53] This is remarkably clear evidence for the close relationship among the terms *cantata*, *madrigal*, and *oratorio*. In Savioni's view a complete cantata for

51. For seventeenth-century pictures of the interior of the oratory and church, see Hager, *S. Maria*, figs. 6 and 3.

52. The entire description is quoted in Bevignani, *Arciconfraternita*, pp. 133–34. Such scenic representations, survivals of the *sacre rappresentazioni*, must have been rare in Roman oratorios of this period, as this is the only known description of one.

53. Translated from the preface of Savioni's *Concerti*, p. 5.

an oratory consists of one of his moral or spiritual concertos *a 3* (which could have been called cantatas)[54] followed immediately by a madrigal *a 5*. In regarding a madrigal as a suitable conclusion of a cantata for an oratory, Savioni is following a practice and terminology prominent in his time; the term *ultimo madrigale* (final madrigal) frequently occurs in this period for the final chorus of a work called an oratorio. Savioni's description of a complete cantata for an oratory perfectly fits his only known composition that is called an oratorio in its source: his *Oratorio per ogni tempo* ("Oratorio for Any Time [of the Church Year]")[55]—a brief, one-part work in several sections using soloists for short recitatives, ariosos, arias, duets, and trios and concluding with a madrigal *a 5*. The work is a dialogue between a faithful spirit and a repentant sinner and includes a narrator's part. A few of Savioni's *Concerti morali e spirituali* are also dialogues, but most use reflective texts with no narrative or dramatic elements.

Compositions in one movement with several sections that employ spiritual or moral texts suitable for oratories are given a variety of terms—the most common being *cantata*, concerto, *dialogo*, and *oratorio*. Any of the first three terms might be combined with an indication that the music is for an oratory or modified by the adjectives *morale* or *spirituale*; the term *oratorio* itself, however, implies a moral or spiritual content and thus is not modified by these adjectives. It is noteworthy that reflective, narrative, and dramatic texts were all used for cantatas performed in oratories, and it is difficult to assert, on the basis of extant sources, that any one of these types was favored over the others. Among the composers of cantatas appropriate for oratories—in addition to Mario Savioni—are Pietro Della Valle, Luigi Rossi, Domenico Mazzocchi (all three treated below), Agostino Diruta for his *Poesie heroiche morali e sacre* ([Rome], 1646), and Teodoro Massucci for his *Dialoghi spirituali* (Rome, 1648).[56]

In larger works called oratorio and employing a twofold structural division, the terms *prima cantata* and *seconda cantata*

54. Savioni's *Concerti* is considered a book of cantatas in Eisley, *Savioni*. The vast majority of the cantatas in this period, however, are secular rather than moral or spiritual.

55. MS in I/Rf: H/II/23.

56. Several anonymous works of this type are in I/Bc: codex Q 43. Three of the four sacred librettos in Tronsarelli, *Drammi*—which are mentioned in Schering, *Oratorium*, p. 123—appear to have been intended for cantatas of this type: *La figlia di Iefte*, *La contesa delle virtù*, and *L'essequie di Christo*; the fourth, however, *Faraone sommerso*, is a large work in three parts, possibly intended to be staged.

are often applied to the two structural parts, although *prima* and *seconda parte* are also used. In a spiritual exercise the two parts of such a composition were separated by a sermon. Archangelo Spagna (ca. 1636–after 1720), an oratorio librettist who published in 1706 the earliest known sketch of the history of the oratorio as a musical-poetic genre,[57] says that in the earliest period of the oratorio at Chiesa Nuova "two simple cantatas, spiritual or moral," were separated by "a profitable sermon." These were unsatisfactory, however, since the two cantatas were so much alike and had no connection with each other; thus, "there was introduced the representation of some story or event from the Sacred Scripture so that the curiosity of hearing the conclusion would all the more entice people to stay there until the end."[58] The Oratorians' practice of using music before and after a sermon began in the sixteenth century and was continued in the period of Anerio's *Teatro*, when two madrigals were performed in a service. Thus a spiritual exercise in the period under consideration still evidently used two "cantatas": two one-part compositions of the type defined above by Savioni or an oratorio in two "cantatas," or structural parts. The two-part oratorio became standard in the later seicento, but one-part works also continue to be composed.

Examples of the Oratorio Volgare

The nature of the oratorio as a new musical genre is revealed in the compositions discussed below. Not all these works are called oratorios in their sources, but most are and all could have been, since those not called oratorios conform to a conception of the oratorio derived from those so designated. All the composers represented took part in the formulation and development of the new genre, and only one, Giacomo Carissimi, lived beyond the 1660s. His oratorios in Italian cannot be dated, but in style and structure they relate closely to this period.

The following compositions are presented in a hypothetically chronological order; although most of the works have not been precisely dated, their relative chronological positions have been tentatively assumed from their stylistic and structural features.

57. Spagna, "Discorso," reprinted in Schering, "Beiträge."
58. Schering, "Beiträge," p. 51.

The compositions by Mazzocchi and Della Valle and the librettos by Balducci seem to represent an early stage, and the oratorios by Carissimi and the anonymous *Daniele* (perhaps by Francesco Foggia) seem to represent a slightly later development. Although the oratorios by Marco Marazzoli and the two-part oratorios attributed to Luigi Rossi are possibly contemporary with some of those discussed before them, they are stylistically and structurally closer than the others to the *oratorio volgare* in the second half of the century and are therefore placed at the end of the discussion.

Domenico Mazzocchi

Both of the Mazzocchi brothers, Domenico (1592–1665) and Virgilio (1597–1646), were active in the early development of the *oratorio volgare*; all of Virgilio's works in this genre are lost.[59] Domenico was born in Civita Castellana and was educated both there and in nearby Rome.[60] By 1614 he was living in Rome; by 1619, when he became a priest, he had received a doctorate of laws, which then consisted of a broadly humanistic education. Nothing is known of his musical education.[61] He was in the service of the Aldobrandini (from 1620) and the Borghese (from 1631), and at times he also served the Barberini and Duke Odoardo Farnese. He is well known for his opera *La catena d'Adone* (1626), with a text by O. Tronsarelli based on G. B. Marino's *L'Adone*. Although his various spiritual cantatas and dialogues have long been known, the music of his chief composition relating to the history of the oratorio—*Coro di Profeti*, on a text by Giovanni Ciampoli (1589–1643)—has only recently been discovered.[62] Ciampoli's libretto is extant, but Mazzocchi's music is only partially so; it is probable, however, that the composer set the entire text to music before 1638.[63]

The libretto of the *Coro* was published in Ciampoli's *Poesie*

59. For references to four of Virgilio's Italian oratorios in a 1682 inventory of the Bologna Oratory, see Mischiati, "Bologna," p. 170.

60. For D. Mazzocchi's life and works, see Witzenmann, *Mazzocchi*.

61. Cf. ibid., p. 8, where his alleged study with G. B. Nanino is shown to be speculation.

62. The discovery was made by W. Witzenmann. For a full treatment of the work, see ibid., pp. 22, 134–41. For negative criticism of Ciampoli's text, see Pasquetti, *Oratorio*, pp. 177–79. Mazzocchi's *Il martirio de' santi Abundio prete*—called an oratorio in Rolandi, *Libretto*, p. 161—was a *sacra rappresentazione* or an opera, according to Witzenmann, *Mazzocchi*, p. 244; only its libretto is extant.

63. Witzenmann, *Mazzocchi*, pp. 134–35.

sacre (Bologna, 1648). The full title is *Coro di profeti, per la festa della Santissima Annuntiata, cantata nell'Oratorio della Chiesa Nuova* ("Chorus of the Prophets, for the Feast of the Most Holy Annunciation, Sung in the Oratory of the Chiesa Nuova"). The libretto is a large epic-lyric work divided into three parts, of which the long *Parte prima* and *Parte terza* are separated by a brief *Parte seconda* that functions as a transition between them; thus the ostensibly three-part work is essentially in two parts. Part I consists of a series of narrative texts based on Old Testament stories and surrounded by lyric reflections on the significance of the narratives. The stories are those of Adam and Eve's expulsion from Paradise, Cain's slaying of Abel, the crossing of the Red Sea, Judith's beheading of Holofernes, and Abraham's sacrifice of Isaac. Throughout part I a ray of hope shines within the darkness, and the closing line looks forward to the appearance of the Virgin, who will "crush the horrible head of the Stygian dragon." In part II, which is entirely lyric, spring is used as a symbol of hope and of the birth of the Savior; heaven is asked to open its heart to the world and to burst the chains of Stygian bondage. In part III, entitled *Coro d'angeli e di profeti* ("Chorus of Angels and Prophets"), the image of spring and its perfumed flowers, together with that of a beautiful and tranquil dawn, is still used. The Angels relate the story of the Annunciation; they describe not only the Virgin's reaction but that of the entire world: the rivers and the wind are silent, the sea does not tremble, and both heaven and earth listen to the announcement of peace. An Angel relates that the Virgin breaks this universal silence with her words, "behold the handmaid of the Lord"— whereupon choruses of "alleluia" and "osanna" are heard through the world, and Mary is crowned with gold. Concluding choruses acclaim Mary as a dove in peace and an eagle in war, a lamb to the just and a lion to the impious; Mary reigns; Jesus will be born.

Although parts I and II employ no personages, each subdivision is labeled with the performing forces that either the poet intended or the composer selected for the musical setting performed at the oratory of the Chiesa Nuova. Six personages, three Angels and three Prophets, are employed in part III, but with their presence the work does not become dramatic: their function is to narrate.

Although no composer's name appears in the libretto, it is probable that Domenico Mazzocchi set the entire work to music

FIGURE IV-6. Title page of Domenico Mazzocchi's *Musiche sacre e morali* (Rome, 1640).
(Courtesy of I/Rsc.)

and subsequently published portions of his setting. All of part II is printed in his *Madrigali à cinque voci et altri varij concerti* (Rome, 1638) as madrigal numbers XXII, *a 4, Coro di soprani,* "Verginelle festeggiante"; XXIII, *a 4, Coro di bassi,* "O tempeste furibonde"; and XXIV, *a 8, Tutti insieme,* "Aprite il seno o Cieli." Portions of parts I and III of the oratorio are printed in Mazzocchi's *Musiche sacre e morali a una, due, e tre voci* (Rome, 1640): two recitatives for soprano solo from part I, "Oda, e stupisca il mondo" and "Ecco Bettulia," and an aria for three sopranos from part III, "Colombella che di latte."

The choruses of part II in the *Madrigali a cinque voci* employ basso continuo; although no other instruments are designated, the composer states in his preface that instruments may be used with any work in the book, including those that are written *a cappella.* The first two of the three choruses are in ABA form. All three of the oratorio fragments are characteristic of the late madrigal in their careful attention to textual expression; unlike some of the other compositions in the book, however, they use virtually no chromaticism.[64] Example IV–1 is characteristic of the choruses for its chordal style, frequent passages in parallel thirds, and careful attention to textual expression and specific word painting (see "gorgheggino" ["are warbling"]). The duet for sopranos and

EXAMPLE IV-1. *Coro di profeti,* "Verginelle festeggiante"—D. Mazzocchi (*Madrigali,* Rome, 1638).

Voices of a thousand birds today are warbling . . .

64. For details of the madrigal book, see Einstein, *Madrigal,* 2:867–71, and Witzenmann, *Mazzocchi,* pp. 157–71.

basso continuo, "Colombella che di latte" in the *Musiche sacre e morali*, employs most of the madrigal techniques found in the music just discussed.[65]

Both of the recitatives printed in *Musiche sacre e morali* employ narrative texts: "Ecco Bettulia" is based on the story of Judith and Holofernes, and "Oda e stupisca il mondo," on that of the passage through the Red Sea. The latter recitative is marked "A voce sola, & à 5. accompagnato con le Viole" ("for solo voice accompanied by five viols"), but only a basso continuo part is provided. This is the only indication in the book that an instrumental ensemble is to be used. The marking no doubt indicates the preferred manner of performance, possibly that used when the recitative was sung as part of the oratorio; the basso continuo line seems generally simple enough that it would present no obstacles to an experienced improvising ensemble of viols.[66] The two recitatives have a number of elements in common: an essentially syllabic style with occasional melismas for text expression, a brief passage in triple meter to express a joyful text following the principal climactic event of the narrative, and a conclusion in aria or arioso style. Example IV–2a, the beginning of "Ecco Bettulia," illustrates the essentially syllabic style, over a sustained bass, that predominates; Example IV–2b, depicting the flooding of mountains and valleys, is one of the more striking instances of word painting; Example IV–2c begins with the climactic moment at which Judith decapitates Holofernes, a moment emotionally intensified by ascending runs and a large downward leap as the bloody scene is described—this is followed by a joyful section, in triple meter, concerning the liberation of Bethulia.

In its entirety this festive, epic-lyric oratorio for the Annunciation, with over five hundred lines of poetry set in a mixture of cantata and madrigal styles, would probably have required an hour or more to perform. The performance took place in an oratory that was probably smaller than Borromini's, for his was still under construction at the time the *Madrigali* were published. Since Mazzocchi states in his dedication of the *Madrigali* that the

---

65. In the libretto the text beginning "Colombella che di latte" was designated *Secondo coro*. This is the only instance in which the musical setting differs from the performing force indicated in the libretto. For a hypothesis that this duet is a reduction of a choral setting, see Witzenmann, *Mazzocchi*, pp. 135–36.

66. For comments on improvising ensembles, see Rose, "Agazzari." It is possible that a relationship exists between the viols intended in this work and those of Antonio Barberini mentioned in Mazzocchi's dedication of this madrigal book.

EXAMPLE IV-2. *Coro di profeti,* "Ecco Bettulia"—D. Mazzocchi
(*Musiche sacre*, Rome, 1640).

Example a:

Behold Bethulia afflicted: of happy hopes, among barbaric enemies, . . .

Example b:

Floods the mountains and valleys . . .

Example c:

Her soul was festering, and she severed the veins of his neck. Come,
come, prepare the songs . . .

works in that book "have been hidden away for some time," it is tempting to speculate that this elaborate composition is the one to which the Oratorians objected in 1630, the one that resulted in "scandal and noise" (see p. 160) on the feast of the Annunciation.

The texts of the pieces in the *Musiche sacre e morali* would make them all suitable for performance in oratories. Two of the works are dialogues: *La Notte del Santissimo Natale* ("The Night of Most Holy Christmas"), a dialogue *a 3* that concludes with an aria *a 3*; and a setting of a Marino text, *Christo smarrito* ("Lost Christ"), a dialogue *a 4* that includes a "Lament of the Blessed Virgin." Another Italian work by Domenico Mazzocchi suitable for an oratory is his dialogue *Madalena errante* ("The Wandering Magdalene") from the *Dialoghi e sonetti* (Rome, 1638).[67]

Pietro Della Valle

The earliest documented application of the term *oratorio* to a musical composition is found in a letter written in 1640 by the world traveler, author of travel memoirs, poet, and musical amateur Pietro Della Valle (1586–1652) of Rome to the Florentine musical theorist Giovanni Battista Doni.[68] On 23 December of that year, Della Valle writes that he has composed "another oratorio" for the feast of the Purification.[69] He says he has prepared this "Oratorio della Purificatione" to give to the Chiesa Nuova's Padre Girolamo Rosini, the prefect of music for the Congregation of the Oratory. This letter implies a previous composition that Della Valle calls an oratorio, evidently his *Dialogo di Esther*, performed on 2 April 1640 at the oratory of the Most Holy Crucifix.[70] In fact, in a letter of several years later, Della Valle refers to this piece as his *Oratorio di Esther*.[71] Of these two works,

67. For quotations from the poetry of *Christo smarrito* and *Madalena errante*, see Pasquetti, *Oratorio*, pp. 192, 180.

68. There has been at least one claim of an earlier documentation for this use of *oratorio*: Pasquètti, *Oratorio*, p. 187, quotes from a document of 1636 in the Archive of San Girolamo della Carità ("Relationi diverse . . . " 197:204) in which, he says, the plural of the word refers to musical compositions. Had he quoted a few words more, it would have been clear that the word *oratorij* here refers to services, not to musical compositions: "oratorij . . . con sermoni . . . et con musica" ("oratory [services] . . . with sermons . . . and with music"). The subsequent uses of the word *oratorio* in that document also refer to oratorio services.

69. Della Valle to Doni, 23 December 1640, in Solerti, "Della Valle," p. 289; partial reprint in Alaleona, *Oratorio*, pp. 136–37.

70. Ziino, "Della Valle," p. 100. For a discussion of *Esther*, see chapter 5.

71. Della Valle to Doni, 24 August 1647, in Solerti, "Della Valle," p. 309; partial reprint in Alaleona, *Oratorio*, p. 179.

PER LA FESTA
DELLA SANTISSIMA PVRIFICATIONE
DIALOGO IN MVSICA
A CINQVE VOCI
CON VARIETÀ
DI CINQVE TVONI DIVERSI
CIOÈ
DORIO, FRIGIO, EOLIO,
LIDIO, ET HIPOLIDIO.

Al Prè Girolamo Rosini
Della Congregatione dell' Oratorio

Pietro Della Valle.

Il diuoto diletto, che io soglio prender dalle musiche, le quali
frà mezo a i Sermoni, si fanno nell'Oratorio della Congregatione, sotto la scorta di VP.tà, e l'obligo in che mi pone il ri-
cordarmi di hauere in mia fanciullezza conoscieuto, e di hauer
parlato al beato San Filippo, autore di cotesto santo istituto;
mi hanno spinto (a fine di concorrere anch'io per quel poco che
vaglio in si buone opere) a comporre et a mettere in musica
alcuni pochi uersi, che, secondo'l costume, potrebbero essere
a proposito da cantaruin per la festa della santissima Purificatione. La musica, conforme al mio solito, è di quella
maniera nuoua, ò per dir meglio, antichissima rinouata
dal Sig.re Gio. Battista Doni, che sola io trauo, e che in fin'ad

hora da altri poco si pratica, cioè con mutatione di varij Tuo-
ni al modo de gli antichi; perche nell'altra maniera del cantare ordinario, io, che poco ne sò, non ardirei di propor cose
mie, a paragone di quelle di tanti valent'huomini, che in tali
sacre adunanze tutto'l giorno si cantano. Qualunque sia questo
mio piccolo componimento, a VP. lo dedico, e lo dono; et ella
con l'innata sua cortesia, son certo, che non mancherà di gra-
dirlo, benche sia di poco pregio. E se pur'a sorte vi trouerà cosa,
che in qualche modo le aggradi, esorti, prego, gli amici suoi più
eccellenti nell'arte, che si applichino a comporre in questa guisa
al parer mio di tanta leggiadria, perche al sicuro faranno cose,
non solo senza comparatione molto migliori delle mie, ma che
a rispetto delle altre del modo ordinario indubitatamente
saranno esquisite.

FIGURE IV-7. Title page and dedication of Pietro Della Valle's *Dialogo* for the feast of the Purification.
(Reproduced by permission of I/Rn.)

only the manuscript of that for the feast of the Purification is extant; it is termed a dialogue on its title page: "For the Feast of the Purification: Dialogue in Music, for Five Voices, with a Variety of Five Different Tones, Being Dorian, Phrygian, Aeolian, Lydian, and Hypolydian" (see the title page in Fig. IV–7).[72] Della Valle's casual vacillation between the terms *dialogue* and *oratorio* reflects the uncertain state of terminology for such works at this time.

The text of Della Valle's dialogue, his own writing, is a short poem of fifty-nine lines based on the account of the Purification in Luke 2:22–40. The dialogue is divided into six sections: (1) "Colui, che il tutto regge"—the Poet (A), or narrator, provides the background of the story and introduces the first character; (2) "Lascia pur, lascia homai"—Simeon (B) sings a monologue based on the canticle "Nunc dimittis"; (3) "Quali cose di tè"—Mary (S) and Joseph (T), in a duet, marvel at Simeon's words; (4) "O di Dio"— Anna the Prophetess (S), Mary, and Joseph sing a trio of rejoicing; (5) "Ecco il fanciul"—Simeon predicts Jesus' work of salvation; and (6) "Cresci, cresci, pargoletto"—the final chorus (SSATB) reflects on Jesus' heavenly origin and anticipates his growth to manhood and the redemption that he will effect.

Della Valle's setting of this dialogue reflects his keen interest in "erudite music" composed according to the conception of ancient Greek modes set forth by his friend Doni.[73] The title page of the manuscript source, quoted above, calls attention to this aspect of the work. The five "tones" mentioned on the title page were thought to be ancient Greek modes, which Della Valle believed could be best played by special instruments constructed for him for the performance of his erudite music. These included the *cembalo triarmonico* (a specially tuned harpsichord with three manuals) and the *violone panarmonico*, the only instruments designated in the manuscript of this composition.

The solo passages in Della Valle's dialogue are in a style that Doni might have called *recitativo arioso*, as is Example IV–3 (p. 178) from Simeon's first solo.[74] This example also reveals the chromatic effects achieved by some of the modes, as the music

72. The MS is in I/Rn: Fondi minori, Mus. 123.
73. For Della Valle's interest in erudite music and for bibliography on Della Valle, see Ziino, "Della Valle."
74. I use the term *arioso* in the sense of *recitativo arioso* in all discussions of seventeenth-century music. Concerning a seventeenth-century precedent for this use of the term, by G. B. Doni, see Palisca, *Baroque*, p. 105.

FIGURE IV-8. Beginning of Della Valle's *Dialogo*.
(Reproduced by permission of I/Rn.)

Divine and blessed Light, to give light to the people, and to the glory of Israel, revealing the lofty secrets of heaven, make earthly man worthy of the stars and make all those happy who believe in his name.

utilizes—in order—the Dorian, Phrygian, Hypolydian, Lydian, Phrygian, and Dorian modes.[75] The duet and trio of the composition employ an imitative style, as does the final chorus. The brevity of this work (about twelve minutes) makes it exceptional among the extant compositions of this period called oratorios, most of which require between twenty minutes and an hour to perform.

Della Valle's work is significant as an early example of a composition written for an oratory and called an oratorio, at least informally, by its composer. It is of greater interest for these reasons and as a curious piece of erudite music than for its intrinsically musical contribution to oratorio literature. Unlike his *Oratorio di Esther* this work was probably never performed in an oratory but only in Della Valle's home. He speaks of some difficulty

75. Example IV–3 has been transposed to concert pitch. The *violone panarmonico* is a transposing instrument, and the high and low manuals (*tastatura alta* and *bassa*) of the *cembalo triarmonico* also require transposition; for details, see Ziino, "Della Valle," pp. 102–4.

in assembling musicians to rehearse the work and of Padre Girolamo's hesitancy in introducing such novel music into the oratory.[76]

Francesco Balducci

A slightly older contemporary of Della Valle, the poet Francesco
Balducci (1579–1642) of Palermo spent much of his life in Rome.
His poetry was admired by Chiabrera, Tronsarelli, Urban VIII, and
Antonio Barberini—among others. His poetic style lies between
that of Chiabrera and Marino, for he draws upon elements used
by both.[77]

Balducci wrote two librettos that were called oratorios in
the posthumous publication of his works in which they first appeared.[78] Spagna considers Balducci to be of primary importance
as the first to use the term *oratorio* for a libretto of a musical
work.[79] When Balducci wrote these librettos is not known, but
from their use of the word *oratorio*, they would appear to be
among his late works.

Balducci's librettos differ considerably both in length and in
character. The longer of the two bears the title *La fede: Oratorio*
("Faith: An Oratorio"),[80] to which Spagna, in his "Discorso,"
adds the appropriately descriptive subtitle *Il sagrificio di Abramo*
("The Sacrifice of Abraham"). This is a narrative-dramatic poem
in two large sections labeled *Parte prima* and *Parte seconda*. In
sharp contrast to Della Valle's brief work, this one, of more than
450 lines, is closer to Ciampoli's *Coro di profeti* and is comparable
to those employed for oratorios of about an hour in duration. The
poem is based on Genesis 21–22, which begins with the birth of
Isaac and includes the episode of Abraham's sacrifice. The narrative passages of the poem are labeled *Historia*, and the personages
are Abraham, Isaac, a chorus of Virgins, and a chorus of Sages.
The words of God, who commands that Abraham sacrifice Isaac,
are placed in the *Historia* passages, since God is not one of the
personages. The most remarkable aspect of the work's structure is
the enormous length of the *Historia* passages—over half of the

76. Solerti, "Della Valle," p. 292.
77. E. Girardi, "Balducci," *Dizionario biografico*, 5:534–36.
78. Balducci, *Rime*, vol. 2. For discussions of his librettos, see Alaleona, *Oratorio*, pp.
141–44; Pasquetti, *Oratorio*, pp. 208–28; and Schering, *Oratorium*, pp. 54–56.
79. Schering, "Beiträge," p. 50.
80. Balducci, *Rime*, 2:329–46. For reprints see Alaleona, *Oratorio*, pp. 293–303;
Schering, *Oratorium*, "Anhang," pp. vii–xiii; and Pasquetti, *Oratorio*, pp. 207–23.

FIGURE IV-9. Francesco Balducci (1579–1642).
(Balducci, *Rime*, 1:fol. [10ᵛ].)

poem is devoted to narrative. Part I of the oratorio is largely nonbiblical, but part II is devoted to biblical material: God's command to Abraham, the trip to the mountain for the sacrifice, and the episode of the sacrifice. Ample attention is given to the emotional aspects of the situation. At the conclusion of each part of the oratorio, there is a reflective, meditative text: the chorus of Sages at the end of part I and two lines of meditation labeled *Historia* at the close of part II. No musical setting of this libretto is known.

The other text, which Balducci calls *Il trionfo: Oratorio* ("The Triumph: An Oratorio"),[81] is aptly subtitled by Spagna, *La incoronazione di Maria Vergine* ("The Coronation of the Virgin Mary"). This poem is of special interest, for a modified version of it was set to music by Giacomo Carissimi under the title *Oratorio della Santissima Vergine* ("Oratorio of the Most Holy Virgin"), discussed below. *Il trionfo*, in one part, is less than half the length of *La fede*. It is a reflective, lyric oratorio—an allegorical vision glorifying the Virgin enthroned in the heavens, crowned with stars, predestined from all eternity to crush the head of the serpent. The Virgin is the only personage, and she alternates several times with the chorus, although the latter has a considerably longer part than the former. The work includes only two narrative passages— the first is the prologue, entitled "L'Aura: Canzonetta morale in bocca all'Istoria, che val di proemio all'Oratorio" ("Dawn: Moral Canzonetta in the Mouth of the Narrator, Which Serves as the Proem to the Oratorio"); the second narrative passage, this time labeled *Historia*, is a brief introduction to a chorus. Parts of the libretto are borrowed from Balducci's earlier publication, *Rime amorose* (1630), and others from the *Rime sacre*, a division of the publication of 1645–46 in which the libretto itself is found.[82] The borrowed source for the final chorus of the libretto is entitled "La croce: canzonetta sovra l'inno *Vexilla Regis prodeunt*" ("The Cross: Canzonetta on the Hymn *Vexilla Regis prodeunt*"). The hymnlike quality of this canzonetta is perfectly suited to the lyric nature of the text as a whole.

81. Balducci, *Rime*, 2:347–57. For reprints see Alaleona, *Oratorio*, pp. 289–93; and IISM–3, 8:viii–ix.
82. For a reprint of all borrowed passages, see IISM–3, 8:vi–viii.

Giacomo Carissimi

All but two of Giacomo Carissimi's oratorios are in Latin; therefore an extended discussion of this important composer of oratorios and his musical style will be reserved for chapter 5. His two Italian works, however, will be considered here, for they contribute significantly to our understanding of the early stages of the *oratorio volgare*. Neither has been dated, but both would certainly date from after December 1629, when Carissimi assumed his duties in Rome; both seem to represent an earlier stage in the *oratorio volgare* than the works by Marazzoli and those attributed to Luigi Rossi, discussed below.[83]

Except for a brief narrative portion, the *Oratorio della Santissima Vergine*[84] is a reflective work, as is Balducci's *Il trionfo* on which it is based; unlike *Il trionfo*, however, it is cast in two parts. The only personage indicated in the score is the Virgin (S); unnamed participants sing solos (A, T, B), ensembles (SS, ATB), and choruses (SSATB). The instruments (two violins, violone, lute, and basso continuo) play a sinfonia at the beginning, occasional ritornellos, and supporting parts for the choruses.

Part I of the libretto is entirely dependent upon Balducci's printed version. There are modifications, deleted stanzas, and changed words, but virtually nothing new is added. The prologue, which is labeled *Istoria* in the printed version, is set by Carissimi for a soprano duet, but the subsequent entry of the *Historia* is absent from the Carissimi setting. The passages designated for chorus in Balducci's print are sung by soloists in the Carissimi setting, except that an abbreviated version of the final chorus in the print is used by Carissimi as the text of his final chorus of part I.

Since most of Balducci's printed libretto is used in part I, part II is largely new. Here the reflective, allegorical vision undergoes a change to include an element of conflict between the Virgin and evil, called the "serpent" or the "monster." The opening tenor and alto solos prepare for the conflict, which is then narrated by the bass: the Virgin conquers the monster and plunders hell. The remainder of the oratorio is based on texts of rejoicing for the

83. Lino Bianchi, in ibid., p. xiii, considers the *Oratorio della Santissima Vergine* to represent an early style, and he suggests the possibility that Balducci (d. 1642) might have modified his *Il trionfo* for Carissimi.
84. Printed in IISM–3, vol. 8.

victory over evil and of praise for the Virgin; a few of these stanzas are taken from Balducci's print. The concluding chorus, on a new text, presents the final, metaphorical meditation: "Night is never so dark that at the end there is no dawn; after the winter, the meadows adorn the scented spring with flowers."

The musical style of Carissimi's Italian oratorios does not differ significantly from that of his Latin works, discussed in the following chapter. Recitatives and ensembles constitute the major portion of this oratorio, and there is some fluctuation between recitative and arioso styles. A passage in aria style occasionally occurs within an ensemble-solo complex, and some of the *recitativo arioso* passages are nearly arias; but there is no independent section in the oratorio that could be called an aria without qualification. The two choruses, one at the end of each part, differ considerably from each other. The chorus at the end of part I is entirely chordal and is strophic, with three stanzas. The final chorus of the oratorio, however, is more complicated; it begins in chordal style then changes to fugal texture, which is continued up to a brief, chordal conclusion.

Of special interest in the structure of this work are the repetitions, modified or exact, of musical material. For instance, the three stanzas of the opening duet are melodically different from one another but are separated by the same instrumental ritornello; in a series of recitatives of part I in which the Virgin alternates with other voices, she concludes each of her recitatives with the same music and text ("Ne senza me fora"); and in the series of ensembles that constitutes the "rejoicing" section of part II, a trio ("Sù verginelle") is repeated after a long digression. The most interesting of all the repetitions, however, is the melodic pattern of the bass at the beginning of the first and third stanzas of the opening duet and at the beginning of every independent solo of the oratorio. The notes of the pattern are represented in Example IV–4 (p. 184). In these bass lines each note of this example is usually represented by a tied note or repeated notes on the same pitch, supporting an active vocal line. Example IV–4 shows three versions of the opening bass line: version *a* is used only once (in the opening duet); *b*, twice; and *c*, seven times in this form (including transpositions of the pattern up and down a major second) and twice with octave transpositions of some of the notes. Such bass repetitions are similar to those employed for strophic variations in

EXAMPLE IV-4. Repeated bass patterns in *Oratorio della Santissima Vergine*—Carissimi (IISM-3, vol. 8).

opera arias and secular cantatas, including Carissimi's, of the period.[85] Here the repetition is confined to the beginnings of solos and duets; it does not extend throughout the passages, as more frequently happens in opera arias and cantatas. This work appears to be unique among oratorios for its extensive use of repeated bass patterns.

Carissimi's other Italian oratorio, *Daniele*,[86] is based on an excerpt from the Old Testament story of Daniel. The excerpt (Dan. 6:1–16) includes the plot of the satraps against Daniel, their superior, and the sentence of King Darius that Daniel be cast into the lions' den. This particular excerpt, as well as the libretto, stops short of the execution of the sentence and Daniel's miraculous salvation. The libretto, a narrative-dramatic poem in two parts, is anonymous, as are nearly all those of Carissimi's oratorios. If this is the oratorio that was performed on a Wednesday in Lent of 1656 for Queen Christina of Sweden, as A. Sandberger says it might be, then the author of the libretto would be the prince of Gallicano.[87] The personages are the *Testo* (T); Darius (B); Daniel (S); the first, second, and third Satraps (S, S, A, SSA); and the chorus of Satraps (SSSATB). No instruments are employed other than the basso continuo. Part I of the oratorio reveals Darius's faith in Daniel as an adviser, the hatred that the Satraps harbor for Daniel, their plot against him, and their pressure on Darius to have Daniel executed. In part II Darius yields to the pressure of the Satraps while recognizing the injustice of his act; Daniel, brought before them in chains, demonstrates his faith in God and willingness to become a martyr while the Satraps give vent to their hatred. In the final chorus the Satraps call for Daniel's death.

85. Rose, "Carissimi," p. 208.
86. Printed in IISM-3, vol. 7. This oratorio is cited, with a music example, in Parry, *Seventeenth*, p. 166; but Schering, *Oratorium*, p. 171, n. 4, mistakes that reference for one to the anonymous *Daniele*, discussed below and printed in Torchi, *Arte*, 5:117–85.
87. Sandberger, "Christine," p. 129.

The text of this work is closer than any discussed thus far to the typical oratorio of the late seventeenth century. The role of the *Testo* is characteristic: he narrates past events, introduces characters, describes situations and actions in the present, relates what has happened during a lapse of time in the course of the drama, and occasionally reflects on the situation, as in his "O stato miserabil de' grandi" ("Oh wretched state of great men"). In later oratorios such reflective passages in a *testo*'s role are occasionally set as arias, but usually, as here, a *testo* sings in recitative throughout. Except for his opening narration, the *Testo*'s passages in this work are characteristically brief. In its dramatic aspect, as revealed in the dialogues between personages, this oratorio is more like those of the later seventeenth century than are the works discussed above. In part I there are dialogues between Darius and Daniel, among the three Satraps, and between Darius and the Satraps; toward the end of part II a more rapid exchange of dialogue between Daniel and the Satraps occurs. Nevertheless the dialogues seem formal and stylized rather than natural; none of them employs the quick, conversational exchange between personages that is found in opera of this period.

As in Carissimi's other *oratorio volgare*, most of the text is set in recitative or arioso. This work seems slightly more mature, however, for it includes five brief arias: four in part I (Daniel: "Gl'imperi più grandi"; Darius: "Si, son degni"; second Satrap: "È Dario si folle"; third Satrap: "Nò, non fia vero") and one in part II (Daniel: "Hor chi sospende"). All are in triple meter, and those in part I are much alike in style, with similar melodic and rhythmic patterns, despite remarkably differing texts. Daniel's "Gl'imperi più grandi" is considerably longer than the others and is strophic, each strophe ending with a modified repetition of the last two poetic lines. A similar form is also employed in the brief arias of the Satraps, which are preparatory to their trio, "Nò, non fia vero."[88] The ensembles and choruses of the Satraps are predominantly imitative, except for the final chorus, which is chordal and antiphonal.

88. This form vaguely suggests the ABB' structure, which is of importance in Carissimi's Latin oratorios as well as in the seventeenth century in general. (See p. 237.)

An Anonymous Daniele

It is of interest to compare an anonymous oratorio on the story of Daniel with the one by Carissimi. Both its text and the music are anonymous, but the work appears to be of Roman origin and is possibly by Francesco Foggia.[89] No genre is designated in the source; the two parts of the work are simply called *Daniele, Parte Prima* and *Daniele, 2.a Parte.* Unlike Carissimi's oratorio on the same subject, this one carries the story as far as Daniel's salvation from death in the lions' den and the king's acceptance of Daniel's God for the entire realm (Dan. 6:1–27). Daniel is a soprano, as he is in Carissimi's oratorio; the other vocal parts, differing from those of Carissimi's work, are the *Testo* (S), the King (T), and the three Satraps (A, T, B). The choruses (SSATB) do not represent identified personages: the final choruses of parts I and II point out the moral of the story, and the other choruses (part II: "O Re sovrano" and "Mira O Re") play the role of an unidentified group of persons commenting to the King about the miracle of Daniel's salvation. The composer or copyist evidently assumed that the choruses would be performed by an ensemble of the soloists, since each part of every chorus is marked in the manuscript (and in Torchi's edition) with the name of a character having the appropriate range for the part. No instruments are designated other than the basso continuo.

In part I of the oratorio, the Satraps plot against Daniel; he is captured, sentenced, and sealed into the lions' den. Part II begins at dawn of the next day when the King, after a sleepless night of weeping, goes to the lions' den and finds Daniel alive. This discovery is followed by rejoicing and praise for the God of Daniel (sung by the King, the chorus, and Daniel), the casting of the Satraps into the lions' den, the King's acceptance of Daniel's God, and the moralizing of the final chorus. The text of this oratorio is considerably more varied and eventful than that set by Carissimi, but it lacks the psychological penetration of the principal characters found in the text of Carissimi's work.

89. Printed in Torchi, *Arte,* 5:117–85; MS source I/Bc: Q 45, fols. 46–72v. Codices Q 43–48 at I/Bc appear—from their composers, styles, and genres—to constitute a Roman repertory. Codices Q 44–46 bear the label (on the spine) "Autori romani," in what appears to be a seventeenth-century hand. An inventory of music owned by the Bologna Oratory in 1682 cites the following: *Daniello. Oratorio a 5. "Fa seren, fa sicuro." Musica del Sig. R Fran.co Foggia.* (Mischiati, "Bologna," p. 155, inventory no. 272 [259].) The incipit "Fa seren, fa sicuro" is that of the final chorus of this anonymous *Daniele* (Torchi, *Arte,* 5:139).

Most of this text is set in recitative and arioso styles, but there are two brief, through-composed arias (both sung by Daniel in part II: "Frena il pianto" and "Non ha tant'erbe"); six duets; and four choruses. Thus there is more emphasis on ensembles than in Carissimi's oratorio; the ensembles are the most attractive parts of the work. The choruses are set in madrigal style, with greater variety of textures and less emphasis on chordal texture than in Carissimi's oratorio. All four of the duets in part I are sung by the Satraps; the two in part II are settings of lines that reveal the tragic fate of the Satraps and are thus essentially narrative.[90] It is unusual in the *oratorio volgare* for narrative texts to be set for ensemble, although such settings are common in Latin oratorios of this period. The duets employ a mixture of parallel thirds and imitation.

Marco Marazzoli

Born in the first decade of the seventeenth century, probably at Parma, Marazzoli had settled in Rome by 1637.[91] In that year he participated in the first performance of the opera *Il Falcone* (later called *Chi soffre speri*), on which he and Virgilio Mazzocchi had collaborated. From 1637 until his death in 1662, Marazzoli was active mainly in Rome, but he made brief visits to Ferrara, Venice, and Paris. He was a singer in the papal chapel, was in the service of Antonio Barberini, and was well known as a composer of operas, secular cantatas, and oratorios. The late Baroque composer and writer Andrea Adami da Bolsena mentions in his *Osservazioni* (Rome, 1711) that Marazzoli "was an excellent composer of oratorios that were much applauded in his time, and I myself have heard them sung several times in the Chiesa Nuova."[92] Among the works that may be reliably attributed to Marazzoli, a number of the shorter pieces were no doubt intended for oratories, but only the two longest compositions appropriate for oratories are designated oratorios in their sources: *Per il giorno di Resurrettione*,

90. The designations of "personages" for the duets of part II in the MS and the modern print are evidently intended to indicate singers rather than personages. The duets in Torchi, *Arte*, 5:168, 172, which are designated "Testo/Satrapo" and "Daniele/Satrapo," use narrative texts. (The latter duet narrates the death of the Satraps in the lions' den; it would be illogical for a Satrap, as a personage, to take part in the narration.)

91. For a summary of Marazzoli's biography based on the most recent research, see Grace, "Marazzoli," pp. 16–56.

92. Quoted in Pasquetti, *Oratorio*, p. 182.

FIGURE IV-10. Beginning of Marco Marazzoli's oratorio for the Resurrection.
(Reproduced by permission of I/Bc.)

oratorio à 6 and *San Tomaso, oratorio à 5.*[93] The first is a reflective work, and the second is narrative-dramatic. Neither oratorio has been dated.

Resurrettione is set for soloists (S, A, T, B), ensembles (SS, SSA), chorus (SSSATB), and basso continuo. The nonbiblical text, in two parts and without designated roles, praises the risen Redeemer with reflections on the significance of the Resurrection. Part I expresses joy and praise for the Resurrection and for the triumph of God. Although part I is not labeled in the manuscript, part II is called *Seconda cantata.* The beginning of part II represents a change of mood, with exhortations to turn away from the world and toward God for true happiness; this part includes reflections on the imperfection of worldly goods, the evils of vanity and worldly honor, and the perfection of heavenly peace. Part II closes with a return to the spirit of rejoicing that prevails in part I.

Because of the festive nature of this work, it is appropriately dominated by clearly metrical, dancelike numbers: three brief through-composed arias, two duets, three trios, and two choruses. Recitative plays a relatively small role in part I but is somewhat more prominent in part II. The two structural parts of the oratorio are balanced in that each has nine sections and concludes with a chorus of six voices preceded by a duet. The only repeated section in the oratorio is the opening aria, "Ai canti ai suoni" (see Example IV–5a, p. 190), which provides the material for a trio (see Example IV–5b) that occurs after three intervening sections and is typical of the work's festive spirit.

Marazzoli's *San Tomaso* is based on the Gospel story of St. Thomas's disbelief in the Resurrection. Found in John 20:19–29, this was the Gospel reading of the mass on the first Sunday after Easter. Thus, it immediately follows the oratorio *Resurrettione* in the liturgical calendar, as it does in its manuscript source.[94] None of the personages of the oratorio are indicated in the source, but they are readily inferred from the text: the Apostles (solos: S, A, T,

93. MS sources, *Resurrettione* and *San Tomaso,* I/Bc: Q 43, fols. 110–20, 122–33. For a quotation of several stanzas of poetry from the beginning of *Resurrettione,* see Pasquetti, *Oratorio,* p. 183.

94. Codex Q 43 in I/Bc carries the label "Settimana santa oratori" on the spine, in what appears to be a seventeenth-century hand. The codex includes music for Holy Week, both Latin liturgical and Italian paraliturgical works, as well as music for Easter and the post-Easter period.

Example a:

Example b:

With songs, with music . . .

B; ensembles: SSA, AT, SAB; chorus: SSATB), St. Thomas (A), St. Peter (B), *Testo* (S), and Jesus (T). The basso continuo is the work's only instrumental requirement. Part I of the libretto is devoted primarily to a dialogue between Thomas and the other Apostles. Thomas affirms his adoration for Jesus but insists that he must see and touch Him if he is to believe in the Resurrection. The Apostles urge Thomas to have more faith and not to trust his senses. They cite examples of others of great faith whom he should imitate. At the beginning of part II, the *Testo* enters, for the only time in the oratorio, to describe Jesus' coming before the Apostles and to introduce his first speech. Jesus invites Thomas to touch him and to believe. After Peter reflects on this tense moment, there is a brief dialogue between Thomas and Jesus; the remainder of the oratorio is devoted to the Apostles' reflections on the blessedness of faith.

The more dramatic nature of *San Tomaso* results in more recitative than is included in the *Resurrettione*. There are nine short, through-composed arias; two duets; and two trios. The only choruses occur at the ends of the two parts; these are immediately preceded by an ensemble and a group of arias. The most intense, and the most musically moving, moment of the oratorio is the scene of Jesus' invitation for Thomas to touch him: Peter sings an aria, "Che fai, che pensi," that becomes increasingly ornate as it unfolds over four complete and two partial statements of the *Romanesca* bass (see Example IV–6a, p. 192, for the beginning of the aria and IV–6b for part of the last section);[95] and Thomas asks Jesus for forgiveness in a highly effective arioso (see Example IV–6c for its beginning).

An anonymous *Oratorio di Santa Caterina* that has been attributed both to Luigi Rossi and Marco Marazzoli has been grouped here with Marazzoli's works because its style, both in recitatives and arias, seems closer to his than to Rossi's.[96] Although its authorship remains in doubt, it is an excellent example of the oratorio in the mid-century, for it is longer and more fully developed in the narrative and dramatic aspects of its libretto than the two works just treated. The libretto, probably by Lelio Orsini, is based on the traditional story of the martyrdom of St. Catherine of Alexandria (sometimes called St. Catherine of the Wheel). In part I (*Prima cantata*) of the libretto, St. Catherine (S) bears witness to her Christian faith in Alexandria and thus provokes the anger of Emperor Maximinus (B). He is enamored of her and makes advances that she rejects. Maximinus repeatedly threatens St. Catherine with torture and death, but she scorns his threats and asserts that for her martyrdom is a source of happiness. Finally she is condemned to be placed in chains and left in prison to starve. Her courage is supported by a duet of Faith (S) and Hope (A) and by the closing *madrigale* (SSATB) of part I. At the beginning of part II (*Seconda cantata*), Maximinus discovers the miracle of St. Catherine's survival, and he orders the torture wheel to be prepared

95. For an edition of the beginning of part II of the oratorio, as far as Peter's aria over the *Romanesca* bass, see Massenkeil, *Oratorium* (and Massenkeil, *Oratorium*-Eng.), pp. 36–41. (In that edition it is not made clear what character sings the aria; as it is sung by a bass, however, it would no doubt be Peter.)

96. MS source is I/Rvat: Barb. lat. 4209. The oratorio is attributed to Luigi Rossi in Ghislanzoni, *Rossi*, p. 104, and to Marco Marazzoli in Mischiati, "Bologna," p. 135. The 1682 inventory of the Bologna Oratory—printed in Mischiati, "Bologna"— cites a title and incipit identical to those of this oratorio and identifies the composer as Marazzoli and the librettist as Lelio Orsini.

EXAMPLE IV-6. *San Tomaso*—Marazzoli (I/Bc: codex Q 43, fols. 128^v, 129^r, and 129^v).

Example a:

What are you doing? What are you thinking? Are you still in doubt that our noble leader is immortal?

Example b:

And until the sun spreads its golden traces . . .

Example c:

O my Lord and God, pardon my failing!

for her. She is about to be placed on the wheel, when at her touch it miraculously falls to pieces on the ground. At Maximinus's order his soldiers kill her with their swords; she dies while kneeling and asking forgiveness for her sins—she maintains her serenity to the end. Evidently a convert now, a Soldier (T) who had pitied her exhorts the people to abandon their earthly desires and to treasure heaven above all else; the final chorus repeats his words.

In this libretto the contrast between the brutality of Maximinus and the purity and steadfastness of St. Catherine is generally presented through their own speeches; but the *Testo*, who speaks several times in both parts I and II, is of special importance in describing the miraculous events and in conveying the scene of St. Catherine's death. The villain, Maximinus, is a type rarely found in oratorios of this period; but his type is found later in the so-called erotic oratorios of the late seventeenth century, often based on the lives of virgin martyrs. By his amorous advances and threats of violence, he gives his victim a choice of moral or physical destruction. As in so many later oratorios the conflict here is between heavenly and worldly love. St. Catherine, sustained by her faith, never laments her misfortune; rather, she anticipates the joy of meeting her Creator. Thus heavenly love, of which she is the symbol, is victorious.

The only instruments required for this oratorio, other than the basso continuo, are two violins, which play an introduction at the beginning of part I, an occasional ritornello, and support for the final chorus. The *lira*, probably a *lira da gamba*, is designated at one point to realize the continuo; it accompanies a soldier's lament, "Piango la tua sventura," for St. Catherine just before her death.[97]

This oratorio makes more use of recitative and arioso than *San Tomaso* because of the longer dialogues between characters and the greater importance of the *Testo*, whose lines are always set in those styles. There are eight arias in the work: three through-composed, two in ABA form, one in ABA'C, and one ("Piango la tua sventura") in an ABC form in which A concludes in recitative style and B consists of a small abb' form. The longest aria, "Deh non più signor," St. Catherine's expression of her steadfast faith, immediately precedes Maximinus's order for his soldiers to pre-

97. This use of the *lira* agrees with the statement in Kircher, *Musurgia*, 1:487, where the instrument is considered particularly suitable for the affections of grief and lamentation.

pare the torture wheel; the aria is relatively simple in style but unusually elaborate in structure: ABCA'BDA', with a brief ritornello for the basso continuo used at the beginning of the aria and following each section. The duet of Faith and Hope, using a kind of strophic-variation procedure, is also structurally elaborate: the melodic structure is ABA'CDA'C, but the bass is similar for each section. As in the other two works by Marazzoli, choruses are used to conclude parts I and II; otherwise, the chorus enters only once, to represent a group of soldiers.

Four additional works in Italian that are anonymous in their sources have been considered to number among Marazzoli's oratorios.[98] These are relatively brief dialogues characteristic of works performed in oratories. The texts are based on Gospel stories of the Nativity ("Poiche Maria dal suo virgineo seno"), the Circumcision ("Qual nume omnipotente che diè leggi"), Palm Sunday ("Ecco il gran rè di regi"), and Christ with the Pharisees ("Udito habbiam Giesù").[99] Each is in one structural part and employs soloists, ensembles, chorus, and basso continuo. The texts consist of a combination of narrative, reflective, and dramatic elements, but the dramatic element is the least prominent. The musical style of these dialogues is much like that of the longer oratorios by Marazzoli discussed above, except that there are no arias, the solo passages being set entirely in recitative and arioso styles.

Five more works in Italian attributed to Marazzoli are cantatas appropriate for oratories. Two of these are dialogues, "Speranza che vuoi?" (between Faith, Hope, and Charity) and "Vincerò regnarò" (between Heresy and Faith),[100] and the other three are settings of reflective, spiritual texts.[101] All five include recitatives, arias, and ensembles with basso continuo, and one requires violins.

Oratorios Attributed to Luigi Rossi

Comparable in significance to the *Santa Caterina* that has been attributed to both Marazzoli and Luigi Rossi, are the other orato-

98. Capponi, "Marazzoli," p. 105. In Witzenmann, "Marazzoli," p. 64, these are called dialogues, rather than oratorios, because of their brevity. Their MS sources bear no designations of musical genres.

99. MS sources, in the above order, are I/Rvat: Chigi lat., Q.VIII.188 fols. 44v–48, 51v–56, 58v–62, 63v–68. For descriptions of the sources, see Witzenmann, "Marazzoli," pp. 65–68.

100. MS sources are I/Rvat: Chigi lat., Q.V.69 and Q.VIII.186–87.

101. MS sources are I/Rvat: Chigi lat., Q.V.69, "Col fausto augurio" and "Ritornate a Giesu"; Q.VIII.179, "Deh mirate, mirate turbe."

rios attributed to Rossi (ca. 1598–1653). Born at Torremaggiore, in southern Italy, Rossi received his early training at Naples with Giovanni de Macque.[102] Around 1620 he went to Rome, where he became a musician for Cardinal Antonio Barberini. After the Barberini had fled to France, Rossi and many of their other musicians were invited to Paris by Cardinal Mazarin. Rossi traveled to Paris in 1646, and there in the following year his *Orfeo*, which was the first Italian opera composed specifically for Paris, was performed. After a return trip to Rome and another sojourn in Paris, Rossi spent his final few years in Rome.

Rossi's principal oratorio activity would probably have occurred between 1641 and 1645—that is, between the time that he entered the service of the Barberini and the time of their departure from Rome. Francesco Barberini was the protector of the archconfraternity of San Girolamo della Carità, and both he and his brother Antonio were interested in the oratory of the Chiesa Nuova. The oratorios attributed to Rossi may have been performed at these oratories.

The two oratorios attributed to Rossi that are the most significant from the standpoint of the development of the *oratorio volgare* are *Giuseppe* ("Joseph, [Son of Jacob]")—with a libretto attributed to Francesco Buti, the librettist of Rossi's opera *Orfeo* —and *Oratorio per la Settimana Santa* ("Oratorio for Holy Week"), with a libretto by Cesare Raggioli.[103] Both are dramatic oratorios, but only *Giuseppe* is also narrative, for it includes a *testo* role. Both are slightly less than one hour in duration and are divided into two parts.

The librettos of these oratorios are significantly different from most of their forerunners and contemporaries, and they point to the future in their markedly dramatic nature. The dramatic conflicts are clearly defined, as are the contrasts between the principal

102. For Rossi's life and works see Ghislanzoni, *Rossi*.

103. Of the works attributed to Rossi that are either oratorios or cantatas appropriate for oratorios, *Giuseppe* is the one for which there is strongest evidence to support the attribution. In the eighteenth century Charles Burney saw, in the Magliabecchi Library of Florence, a scene from *Giuseppe* (presumably this work) that bore the name of Luigi Rossi as composer and the title *Giuseppe, figlio di Giacobbe*; the MS that he saw is no longer extant (Burney, *History*, 2:618; Ghislanzoni, *Rossi*, p. 94; Becherini, *Catalogo*, p. 6). On the attributions of Rossi's oratorios and for brief comments about the works, see Ghislanzoni, *Rossi*, p. 94ff., and Ghislanzoni, "Oratori." The MS sources of *Giuseppe* and *Settimana Santa* are I/Rvat: Barb. lat. 4194–95 and 4198–99. Modern editions of *Giuseppe* (by Claude Palisca) and of *Settimana Santa* (by the present author) are in progress.

FIGURE IV-II. Beginning of *Giuseppe*, attributed to Luigi Rossi.
(Reproduced by permission of I/Rvat.)

characters. In its absence of a *testo*, *Settimana Santa* anticipates the tendency at the end of the century for dramatic oratorio to draw closer to opera. Both librettos include quick exchanges in the dialogue between characters and lyrical moments for arias, ensembles, or choruses. Except for the final choruses, which either address the audience with a moral or repeat the ideas of the last character who sang, the chorus represents a group of personages in the drama.

The libretto of *Giuseppe* is based on the story of Joseph and his brothers in Genesis 42–45. In part I (*Prima cantata*) Joseph's brothers (the sons of Jacob, sung variously by SSATB, SSAT, ATB, SST, S, and T) arrive in Egypt to buy grain to alleviate the famine in their land. Joseph (B), the governor, unrecognized and pretending not to recognize his brothers, accuses them of robbery; they protest their innocence. After questioning a Son of Jacob at length about their father and family, Joseph permits their return home, providing they leave a hostage in Egypt until they come back with

Benjamin. By the beginning of part II (*Seconda cantata*), the Sons have traveled home and back; they are leaving Egypt again when they are arrested by the *Turba di servi* (Crowd of [Joseph's] Servants, ATB) and accused of stealing a cup that is eventually found in Benjamin's sack—it had been secretly placed there at Joseph's command. After feigning rage, Joseph calls for an end to his brothers' anguish and lamentation, and he reveals his identity and the truth about the cup. Joseph, filled with emotion, forgives his brothers for their past offenses against him. The final chorus (*Madrigale ultimo*) has a summarizing and moralizing text.

In this libretto Joseph is a heroic figure, and his brothers are anxious and humble as they plead for mercy. The strong conflict that develops between them employs the theatrical technique of concealed identity, which was also an essential feature of the scriptural story. The role of the *Testo* (A) is essential in this work, and he functions much as he does in Carissimi's *Daniele* and the *Santa Caterina* discussed above. Although the libretto treats its biblical source in a free manner by retaining only the central points of the story and focusing on the contrast between Joseph and his brothers, it is nevertheless closer to its source than is the *Oratorio per la Settimana Santa*.

Settimana Santa, quite freely based upon the events of the Passion story, is the earliest known Passion oratorio. In part I the *Turba* (ATB) calls for the release of Barabbas and the death of Jesus. Pilate (B) hesitates but finally declares his innocence, washes his hands, and gives them Barabbas. At this point a Demon (B) calls for weeping to cease in the underworld and for all to rejoice at their victory. As the finale of part I, the Demons (SSATB) sing a joyful, triumphant chorus with echoes that resound through the halls of hell. At the beginning of part II, one Demon urges the others on to greater merriment, and their chorus cheerfully anticipates the Crucifixion. When suddenly the voice of the Virgin Mary (S) is heard in a brief cry for pity, the Demons relate that Jesus has died. The Virgin laments the loss of her Son, and the Demons comment on her misery and on the folly of faith. The final chorus concludes the Virgin's lament.

The angry, violent *Turba* and the indecisive, anguished Pontius Pilate are, of course, Passion figures; but the Demons and the Virgin are theatrical additions. In fact this libretto is strikingly theatrical, the more so because it does not employ a narrator. An unusual text, indeed, for the most solemn moment in the church year, it is remarkably full of pretexts for composing diabolically joyous music. Demons had appeared in fifteenth- and sixteenth-century *sacre rappresentazioni* for Holy Week; they continued to appear in early operas, but they were virtually absent from spiritual and moral dialogues of the first third of the seventeenth century.[104] The inclusion of demons here, however, foreshadows their rather frequent inclusion in later seventeenth-century oratorios, although these demons are lighter and more cheerful than are their successors. Their diabolical festivities intensify the dramatic impact of the Virgin's lamentation. Her role is akin to that of the operatic Arianna, but it is also rooted in the laments of the Virgin and the Magdalene—which recur time and again in the *laude*, madrigals, and monodies of the late sixteenth and early seventeenth centuries and which have medieval origins. Like the sorrowful mother of the *Stabat Mater*, the Virgin here is a deeply pathetic figure. Here she stands alone—abandoned, tormented by the howling inhabitants of hell—as she pours forth the anguish of her soul.

The musical settings of these texts have so many characteristics in common that they may be considered together. Both oratorios require four soloists, a five-part chorus, two violins, and basso continuo. Cembalo is designated for the continuo throughout *Giuseppe*; there are also some continuo lute parts for *Giuseppe* and *Settimana Santa*. The *lira* is designated for the continuo twice in *Giuseppe* and once in *Settimana Santa*; in both works the *lira* is specified only for the accompaniment of texts expressing deep sorrow, as it is in the *Santa Caterina* discussed above.

The only independent instrumental pieces in the oratorios are the brief introductions to parts I and II. The violins are used with arias for ritornellos and occasionally for accompaniment; sometimes they support the choruses.

The chorus plays a prominent role in both: it enters frequently throughout each oratorio to represent groups of personages, and it consumes about one-third of the time of each work. The choruses in both oratorios use a mixture of imitative and chordal styles; they are generally diatonic, but for particularly expressive purposes they become chromatic and employ the musical-rhetorical figure *pathopoeia*, as in the striking lament of the Sons of Jacob in

104. Early operas in which demons appear are A. Agazzari's *Eumelio*; M. da Gagliano's *La Regina S. Orsola*; and S. Landi's *Sant'Alessio*.

part I of *Giuseppe* (see Example IV–7).[105] Near the beginning of *Settimana Santa*, choral repetitions alternate with solo passages, in quasi-ritornello fashion, to create a large formal structure. In this section the *Turba*, in dialogue with Pilate, calls four times for the release of Barabbas; these brief choruses of the *Turba* are textually identical and musically similar (see Example IV–8).

EXAMPLE IV-7. *Giuseppe*—Attrib. to L. Rossi (I/Rvat: codex Barb. lat. 4194, fol. 15^v).

Wretched, and what would happen [to us]

EXAMPLE IV-8. *Oratorio per la Settimana Santa*—Attrib. to L. Rossi (I/Rvat: codex Barb. lat. 4198, fol. 3^r).

Let Barabbas be given to us!

105. For a more extended treatment of musical-rhetorical figures, see the discussion in chapter 5 of their use by Carissimi.

The three solo styles in these oratorios (recitative, arioso, and aria) are clearly distinguished but frequently mixed: especially at cadential approaches, a recitative will often include a few measures "in aria" (sometimes so designated in the source), and an aria will frequently include one or more recitative passages. Arioso style is occasionally found within arias and recitatives; extended arioso passages are reserved for texts of an unusually intense emotional quality. In *Settimana Santa*, for example, arioso style is used for Pontius Pilate's final and most moving solo, "O di colpo mortale," in which he recognizes the injustice of the agonizing decision forced upon him; yet condemning Jesus to death, he washes his hands and releases Barabbas (see Example IV–9). In this passage, a clear example of *recitativo arioso*, the long notes in the basso continuo are like those in the accompaniment of recitative, but the declamatory vocal line differs from recitative in revealing fewer

EXAMPLE IV-9. *Oratorio per la Settimana Santa*—Attrib. to L. Rossi (I/Rvat: codex Barb. lat. 4198, fol. 10ʳ).

Oh, from the mortal blow, from the harsh piercing, retreat, my zeal! The anger of heaven will punish so great an error, so grave a fault. Of the blood of a just man, and heaven well knows it, I am innocent. I wash my hands and give you Barabbas.

repeated notes, greater rhythmic variety, and more melodic sequences (note the musical-rhetorical *climax* on "cedi, cedi mio zelo") and analogous phrases.

Most of the arias in these works are brief and through-composed. All eleven of those in *Giuseppe* are of this type, as are four of the five in *Settimana Santa*. The composer is clearly interested in revealing the attitudes of his characters through aria and arioso styles. For instance, in Pilate's arioso cited above (Example IV–9), elements contributing to the expression of his anxiety are the rest after the first note, which calls attention to the opening exclamation; the dissonances (mm. 2, 10, and 15); the predominantly minor mode; and the *lira* accompaniment. In *Giuseppe* the first entrance of Joseph, the aria "Chi d'Egito" (see Example IV–10), shows him to be Egypt's powerful governor, angered by intruders into his empire; the bold melodic leaps and the marchlike rhythm contribute to this effect. In *Settimana Santa* the lament of the Virgin, "Tormenti non più" (a long ABA'C structure; see Example IV–11 for the beginning of A), skillfully reflects her sorrow and frustration as she hears the Demons' joyful triumph over the death of Jesus; contributing to this effect are the smooth style of the melodic line and the special treatment of certain words. In Example IV–11, for instance, the Virgin's melodic line rises to its peak at "con gridi orribili" ("with horrible screams"), and it approaches its cadence with harsh dissonances and parallel fifths in the violin parts on the word "inferno." Section B of the aria is a brief recitative passage, and section C is a highly effective declamatory vocal line over a chaconne bass, often used in this period to express texts of lamentation.

EXAMPLE IV-10. *Giuseppe*—Attrib. to L. Rossi (I/Rvat: codex Barb. lat. 4191, fol. 12ʳ).

(EXAMPLE IV-10, continued)

Who in this vast empire of Egypt made you penetrate as robbers? Of what king these machinations and plots? You lie in your hearts and in your thoughts.

EXAMPLE IV-11. *Oratorio per la Settimana Santa*—Attrib. to L. Rossi (I/Rvat: codex Barb. lat. 4199, fols. 10ᵛ–11ʳ).

(EXAMPLE IV-11, continued)

con gri-di or-ri-bi-li,con vo-ci di scher-no,ri-der gl'ab-bis-si e fe-steg-giar l'in-fer - - - no.

No more torment! Wretched, and what do I hear: a happy victor, with shouts and hisses, with horrible screams, with voices of scorn, the abysses laughing and inferno celebrating.

Of the oratorios attributed to Luigi Rossi, the two just treated are the most dramatic and thus the most forward looking; there are others attributed to him, however, that are of interest for the light they shed on the reflective oratorio. The six works of this type attributed to Rossi, all with texts by Giovanni Lotti, are listed below with the titles found in their manuscript sources. The titles are of interest for their mixtures of the terms *oratorio* and *cantata*.[106]

1. *Oratorio. Un peccator pentito,* "Mi son fatto nemico." *Cantata à 5 con stromenti.*
2. *Una cantata morale per oratorio. Cantata à 5* . . . , "Ancor' satio non sei."
3. *Oratorio* . . . *Prima cantata. Cantata à 5.* "Inferno."
4. *Seconda cantata per oratorio à 5 morale, con instromenti se si vuole.* "Disperar di se stesso . . . . "
5. *Oratorio* "O cecità," *cantata à 5 con stromenti se si vuole* . . . .
6. *Predica del sole. Cantata à 5 morale,* "Ergi lamente al sole."

Items 1, 2, and 5 may be considered one-part oratorios, or cantatas to be sung in an oratory, as is specified in the title of item 2. Items 3 and 4 appear to be parts I and II (*Prima* and *Seconda*

106. In this list italics indicate titles and designations of genres, and quotation marks indicate incipits; the information is recorded in the order in which it is found on the title pages or covers (in the absence of title pages) of the MSS. The name of the poet, the same for all, has been deleted. For the attributions to L. Rossi, see Ghislanzoni, *Rossi*, pp. 217–18; for brief descriptions of some, see ibid., pp. 108–15. MS sources are I/Rvat: Barb. lat., (1) 4191; (2) 4190 and 4192; (3) 4189; (4) 4188; (5) 4218 and 4193; (6) 4187.

cantata) of a two-part oratorio. Item 6 is not designated an oratorio in its source, but since it is a "moral cantata," as is item 2, it would probably have been used in an oratory. All six items employ reflective texts: the first four deal with reflections of penitent sinners; item 5, with exhortations for blind and miserable mortals to leave the things of the world and to turn to heaven; and item 6, with reflections on the superiority of heavenly light over the splendor of the sun. None of the works employ personages except item 6, essentially a reflective dialogue between the Sun (B) and Mortals (SSATB). Each of the six items is about as long as one part of the two-part oratorios attributed to Rossi that have been treated above. They all employ two violins (indicated as optional in items 4 and 5), basso continuo (including *lira*), from one to four soloists, and chorus (SSATB). The styles and structures are similar to those of the two-part works described above.

The Chief Characteristics of the Oratorio Volgare

By about 1660, the end of the period under consideration in this chapter, the term *oratorio* when applied to works with Italian texts designated a composition with the combined elements of the cantata for a few voices and the polyphonic madrigal. Oratorios were usually either in one structural part of about twenty to thirty minutes, with exceptions as short as ten minutes in duration, or they were in two parts, totaling from about forty-five minutes to an hour. An oratory exercise normally employed its principal music before and after a sermon; thus either a two-part oratorio or two one-part oratorios could be used.

The texts of Italian works called oratorios are either reflective or dramatic. The dramatic type usually employs the narrative element; when it does, that element is set forth by a narrator—called *Poeta*, *Testo*, *Istoria*, or *Historia*. On the basis of extant sources, one could conclude that the reflective and dramatic types were of approximately equal prominence in this period; since the extant sources are relatively few, however, and since the later development of the oratorio is largely dramatic, that type might well have predominated in this period also.

Recitative texts in oratorios with Italian texts are poetic, and they usually employ a free mixture of seven- and eleven-syllable lines; aria and chorus texts generally use lines of one length throughout, with those of four, six, and eight syllables being common. In this period most oratorio texts are relatively simple; they use few rhetorical devices, for the oratorios were intended to communicate to the widest possible audience and attract persons of all walks of life into the oratories. The two texts by Balducci, however, occasionally reveal the influence of Marino's style in the extravagance of their similes and metaphors, and the texts of Ciampoli and Lotti, while further from Marino, reveal the considerable poetic skill of their authors.

The sources of texts are the Old Testament, the New Testament, hagiography, and spiritual and moral subjects similar to those of the *laude* in the period of Philip Neri. The biblical and hagiographical texts treat their subjects freely: they embellish them for interest and edification, and scriptural quotation is rare.

The dramatic texts are usually set to music with one singer per character, although the lines of the narrator are occasionally set for ensembles. Choruses and ensembles are used to represent groups of characters or crowds; except for the final choruses, which are characteristically moralizing in content, choruses rarely reflect on the plot from outside the dramatic action. Most oratorios close with a chorus, and many use the chorus only at the end of the work or of each part in a two-part oratorio.[107] Occasionally, however, an oratorio ends with a solo passage: Cesare Mazzei's libretto *Abele e Caino*,[108] a work possibly dating from his period as prefect of music for the Congregation of the Oratory (1653–56), concludes with Cain's lament for his murder of Abel.

The solo styles (recitative, arioso, and aria) are those characteristic of operas and secular cantatas of the period, and the blending of two or even all three of the styles within a relatively brief passage is common. The numerous aria forms and procedures that are found include the through-composed, strophic, strophic variation, ground bass, and ABA forms; various rondolike schemes; and binary forms with repeated sections. The da capo sign, so common later, is not seen in oratorios of this period. Ensemble styles are both imitative and chordal, in the manner of the poly-

107. The choruses in oratorios were probably sung by ensembles of the participating soloists when the chorus played a relatively minor role. (See the character designations in the choruses of the anonymous *Daniele*, discussed above.)

108. Printed in Alaleona, *Oratorio*, pp. 303–12.

phonic madrigals of the period. Although difficult vocal ornaments were no doubt added in performance, vocal virtuosity is rarely required for singing the oratorios as notated, since neither the ranges nor the passage work tends to be taxing; there are some notable exceptions, however, especially in the solo passages of the oratorios by Domenico Mazzocchi and Mario Savioni.

When instruments other than those for the basso continuo are designated, they are two violins; other instruments might well have been used, of course, in an improvisatory capacity. The instruments play primarily introductions to oratorios, supporting passages during choruses, and ritornellos for choruses, ensembles, and arias; only occasionally do they accompany a solo voice.

CHAPTER V

Mid-Century Rome II: Carissimi and the Oratorio Latino

§♥ From a musical standpoint the *oratorio latino* and *volgare* are not separate genres but one genre in different languages. They developed at approximately the same time, in Rome, from the early Baroque's interest in musical settings of narrative and dramatic texts. Some of the same composers set to music oratorio texts in both languages and used the same style for both types. From a literary standpoint, however, the *oratorio volgare* and *latino* differ considerably in this early period of their development: while the former uses a poetic text throughout—as is normally true of *laude*, madrigals, cantatas, and operas—the *oratorio latino* employs a text largely in prose, as do most motets. Thus motets with narrative and dramatic texts, such as the dialogues described in chapter 3, must be considered the chief antecedents of the *oratorio latino*.

Rome's Latin Oratory and Its Music

The use of the Latin language assumed a well-educated audience, which would be drawn from a relatively small segment of the population. Only one oratory in Rome is known to have fostered the performance of Latin oratorios; it was called the Oratorio del Santissimo Crocifisso (Oratory of the Most Holy Crucifix, hereafter called "Crocifisso"), near and administratively related to the

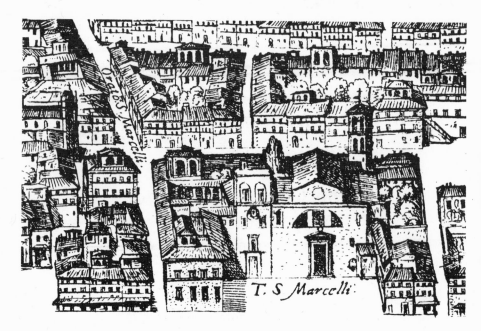

FIGURE V-1. Detail from a 1593 map of Rome showing the church of
San Marcello (marked "T. S. Marcelli") and the Oratorio
del Santissimo Crocifisso, or Oratorio di San Marcello
(the churchlike structure to the left of the marking
"Orato.^re S. Marcelli").
(Tempesta, *Roma*.)

church of San Marcello.[1] Founded by a group of Roman noblemen, the society for which that oratory was constructed dates
from the early sixteenth century. On 25 May 1519 a fire destroyed
the church of San Marcello; yet a large crucifix, completely intact
and with a lamp still burning before it, is said to have been found
in the ruins. Thereafter venerated as a miraculous image, this
crucifix played a prominent role in an effort of 1522 to relieve
Rome of a fierce pestilence. On Good Friday of that year the
crucifix was carried in a solemn procession from its church of San
Marcello to San Pietro in Vaticano; it was

1. In early sources this oratory is sometimes called the Oratorio di San Marcello because of its association with the church.

accompanied by numerous nobility, prelates, and every sort of Roman citizen in penitential habit, and among others by many innocent boys, who, barefoot and covered with ashes, in a single, high voice interrupted only by the sobs and sighs of those who were accompanying them, exclaimed: Misericordia Santissimo Crocifisso. The above-mentioned sacred image was carried as far as the Vatican Basilica. The described prayer had not even been finished, nor had the image been replaced, when the pestilence was observed to cease, and Rome, so desolate that it was almost completely destroyed, returned to normal.[2]

Following this demonstration of the apparent efficacy of the crucifix, numerous noblemen and prelates formed a society called the Company of the Most Holy Crucifix. The statutes of the company were soon formulated and were approved by Pope Clement VII in 1526. Later in the sixteenth century the company was given the title of Archconfraternity of the Most Holy Crucifix; the oratory constructed for their services was completed in 1568.[3]

The chief ceremonies of the archconfraternity in the sixteenth and seventeenth centuries took place during Lent. Of primary importance was the annual procession on Maundy Thursday or Good Friday, in which the crucifix was carried from San Marcello to San Pietro. These processions grew into magnificent affairs, with as many as fifteen thousand participants reported in the Holy Year of 1650; the processions included decorated carriages and floats and vocal and instrumental music, which was supplied by the best musicians in Rome.[4] From the sixteenth until the early eighteenth century, Divine Office was sung in the oratory throughout Holy Week, and services in which music was especially prominent were held there on five Fridays in Lent.[5] In 1650, and prob-

2. Translated from *Statuti*, p. 7. For a sketch of the early history of the archconfraternity, see ibid., pp. 6–9; see also the summary in Alaleona, *Oratorio*, pp. 163–64.

3. Alaleona, *Oratorio*, p. 329.

4. Ibid., p. 165. The 1650 procession is described in Gio. Simone Ruggieri, *Diario dell'Anno Santis. Giubileo 1650 celebrato in Roma dalla Santità d. N. S. Papa Innocentio X* ([Rome], 1651), p. 86, quoted in Alaleona, *Oratorio*, p. 165, n. 1; the same procession is briefly described in Lassels, *Voyage*, pp. 2, 197–98.

5. The musically prominent five Fridays in Lent appear to have begun with the second Friday and ended with Friday of Passion Week. In 1650, for instance, the five Fridays were 11, 18, and 25 March and 1 and 8 April (cf. Alaleona, *Oratorio*, p. 179, n. 3). From Ruggieri's *Diario* quoted in Alaleona, *Oratorio*, pp. 160 and 179, n. 3, it is clear that the last Friday, 8 April 1650, was Friday of Passion Week. In Grace, "Marazzoli," pp. 100–101, similar conclusions regarding which five Fridays of Lent were the musically prominent ones are reached.

ably every year thereafter, the music for the five Fridays was the responsibility of five guardians, all noblemen, of the archconfraternity. Each guardian would select a maestro di cappella for his Friday and would pay the expenses for the music.[6]

No record is known to exist of the compositions performed at Crocifisso during the late sixteenth and early seventeenth centuries. Evidently no corpus of music was composed specifically for this oratory as the *laude* and G. F. Anerio's *Teatro* were for the oratories of the Chiesa Nuova and San Girolamo della Carità. Since Latin was the language of the text set to music, motets would have been used in addition to music for the Divine Office of Holy Week, such as the Lamentations of Jeremiah and the responsories. Among those who were in charge of the music at Crocifisso from the later sixteenth to the mid-seventeenth centuries are some of Rome's most famous composers, whose music represents a variety of styles including both the *stile antico* and *moderno*: Palestrina, Luca Marenzio, G. F. Anerio, Paolo Quagliati, Giovanni Maria and Giovanni Bernardino Nanino, Ottavio Catalano, Paolo Tarditi, Stefano Landi, Ruggiero Giovanelli, V. Mazzocchi, F. Foggia, Loreto Vittori, Carissimi, and others.[7] Since the oratorio was beginning to develop at San Girolamo della Carità and the Chiesa Nuova in the first third of the century, as G. F. Anerio's *Teatro* indicates, it is reasonable to assume that it was also developing at Crocifisso and that some of the motets performed there in the same period were dialogues such as those described in chapter 3. In fact, Archangelo Spagna traces the origin of the Latin oratorio directly to the motets that were used as substitutions for parts of the liturgy: "The Latin oratorios, in the beginning, were like those motets which are continually sung in the choirs of the religious and formerly were heard on every feast day instead of the antiphons, graduals, and offertories."[8]

By 1639 oratorios, or at least incipient oratorios, were being performed at Crocifisso, according to the account of the French violist André Maugars, who was visiting Rome in that year. His

6. For lists of those who supported the oratory services in 1650 and in various years thereafter, see Alaleona, *Oratorio*, pp. 340–50.

7. For documentation from the archive of Crocifisso regarding composers and performers active there from the sixteenth to the eighteenth centuries, see ibid., pp. 325–50, and Liess, "Musikerlisten."

8. Translated from Schering, "Beiträge," p. 65.

published reply to an inquiry about the music he heard in Rome is an invaluable document.[9] Among other descriptions, Maugars includes the following one of music at Crocifisso:

There is yet another kind of music, which is not at all in use in France, and which for that reason well merits my giving you a detailed account. It is called *stile récitatif*. The best that I have heard has been in the Oratory of San Marcello, where there is a congregation of the Brothers of the Holy Crucifix, composed of the most important gentlemen of Rome, who consequently have the means to assemble the rarest that Italy produces; and in fact, the most excellent musicians pride themselves in being there, and the most competent composers solicit the honor of having their compositions heard there and try to show in them all the best results of their study.

This admirable and ravishing music is performed only on the Fridays of Lent from three until six o'clock. The church is by no means as large as the Sainte-Chapelle in Paris; at the end of [the church] there is a spacious loft [*Jubé*] with a medium-sized organ, very soft and very suitable for the voices. On the two sides of the church there are two more small stages [*Tribunes*] where there were the most excellent instrumentalists. The voices would begin with a psalm in motet form, and then all the instruments would play a very good symphony. Afterwards the voices would sing a story [*une histoire*] from the Old Testament in the form of a spiritual play, such as that of Susanna, Judith and Holofernes, or David and Goliath. Each singer represented a personage of the story and expressed perfectly the force of the words. Then one of the most celebrated preachers would give the exhortation. That finished, the singers performed the Gospel of the day, such as the story of the Samaritan woman, the woman of Cana, Lazarus, the Magdalen, or the Passion of our Lord; the singers imitated perfectly the different personages whom the Evangelist mentioned. I could not praise enough that *musique récitatif*; it is necessary to have heard it on the spot to judge well its merits.

As for instrumental music, it consisted of an organ, a large harpsichord, a lyra, two or three violins, and two or three archlutes.[10]

Thus Maugars attests to the excellence of the music at Crocifisso and the prestige attached to performances there. In describing the order of events in the service as (1) a motet with a psalm text,

9. Maugars, *Response*; for a modern edition see Thoinan, *Maugars*; for translations into English and German, respectively, see Shedlock, "Maugars" and Wasielewski, "Musikbericht."
10. Translated from Thoinan, *Maugars*, pp. 29–30.

(2) an instrumental number, (3) a musical setting of an Old Testament story, (4) a sermon, and (5) a musical setting of a New Testament story, Maugars uses neither the term *oratorio* nor any other genre name except *motet*. His term *story* (*histoire*) apparently refers to the text, a narrative from the Bible.[11] The performance before and after the sermon of two independent compositions (dialogue motets or brief oratorios) parallels the early practice in the oratories that used the Italian language.

In 1640, the year following that of Maugars's letter, Pietro Della Valle entered in his diary an account of a performance at Crocifisso of a work that he calls his *Dialogo di Esther*; but he also refers to it as an oratorio in a letter to G. B. Doni in the same year and again in a letter of 1647.[12] This is the earliest Latin composition known to have been called an oratorio by its composer. Since the work is lost, the description of it in the composer's diary is of special importance:

2 April [1640]. Monday of Holy Week. I had my Dialogue of Esther sung in the Oratory of the Most Holy Crucifix; [it was] written and set to music by me with a variety of ancient tones conforming to the doctrine of signore Giovanni Battista Doni. A most noble audience of ladies, cavaliers, prelates, and other personages were there with a very large crowd of other people. Of the cardinals there was only Cardinal Crescentio, who, since he was alone, did not stay below but up with the chorus of musicians. It succeeded rather well, although the musicians had never practiced it except at my house the same morning where I kept them all to dine. To the learned and to the connoisseurs of the art it was rather pleasing, but not to the ordinary people, because of the scarcity of the instruments which were there, no others being played but my *cembalo triarmonico*, my *violone panarmonico*, and my *violini delle tre armonie*.[13]

Continuing his description, Della Valle indicates that there were only three instrumentalists, one (V. Mazzocchi) for the *cembalo*

---

11. The Italian and Latin equivalents, *istoria* and *historia*, were often used in that manner (cf. Griffi's preface to Anerio's *Teatro*, above). These terms are not known to have been used by Italians to designate a musical genre in this period.

12. Della Valle to Doni, 24 November 1640 and 24 August 1647, in Solerti, "Della Valle," pp. 285, 309. During carnival of 1647—according to the letter of that year—this oratorio was performed in Della Valle's home as a spoken play with scenery and costumes; the play was recited by young girls, and only the choruses were sung.

13. Diary of Della Valle, 2 April 1640, translated from Ziino, "Della Valle," pp. 107–8; see also Ziino's comments, p. 100.

triarmonico, another for the *violone panarmonico*, and a third for the three *violini delle tre armonie*. Five singers performed the parts of Assuerus (B), Mardochai (T), the Poet (T), Aman (A), and Esther (S). Della Valle mentions "signore Mariuccio" (a "contralto famoso," possibly Mario Savioni) who not only sang the part of Aman but conducted very well; Della Valle assisted by indicating tempo changes.[14] From Della Valle's description and his letters to Doni, it appears that in several respects his *Esther* parallels his *Purificatione*, described in chapter 4: both were termed oratorios in 1640, both are "erudite" compositions (that is, they employ ancient Greek modes according to Doni's teaching), and both use four characters plus a narrator, called the Poet. Although it is impossible to estimate the duration of *Esther*, the fact that the only rehearsal for this piece with strange and probably difficult intonation was in the morning on the day of the performance might indicate that it was as brief as his *Purificatione*, which is about twelve minutes long.

In Spagna's discussion of the Latin oratorio at Crocifisso, he confirms part of Maugars's report and describes certain aspects of a later practice. He states that the early oratorios performed there

were different in each part of the oratory service, without a connection of the first with the second. The subjects were taken from the sacred scripture; the recitatives were in prose with the same words as the sacred text (*sacro testo*), and that is why more appropriately it [the narrative portion] was given the name *text* (*testo*). The greatest attention was paid to the multiplication of musical instruments [by] separating them into various choruses for the grandiosity of the pomp; and, to make room for the great number of singers who performed there, various platforms were constructed; but these, larger and more decorated, now serve to accomodate many gentlemen and ladies who are invited there and assemble to listen. Then the same subject was divided into two parts, in imitation of the *oratorii volgari*, and the *testo* was abolished, as has been stated.[15]

Writing in the early eighteenth century, Spagna thus surveys three seventeenth-century developments: (1) that from the early practice of performing two unrelated works, before and after the sermon, to the later one of using a single work in two parts; (2) that from

14. Diary of Della Valle, 2 April 1640, in Ziino, "Della Valle," p. 109.
15. Translated from Schering, "Beiträge," p. 65.

the early practice of using a large number of singers and instrumentalists to the later one of using a smaller performing group, no doubt because of the diminished importance of the chorus—thus the platforms had changed from their former function of seating the performers to that of seating some of the audience; and (3) that from the early practice of using a *testo* to the later (albeit inconsistent) one, of which Spagna was a strong advocate, of omitting the *testo* and making the libretto thoroughly dramatic.

A report by the traveler Francis Mortoft, writing in 1659, helps to clarify Spagna's point regarding the number of singers used at Crocifisso in the mid-seventeenth century and provides further testimony regarding the excellence of the music. On 7 March, the second Friday of Lent, Mortoft relates,

Wee went to A little Church called the Auditory [i.e., oratory] of St. Marcel, which is behind the Corso, where wee heard Musicke. This place being appointed for the purpose, there being every Friday in the lent a Consort of the best voyces in Rome at this place. I thinke there was in this little Church all the strangers about Rome, where having waited some two howers, at last Musicke began with some a douzen voyces. A Lute, Violin and Organs, which sounded most sweetly, especially the Lute and Violin was so rare, that being once out of Rome it must never be expected to heare the like againe: the Subject that the musicke was upon was in the Praise of Thomas Aquinas, which A Dominican Priest extolled to the Skyes, calling him his Saint, and praying to him, that I beleeved the Priest lookes onely to be saved by the merrits of St. Thomas, and not by the Merrits of Christ.[16]

Again, on the fourth Friday of Lent, 21 March, Mortoft visited the same oratory "and there heard the most sweete and harmonious musicke, which one, being once out of Rome, must never upon Earth be expected to heare the like. It was composed of at least 20 voyces, organes, Lute, Violl, and two Violins, all which made such melodious and delightful musicke that Cicero with all his eloquence could never discribe the sweetnesse of this more than sweete and harmonious musicke."[17] Thus Mortoft heard about a dozen singers at one performance, at least twenty at another, and

16. Mortoft, *Travels*, p. 145. For the report of another traveler, Aerssen de Sommelsdyck, who visited Crocifisso in 1654 and praised its music, see ibid., n. 1.
17. Ibid., p. 153.

both services employed at least two organs and a few other instruments. These performing forces are comparable to those indicated by the extant payment records for musicians who performed in oratorios at Crocifisso in the 1660s.[18] Polychoral works, which at that time were common there, appear to have employed two or three choruses with one person on each part, an organ for each chorus, and an ensemble of instruments ranging from three to fifteen pieces. By the 1690s, however, the normal performing force seems to have been six voices, one organ, and three to six other instruments—this number confirms Spagna's remarks concerning the reduction in the number of musicians used at Crocifisso in the late Baroque.

Crocifisso remained the Roman center for the performance of Latin oratorios until 1710, when the archconfraternity ceased sponsoring them. Only in the Holy Year of 1725 was the Lenten practice revived. Two of the best-known composers active there in the later period are Alessandro Stradella and Alessandro Scarlatti.[19] Although most of the music of the oratorios performed at Crocifisso has not survived, numerous printed librettos are extant from 1678–1725.[20] Intended to assist the listener, these librettos include the entire Latin text, a summary of the story in Italian, and occasionally an Italian translation of the text.

Giacomo Carissimi

Biography and Environment

By far the most famous composer of Latin oratorios in the mid-seventeenth century was Giacomo Carissimi (1605–74). His reputation and influence as an oratorio composer reached beyond Rome and Italy to northern Europe in his own time, and today

18. For these payment records see Liess, "Musikerlisten," pp. 142–68; for further payment records from Crocifisso in the 1660s, see Wessely-Kropik, *Colista*, pp. 57–61.

19. For archival documentation see Alaleona, *Oratorio*, pp. 342, 344. For archival documents listing maestri di cappelle at Crocifisso from the sixteenth to the eighteenth centuries, see ibid., pp. 325–50; for documents listing musicians at Crocifisso in the period 1664–1725, see Liess, "Musikerlisten."

20. For a bibliography of extant librettos of oratorios performed at Crocifisso, see Alaleona, *Oratorio*, pp. 351–62, and Liess, "Oratorienlibretti."

FIGURE V-2. The German College (right) and its church of Sant'Apollinare.
(Vasi, *Magnificenze*, pt. 7, no. 164.)

more of his Latin oratorios are extant than are those of any of his
contemporaries.

Born in the hill town of Marino, near Rome, Carissimi became
a singer at the cathedral of nearby Tivoli at seventeen or eighteen
years of age, and from 1624 to 1627 he was the organist there.
From 1628 to 1629, he was the maestro di cappella at the church
of San Rufino at Assisi. By 15 December 1629[21] he had begun his
long tenure as a teacher at the German College in Rome and as the
maestro di cappella at the college's church, Sant'Apollinare, a
position that he held until his death.

The German College, founded in 1552 in an effort to strengthen
German Catholicism, was managed by the Jesuits; its specific
purpose was to train young Germans for the priesthood. Beginning
in the 1570s, music became increasingly important at the col-

21. Culley, *German*, p. 173; Culley, "Influence," p. 5.

lege.[22] By the time Carissimi assumed his duties there, Sant'Apollinare had established an outstanding reputation for its music. According to a report of 1608, the services of Sant'Apollinare were "frequented by cardinals, ambassadors of princes, prelates, etc."[23] Two reports of 1611—one of which was written by Bernardino Castorio, the rector of the college from 1600 to 1634—indicate that "the excellence of the music there was the sole reason for its being one of the most frequented churches in Rome," that "the best music of the city was to be found at the college, that it was listed in books as one of the marvels of Rome, and that all the tourists wanted to hear it"; furthermore, "the music of the college was famous not only in Rome, but throughout Italy and Germany as well."[24] Francis Mortoft was evidently no exception among foreign tourists in Rome, for in 1659 he reports having gone to Sant'Apollinare specifically to hear its music.[25] He mentions hearing beautiful music there on each of his several visits,[26] and being impressed at learning "that the Musicke Master [Carissimi] has 3 thousand Crownes a yeare out of the Colledge to maintaine Musicke every Sunday in the yeare."[27]

Carissimi's period at the college continued the institution's previous brilliant musical tradition; his was also a period of increase in musical professionalism and, apparently, of a corresponding decrease in attention to the college's students. Professionalism in music at the expense of the students came under attack prior to the college's musical reform of 1657, which took place in the wake of Pope Alexander VII's decree of that year concerning the reform of music in churches and oratories. (Passages from the decree are quoted in chapter 4.) The following excerpts from reports written before 1657 point out some of the specific abuses considered to be in need of reform, and they provide valuable information about musical practice at the German College:

Little by little after the death of the first rectors, Father Castorio introduced paid, secular musicians; and all the privileges of those student

22. Culley, *German*, p. 18.
23. Quoted ibid., p. 167.
24. Culley's summary of the reports, ibid.
25. Mortoft, *Travels*, p. 143.
26. Ibid., pp. 118, 140, 143.
27. Ibid., p. 143.

musicians have gone to these seculars without reason, since they are paid. . . . And this abuse of secular music has increased in such a way that it is of the greatest expense for the college; for a room of castrati, with [a] prefect, is kept (which costs the college more than six hundred scudi), and the present maestro di cappella [Carissimi], towards the last years of the old age of Father Castorio, introduced two organs and three choirs of music, with great expense for the college. He does not teach the students [any] more, and a thousand other abuses in the way of lunches and dinners for the musicians have been introduced.[28]

But granted and conceded that this [the music] be necessary . . . one ought, however, to manage it . . . with the moderation that is necessary, and not with that pomp and excess which is had now. For today, the extremely long music made with instruments, and the unending motets, do not serve for anything other than to . . . exhaust the students in the choir, who, to while away the tedium in these rainstorms of motets, either talk, read profane books, go late, or leave the choir.[29]

With professional musicians living in the college and evidence of elaborate music performed there, it is clear that all the necessary personnel would have been available for the performance of Carissimi's oratorios at Sant'Apollinare. The performance of such music during Mass is by no means out of the question, for as early as 1628 Lorenzo Ratti, Carissimi's predecessor at the German College, had indicated that some of his dialogues were intended to be substitutes for the offertory.[30] Nearly thirty years later, non-liturgical substitutes were still being used for liturgical items in Roman churches, as Pope Alexander VII's decree of 1657 makes clear. Spagna, in his historical sketch of the Latin oratorio, refers to the use of oratoriolike motets as substitutes for antiphons, graduals, and offertories, as indicated above. In fact, it was evidently to prevent further use of Carissimi's oratorios in the church that they were not printed in his lifetime; such, at least, is the implication of the following excerpt from a letter of 24 February 1665, written by René Ouvrard in Paris to Claude Nicaise, who was visiting Rome: "They have wanted to convince me that the present pope, two years ago, forbade the stories in music [*les*

28. Translated in Culley, *German*, pp. 198–99; original printed, ibid., p. 376.
29. Translated ibid., p. 199; original printed, ibid., pp. 361–62.
30. Smither, "Dialogue," p. 414; Chauvin, "Ratti."

histoires en musique], not wishing that anything be sung in church which was not contained, word for word, in Holy Scripture or in the breviary. That would have meant cutting off the wings of the angel of Music. . . . In addition, a man who arrived two months ago from that country there told me that Signor Carissimi had not obtained permission to have printed those which he has composed."[31] With considerable evidence that oratoriolike pieces were sometimes used in churches as motets, it is possible that at least some of Carissimi's shorter oratorios might have been among the "unending motets" and "rainstorms of motets" performed at Sant'Apollinare.

In addition to his normal activity at the college, Carissimi occasionally worked elsewhere in Rome. There are records of his having served as the director of music at Crocifisso on the fourth Friday of Lent in 1650, the fifth in 1658, and the fourth in 1659 and 1660;[32] he might have served there at other times too, for the records of Crocifisso are incomplete. For the second of these performances, the following excerpt from a diary of the college for 5 April 1658 provides some useful background:

This evening, the Father Rector having to preach the sermon in the Oratory of San Marcello, . . . the older [students] asked to go there. And the Father Rector granted it to them, on account of having been informed that, on a similar occasion even the Father Olivia permitted them to go to the Oratory of S. Filippo, of the Chiesa Nuova. The . . . older [students] went, leaving the house at about twenty-one hours [i.e., about three hours before sundown]; wherefore they did not go to school. Two servants with torches were sent to bring them home. Also, our *maestro di cappella* made the music this evening in the said Oratory.[33]

Thus for this oratorio service, and surely for others at Crocifisso and at other oratories, students formed a part of the audience. It is

31. Ouvrard to Nicaise, 24 February 1665, translated from Prunières, *Opéra*, pp. 314–15. I am grateful to Professor Albert Cohen for providing me with a transcription of more of this letter than Prunières gives and thus clarifying the meaning of this passage. The person to whom the letter is addressed is clearly Claude Nicaise, not Marc-Antoine Charpentier, as indicated in Culley, *German*, pp. 267–68. For details regarding the correspondence of Ouvard and Nicaise, see A. Cohen, "Ouvard-Nicaise."

32. For archival documentation see Alaleona, *Oratorio*, p. 174.

33. Diary of the German College, 5 April 1658, translated in Culley, *German*, p. 178; original printed, ibid., p. 305.

of interest that this was an afternoon service, as was that at Crocifisso reported almost twenty years earlier by Maugars. What music the students heard is not known; nor are there records of any particular compositions by Carissimi having been performed at Crocifisso. It has been assumed that all his oratorios were intended for that oratory;[34] some no doubt were, especially those performed there when he was director of the oratory's music, but the possibility of church performances, as mentioned above, should not be excluded.

A position of considerable distinction that Carissimi held outside the German College is that of *maestro di cappella del concerto di camera* of Queen Christina of Sweden. He was appointed to the position in July 1656,[35] about six months after the queen had taken up residence in Rome. Carissimi probably found occasion to perform his numerous secular cantatas as well as his other secular and sacred works, including oratorios, at the palace of this extremely active patron of music.[36]

Carissimi's reputation among his contemporaries in Rome was, according to the theorist Athanasius Kircher, that of "a very excellent and famous composer, . . . [who,] through his genius and the felicity of his compositions, surpasses all others in moving the minds of listeners to whatever affection he wishes. His compositions are truly imbued with the essence and life of the spirit."[37] Extant letters testify to Carissimi's excellent reputation and influence throughout Italy and even in northern Europe.[38] His influence was spread through the circulation of prints and manuscript copies of his music as well as by his students, both Italian and foreign. Among his Italian students was Giovanni Paolo Colonna, an outstanding Bolognese composer whose works include oratorios; the foreigners included Marc-Antoine Charpentier and Kaspar Förster, Jr.,[39] both of whom became excellent composers of Latin oratorios.

34. Alaleona, *Oratorio*, p. 174; Pasquetti, *Oratorio*, p. 243; and Bianchi, *Carissimi*, pp. 149–50.

35. Culley, *German*, p. 178; for a facsimile of the appointment document, see ibid., p. ix.

36. For information about Queen Christina's patronage of Carissimi, see ibid., pp. 178–80; and Sandberger, "Christine," pp. 126, 129.

37. Kircher, *Musurgia*, 1:603, as translated in Palisca, *Baroque*, p. 115.

38. Culley, *German*, pp. 181–93.

39. Ibid., pp. 176–77. For the musical influence of the German College and Carissimi

Latin Oratorios

Terminology and Classification. Considerable confusion of terminology exists in writings about Carissimi's compositions with Latin texts. The reasons for the confusion begin with the sources.[40] Although Carissimi left all his music to the German College, his entire collection disappeared sometime after the early eighteenth century;[41] thus no sources of the oratorios are extant in the composer's hand. The bulk of the sources are manuscript copies by French and English scribes, and the terminology in the sources may or may not be that of the composer. Seven of Carissimi's works in a French manuscript are designated by the term *oratoires*;[42] all others that are called oratorios by various twentieth-century writers are designated in the sources as *histoire, historia,* or *motet.*

In the period under consideration, as pointed out above, the genre was only beginning to be identified by the term *oratorio,* and other terms were applied to it as well. Just as Mario Savioni used the expression "cantata for an oratory" to designate a work with an Italian text similar to one for which he used the term *oratorio,* so the expressions "dialogue for an oratory" and "motet for an oratory" were no doubt used for works with Latin texts that resemble the oratorio as a genre.[43] Although the genre took its name from the building and the religious service in which it was employed, one cannot assume that all motets performed in oratories were oratorios in the sense of a distinct musical genre; this is clear from a letter to Carissimi written by Landgrave Friedrich (probably of Hesse-Darmstadt) and dated at Florence 29 March

---

in Germany, see Culley, *German,* pp. 270–74 and Culley, "Influence." For Carissimi's influence in France, see Prunières, *Opéra,* p. 17, n. 4, and p. 316.

40. For writings on the principal Carissimi sources, see Chrysander, "Carissimi"; Chrysander, "Jephta"; Brenet, "Carissimi"; and the introductory notes of the modern editions in IISM–3. For a partial list of sources of Carissimi's music with Latin texts, see Beveridge, "Carissimi," pp. 214–87. For a study of the questions of terminology raised by Carissimi's Latin oratorios, see Smither, "Carissimi."

41. For a summary of the theories about the fate of Carissimi's MSS, see Culley, *German,* p. 196.

42. The MS is D-brd/Hs: M C/270. The works called oratorios in that MS are *Judicium extremum, Diluvium universale, Judicium Salomonis, Lamentatio Damnatorum, Foelicitas beatorum, Martyres,* and *Dives malus.* (Cf. figure V-3.)

43. It is of interest that in 1650 Carissimi's *Jephte* was called a dialogue in Kircher, *Musurgia,* 1:603.

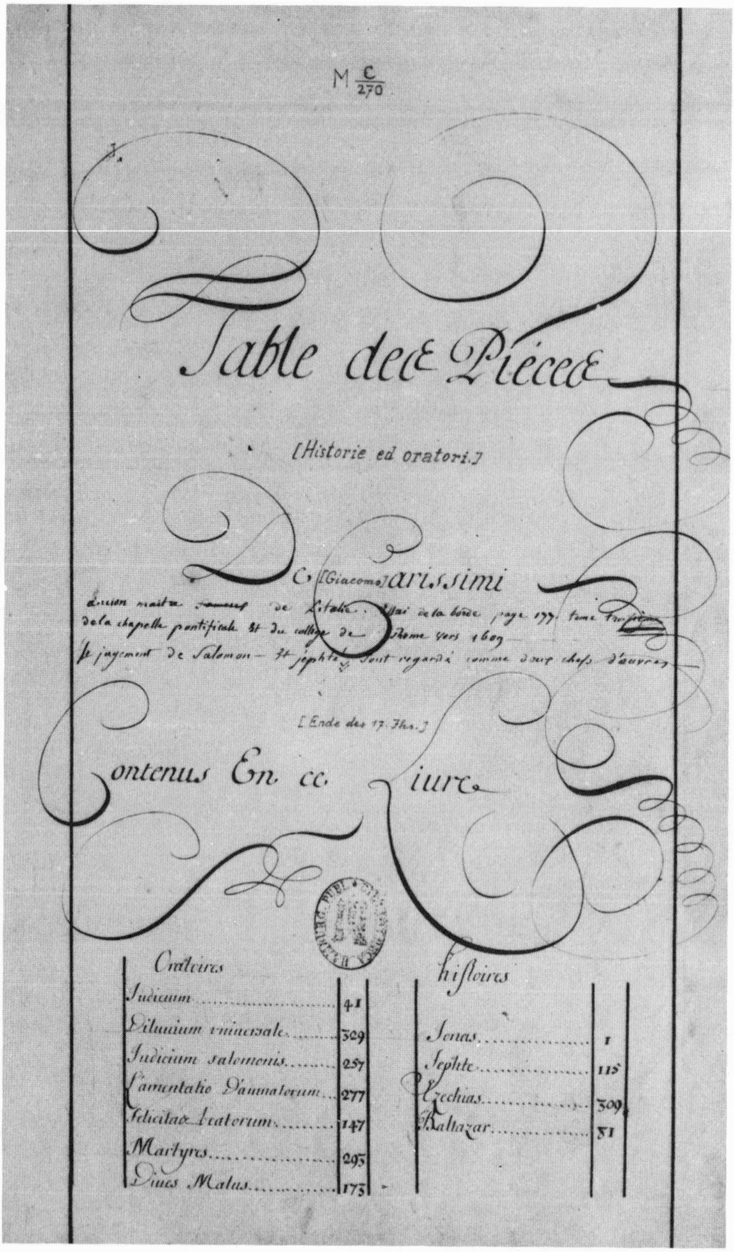

FIGURE V-3. Table of contents of a late seventeenth-century French copy of some sacred Latin works by Carissimi. The works are grouped into "Oratoires" and "Histoires."
(Reproduced by permission of D-brd/Hs: MC 270.)

1642. Friedrich asks the composer to send him "three motets, for four, five, or more voices (as you will think fit), which are to serve for an oratorio [that is, a service in an oratory] which is to be given Friday at eight, at the Jesuit Fathers', who have asked me [for them] so insistently. One of these [motets], if it seems fitting to you, could be *Clama ne cesses*, for four voices."[44] It is not known what compositions Carissimi might have sent for this oratory service; some of them might have been pieces that could be termed oratorios in the sense of a musical genre, but a motet on the text of "Clama ne cesses," as requested in the letter, would appear to be nothing like an oratorio.[45]

Considerable differences of opinion regarding the number of Latin oratorios by Carissimi have arisen in musicological writings: none at all, seven, twelve to sixteen, and thirty-three.[46] These discrepancies result from widely varying criteria for applying the term *oratorio*. In an effort to clarify terminology, the present author has examined all known musical compositions that are designated by the term *oratorio* in sources of Italian provenance from the mid-century period.[47] The composers of the works examined are men who worked entirely or primarily in Rome during Carissimi's time; they are treated in this chapter and in the preceding one. The results of that study show that one criterion of the time for calling a dialogue an oratorio was that of its function —virtually any sacred Latin dialogue could have been called an oratorio if it were intended for or performed in an oratory. Since no information has been found regarding the intention or place of performance of Carissimi's Latin works, however, the criterion of function cannot be applied to them today. Nevertheless, other criteria of the time, criteria relating to the oratorio as a musical genre, can be applied to them. "Using these criteria, one may assume that Carissimi's Roman contemporaries would consider one of his Latin dialogues an oratorio (1) if it were a setting of a

44. Friedrich to Carissimi, 29 March 1642, translated in Culley, *German*, p. 188; original printed, ibid., pp. 330–31, and Loschelder, "Carissimi," p. 227.

45. I know of no motet by Carissimi on this text. The introit text—"Clama ne cesses," as printed in Marbach, *Carmina*, p. 325—is neither narrative nor dramatic.

46. See Smither, "Carissimi," for a tabular presentation of the discrepancies in the lists of Carissimi's oratorios found in Bianchi, *Carissimi*, pp. 214–15; Brenet, "Carissimi," pp. 465–66, 470–73; F. Ghisi, "Carissimi," in *MGG*, 2:col. 843; Schering, *Oratorium*, p. 71; Massenkeil, "Oratorische," p. 5; and Massenkeil, "Wiederholungsfiguren," p. 44.

47. Smither, "Oratorio," and Smither, "Carissimi," pp. 66–69.

dramatic text based on a biblical story, the life of a saint, or some other spiritual subject, with dialogue among the personages and with the possible inclusion of narrative passages; (2) if it were either in one or two structural parts; and (3) if its duration were between about sixteen and sixty-four minutes, or quite exceptionally, if it were as brief as eight minutes."[48] Applying these criteria to the classification of Carissimi's Latin dialogues, of which there are at least thirty-three,[49] and using the term *oratorio* in a sense common with Carissimi's Roman contemporaries, one finds that the following eight works could have been called oratorios: (1) *Baltazar*, (2) *Ezechia*, (3) *Diluvium universale*, (4) *Dives malus*, (5) *Jephte*, (6) *Jonas*, (7) *Judicium extremum*, and (8) *Judicium Salomonis*.[50] All eight of these works have texts based on a biblical story, include both dialogues among personages and narrative passages, last from about fifteen to thirty minutes, and—with the possible exception of *Jephte*, which could be viewed as a two-part oratorio—are in one structural part. *Jephte* is by far the best known of these; *Diluvium universale*, incomplete in its manuscript source, is probably the least known, since it is the only one not published in a modern edition. Not only are these eight works the longest of Carissimi's dialogues, they also require the largest performing groups and, except for *Ezechia* and *Judicium Salomonis*, they make the most extensive use of the chorus.

Carissimi's contemporaries would no doubt have considered the works in the following group to be exceptional oratorios: (9) *Abraham et Isaac*, (10) "Duo ex discipulis," (11) *Job*, (12) *Mar-*

48. Smither, "Carissimi," p. 70; my conclusions in that article, and in the present book, regarding which works by Carissimi might be best called oratorios must be considered provisional until the completion of the research of three Carissimi specialists: Dr. Iva Buff, whose catalogue of Carissimi's sacred Latin works is in progress; Professor Beekman C. Cannon, whose book on Carissimi's music is in progress; and Lino Bianchi, whose edition of Carissimi's oratorios (IISM–3) is in progress. A recent publication, Sartori, *Carissimi*, appeared too late for inclusion in the present study.

49. See the list in Bianchi, *Carissimi*, pp. 214–15; that list is reproduced in Smither, "Carissimi," p. 56, table 1.

50. The titles of these works differ in various MS sources; the titles used here are adapted from those of the most recent modern editions. Among the modern editions of these works are the following: (1) IISM–3, vol. 3. (2) ibid., 1:14–34. (3) Beveridge, "Carissimi," p. 531 (chorus "Agite, ruite" only—this work is incomplete in D-brd/Hs: M C270, its only source). (4) IISM–3, vol. 5. (5) DT, vol. 2; CDMI, vol. 4; Carissimi, *Jephte*-B; Carissimi, *Jephte*-C; Carissimi, *Jephte*-W; Carissimi, *Jephthah*-P. (6) DT, vol. 2; CDMI, vol. 5; Carissimi, *Jonah*. (7) IISM–3, vol. 4. (8) DT, vol. 2; CDMI, vol. 5. No. 8 is the work identified as *Judicium Salomonis* I ("A solis ortu") in Bianchi, *Carissimi*, p. 163.

tyres, and (13) *Vir frugi et pater familias*.[51] The characteristics of these five works are similar to those in the first group, except that the approximate durations are between nine and fourteen minutes; two works (numbers 12 and 13) are not based on biblical stories; three works (numbers 11, 12, and 13) do not include narrative passages; and none of the works emphasizes the chorus, as do most of those in the first group. The other Latin works by Carissimi that have at times been classified as oratorios in musicological writings would probably have been referred to as dialogue motets in his time.[52] Although little of Carissimi's music can be dated, at least three of the works listed above (numbers 5, 6, and 10) had been composed by 1649, for they have been found in a French source bearing that date.[53] The following discussion of Carissimi's oratorios summarizes the styles and structures of the thirteen works listed above and classified here as oratorios.

Texts. All the texts of Carissimi's Latin oratorios are anonymous. Their author might have been one of the fathers at the German College or perhaps the composer himself.[54] Eight of the texts are based on stories from the Old Testament and two, on those from the New Testament;[55] one is a "patchwork" text employing frag-

51. Modern editions: (9) IISM-3, 2:1–22; (10) ibid., 6:12–46; (11) ibid., 1:1–13; (12) Beveridge, "Carissimi," p. 595; (13) IISM–3, 2:23–41. No. 9, *Abraham et Isaac*, apparently could not be the same work as the *Sacrificio d'Isacco* performed for Queen Christina of Sweden in 1656 at the German College, as is stated in F. Ghisi, "Carissimi," in *MGG*, 2:col. 843, and in F. Ghisi, "Carissimi," in *Enciclopedia d. mus.*, 1:413. For documentary information about a performance of the *Sacrificio d'Isacco*, which lasted several hours, see Culley, *German*, p. 179. This *Sacrificio*, performed for the queen, was no doubt a *sacra rappresentazione*—as indicated in Schering, *Oratorium*, p. 71, n. 4—rather than an oratorio—as indicated in Culley, *German*, p. 179.

52. Two works, *Historia Davidis et Jonathae* and *Lucifer*—listed in Bianchi, *Carissimi*, pp. 151, 161 and also in Schering, *Oratorium*, p. 71—are not considered here: the first is like an oratorio but of doubtful authenticity (cf. Brenet, "Carissimi," p. 463), and the second is a motet for bass solo and as such is far removed from the oratorio. No. 13, *Vir frugi*, in the above list, is included only with reservations; the MS source bears Carissimi's name, but the work differs considerably from his style.

53. Rose, "Portrait," p. 403.

54. Massenkeil, "Wiederholungsfiguren," p. 60.

55. For a detailed comparison of Carissimi's oratorio texts with their biblical sources, see ibid., "Anhang I." The following is a list of the oratorios (according to the numbers used above), their subjects, and their text sources. *Old Testament stories*: (1) Belshazzar's feast, Dan. 5:1–30; (2) Hezekia's illness and recovery, Isa. 38:1–8 and Pss. 88:32, 117:16–17; (3) the flood, Gen. 6–7:16 (incomplete oratorio); (5) Jephthah, Judg. 11:28–38; (6) Jonah, Jon. 1–3; (8) Solomon's judgment, Ps. 106:3 and 3 Kings 3:16–28; (9) Abraham's sacrifice, Gen. 22:1–18; (11) Job's patience and resignation, Job 4:6, 1:14–21, 5:16–18. *New Testament stories*: (4) the rich man and Lazarus, Luke 16:18–31; (10) two disciples from Emmaus meet Jesus, Luke 24:13–33.

ments from the Old and New Testaments, and two are nonbiblical.[56] The oratorios based on biblical stories generally employ only narrative and dialogue texts, with the narrative passages (sometimes designated *historicus*) set to music for one or more soloists, an ensemble, or a chorus and with the characters in the drama represented by soloists. Only two of the oratorios based on biblical stories include texts of reflection or commentary other than those at the conclusion;[57] the final choruses of the oratorios are usually reflective.

Exact biblical quotations of more than a verse or two are rare, but extended biblical paraphrases are common. The following is a comparison of the beginning of Carissimi's *Jonas* and the parallel passage from the Vulgate; the text of the oratorio is characteristic in its combination of paraphrase and quotation:

Jonas—Carissimi	*Jonas—Vulgate*
HISTORICUS—Cum repleta esset Ninive iniquitate vox peccatorum ejus clamavit de terra ad Dominum, qui locutus est ad Jonam prophetam de coelo dicens:	1:1—Et factus est verbum Domini ad Jonas filius Amathi, dicens:
DEUS—Surge, Jona, surge et vade in Ninivem civitatem grandem et praedica in ea, quia malitia ejus ascendit coram me.	1:2—Surge, et vade in Ninivem civitatem grandem, et praedica in ea: quia ascendit malitia ejus coram me.
CANTUS I [HISTORICUS]—Audivit Jonas vocem Domini et timuit timore magno et descendit in navim euntem in Tharsim, ut fugeret et eriperet se a facie Domini.	1:3—Et surrexit Jonas, ut fugeret in Tharsis a facie Domini, et descendit in Joppen, et invenit navem euntem in Tharsis: et detit naulum ejus, et descendit in eam ut iret cum eis in Tharsis a facie Domini.

Translation

NARRATOR—When Nineveh had become
filled with iniquity, her voice, [that]
of sinners, cried out from earth unto

56. The oratorio with a "patchwork" text is no. 7. Those with nonbiblical texts are nos. 12 and 13.
57. "Duo ex discipulis" (see the chorus "Ite felices") and *Diluvium universale* (see the soprano solo "Age, age, Jupiter," among other reflective passages in this work).

the Lord who spoke from heaven
to the prophet Jonah, saying:

1:1—Now the word of the Lord came
to Jonah the son of Amathi saying:

GOD—Arise, Jonah, arise and go to
Niniveh the great and mighty city
and preach in it, for her wickedness
ascends before me.

1:2—Arise, and go to Niniveh the
great city, and preach in it, for
the wickedness thereof comes up
before me.

NARRATOR—Jonah heard the voice of
the Lord, and he feared with a
great fear and boarded a ship
going to Tharsis to flee and
to remove himself from
the presence of the Lord.

1:3—And Jonah rose up to flee into
Tharsis from the presence of the Lord,
and he went down to Joppe, and found
a ship going to Tharsis. And he paid
the fare thereof, and went down into
it, to go with them to Tharsis from
the presence of the Lord.

The biblical stories are often elaborated by the insertion of original material, sometimes combined with psalms or other scriptural passages that are either narrative or dramatic. The insertions are usually in prose but often in an oratorically ornamented style approaching poetry; occasionally they are poetic, with clear meters and rhyme schemes. The first chorus in *Jonas*, quoted below, is largely an original prose insertion elaborating the narrative of the storm at sea; only its conclusion (in italics) paraphrases the Vulgate Bible (Jonas 1:5):

Jonas—Carissimi

Et proeliabantur venti et
notus et auster et Africanus
fremuerunt contra navim, nubes
et nimbi, fluctus et turbines,
grandines et fulgura, tonitrus
et fulmina, impetu horribili
fremuerunt contra navim
ceciderunt super mare, et
facta est tempestas magna in
mari *et terruit nautas
clamantes ad deos suos et
dicentes:*

And the winds battled, and the
south wind, the African wind, raged
against the ship; thick clouds,
waves and whirlwinds,
hail storms and lightning, thunder
and lightning, with horrible force
raged against the ship and
waged war upon the sea, and
a great tempest was made
on the sea and terrified the sailors
who were crying to their god,
saying:

Near the beginning of *Baltazar*, the long, inserted description of Belshazzar's feast, intended to emphasize the voluptuousness of the scene, is partially in poetic style, with an *a a b* rhyme scheme and four trochees per line:

Baltazar—Carissimi

Inter epulas canori	During the feast let harmonious
exultantes sonent chori	choruses, rejoicing, resound
regis nostri gaudia.	the joys of our king.
Agant plausus convivales,	Let those feasting applaud,
mensae nitent dum regales	while the royal tables glitter,
oneratae dapibus.	burdened with delicacies.
Leves saltus, molles luctas,	Sprightly dancing, pleasant struggles,
blanda suscitet voluptas	seductive desire rises up
ad sonantem cytharam.	at the sound of the lyre.

Seventeenth-century interest in rhetorical devices, as evidenced by the poetry of Marino and his followers, is reflected in the nonbiblical, usually prose insertions in most of Carissimi's oratorios. Repetition is the most commonly employed rhetorical device; its use sometimes results in a free style of poetry—as it does in the first chorus of *Dives malus*, in which the Demons recall the Rich Man's sins and pronounce his sentence:

Dives Malus—Carissimi

Iam satis edisti,	Enough have you eaten,
iam satis bibisti,	enough have you drunk,
iam satis plausisti,	enough have you applauded,
iam satis lusisti,	enough have you played,
iam satis voluptatis hausisti.	enough have you drawn on lust.
Et nunc tibi est moriendum	And now you must die
et pro flagittiis	for your crimes
et pro peccatis.	and for your sins.
Et in chaos horrendum	And you must descend with us
nobiscum descendendum	into horrid chaos
ubi semper torqueberis	where you will be tortured forever
et mille undique repleberis.	and filled with thousands of evils on every side.

Music. Corresponding to the rhetorical aspect of Carissimi's texts is his extensive use of rhetorical figures in music—that is, musical figures conceived as analogous to rhetorical figures.[58] By the time of Carissimi's oratorios, such figures had become well-established elements of Baroque musical style. Around 1600 a comprehensive theory of musical figures (*Figurenlehre*) was established in three treatises by Joachim Burmeister—his *Hypomnematum musicae poeticae* (Rostock, 1599), *Musica autoschediastike* (Rostock, 1601), and *Musica poetica* (Rostock, 1606). Throughout the Baroque era theoretical treatises, particularly those published in Germany, continued to include sections on musical figures and to give the figures Latin and Greek rhetorical terms. Although the theory of figures was essentially a German contribution, the practice of composing with such figures was a part of Baroque style in general. Carissimi was well known for his skillful expression of texts, and his use of figures was an important means to that end. The Italians are said to have called him a "musical orator";[59] Kircher considered him superior to all others in "moving the minds of his listeners to whatever affection he wishes."[60]

Musical-rhetorical figures of repetition are among the most immediately noticeable aspects of Carissimi's oratorios, and they are among the most frequently employed figures in his period. Carissimi occasionally repeats the same group of tones at the same pitch level (a figure called *palillogia* in the musical-rhetorical terminology of the time), as he does in Example V–1 (p. 230) to emphasize King Solomon's threat to cut the child in half; more often, however, he employs figures involving melodic sequence. The most common of the latter is sequential repetition at the interval of a perfect fourth or fifth (a type within the classification of *epizeuxis*)—as illustrated in Example V–1 by the sequential relationship of the two *palillogia* figures, the second of which is stated at the lower fourth. Among other intervals of sequential

58. For a summary of the history and theory of rhetorical figures in music, see A. Schmitz, "Figuren, musikalisch-rhetorische," in *MGG*, 4:cols. 176–83. For studies of rhetorical figures in Carissimi's oratorios, see Massenkeil, "Oratorische," and Massenkeil, "Wiederholungsfiguren"; the latter is based on a portion of the former. The terminology for musical-rhetorical figures used in the present volume is based on that of these two writings by Massenkeil; his terminology represents a synthesis of writings on musical-rhetorical figures that span the entire Baroque era.

59. Johann Valentin Meder to Christoph Raupach, 21 May 1708, translated from Mattheson, *Ehren-Pforte*, p. 220.

60. Translated from Kircher, *Musurgia*, 1:603.

repetition is the one at the upper second (called *climax*), as used in Example V–2 to heighten the tension in the description of the voice of God condemning sinners to eternal damnation. Carissimi often repeats words or phrases in the text for rhetorical effect while employing sequential repetition in the music, as in Examples V–1 and V–2; but the texts themselves frequently exhibit rhetorical parallelism, which Carissimi's music reinforces by sequential repetition. At the beginning of the lament of Jephthah's daughter (Example V–3), the repetitions of "plorate" and "dolete" (set to music as modified *climax* figures) are no doubt the composer's and are not essential to the text; but the text itself exhibits a grammatically parallel construction, and the sounds of the final syllable of each phrase are similar (*homoeoteleuton*, in rhetorical terminology): "Plorate coll*es*,/dolete mont*es*." The composer reinforces this textual parallelism by the *epizeuxis* figure, the melodic sequence at the upper fourth.

EXAMPLE V-1. *Judicium Salomonis*—Carissimi (*DT*, 2:37).

Divide the living child!

EXAMPLE V-2. *Judicium extremum*—Carissimi (IISM-3, 4:49).

O sad and deadly voice . . .

EXAMPLE V-3. *Jephte*—Carissimi (Carissimi, *Jephte*-W, p. 29).

Weep, ye hills, grieve, ye mountains . . .

A particularly striking figure in Carissimi's oratorios, and one frequently employed in the Baroque period for expressions of pathos, is the melodic progression in minor seconds (*pathopoeia*). This figure, descending more frequently than ascending, is employed in the vocal parts, in the continuo, or in both. In Example V–4, a moment of pathos in which Jephthah's daughter offers herself as a sacrifice, the *pathopoeia* expresses the affection first in the vocal line as a progression of two ascending minor seconds and then in the continuo part, where it spans the interval of a descending perfect fourth. In Example V–2 *pathopoeia* is employed in the continuo to express the phrase "O sad and deadly voice" in reference to the Last Judgment. A particularly extensive and highly expressive use of this figure in *Jephte* is the trio or chorus (SSA), "Et ululantes filii Ammon," which uses a long series of consecutive chromatic progressions to convey the affection of the vanquished Ammonites.

EXAMPLE V-4. *Jephte*—Carissimi (Carissimi, *Jephte*-W, p. 26).

. . . behold, I, your only daughter, offer myself as a sacrifice for your victory . . .

Word painting (*hypotyposis*) abounds in Carissimi's music, as it does in his period in general; words denoting motion, direction, and sound are painted with considerable consistency (see Examples V–5, a–d). In expressions of the sense or affection of a word or phrase, coloratura passages are frequently used for joy, glory, or exaltation (see Example V–5e); a particular type of *stile concitato*, a dactylic pattern, expresses excitement of many kinds—including that of war, of the raising of the dead at the Last Judgment, and of applause for King Solomon (see Examples V–5, f–h).

EXAMPLE V-5. Examples of Word Painting—Carissimi.

Example a:
Dives malus (IISM-3, 5:5).

. . . and was taken up by angels . . .

Example b:
Dives malus (IISM-3, 5:81).

Descend with us into hell . . .

Example c:
Judicium extremum (IISM-3, 4:4).

Then with a horrible sound the clanging trumpets . . .

(EXAMPLE V-5, continued)

Example d:
Baltazar (IISM-3, 3:4).

. . . and singing such a song: . . .

Example e:
Ezechia (IISM-3, 1:26).

. . . and he exalted me . . .

Example f:
Jephte (Carissimi, *Jephte*-W, p. 11).

Flee, yield, impious ones . . .

Example g:
Judicium extremum (IISM-3, 4:20).

Arise, dead ones . . .

(EXAMPLE V-5, continued)

Example h:
Judicium Salomonis (DT 2:47).

... applaud for Solomon.

Important in the general structure of Carissimi's oratorios are repetitions of instrumental ritornellos, choruses, and solo passages in aria style: in *Dives malus*, for instance, virtually the same brief ritornello is used at three widely separated points in the work, the first two occurrences following similar choral passages;[61] in *Judicium extremum* the chorus "Quam magna," which first appears about the middle of the work,[62] is repeated as the final chorus; in "Duo ex discipulis" the first chorus, "Ite felices," is repeated after an intervening narration and dialogue;[63] and in *Baltazar* the chorus "Regi nostro complaudamus" is repeated after a long interval during which a sinfonia, chorus, sinfonia, and soprano solo are heard.[64] The brief oratorio *Job* is unified by a short refrain in aria style, "Sit nomen Domini," that recurs eight times in the course of the work.[65] In these instances, selected from many, both the same music and the same text return for the purpose of unification. There are other instances, however, in which the text returns with new music, and still others in which the music returns with new text. In *Jephte* the first part of the text of the bass solo "Fugite, cedite" is used again at the beginning of the following chorus, with new music but with some of the same rhythmic figures.[66] Repetitions of text with new music and of music with new text are found in the victory-celebration section of *Jephte*, to be pointed out in the discussion of that work.

Solo passages in Carissimi's oratorios are usually assigned to characters in the drama or to the *historicus*; occasionally, however,

61. IISM-3, 5:46, 86, 114.
62. Ibid., 4:27.
63. Ibid., 6:13, 26.
64. Ibid., 3:9, 24.
65. For the first occurrence see ibid., 1:2.
66. Carissimi, *Jephte*-W, pp. 9, 11.

solos have reflective texts, with no personages identified, which are similar to the lines of a commenting chorus in ancient Greek drama.[67] The solo styles range from relatively simple recitative through a more expressive *recitativo arioso* to a clearly structured aria style. Although Carissimi sets some passages of considerable length in only one of the three styles, he more often slips from one to another within a single solo to express changing attitudes in the text. The simple recitative consists of numerous repeated notes and triadic skips in the melody, a slowly moving basso continuo, and a primarily consonant relationship between the two parts. This type of recitative, which might well be termed narrative style,[68] is frequently used for the *historicus* (Example V–6a), although it is occasionally used for narrative passages sung by the characters in the drama (Example V–6b).

EXAMPLE V-6. Examples of Simple Recitative—Carissimi.

Example a:
Baltazar (IISM-3, 3:3).

Belshazzar, most opulent king of the Assyrians, for his thousand courtiers [prepared a splendid banquet].

Example b:
Judicium Salomonis (DT, 2:32).

I and this woman dwelt in one house and I was delivered of a child with her in the chamber . . .

67. For example, see "O vox minimum" and "O vox tristis" of *Judicium extremum,* IISM-3, 4:48–49.
68. *Narrative* is one of G. B. Doni's terms for this style. Cf. Doni's *Annotazioni sopra il Compendio de' generi, e de' modi della musica* (Rome: Andrea Fei, 1640), pp. 60–62; Palisca, *Baroque,* p. 33; and Witzenmann, *Mazzocchi,* p. 60.

In the more expressive *recitativo arioso* style the vocal line includes more phrases in melodic sequence and more skips of augmented and diminished intervals than it does in the simple, narrative style; the continuo line is similar to that of the simple style or slightly more active; and suspensions and unprepared dissonances are common between the continuo and vocal lines. The longer arioso passages often employ one or more phrases that function as a refrain, sometimes in aria style. The most expressive arioso sections occur at emotionally climactic points: in *Jephte*, for instance, Jephthah's moving lament, "Heu, heu mihi" (for its beginning see Example V–7), is an outstanding illustration. Other and longer examples are the lament of Jephthah's daughter (for its beginning see Example V–3); Jonah's prayer, "Justus es, Domine,"

EXAMPLE V-7. *Jephte*—Carissimi (Carissimi, *Jephte*-W, p. 24).

Alas! My daughter, alas, you have deceived me, my only daughter, . . .

which he utters from inside the great fish in *Jonas*;[69] and Hezakia's prayer, "Obsecro, Domine," in *Ezechia*.[70] These last three passages in arioso style are similar in that all use repeated material functioning as a refrain and all are intensely emotional lamentations in several sections. In the examples from *Jonas* and *Ezechia*, a vocal refrain followed by an instrumental ritornello marks the divisions between the sections; in that from *Jephte*, as pointed out below, an echo *a 2* concludes the first three sections, and a chorus concludes the last one. Although arioso style is usually given to characters in the drama, it is occasionally given to the *historicus*, especially when he describes a particularly emotional scene.

Aria style, with its clearly metrical and often dancelike vocal line and basso continuo, is frequently employed for brief passages

69. *DT*, 2:110–13.
70. *IISM*-3, 1:18–22.

of two to ten measures within a solo-chorus complex[71] or at the conclusion of a recitative.[72] Longer independent sections, which may be called arias but are not so called in the sources, occur in most of the oratorios. The arias range from about fifteen to forty measures in length. The shortest arias tend to be through-composed, with brief phrases immediately repeated but without clearly sectional structure. For the longer, sectional arias the most common structures are AB, ABB′, and strophic variations; the ABA structure does not appear in Carissimi's oratorios, although it occasionally appears in his secular cantatas.[73] The ABB′ structure is prominent for arias in oratorios and operas until the end of the seventeenth century,[74] when the da capo aria begins to dominate. When the ABB′ structure is used in Carissimi's oratorios, the B′ is usually a transposition to the perfect fourth or fifth and an expansion and elaboration of the first B. In *Ezechia* the long, florid aria in which Hezekiah praises the Lord, "Dextera Domini fecit,"[75] illustrates the ABB′ form with an extensively elaborated and expanded B′ section. An example of the AB form in an aria is the brief, warlike bass solo "Fugite, cedite impii" in *Jephte*.[76]

A characteristic strophic-variation aria in the oratorios consists of three strophes—that is, three statements of the same or approximately the same continuo line supporting melodies that may or may not be similar; the strophes are sometimes separated by an instrumental ritornello. The aria "En vitae suprema" in *Dives malus* (with an ABB′C form for each strophe) is typical,[77] as is "Aquis arva demerguntur" in *Diluvium universale*;[78] in the last-named aria the third strophe and its ritornello are followed by a through-composed section. Of special interest is the strophic-variation aria *a* 2, "Sat mensas mille" in *Dives malus*, in which two Demons recite some of the Rich Man's sins and pronounce his sentence.[79] This aria consists of five strophes, each only five measures long including the two-measure instrumental ritornello at

71. For example, see *Baltazar*, in IISM-3, 3:31, 41, 51.
72. For example, see *Job*, ibid., 1:1.
73. Rose, "Carissimi," p. 208.
74. For a discussion of this form, where it is considered so prominent in the period that it is termed *Seicentoform* (probably an exaggeration), see Lorenz, *Scarlatti*, 1:213–18.
75. IISM-3, 1:25.
76. Carissimi, *Jephte*-W, p. 9.
77. IISM-3, 5:56.
78. D-brd/Hs: M C 270, p. 365.
79. IISM-3, 5:47.

the cadence and each stated in a different major key (F, G, A, C, and D). The first, third, and fourth strophes are sung by a soprano; the others, by a tenor.[80] All five strophes begin with an ascending sixteenth-note run spanning a perfect fifth, a type of aria beginning that is fairly common in the period and is found several times in Carissimi's oratorios.[81] Functioning as a striking conclusion to this aria is an ominous pronouncement of the Rich Man's sentence: that he be tortured in hell. He is sentenced in a chantlike recitation style ("Ubi ab igne vocaberis") on one tone, in triple meter, with a descending minor-third cadence; the same passage is chanted twice by a soprano—first on e″, then on d″. Similar to "Sat mensas mille" in its use of strophic variation with changing keys is the arioso section in *Baltazar* where Daniel interprets the mysterious handwriting on the wall.[82] The three brief strophes proceed in successively higher keys: F, G, and A. Each strophe begins with Daniel's pronunciation, in triple meter, of one of the three enigmatic words ("Mane," "Thecel," and "Phares"), after which the meter changes to duple for the word's interpretation.

Ensembles in Carissimi's oratorios have several functions. Duets represent two characters in the drama, such as the "Nos autem sperabamus" of the two disciples in "Duo ex discipulis"[83] and the "O, o felix" of Abraham and Isaac in *Abraham et Isaac*;[84] duets also have a narrative function, as in "Tunc, iubente rege" of *Baltazar*,[85] "Et clagebant tubae" of *Jephte*,[86] and the duets in *Ezechia*;[87] and duets are used to set reflective texts in chorus-solo-soli complexes such as the one that ends *Baltazar*.[88] The voices of the duets generally move either in parallel thirds and sixths or in imitation, and the characteristic melodic and rhythmic styles are those of an aria. A curious exception to the normal style is a six-

---

80. Cf. ibid, where the editor divides the soprano solos between two singers, cantus I and II, and thus interprets this as an aria *a 3* (S, S, T); that division, however, is not in the MS source, F/Pn: Vm¹ 1476, fol. 16v.

81. For other examples of this aria beginning in Carissimi's oratorios, see the following arias, mentioned above: "Aquis arva demerguntur" in *Diluvium*; "Quid fugacius" in *Foelicitas*; and "Fugite, cedite impii" in *Jephte*. For this aria beginning in a work by another composer, see "Frena il pianto" in the anonymous *Daniele* (Torchi, *Arte*, 5:157), discussed in chapter 4.

82. IISM-3, 3:38–39.

83. Ibid., 6:22.

84. Ibid., 2:7.

85. Ibid., 3:40.

86. Carissimi, *Jephte*-W, p. 8.

87. All the narrative passages of this work are duets: IISM-3, 1:14, 15, 17, 24.

88. Ibid., 3:42, 45, 50, 55.

measure recitative for the two disciples in "Duo ex discipulis" (for the beginning of the recitative, see Example V–8).

EXAMPLE V-8. "Duo ex discipulis"—Carissimi (IISM-3, 6:36).

Was not our heart burning within us . . .

The chorus plays a more prominent role in Carissimi's oratorios than in most of those of his contemporaries. Its function is often to represent a group of personages in the drama—such as the choruses of Demons in *Dives malus*, the Sailors in *Jonas*, and the Just and the Sinners in *Judicium extremum*. As mentioned above, the chorus also functions as a narrator; examples of this function are "Transivit ergo Jephte," which tells of the battle in *Jephte*,[89] and "Et proeliabuntur venti" (see the text quoted above), which describes the violent storm at sea in *Jonas*.[90] Another function is similar to that of the chorus in ancient Greek tragedy, which reflects on the action and sometimes clarifies the meaning of the drama. Although most reflective and moralizing choruses are found at the ends of the oratorios, they occasionally occur within a work, as does "Ite felices" in "Duo ex discipulis."[91] All the oratorios except *Job* close with a chorus.[92] Most of the concluding choruses praise God or the central character; two oratorios conclude with moralistic choruses (*Baltazar* and *Dives malus*); two, with choruses restating reflective ideas that have just been expressed (*Jephte* and "Duo ex discipulis"); and one, with a chorus that constitutes the final episode of the story (*Jonas*, the chorus of Ninivites).

The choruses range in size from *a 3*[93] to triple choruses *a 12*.

89. Carissimi, *Jephte*-W, p. 6.
90. *DT*, 2:86.
91. IISM-3, 6:13, 26.
92. *Job* closes with a duet (which begins as a trio) of personages (see ibid., 1:9–13).
93. Trios virtually always function as choruses, rather than as a group of three individuals. An exception is the trio in *Job*, "Quae me vox agitat" (ibid., 1:9).

In a few of the works, the same voices are required for the choruses as for the solo roles. *Judicium Salomonis*, for example, requires four soloists for the personages (the two Women, S,S; the *Historicus*, A; and Solomon, B), and the only chorus in the composition, the concluding number, is limited to those four voices. Such a limitation, found only in works in which the chorus is little used, suggests that the choral parts were intended to be performed by the four soloists.[94] In about two-thirds of the oratorios, however, more voices are required for the chorus than for the solo passages. The works requiring the greatest number of voices are those making the most frequent use of choruses, and they are also the longest oratorios: *Baltazar* (SSATB), *Jephte* (SSSATB), *Jonas* and *Dives malus* (double choruses: SATB-SATB), *Judicium extremum* (triple chorus: SSATB-ATB-ATB), and *Diluvium universale* (triple chorus: SS-SSATB-SSATB).[95]

Chordal style prevails in Carissimi's choruses, the rhythms of which are usually based on the accents of the text; fugal texture plays only an incidental role. In the double and triple choruses an overlapping antiphonal style is used, often in quick alternation, with the entering chorus beginning on the final pitches of the concluding one, as in "Et proeliabantur venti" in *Jonas*.[96] The double and triple choruses are also used in imitation, as in "Tunc horribili sonitu" of *Judicium extremum*.[97] The harmonic style of the choruses, and of the oratorios in general, tends to be simple and diatonic. Carissimi employed all the harmonic resources of his time, including a fairly strong fuctional tonality with little modulation, in the oratorios; he is economical in his use of chromaticism, however, which is employed primarily to express the pathos of the text, as indicated above.[98]

Instrumental parts other than the basso continuo are written in the sources of only nine of the thirteen oratorios; *Jephte* is exceptional among the longer compositions for the absence of

94. In addition to *Judicium Salomonis*, the limitation is found in *Ezechia*, *Martyres*, and "Duo ex discipuli."

95. The two-soprano group in the latter triple chorus might be intended for soloists, since its style is more elaborate than that of the other groups.

96. *DT*, 2:86.

97. IISM-3, 4:5.

98. For a study of Carissimi's harmonic style in the oratorios, see Müller-Blattau, "Carissimi."

instruments.[99] The sources usually do not indicate the instruments to be used but show only that two instruments in the soprano range and sometimes a bass instrument separate from that of the continuo are required. The two upper parts are always written in the G clef, and whenever an instrument is named, it is a violin;[100] the bass instrument is never designated. Except *Dives malus*, all the oratorios using instruments begin with a sinfonia ranging in length from about sixteen measures (*Jonas* and *Ezechia*) to about forty measures with two or more contrasting sections (*Baltazar* and *Judicium Salomonis*). The instruments are used for brief ritornellos within and at the ends of arias, arioso sections, and choruses; they never support the voice in recitatives and rarely do so in sections of arioso or aria style. The instruments are frequently used simultaneously with the chorus, either to double some of the voices or to fill out the sonority.

Jephte. Carissimi's best-known Latin oratorio, *Jephte*, is among the greatest oratorios of the seventeenth century. It is known to have been composed by 1649, because one of its French sources bears that date[101] and because Athanasius Kircher describes part of it in his treatise *Musurgia universalis* (Rome, 1650). Information is lacking, however, regarding either an occasion for which it was composed or the place where it was first performed.

   Jephte's anonymous text is drawn from an Old Testament story (Judg. 11:28–38). This oratorio seems clearly to have been conceived as a one-part work, as are all the rest of Carissimi's Latin oratorios, and thus seems intended to be performed straight through, without a pause for a sermon at the midpoint. Nevertheless, one may subdivide the work on the basis of dramatic action into two large sections, the first with three subsections emphasizing optimistic affections and the second with two subsections of lamentation. The first subsection, that of Jephthah's vow, quotes and paraphrases Judg. 11:28–31. Jephthah (T), who is about to lead

99. Although some of the sources of *Jephte* include instrumental parts, the most reliable ones do not (Beat, "Carissimi," p. 342). In addition to *Jephte*, the only oratorios without instrumental parts in their sources are nos. 9, 10, 11, and 13 of the above list. The absence of instrumental parts in the sources, however, would not preclude the use of instruments to play sinfonie, to double the choral parts, and to improvise from the basso continuo part.
   100. See, for instance, the MS of *Divitis* in F/Pn: Vm¹ 1476, fol. 2.
   101. See above, n. 53.

FIGURE V-4. Beginning of Carissimi's *Jephte*.
(Reproduced by permission of D-brd/Hs: MC 270.)

the Israelites in war against the Ammonites, makes a vow to God: "If the Lord will deliver the children of Ammon into my hands, whosoever shall first come forth out of my house to meet me I will offer to the Lord in holocaust." The second subsection (beginning "Transivit ergo Jephte") is that of the battle, in which the Israelites are victorious. At the beginning and ending of this subsection, a few fragments from Judg. 11:32–33 are quoted, but most of the subsection consists of a nonbiblical narrative-dramatic interpolation describing the battle, quoting the Israelites who cry out for the enemy to flee, and commenting on the lamentation and humiliation of the defeated Ammonites. The third subsection ("Cum autem victor Jephte") constitutes a kind of victory celebration. At the beginning the text quotes and paraphrases Judg. 11:34, describing Jephthah's victorious return to his home; his only Daughter (S) is the first person to meet him, and she greets him joyfully with timbrels and dancing. Except for the opening narrative passage this subsection consists entirely of freely invented texts inserted into the biblical story to emphasize and dramatize the rejoicing of the Daughter and of the chorus. At the beginning of the second large section ("Cum vidisset Jephte"), the affection changes drastically as Jephthah, in a deeply moving lament and dialogue with his Daughter, reveals to her the vow that will force him to sacrifice her. The dialogue quotes and paraphrases Judg. 11:35–38, and it closes with the request of Jephthah's Daughter to go with her companions into the mountains for two months to lament her virginity. The final subsection ("Abiit ergo in montes") consists of the lament of the Daughter and her companions; except for the brief narrative introduction the section is entirely nonbiblical. The oratorio's final chorus concludes the lament.

The narrative passages, usually marked *Historicus* in the sources but sometimes left unmarked, are given a variety of settings. Of the seven narrative passages four are written for soloists (one each for S and B, and two for A), one for a duet or two-part chorus (SS), one for a trio or three-part chorus (SSA), and one for a quartet or four-part chorus (SSAB). The distribution of the narrative passages among two or more soloists and/or choruses is found in a number of Carissimi's other oratorios (*Baltazar*, *Diluvium universale*, *Dives malus*, "Duo ex discipulis," and *Jonas*), but such a distribution is unusual for the oratorio in general during this period. More characteristic would be the consistent use of one voice throughout an oratorio for the narrative passages.

As is often the case with oratorio sources in this period, those of Carissimi's *Jephte* do not always distinguish between choruses and ensembles of soloists. It would seem appropriate, however, to perform at least four of the numbers in *Jephte* by a chorus: "Transivit ergo Jephte," "Fugite, cedite impii," "Cantemus omnes Domino," and "Plorate filii Israel." Only the first and fourth of these numbers are marked with the word *Chorus* in a manuscript source.[102] Nevertheless, all four are six-voice settings (SSSATB) and are stylistically similar; thus it would seem reasonable to use the same performing group for them all. For reasons of style and function, five other numbers would lend themselves to choral performance, although none is marked by the word *Chorus* in a manuscript source: "Et clangebant tubae" (SS), "Et ululantes filii Ammon" (SSA), "Hymnum cantemus Domino" (SS), "Abiit ergo in montes" (SSAB), and the echo parts (SS) of the Daughter's lament, "Plorate colles."[103] Of the nine numbers just mentioned, particularly interesting are three of those in the battle section of the work—"Et clangebant tubae" (with its militaristic, triadic fanfare lines in imitation), "Fugite, cedite impii" (with its emphasis on the dactylic *concitato* pattern mentioned above and illustrated in Example V–5f), and "Et ululantes filii Ammon" (a highly chromatic number, mentioned above as an example of the rhetorical figure *pathopoeia*, expressing the weeping of the defeated Ammonites). Also of special interest is the oratorio's final chorus, "Plorate filii Israel," with its affective dissonances in the section beginning "in carmine doloris," a chorus that provides a fitting conclusion to the oratorio's final section of lamentation. (Handel used this chorus as a model and borrowed elements from it for the chorus "Hear Jacob's God" in his oratorio *Samson*; this would appear to be the only borrowing from Carissimi in Handel's oratorios.)

The scene of the victory celebration is a convincing expression of the joy of Jephthah's Daughter, and it is also of interest from the structural standpoint. The main body of the celebration scene consists of six sections, in which there are both the return of a

102. For the markings in the MS sources, see Carissimi, *Jephte*-W, in which the indications in the various sources are clearly distinguished from editorial additions.

103. Cf. ibid., where these are editorially marked "Chorus ad lib." Another number with the same editorial marking is "Fugite, cedite impii" for bass; but this number is marked "Basso solo" in one of the MS sources, and it would therefore seem best performed with a soloist rather than a chorus.

section of text with new music and the return of a musical passage with new text, as may be seen in the following outline:

Form	Sig.	Character	Text Incipit
A		Daughter	"Incipite in tympanis"
B	3/2	Daughter	"Hymnum cantemus"
C		Daughter	"Laudemus regem coelitum"
D	3/2	à 2 (SS)	"Hymnum cantemus"
C'		Daughter	"Cantate mecum Domino"
E		Chorus (SSSATB)	"Cantemus omnes Domino"

All the passages sung by the Daughter are in aria style. Sections C and C' are melodically similar but textually different; B and D are similar in text and meter but different in melody and texture. Sections A, B, and C could be interpreted as a single aria in three sections—the second two of which conclude with brief, transposed repetitions of material; also sections D and C' conclude with comparable repetitions of material. Although it is perhaps an exaggeration of the importance of these concluding repetitions to interpret sections B through C' as four small examples of the abb' form common in Carissimi's oratorios, these sections are not far removed from that form.

A procedure that Carissimi used for the expression of contrasting affections is the "mutation of mode" (*mutatio toni* or *modi*). Athanasius Kircher considers mutation of mode to be a technique of strong emphasis, and he illustrates it by printing an example from a cantata by Carissimi in which the word *ridere* ("to laugh"), set in the major form of a scale, is followed immediately by *piangere* (to weep) in the minor form.[104] A similar mutation takes place in Carissimi's *Jephte* at the change from the victory celebration, predominantly in G and C major, to the tragic episode that follows, predominantly in A minor. Kircher found this moving scene and its mutation of mode worthy of special mention in his *Musurgia*: "In [*Jephte*], after victories, triumphs, and ceremonies, Jephte's daughter approaches him with instruments and dances of all sorts to congratulate him. In a musical style called recitative, Carissimi gives expression to the bewildered father with singular genius and piercing tones. Jephte is suddenly transported

104. Kircher, *Musurgia*, 1:673. The example is reproduced in Massenkeil, "Oratorische," p. 102.

from joy to sadness and lamentation as his daughter unexpectedly runs toward him, because the irrevocable decree of the vow must fall on her for this fateful greeting. Carissimi achieves this transition to the opposite affection beautifully with a mutation of mode."[105] The tragic mood of this section is conveyed not only by the mutation of mode but also by the highly effective arioso style of Jephthah's lament. What Kircher calls "piercing tones" are no doubt the harsh dissonances, especially those approached by leap, that are characteristic of the lament, the beginning of which is shown in Example V–7 (p. 236). The first section of the lament returns after brief passages sung by the Daughter and Jephthah. The dramatically significant point in the dialogue between the father and daughter, when the latter offers herself in holocaust because of her father's vow, has been mentioned above (see Example V–4, p. 231) for its use of the figure *pathopoeia*.

Although the dramatic climax of this oratorio occurs early in the second large section, the musical climax occurs later—during the Daughter's lament, which is among the most moving passages in all of Carissimi's oratorios. The beginning of this lament, in arioso style, has been discussed in terms of its use of the figures of *climax* and *epizeuxis* (see Example V–3, p. 231). The Daughter's lament divides into four episodes, each of which is concluded by an ensemble or chorus. The first two of these concluding passages are similar, and they are polyphonic echoes of the immediately preceding cadential passages sung by the Daughter; the third concluding passage is also an echo of the Daughter's cadential passage, but it is different from, and more elaborate than, the earlier ones. The last concluding unit is the final chorus, presumably intended to be understood as sung by the Daughter's companions.

Some Contemporaries of Carissimi

When one thinks of the oratorio in mid-seventeenth-century Italy, one almost automatically thinks of Carissimi. The extensive writ-

105. Kircher, *Musurgia*, 1:603, translated in Palisca, *Baroque*, p. 115. I am grateful to Dr. Eva Buff for calling to my attention that in one of the several French MSS of *Jephte* (F/Pn: Rés. F 934a) the two large sections are labeled as parts I and II. This could imply a pause, perhaps for a sermon, between the Daughter's victory celebration and Jephthah's anguished reaction. Such a pause is of doubtful authenticity, however, for it would destroy

ings about his oratorios, as well as the numerous modern editions and recordings, have conditioned our thinking in this respect. To be sure, Carissimi is among the outstanding composers of his time, and some of his Latin oratorios are truly great works. Nevertheless, to view the Latin oratorio of his time only through his works is to underestimate the importance of a number of his contemporaries, some of whom are treated briefly below. Detailed comparisons between Carissimi's oratorios and those of his contemporaries must await more modern editions and studies of the latter.

Domenico and Virgilio Mazzocchi

Seven compositions by Domenico Mazzocchi, most of which are called dialogues in their source, may be classified as oratorios in the sense of a musical genre; they are comparable in length and certain other respects to Carissimi's shorter oratorios. The title page of the book in which they were published—*Sacrae concertationes binis, ternis, quinis, octonis, novenisque vocibus, a Dominico Mazzocchio pro oratoriis modis musicis concinnatae* ("Sacred Concertos in Two, Three, Five, Eight, and Nine Voices, Composed in Musical Ways by Domenico Mazzocchi for Oratories," Rome, 1664)[106]—clearly indicates that the book was intended for use in oratories. Thus all the works in the book could be called oratorios in the general functional sense, but most of them lack the essential traits of the oratorio as a genre. Although this book was not published until 1664, the music is probably from an earlier period, perhaps from the 1630s.[107] Domenico Mazzocchi is not known to have directed performances at Crocifisso, but his brother, Virgilio, was the director of the music there throughout Lent of 1634. Since it is known that the two brothers cooperated professionally and since the texts of Domenico's eight works would be appropriate for the Lenten services at Crocifisso, it is possible that Virgilio performed some of his brother's works there in addition to his own.

---

the effect that Kircher describes here as sudden—and it would seem likely that Kircher heard the work under Carissimi's direction.

106. This book is an unicum in I/Ls. (Maggini, *Lucca*, pp. 154–55.) For a modern edition by Wolfgang Witzenmann, see *ConM*, vol. 3. I gratefully acknowledge the help of Dr. Witzenmann, who made the manuscript of his edition available to me prior to its publication.

107. For support of the early date and the possible use of Domenico's works at Crocifisso, see Witzenmann, *Mazzocchi*, pp. 24–26.

The seven compositions under consideration here are grouped together in the print as numbers thirteen through nineteen:[108] (13) *Dialogo del Prodigo* ("Dialogue of the Prodigal [Son]"), (14) *Dialogo di Lazaro* ("Dialogue of Lazarus"), (15) *Dialogo di Gioseppe* ("Dialogue of Joseph [and His Brothers]"), (16) *Dialogo della Maddalena* ("Dialogue of the Magdalene"), (17) *Dialogo dell'Apocalisse* ("Dialogue of the Apocalypse"), (18) *Lamento di David* ("Lament of David"), and (19) *Concilio de' Farisei* ("Council of the Pharisees"). The texts of all are based on biblical passages: two, on the Old Testament (nos. 15 and 18) and the others, on the New Testament. Four of the works are based on biblical stories,[109] and the other three are patchwork texts made up of fragments from several books of the Bible.[110] The biblical sources are sometimes literally quoted but more often shortened and paraphrased. Unlike Carissimi's texts these seldom employ original insertions, and rhetorical figures are rare; only one of the works, *Lazaro*, closes with a nonbiblical text.

The solo styles in Domenico Mazzocchi's oratorios range from simple recitative to highly expressive arioso; aria style is rare and tends to last for only a few measures.[111] Among the more expressive moments of these oratorios are David's lament, "Considera Israel," near the end of *David* and Mary Magdalene's lament, "Tulerunt Dominum meum," following the opening chorus of *Maddalena*. The latter lament, in arioso style, begins with a sequentially repeated phrase (see Example V–9) reminiscent of the lament "Plorate colles" in Carissimi's *Jephte* (Example V–3, p. 231). Various musical-rhetorical figures, including repetitive figures such as this one, are found in Domenico Mazzocchi's oratorios, but they are by no means as prominent as in Carissimi's works.

Ensembles and choruses are used for groups of characters as

108. No. 9 of the print, *Dialogo della cantica*, based on a modification of passages from the Canticle of Canticles, is less dramatic, shorter, and less like an oratorio than the works listed.

109. For text sources see Witzenmann, *Mazzocchi*, pp. 242–43. Biblical stories: (13) Luke 15:11–32; (14) John 11:1–43; (15) Gen. 37:2–33; (18) 2 Kings 1:1–27.

110. Patchwork texts: (16) Matt. 28:1–10, Mark 16:1–8, Luke 24:1–10, John 20:1–13, Cant. 8:7; (17) Apoc. 15:2–4, Ps. 95:11, Jer. 49:13, Apoc. 19:1, 6, 7; (19) John 11:47–50, Luke 23:2, Jer. 11:19, Wisd. 2:20—no. 19 concludes with a text from the sixth responsory for matins of Holy Saturday.

111. For a discussion of the style and structure of these works, see Witzenmann, *Mazzocchi*, pp. 97–113.

They have taken away my Lord and I know not where they have laid him.

well as for narrative and reflective texts. Chrous sizes range from *a 3* to double-chorus *a 9*. Both the chorus and the fugal writing are somewhat more prominent here than in Carissimi's smaller oratorios. The choruses tend to be harmonically as simple as Carissimi's, but they are more strongly rooted in the church modes and less oriented toward functional tonality.

No instruments other than the basso continuo are used in these compositions. *Prodigo* includes an indication, during the festive scene of the return of the Prodigal Son, that a sinfonia may be played, but none is provided. In *David* a note at the beginning of the lament section indicates that the *lira*—probably the *lira da gamba*—may realize the continuo part.[112]

Virgilio Mazzocchi (1597–1646), maestro di cappella at St. Peter's from 1629 until his death, was in charge of the music at Crocifisso throughout Lent of 1634.[113] Although he would have needed oratorios or motets for five Fridays of Lent, only one extant composition of his, "Ego ille quondam," is called an orato-

112. The use of the *lira* to accompany a lament was also noted above in the Italian oratorios attributed to Marco Marazzoli and Luigi Rossi.

113. For archival documentation see Alaleona, *Oratorio*, p. 340.

rio in its manuscript source.[114] The same work is called both a dialogue and a concerto by Domenico Mazzocchi, who includes it in his *Sacrae concertationes* and states in the preface of that publication that it is his brother's "last and celebrated dialogue which he composed shortly before the end of his life."[115] In the printed source the work bears the title *Fumo è la nostra vita* ("Our Life Is Smoke"). The text of this oratorio begins with a quotation from Job 16:13 and reflects on the transitory nature of life. There are no personages in the work, as it is entirely reflective; it is cast in one large structural part, unified by repeated sections. Composed for two violins (deleted from the printed version), organ continuo, and eight voices, the work consists of solo passages in recitative and arioso styles, duets, and double choruses (SATB-SATB).

Marco Marazzoli

Marazzoli, whose biography is briefly sketched in chapter 4, was among Rome's best-known composers—primarily for his operas, cantatas, and oratorios. In addition to his oratorios with Italian texts, he is known to have composed five oratorios with Latin texts,[116] works similar in length and some aspects of style to those by D. Mazzocchi. The manuscript source that includes the Latin oratorios by Marazzoli bears no designations of genres, but from their texts and musical settings the five Latin works considered here may be readily classified as oratorios.[117] Although the incomplete extant records of musicians active at Crocifisso do not name Marazzoli, it has been inferred from the nature of these oratorios that he directed the services there for all the Fridays of at least one Lenten season.[118] Four of these oratorios—"Erat quidem

114. I/Bc: Q 45, fols. 155–68. Virgilio Mazzocchi's "Beatum Franciscum" in the same MS (fols. 73–77)—described as an oratorio in Schering, *Oratorium*, pp. 83–84—is not like an oratorio in the sense of a musical genre and is not called an oratorio in its source.

115. Translated from the preface to the publication printed in Maggini, *Lucca*, p. 154.

116. For a study of Marazzoli's Latin oratorios, with music examples, see Grace, "Marazzoli." These Latin oratorios are anonymous in their source (I/Rvat; Chigi Q. VIII. 188), but they have been reliably attributed to Marco Marazzoli. For full information on the attribution and for a description of the MS, see Witzenmann, "Marazzoli," pp. 65–68; and Grace, "Marazzoli," pp. 6–15, 94–97. I gratefully acknowledge the assistance of Dr. Michael Grace, who generously supplied me with information and transcriptions of music while his dissertation on Marazzoli's oratorios was in progress.

117. For a discussion of the classification of these works, see Witzenmann, "Marazzoli," pp. 63–64; and Grace, "Marazzoli," pp. 103–26.

118. Witzenmann, "Marazzoli," pp. 63–64.

languidus" (on the story of the cure at the pool of Bethsaida, John 5:1ff.), "Homo erat paterfamilias" (on the parable of the vine dressers, Matt. 21:33ff.), "Venit Jesus in civitatem Samariae" (on the story of the Samaritan woman, John 4:5ff.), and "Erat quidam languens" (on the raising of Lazarus, John 11:1ff.)—use narrative-dramatic texts based on the Gospel passages read in Mass on the first four Fridays of Lent. These texts make them perfectly appropriate for the second of the two oratorios required for each service at Crocifisso on those days. Another composition, "O mestissimi Jesu," in the same manuscript is nondramatic and is not an oratorio in the sense of the genre; this work would be appropriate for performance on Good Friday. If the works were performed at Crocifisso, it would no doubt have been prior to 1650, for after that date a different composer was used for each of the Fridays of Lent. Since some of the stories on which these oratorios are based are the same as those that Maugars mentions in his report of 1639, it has been suggested that these Latin oratorios by Marazzoli were composed for the Lenten season of 1639 and were among those that Maugars heard at Crocifisso.[119] A fifth oratorio by Marazzoli, "Erat fames in terra Canaan" (on the story of Joseph and his brothers, Gen. 42:5ff.), in the same manuscript, is a narrative-dramatic work possibly performed at Crocifisso, but its position within the Lenten season is not clear.

The texts of these five oratorios treat their biblical sources freely; sometimes they quote brief passages, but more often they rearrange phrases, modify the vocabulary, and freely paraphrase the Bible to increase the dramatic element. All the texts employ a narrator, called *Textus* or *Testo*. Three of the texts ("Erat quidem languidus," "Homo paterfamilias," and "Venit Jesus in civitatem Samariae") are closer to those of Carissimi's oratorios than to D. Mazzocchi's in that they employ nonbiblical insertions. In these works insertions are used to expand the dramatic dialogue sung by soloists representing personages and to provide passages of reflection and commentary sung by the chorus. In addition to reflecting and commenting on the action, the chorus represents groups of personages in the drama. The final choruses plea for mercy, praise God, and warn sinners of the consequences of their acts.[120]

119. Grace, "Marazzoli," p. 94.
120. The final choruses of two of the oratorios ("Erat quidam languens Lazarus" and "Erat quidem languidus") do not have texts in the MS.

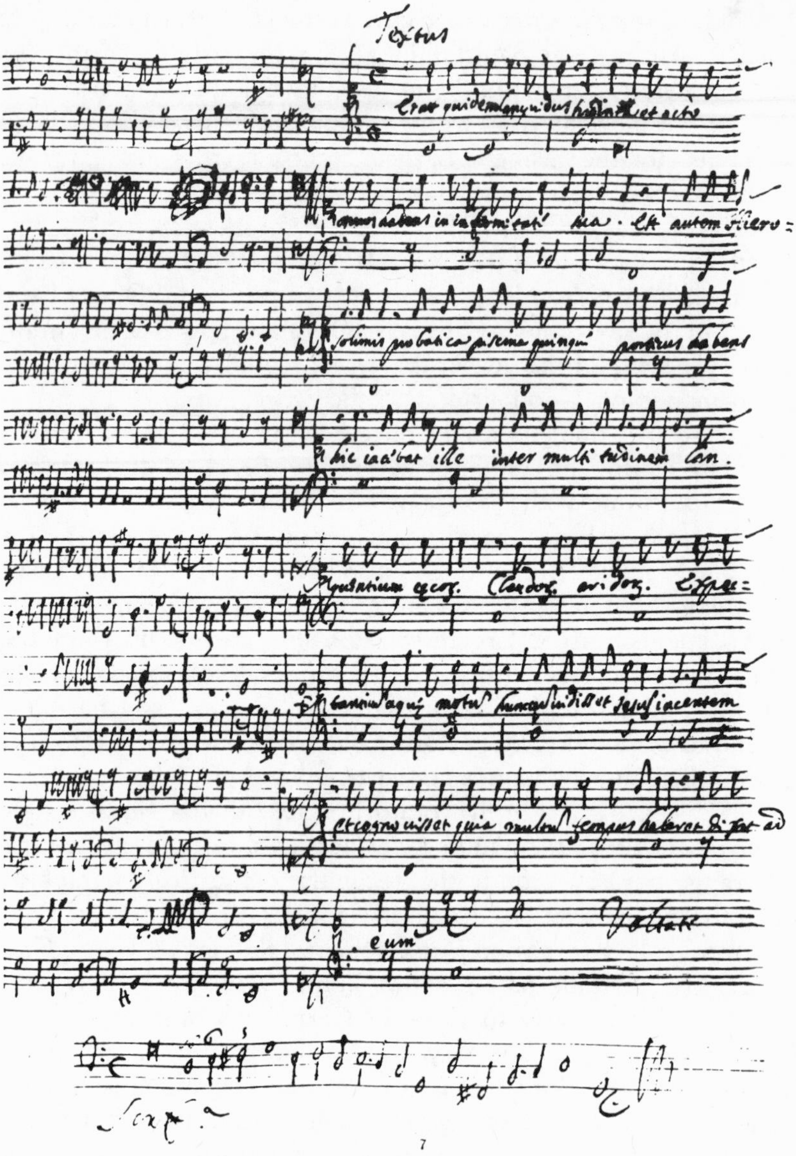

FIGURE V-5. Beginning of Marazzoli's Latin oratorio "Erat quidem languidus." In this rough MS with corrections, probably the composer's first draft, the oratorio begins with the narrator's part labeled "Textus," at the top of the page.
(Reproduced by permission of I/Rvat.)

The solo passages of these works employ recitative, with occasional melismatic passages for expressive purposes. Example V-10 illustrates their characteristic recitative style with its numerous repeated notes in the vocal line, generally sustained or slowly moving continuo part, and brief moments of word painting, as at "descendit" and "surge, tolle." In striking contrast to Marazzoli's oratorios in Italian (treated in chapter 4), which employ numerous arias, these works include neither arias nor aria style. In fact they are among the very few oratorios of the period, in either Latin or Italian, in which aria style is absent; the continuing emphasis upon recitative contributes to the general impression of simplicity and seriousness that they convey.

EXAMPLE V-10. "Erat quidem languidus"—Marazzoli (I/Rvat: codex Chigi, Q. VIII. 188; after a transcription by M. Grace).

CHRIST—Dost thou want to get well? SICK MAN—Sir, I have no one to put me into the pool when the water is stirred; for while I am coming another steps down before me. CHRIST—Rise, take up thy pallet and walk.

The ensembles and choruses, ranging from *a 2* to double choruses *a 10*, resemble those of D. Mazzocchi's works more than Carissimi's in their somewhat greater use of imitation. Like Mazzocchi's oratorios these make more frequent use of the chorus than do the shorter of Carissimi's oratorios, which are comparable to these in length.

Instruments are occasionally used to double the vocal parts in choruses. In only one of the works, "Erat fames in terra Canaan," do the instruments (undesignated, but probably two violins with continuo) play a brief, independent sinfonia, which is repeated once after some intervening vocal passages.

Francesco Foggia

Born at Rome in 1604, Francesco Foggia received his musical training there before serving at courts in Cologne and Munich. Returning to Rome, he worked at Santa Maria in Trastevere and as maestro di cappella at San Giovanni in Laterano (1636–61), San Lorenzo in Damaso, and Santa Maria Maggiore (1677 until his death in 1688). Records show that he was in charge of the music at Crocifisso for Lent of 1641, the first Friday of Lent in 1658, the second in 1660 and 1665, and the first in 1679.[121] Thus his activity there, which might have been greater than the incomplete records indicate, extended through a period of nearly forty years.

Foggia was a prolific composer of motets, some of which he might have used at Crocifisso, but only three of his known works are oratorios: *Victoria Passionis* ("Victory of the Passion"), *David fugiens a facie Saul* ("David Fleeing from the Presence of Saul"), and *Tobiae oratorium* ("Oratorio of Tobias").[122] Both of the two last-named works are in one structural part, but they differ remarkably in length: *David* is a work of about twenty minutes, but *Tobiae* is extremely brief, about eight minutes long, which makes it the shortest known Latin work called an oratorio in its source. Both are dramatic compositions based on biblical stories and using biblical quotations and paraphrases.[123] The text of *Tobiae* is clos-

---

121. For archival documentation see Alaleona, *Oratorio*, pp. 340–43.

122. Professor Beekman C. Cannon kindly called my attention to Foggia's *Victoria Passionis* (F/LY: Ms. 134.025), a work about which I learned too late to consult it for this study. The MS sources for *David* and *Tobias*, respectively, are I/Bc: Q 43, fols. 161–76, 179–84.

123. *David* is based on 1 Kings 18:6ff. and 21:10ff., and *Tobias*, on Tob. 12:1ff. and 15.

est to its source; this brief oratorio is much like the dialogue motets of the first third of the century in its text, musical setting (except for a clearer tonality), and duration. *David*, on the other hand, is more like the oratorios of Carissimi both in text, which includes original insertions, and in music. In *Tobiae* the narrative parts are all sung by a duet; the characters are represented by soloists in recitative or arioso style (but not in aria style); the chorus enters only at the end; and no instruments are required other than the basso continuo. In *David* the parts for the narrator and characters are sung by soloists in recitative, arioso, and aria styles. Functioning as a group of virgins and a commentator on the action, the chorus plays a prominent part in the work and provides a moralizing conclusion. Two undesignated instrumental parts in the G clef—probably violins—play a *symphonia* at the beginning and several others during the course of the work. Particularly effective in *David* is the long victory celebration near the beginning, as David and Saul return from battle; this section— composed of solos, ensembles, choruses, and *symphoniae*—is in triple meter throughout and is further unified by repeated *symphoniae*.

Bonifazio Graziani

Marino, the birthplace of Carissimi, is probably that of Graziani, born in 1604 or 1605. In 1648 Graziani became maestro di cappella at the Jesuits' church in Rome, the Giesù, and at the Roman Seminary. He directed the music at Crocifisso at least once—on the fifth Friday of Lent, 1650.[124] Graziani died in 1664 in Rome.

A list of Graziani's sacred works compiled in 1676 includes the title of a lost collection, *Dialoghi oratorij à 2, 3, 4, e 5, con sinfonie e senza*.[125] His only known oratorios, however, are *Adae oratorium* ("Oratorio of Adam") and *Filii prodigi oratorium* ("Oratorio of the Prodigal Son").[126] An important aspect of these works is their two-part structure; they are the only known two-part Latin oratorios from this period, and in this respect they

124. For archival documentation see Alaleona, *Oratorio*, p. 341.
125. L. Tagliavini, "Graziani," in *MGG*, 5:col. 746.
126. The sources are I/Bc: Q 43, fols. 134–47, 149–59. For a modern edition of the beginning of part II of *Adam*—including a dialogue among God, Adam, and Eve—see Massenkeil, *Oratorium* (and Massenkeil, *Oratorium*-Eng.), pp. 50–54.

anticipate the normal structure of both Latin and Italian oratorios of the later seventeenth century. Both works treat their biblical sources freely but include occasional biblical quotations. The only original insertions in *Adam* are the texts of the concluding sections (for solos and choruses) of the first and second parts. In *Prodigal* long sections of rejoicing based on original texts are found at the end of part I and the beginning of part II. A brief, original, moralizing text concludes the oratorio. In both works solos are used for narrative texts and to represent personages; the solo styles include recitative, arioso, and aria, with aria style more prominent in *Adam* than in *Prodigal*. Ensembles and choruses represent groups of personages, and the final choruses of the first and second parts in both works are reflective and moralistic. In *Adam* no instruments are used other than the basso continuo. In *Prodigal*, however, a number of *symphoniae* are required, but only the basso continuo is supplied, the upper staves having been left blank in the manuscript. *Prodigal* is of special interest for its recurring ritornellos and choruses during the celebration scene at the beginning of part II.

The Chief Characteristics of the Oratorio Latino

Most extant oratorios with Latin texts from Carissimi's time are in one structural part and may be considered expansions of the dialogue motet. The only known two-part oratorios from the period are the two works by B. Graziani. Of the Latin works designated *oratorio* in their seventeenth-century sources, the shortest is about eight minutes (F. Foggia's *Tobiae*) and the longest, about forty minutes (B. Graziani's *Prodigal*). Of the thirteen works by Carissimi that relate, in varying degrees, to the genre of the oratorio, the longest lasts about thirty minutes and the shortest, about nine minutes.

Narrative-dramatic texts predominate, and the texts are virtually always based on biblical stories. In this respect the Latin oratorios of the period differ from those in Italian, for the latter employ texts based on hagiography as well as on the Bible. Exact biblical quotations are usually brief in the oratorios; paraphrases and modified wording are more common. Passages of original text are often inserted into the biblical stories for the purpose of expanding their dramatic, descriptive, or reflective aspects. Rhetorical devices are particularly prominent in the original passages of Carissimi's texts, and some of these passages are poetic in language and structure. Reflective oratorios use original texts, fragments selected from a variety of biblical books, or a combination of these.

As in the *oratorio volgare* the roles of personages are sung by soloists in narrative-dramatic oratorios, but the narrative passages are less consistently restricted to a certain voice or ensemble. Narrative passages are sometimes sung by a soloist designated *Historicus* or *Textus*, but such passages are often divided among various vocal forces (soloists of several ranges, ensembles, and choruses) within one work. Narrative, reflective, and descriptive choruses are more common in the *oratorio latino* than in the *volgare*; the former, like the latter, characteristically closes with a chorus, usually reflective or moralistic in nature.

Although the text and structure of the Latin oratorio point to its derivation from the early dialogue motet, the musical style, particularly that of solo passages, is closer to that of contemporary operas and cantatas. The recitative style varies from the extremely simple, "dry" recitative of Marazzoli's oratorios to the highly expressive *recitativo arioso* style of Carissimi's. Arias tend to be less common in the *oratorio latino* than in the *volgare*, there being no arias at all in the oratorios of D. Mazzocchi and Marazzoli and relatively few in the works of others. Through-composed, ABB', and strophic-variation arias predominate. Ensembles and choruses use both chordal and imitative textures, but Carissimi tends to employ the chordal style more than his contemporaries.

Instruments other than those for the basso continuo are sometimes employed, but the specific instrumentation is rarely designated. The instruments function much as they do in the *oratorio volgare*.

CHAPTER VI *The Later Baroque I:*
Social Contexts,
Patrons, Composers, Poets

The period from the mid-seventeenth to the early eighteenth century was one of increasing oratorio activity, not only in the genre's native Rome, but in other Italian cities and beyond the Alps as well. Among the reasons for the growing interest in the oratorio were the expansion of the Oratorians, who sponsored oratorio performances in many cities of Italy, and the increasingly close relationship between the functions of oratorio and opera. The latter was by far the most popular public entertainment of the Baroque era—a period in which the oratorio was increasingly seen as a viable substitute for opera, particularly during the Lenten season when opera theaters were closed. As a result of this function, the stylistic and structural features of oratorios grew closer to those of operas than they had been in the past. Although oratorios continued to be performed in a more or less devotional context in the oratories of Italy, they were also frequently presented in the palaces of noblemen, where they functioned as quasi-secular entertainments despite the religious basis of their texts. The following treatment of various social contexts, patrons, composers, and poets of the oratorio deals more with Rome than with other cities because of the greater emphasis on the genre there and because more previous research has been done on the Roman development. Nevertheless, with few exceptions the oratorio practices of Rome appear to be representative of those in other Italian cities.

Rome

The chief Roman centers of oratorio performance in a devotional context continued to be the oratories—particularly those of San Girolamo della Carità, the Chiesa Nuova, and Crocifisso.[1] As in the previous period, oratorios in Italian were performed in the first two locations primarily on Sundays and other feast days in the winter months;[2] Crocifisso continued to restrict its oratorios to the Latin language and to the Fridays of Lent. Well before the 1660s these oratories had become famous musical centers, as pointed out above; yet they had not been merely concert halls but also places of prayer and preaching: the music had been viewed as a spiritual instruction as well as an entertainment. This view ostensibly continued in the oratories throughout the present period. Although the sermon was retained between the two structural parts of two-part oratorios, the style of the genre grew ever closer to that of opera, and the oratorio's growing domination of the oratory service turned the prayer hall into a place of entertainment. That some Oratorians at the Chiesa Nuova were disturbed by the increasing emphasis on musical entertainment in the oratory is clear from a letter written in the 1660s by Father Mario Sozzini (1613–80) to the Florentine Oratorians. He does not disapprove of music in the oratory if the expenses be fully covered by patrons; if the prefect of music and the community approve the quality and length of the piece, degree of secularism, hour of the performance, and suitability of the work for the season; and if "the vanity of the music does not distract the devotions of the oratory, for to some degree the Demon has won with our oratory of Rome, where we sweat blood to restrain the disorder of the music and daily we remain at a loss in this matter."[3]

1. This conclusion is based primarily on my survey of extant printed librettos of oratorios performed in Rome during this period. The most important collections of Roman librettos are those of the following libraries: I/Rc, I/Rli, I/Rn, I/Rsc, and I/Rvat. Oratories other than the three mentioned above, such as the oratory of Santa Teresa (Allacci, *Drammaturgia*, col. 279) are rarely mentioned in the librettos as locations of oratorio performances.

2. According to François Raguenet, oratorios were still performed in 1697 at the oratory of San Girolamo della Carità "every Holy Day night from All Saints to Easter; a laudable Institution, design'd to restrain the Populace from more guilty Diversions." (Raguenet, *Comparison*, p. 22, n. 16.)

3. Sozzini to the Florentine Oratorians, [1660s], translated from the MS "Consuetudini e ricordi della Congregazione," vol. 91, fol. 126, in I/Fo. Father Antonio Cistellini, Preposito of the Congregation of the Oratory at Florence, kindly brought this document to my attention and provided the approximate date.

As in the past, the oratorios performed at Crocifisso were financially supported by the noblemen who were members of the archconfraternity to whom the oratory belonged. Various individuals and groups in Rome also sponsored special festive performances at other oratories. For example, to celebrate the Holy Year of 1675 the Venerabile Compagnia della Pietà della Natione Fiorentina, a society of Florentine gentlemen living in Rome, sponsored performances of fourteen oratorios from January to April of that year.[4] The headquarters of the society was the church of San Giovanni dei Fiorentini, the parish church of Florentines in Rome, and the performances took place in the oratory of that church.[5] The composers represented in the series were Antonio Masini, Ercole Bernabei, Alessandro Melani, Giovanni Battista Di Pio, Bernardo Pasquini, and Alessandro Stradella. Performances were also sponsored at the oratory of the Chiesa Nuova by such distinguished patrons as Queen Christina of Sweden,[6] Cardinal Pietro Ottoboni,[7] Prince Francesco Maria Ruspoli,[8] and Pope Clement XI (1700–21).[9] In 1703 Clement XI issued an edict that prohibited carnival activities, including opera, for five years as an act of thanksgiving to God for having protected Rome from the series of violent earthquakes that had devastated the immediately surrounding area.[10] Thus in 1704, apparently to help fill the void created by the absence of opera, the pontiff recommended that the Oratorians at the Chiesa Nuova present during the carnival season "the most beautiful oratorios," that they produce "something extraordinary, there being no other entertainment in Rome"; and he offered to pay the expenses for this special carnival entertainment.[11]

Educational institutions, too, were often the locations of performances supported by the nobility. Cardinal Benedetto Pamphilj,

4. For a documentary study of this oratorio series, see Casimiri, "Oratorii."

5. The oratory is mentioned in a document in ibid., pp. 163–64, 166. For more information about this oratory, see above, chapter 2, p. 45; see also Figure II-5 and the end paper, no. 2. Regarding the origin of this society and the function of this church, see Totti, *Roma*, pp. 244–46.

6. Gasbarri, *Oratorio rom.*, p. 292.

7. Marx, "Ottoboni," p. 153.

8. Gasbarri, *Oratorio fil.*, p. 65.

9. Ibid.

10. Regarding the earthquakes and the edict, the latter also prohibiting for five years the participation of women in public performances, see Ewerhart, "Händel-Handschriften," p. 121; and Zanetti, "Haendel," p. 9.

11. Gasbarri, *Oratorio fil.*, p. 65.

the protector of the Clementine College, sponsored several oratorios in the theater of that institution.[12] A particularly festive performance that took place there under his sponsorship in 1705 was dedicated to Sister Maria Grazia, a Carmelite and the niece of Clement XI; a contemporary record states that "no expenses were spared" for the stage decorations, designed by the architect Carlo Fontana (1634–1714).[13] The libretto of the work, *Oratorio di Santa Maria Maddalena dei Pazzi*, was written by Pamphilj and set to music by Alessandro Scarlatti. Oratorios were also presented at other colleges in Rome and at the Jesuits' Roman Seminary.[14]

Performances of oratorios in an essentially secular context frequently took place in the private palaces of such patrons as Queen Christina of Sweden, Cardinals Pamphilj and Ottoboni, and Prince Ruspoli. That oratorios were performed in Queen Christina's palace has been mentioned with relation to her patronage of Carissimi. The palace of Benedetto Pamphilj (1653–1730)—a prince, poet, patron of the arts, and cardinal—was a cultural center of primary importance in the Rome of his time (see Figure II–2, no. 5). Pamphilj's interest in oratorios was more than that of a patron: he was also the author of several oratorio texts, the best known of which is *Il trionfo del Tempo e del Disinganno*, set to music for him by Handel in 1707. Pamphilj's interest in the oratorio began shortly after Rome's theaters closed in the wake of a scandal occurring in the carnival season of 1677.[15] Pope Innocent XI (1676–89) had not only closed the theaters but was also carefully scrutinizing the morality of entertainments given in private palaces. Since oratorio was an accepted substitute for opera, Pamphilj turned to it both as a patron and a poet.[16] His earliest oratorio, *Abel*, set by Alessandro Melani, was first performed in 1678 at the palace of Cardinal Pio.[17] Pamphilj continued his sponsorship of oratorios, in his own palace and in other locations, throughout his life. Bernardo Pasquini was among those who composed oratorios for Pamphilj, and Arcangelo Corelli served this patron a few years, no doubt performing in the orchestra for the oratorios presented at his palace.

12. For details of Pamphilj's patronage of music, see Montalto, *Mecenate*, pp. 309–39.
13. Ibid., pp. 334–35.
14. For oratorios performed at the Roman Seminary, see Sommervogel, *Bibliothèque*, 7:74–77.
15. Regarding this scandal and the pope's reaction, see Ademollo, *Roma*, pp. 150–52.
16. Montalto, *Mecenate*, pp. 312–13.
17. Ibid., pp. 207–9.

Obÿt die 22 Martÿ 1730.

BENEDICTVS S.R.E. PRIMVS DIACONVS
CARDINALIS PAMPHILIVS ROMANVS
SIGNATVRÆ GRATIÆ PRÆFECTVS
BASILICÆ LATERANENSIS ARCHIPRESBYTER
CREATVS DIE I. SEPTEMBR. M.DC.LXXXI.

Io Iacobi de Rubeis Formis Romæ ad Templ. S.M.de Pace cum Priu. S.Pont.

FIGURE VI-1. Cardinal Benedetto Pamphilj (1653–1730).
(From De Rossi, *Effigies*, 1:147.)

FIGURE VI-2. The Clementine College and the Ripeta Port on the Tiber. Detail from Giovanni Battista Piranesi's engraving of the Ripeta Port.
(Reproduced by permission of the Gabinetto Nazionale delle Stampe, Rome.)

Francesco Maria Ruspoli (1672–1731), one of the most influential men in Rome, held the title of marquis before 1709, when Pope Clement XI named him Prince of Cerveteri in gratitude for his powerful military assistance. Ruspoli's patronage of the arts was every bit as active as Pamphilj's. Like most of the music patrons of the city, he retained a small company of musicians as regular members of his household and employed additional performers for special events.[18] Antonio Caldara (1670–1736) was Ruspoli's maestro di cappella from 1709 to 1716; a number of his oratorios were first performed at Ruspoli's residence, the Palazzo Bonelli (see Figure II–2, no. 3).[19] During this period oratorio performances were given at his residence primarily in the Lenten and Easter seasons. Although the number of oratorios each season varied, in some years an oratorio was performed on every Sunday evening of Lent and on Easter. At the Ruspoli residence, as at others, oratorio performances were essentially secular concerts, entertainments that substituted for opera in the ostensibly solemn season when the theaters were closed. Neither prayers nor sermons would form a part of the usual evening of oratorio in a private palace; instead, refreshments would be served at the intermission between the two parts of the oratorio.[20]

The most elaborately prepared and heavily attended of the numerous oratorio performances at the Ruspoli residence was that of Handel's *La Resurrezione* on Easter Sunday, 8 April 1708.[21] In this period before Ruspoli was made a prince, he was actively seeking the favor of the oratorio-loving Clement XI: an *Oratorio di San Clemente* (anonymous) was performed during the Lenten musical series,[22] and Handel, the brilliant newcomer who had established his reputation during the previous year by performing and composing for Rome's most distinguished patrons, was chosen

18. For details of Ruspoli's patronage of music, particularly oratorio, see U. Kirkendale, *Caldara*, pp. 44–84; U. Kirkendale, "Ruspoli"; and H. Hucke, "Ruspoli," in *MGG*, 11:cols. 1126–28.

19. From 1705 to 1713 Ruspoli's residence was the Palazzo Bonelli, today the Palazzo della Provincia and the seat of the Prefecture of Rome. In 1713 Ruspoli purchased the magnificent Palazzo Gaetani (Caetani), in Via del Corso, which is the present Palazzo Ruspoli. (U. Kirkendale, "Ruspoli," p. 227; U. Kirkendale, *Caldara*, p. 45.)

20. The French priest G. B. Labat, writing of his visit to Italy in 1709–10, mentions that refreshments were usually served during the intermission at a private oratorio performance in Rome and comments on the extreme frequency of oratorio performances in the city. (Labat, *Voyages*, 3:156–57.)

21. For details of the preparation and performance, see U. Kirkendale, "Ruspoli," pp. 231–39.

22. U. Kirkendale, *Caldara*, p. 49.

to compose his *Resurrezione* as the series' final oratorio. In preparation for the performance of Handel's work, a proscenium-framed and curtained stage was constructed and elaborately ornamented in a large hall (the Stanzione delle Accademie) of Ruspoli's residence (the Palazzo Bonelli); in fact, the hall was virtually transformed, temporarily for this event, into a theater. The stage included semicircular elevations for the orchestra and a special platform for seating the "Concertino de' Violini." Serving as a background for the stage was a large, square painting described by the painter, Angelo Cerruti, as follows: "within the frame, painted 'al naturale,' the resurrection of our Lord with a 'gloria' of *putti* and cherubim, and the angel sitting on the tomb announcing the resurrection to Mary Magdalene and Mary Cleopha, with John the Evangelist in the vicinity of a mountain, and demons plunging into the abyss."[23] Above the proscenium and extending across the full width of the hall was a large representation of an ornate title page bearing the title of the oratorio. Elaborate and colorful drapery was hung on the walls of the stage, and the entire hall was lavishly decorated and illuminated. The room where refreshments were served between the two parts of the oratorio was redecorated especially for the occasion, and an actual waterfall, combined with painted scenery, was installed in an adjoining room for the pleasure of those partaking of the refreshments. The two performances of *La Resurrezione*, on Easter Sunday and Monday, were preceded by three rehearsals at which visitors were expected. The orchestra, consisting of forty-five or forty-six pieces and directed by Corelli, was the largest of any of Ruspoli's musical productions; the usual orchestra for oratorio performances at the Ruspoli palace in this period consisted of only thirteen to sixteen pieces.[24]

Ruspoli's oratorio performances were open to the public, although only the socially elite would normally attend. On 31 March 1715 a German visitor to Rome, Johann Friedrich Armand von Uffenbach (later the mayor of Frankfurt), attended a performance of Caldara's oratorio *Abisai*. His carefully recorded impressions contribute considerably to the understanding of the social context of more modest oratorio performances than those just described:

23. U. Kirkendale, "Ruspoli," p. 234; see also ibid., p. 260, for the document of which this description is a paraphrase.
24. U. Kirkendale, *Caldara*, p. 52.

In the evening was the great, weekly concert in the palace of Prince Rospoli [sic] which, because of the many expenses that he annually allots to it, is the best here; and since he welcomes and permits every foreigner to come in without introduction, we therefore went there together, and were led through a large number of exquisitely furnished rooms to an enormously large and long hall in which, as in the entire house, there is no lack of incomparable paintings and silver work. Everything was most brilliantly illuminated, and on both sides of the entire hall chairs were placed for the listeners; above, however, the place for the musicians was left free where a great number of virtuosos arranged themselves, and three female singers next to a small castrato, belonging to the ambassador Gallas, sat in front. They then gave such an excellent concert, or so-called oratorio, that I was completely delighted and convinced that I had not in my life heard the like, in such perfection. The composition is completely new each time and is composed by the well-known Caldara, papal maestro di cappella, who also conducted here. People listened to the excellent voices so attentively that not a fly stirred, except when a cardinal or a lady arrived, since everyone stood up but afterward sat down again in his old place. I found also that all the voices usually heard in operas fell short short of these; particularly the one called Mariotgi had something quite extraordinary and uncommonly pleasing in her singing. The leading soprano was the wife of Caldara; to be sure, she was very finished in music and sang the most difficult things with nothing but great skill, yet to me, because of the weakness of her voice, she did not long please as well as the one described above. At about the middle of the concert they had an intermission, and then liquors, frozen things, confectionery, and coffee were brought around in quantity and presented to everyone. Afterward was performed the other half of the concert, which lasted altogether four hours. I would have remained even fourteen days with great pleasure, for I certainly left with genuine astonishment, and I have never in my life heard anything to compare with this. In the accompaniment there was a violin that was unusually well played, and many other instruments, all played to perfection. It was midnight when we were finished, but sleep did not hinder me from listening to it all to the end with the greatest pleasure. The auditorium was very full, and there were many ladies, also several cardinals, among others the cardinal Ottoboni of Venice who never misses such things. He went as an ordinary abbot, except that he wore red stockings and heels and also a red calotte; and the remaining cardinals also went similarly dressed. After this was over, we went home and dined.[25]

25. Diary of Uffenbach, 31 March 1715, translated from Preussner, *Uffenbach*, pp. 77–78; and U. Kirkendale, *Caldara*, p. 74. Uffenbach erroneously refers to Caldara as "papal chapelmaster"; he was actually Ruspoli's chapelmaster and only occasionally served the papal chapel, according to U. Kirkendale. *Caldara*, p. 75. For another translation of this passage, see Poultney, "Transformation," p. 589.

At another of Ruspoli's oratorio performances, on 7 April 1715, Uffenbach says that the crowd—even larger—included Cardinal Ottoboni again, that the music was even better, and that refreshments were served. Although everyone was extremely quiet, the "passionate Italians indeed at every moment rolled their eyes and moved all their limbs in admiration, even applauded when something ended, yet with their mantles doubled many times between their hands so that one would not hear it; and that would be out of respect, for clapping is allowed only in the theater."[26]

Pietro Ottoboni (1667–1740), the son of a noble Venetian family and grandnephew of the worldly pope Alexander VIII (1689–91), was named cardinal and vice-chancellor of the holy church in the first year of Alexander's pontificate. At twenty-two years of age, Ottoboni thus became one of Rome's wealthiest men. An extremely enlightened and active patron of the arts, he made his residence, the Palazzo della Cancelleria (the palace of the same name today; see end paper, no. 4), the center of an intense musical life.[27] With its theater, large halls, courtyard, and basilica of San Lorenzo in Damaso, the palace provided a variety of locations for the frequent performances of operas, oratorios, chamber music, and liturgical music. Arcangelo Corelli joined Ottoboni's service in 1690; for the rest of his life, he lived in the palace and functioned as the musical director for most performances, including oratorios, in which instruments took part. Alessandro Scarlatti was briefly in Ottoboni's service from 1705 to 1706, and the best musicians of Rome, including Handel during his visit, performed at this court. Archangelo Spagna—the librettist, theorist, and historian of the oratorio—was the *maestro di casa* of the Cancelleria.[28]

Like Benedetto Pamphilj, Ottoboni was both a librettist and a patron of the oratorio. Among his several librettos are *Il regno di Maria Vergine assunta in Cielo* ("The Reign of the Virgin Mary Taken into Heaven"), set to music by A. Scarlatti, and *Il trionfo della castità* ("The Triumph of Chastity"), set by Caldara. At the Cancelleria oratorios were performed primarily in the large halls that included balconies for the musicians but also in the theater and in San Lorenzo in Damaso.[29] The performance of A. Scar-

26. Diary of Uffenbach, 7 April 1715, translated from Preussner, *Uffenbach*, p. 78; and U. Kirkendale, *Caldara*, pp. 74–75.

27. For details of Ottoboni's patronage of music, see Marx, "Ottoboni," and Hansell, "Ottoboni."

28. Marx, "Ottoboni," p. 111.

29. Ibid., pp. 106, 111, 113.

Obijt die 28 February 1740.

PETRUS EPISCOPUS OSTIENSIS
S.R.E. CARDINALIS OTTHOBONUS VENETUS
SACRI COLLEGIJ DECANUS,
EJUSDEM S.R.E. VICE-CANCELLARIUS, ET SUMMISTA
BASILICÆ LATERANENSIS ARCHIPRESBYTER
CREATUS DIE VII. NOVEMBRIS MDCLXXXIX.

Franc·Trevisani pinx   Gaspar Masei sculp

Domin. de Rubeis Formis Romæ ad Templ S. M. de Pace cum Priuil. S. P.

FIGURE VI-3. Cardinal Pietro Ottoboni (1667–1740).
(De Rossi, *Effigies*, 2:1.)

latti's Passion at the Cancelleria on Wednesday of Holy Week in 1708—just four days before that of Handel's *La Resurrezione* at Ruspoli's palace—may have taken place in the grand salon (the Sala Riaria) or the theater. Some sketches of stage decorations (see Figures VI–4 and VI–5)[30] made by Filippo Juvarra (1676–1736), possibly for the Scarlatti performance, show that the oratorio decorations in Ottoboni's palace were comparable to those in Ruspoli's. It has been suggested that Ottoboni and Ruspoli, friends with common interests, had planned the performances of these two works as a Passion-Resurrection sequence.[31] That the theater in the Cancelleria, designed by Juvarra, was used for oratorio performances is further indicated by a printed libretto of a Christmas oratorio, called a *componimento sacro*,[32] that was Pietro Metastasio's first oratorio libretto and was set to music by Giovanni Battista Costanzi. The work was performed at the Cancelleria in 1727 for the annual Christmas meeting of the Accademia dell' Arcadia, the distinguished literary society of which Ottoboni was a member. According to the description of the performance that was provided in the libretto, the introduction to the work was sung by the Heavenly Genius (Il Genio Celeste), surrounded by a court of other Genii who were seated on a cloud that represented a transparent realm; after the introduction, a message of peace to all mortals, the cloud ascended to reveal an amphitheater where the remainder of the composition was performed. The work is in two parts and is like a normal oratorio in every respect except its theatrical introduction. The libretto is illustrated by two engravings that represent the scenes of the introduction and the amphitheater. In the engraving of the introduction (see Figure VI–6, p. 272), Heavenly Genius is seated on a cloud in the upper center. In the scene of the amphitheater (see Figure VI–7), there appear to be about thirty-six instrumentalists and three singers on stage; in addition, about twenty instrumentalists, including two harpsichordists and two groups of wind performers, are in the orchestra pit. Both the use of a theatrical machine and the similarity between the proscenium arch of the engravings and that of Ottoboni's

30. See pp. 270–71. The sketches are also reproduced in Brinckmann, "Disegni," pls. 188–89, and Viale Ferrero, *Juvarra*, pls. 177–78.

31. For a full statement of this hypothesis and its support, see U. Kirkendale, "Ruspoli," pp. 238–39.

32. *Componimento sacro per la festività del SS. Natale in occasione della solita annua adunanza de' signori Accademici Arcadi nel Palazzo della Cancelleria Apostolica* (Rome, 1727). A copy is in I/Rvat: St. Barb. JJJ. IX. 30, int. 22.

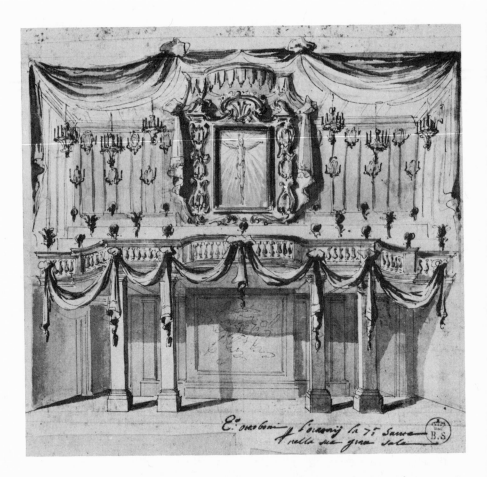

FIGURE VI-4. A stage design by Filippo Juvarra for an oratorio performance in the grand salon, the Sala Riaria, of Cardinal Pietro Ottoboni's palace, the Cancelleria. The design may have been made in 1708 for a Holy Week performance of Alessandro Scarlatti's Passion. (Reproduced by permission of I/Tn: Ris. 59, 4, f. 81 [1].)

FIGURE VI-5. A stage design by Juvarra for an oratorio performance in the theater of the Cancelleria. This may have been intended as an alternate design for that shown in Figure VI-4.
(Reproduced by permission of I/Tn: Ris. 59, 4, f. 23 [1].)

FIGURE VI-6. The stage machine for the prologue of the *Componimento sacro per la festività del SS. Natale* (Rome, 1727), with a libretto by Pietro Metastasio and music by Giovanni Battista Costanzi, that was performed in Ottoboni's theater in the Cancelleria.

(Courtesy of I/Rvat.)

FIGURE VI-7. The appearance of the stage after the prologue represented in
Figure VI-6.
(Courtesy of I/Rvat.)

theater would seem to indicate that his theater, rather than a hall in the palace, was the location of this performance.[33]

In dedicating the second book of his *Oratorii overo melodrammi sacri* (Rome, 1706) to Cardinal Ottoboni, Spagna calls attention to Ottoboni's propensity for this genre of composition, to the nobility of his talent, and to his having had oratorios performed with such royal magnificence that he was applauded as "the only Maecenas of our time." Perhaps Spagna had in mind such festive performances as those of Ottoboni's and Scarlatti's *Il regno di Maria Vergine assunta in Cielo*—given in the courtyard of the Cancelleria on the evenings of 23–24 August 1705, slightly more than a week after the important feast of the Assumption. According to a detailed contemporary report of those performances,[34] the orchestra, under the direction of Corelli, consisted of more than one hundred stringed instruments, plus trumpets and others, and the four best voices of the city sang the oratorio. The report highly praises the performance, the libretto, and the musical setting. For this important occasion a stage was erected on one side of the courtyard and was elaborately designed with balustrades, staircases, large twisted columns, and painted scenes representing the virtues; in the center, at an opening in the front balustrade, was a platform for the singers. The audience was seated in open carriages that had previously been aligned so closely together that they touched one another. The most illustrious personages of Rome and its environs attended the performances. Prior to the beginning of the oratorio on the first evening, a bell was rung, after which Pope Clement XI led the audience in devotions that included the *Ave Maria*, the *Gloria Patri*, and a prayer by the pontiff. At the end of the first part of the oratorio and throughout the second part, sumptuous refreshments were served. On the second evening, 24 August, the performance began at a later hour to accommodate certain nobility who were traveling to Rome from a considerable distance. The audience had similar refreshments, and the performance lasted until about midnight.[35] As usual in a private palace, these performances appear to have

33. For Juvarra's sketches of the theater showing its proscenium arch, see Warner, "Ottoboni," pp. 38, 40; and Viale Ferrero, *Juvarra*, pls. 181, 185.

34. "Oratorio esposto al publico e fatto rappresentare nel cortile della Cancelleria . . . ," a MS in I/Rvat: Urb. lat. 1706, fols. 1– 4v.

35. The performance concluded "alle hore quattro della notte," four hours after sunset—about midnight.

functioned essentially as entertainments; the presence of the pontiff would probably have been responsible for the devotional service that preceded the oratorio on the first evening.

Although the popes generally approved of oratorios, the Vatican Apostolic Palace appears rarely to have been the location of oratorio performances. In the second half of the seventeenth century, however, an old tradition was revived of performing festive music there on Christmas Eve, a practice that eventually provided a context for Christmas oratorios. According to this tradition, after the pontifical vespers the numerous cardinals who had assisted, and who would assist later at matins and midnight mass in the Sistine Chapel, were entertained in the Apostolic Palace by Christmas music with Italian words, followed by a splendid banquet.[36] Following the ideals of the Roman Catholic reform, Pope Gregory XIII abolished these festivities in 1573 because of serious abuses. During the seventeenth-century revival of the tradition, the works performed on this occasion were normally termed *cantata*, *concerto*, or *componimento sacro*. Despite the terminology, however, there seems to have been a gradual development from the cantata to the oratorio in this Christmas Eve music—that is, from the reflective cantata of praise in the 1670s to the one-part narrative-dramatic cantata (or short oratorio) with *testo* and three or four characters in the 1690s and finally to the two-part oratorio from the early eighteenth century until the discontinuation of the festivities later in that century.[37] By the late 1730s the term *oratorio* was common for these compositions; it is used by Charles de Brosses in his eyewitness account of the events at the Apostolic Palace on Christmas Eve in 1739: "The evening began with a very harmonious concert and an oratorio ['un *oratorio* en musique'] in the royal hall, after which they served a splendid repast which

36. Alaleona, *Oratorio*, pp. 11–12.

37. More librettos than music are extant to reveal this development. The three stages of development are represented in the following three librettos: *Celeste annunzio di pace al popolo cristiano musicalmente espresso per la notte del santissimo Natale nel Palazzo Apostolico Vaticano* (Rome, 1678), music by Giovanni Pietro Monesio (I/Rli: 172. A. 8 [26]); *I pastori di Bettlemme annunziati dall'angelo, concerto musicale da cantarsi nel Palazzo Apostolico la notte del santissimo Natale* (Rome, 1691), anonymous (I/Rli: 172. I. 19 [5]); *Cantata da recitarsi nel Palazzo Apostolico la notte del santissimo Natale* (Rome, 1714), music by Domenico Scarlatti (I/Rsc: Carvalhaes, 2648). Other librettos of Christmas music for this purpose exist in I/Rli, I/Rsc, and I/Rvat. It is not known whether A. Stradella's *Cantata per il Santissimo Natale* ("Ah, ah, troppo è ver"; MS in I/MOe: Mus. F. 1145) was intended for performance in the Vatican Apostolic Palace, but it is a reflective work, with personages, of the type performed there in the 1670s. For a study of this Stradella work, see Dietz, "Stradella," pp. 80–92.

even the Abbé de Périgny said could be called a good supper."[38] Brosses's further description, including that of the overindulgence of Cardinal-Vicar Guadagni, who gorged himself and drank wine "like a Templar"—the cardinal later fainted during matins and had to be carried out while people commented that the holy man was weak from fasting—indicates that in some measure the old abuses had returned.

Although the oratorios mentioned in this chapter often functioned as substitutes for opera, sometimes employed lavish decorations, and in one instance even required machinery for a theatrical introduction, none of them appears to have been performed as an opera—with costumes, acting, and changes of scenery. Throughout Italy, and all of Europe as well, such a performance for a work called an oratorio was rare in this period. The only Roman work known to the present author that was labeled *oratorio* but was performed as an opera is *Il martirio di Sant'Eustachio, oratorio per musica* (Rome, 1690); with poetry by Crateo Pradalini and music by an anonymous composer, the work was dedicated to Princess Maria Ottoboni, niece of Pope Alexander VIII.[39] The term *oratorio* seems misused for this work, however, for it is divided into three acts (rather than two parts), each with a number of scenes; the first and second acts are followed by dances; costumes and stage actions are described in the libretto; and it is stated in the dedication that the work is given a scenic representation ("si rappresenta in scena"). According to the normal terminology of the period, this would not be an *oratorio per musica* but a *dramma per musica*, a common designation for an opera.[40]

Among the most prominent composers of oratorios active in Rome during this period were Bernardo Pasquini, Alessandro Stradella, Alessandro Scarlatti, Antonio Caldara, and, briefly, George Frideric Handel. A host of less prominent oratorio composers includes Alessandro Melani, Antonio Massini, Ercole Bernabei, Antonio Foggia, Giovanni Bicilli, Giuseppe Pacieri, Giovan Francesco Garbi, Giuseppe Scalamani, Quirino Colombani, Gregorio Cola,

38. Brosses to the Abbé Cortois de Quincy, n.d. [early in 1740], in Brosses, *Lettres*, 2:112.

39. A copy of the libretto is in I/Rsc: G. IX. 19.

40. For a discussion of several Florentine librettos of genuine, two-part oratorios in which scenes and actions are described but were probably not visually represented, see Schering, *Oratorium*, pp. 127–28; see n. 76, below. For comments regarding the virtual absence of scenic representation of oratorios in Italy before 1750, see U. Kirkendale, "Ruspoli," p. 235, n. 44.

Giovanni Battista Costanzi, Flavio Carlo Lanciani, Domenico Laurelli, Giovanni Lorenzo Lulier, Tommaso Bernardo Gaffi, and Carlo Francesco Cesarini. Most of these men are named as composers in extant printed librettos, but few of their scores for oratorios have survived.

Although the composers of oratorios include some of the greatest figures of the period, the librettists are mostly minor poets, many of whom also wrote for opera. Among the chief librettists of oratorios, in addition to Cardinals Pamphilj and Ottoboni, are Sebastiano Lazarini and Archangelo Spagna. The former published a collection of ten of his librettos under the title *Sacra melodia di oratorii musicali* (Rome, 1678). Spagna, the author of at least thirty oratorio librettos, published a two-volume collection of them, his *Oratorii* (Rome, 1706), mentioned above; he also published a volume of poetry, *I fasti sacri* (Rome, 1720), which contains a few oratorio librettos.[41] Among the more active of the numerous poets whose names appear on librettos printed separately are Silvio Stampiglia, Giovanni Battista Grappelli, Francesco Posterla, Bernardo Sandrinelli, and Francisco Laurentino. Spagna in his "Discorso" lists a number of librettists whom he considers important and singles out Giovanni Francesco Rubini and G. B. Grappelli as worthy of special attention.[42]

In 1690, the year after the death of Christina of Sweden, the Accademia dell'Arcadia was formed by the poets of her circle. In reaction to seicento literary tendencies, particularly those influenced by G. B. Marino, the academy stated that its purpose was "to exterminate bad taste" in Italian literature.[43] Of the librettists mentioned above, Pamphilj, Ottoboni, and Stampiglia were members of the academy, and they might well have attempted to incorporate its ideals of simplicity and clarity into some of their oratorio librettos.[44] These ideals are particularly exemplified, however, in the frequently used oratorio librettos of Pietro Metastasio, who was first introduced to the academy's aims during his youth in Rome.[45]

41. For a list of the thirty oratorios contained in these volumes, see Schering, "Beiträge," pp. 44–45.

42. Ibid., pp. 53, 63.

43. Wilkins, *Literature*, p. 325.

44. The determination of the extent to which they might have been reformers of the libretto must await specialized literary studies.

45. Most of Metastasio's oratorio librettos were written at Vienna during the 1730s. The librettos of Apostolo Zeno and Metastasio are considered in chapter 8.

Other Centers

The popularity of the movement begun by St. Philip Neri increased for more than two hundred years and reached a peak in the mid-eighteenth century. By then over one hundred communities modeled on the Congregation of the Oratory in Rome were active in Italy alone, and communities existed in many other countries of Europe and on other continents.[46] The Italian communities followed the practices of that in Rome as closely as local conditions would permit. This included holding simple spiritual exercises in which *laude* were sung and, from the mid-seventeenth century on, sponsoring performances of oratorios. Particularly in cities in which opera had become a significant part of cultural life, the oratorio was fostered as a closely related genre, and, as pointed out above, as a Lenten substitute for opera. Although churches were seldom the locations of oratorio performances in Rome, they seem to have been used for this purpose more frequently in other cities. The treatment of the oratorio as an essentially secular form of entertainment—in palaces, theaters, and academies—was common throughout Italy, as in Rome. The following comments on the social contexts, patrons, composers, and poets of oratorios in selected Italian cities will further illustrate the function of the oratorio in Italian cultural life.[47]

Bologna and Modena[48]

One of the great musical centers of the Italian Baroque, Bologna was extremely active in the cultivation of opera and oratorio as well as the instrumental and liturgical music for which its largest church, San Petronio, was well known. The Oratorians were es-

46. By 1750 at least seven communities existed in Latin America, three in India, and one in Ceylon. For details see Gasbarri, *Spirito*, pp. 184–87.

47. The cities were selected because previous research has shown them to be important in the history of the oratorio. A number of other Italian cities about which little is known in this regard—in particular Naples, Palermo, Milan, Perugia, Lucca, Brescia, and Ferrara—might well have been as important as some of these in fostering oratorio performances. Specialized studies of these and other cities are needed to determine their relative importance in the development of the oratorio. Mario Borelli of Naples has begun a study of the musical life of the Oratorians in that city in the Baroque era. Policastro, "Catania," pp. 12–24, is a preliminary study of the oratorio in Catania.

48. For much material in this section, I gratefully acknowledge the assistance of Julia Ann Griffin, who supplied me with information—gathered during the research work for her dissertation in progress, Griffin, "Colonna"—from the libraries and archives of Bologna and Modena.

tablished at Bologna in the early seventeenth century. By 1615 spiritual exercises patterned after those of the Roman Oratorians were being held at the home of one Cesare Bianchetti; by Lent of 1616, the exercises had been moved to the church of Santi Barbara e Ippolite. In 1621 Pope Gregory XV (Alessandro Ludovisi, 1621–23) officially recognized the Bologna Congregation of the Oratory and granted it the larger church of Madonna di Galliera, which was to be the permanent church of the Oratorians.[49] The congregation's oratory was adjacent to the church.[50]

Bologna was second in importance only to Rome among the cities of the Papal State, and a particularly close relationship existed between the Oratorians in the two cities. This relationship is revealed in its musical aspect by the 1620 and 1622 inventories of music owned by the Bologna community. That a close contact with Rome was also maintained later in the century is shown by another inventory, dated 1682;[51] Roman composers dominate the inventory, and most of the 392 works it lists are oratorios. This relationship with Rome, together with Bologna's keen interest in opera,[52] would lead one to expect fully developed oratorios to have been performed there in the 1640s, as they were in Rome. Although this might have been the case, the earliest documentary evidence of an oratorio performed at Bologna is the extant libretto printed in 1659 for a performance of Maurizio Cazzati's oratorio entitled *La morte di S. Gioseppe* ("The Death of St. Joseph").[53] In 1661 two oratorios by Giulio Cesare Arresti, *Licenza di Giesù da Maria* ("The Departure of Jesus from Mary") and *L'Orto di Getsemani glorioso ne' sudori di Cristo* ("The Garden of Gethsemane, Glorious in the Sweat of Christ"), were performed at Bologna in the private residence of the abbot Carlo Antonio Sampieri.[54]

Judging primarily from the extant librettos printed at Bologna,[55] one may conclude that oratorios were sponsored, not only by

49. Comelli, *Bologna*, p. 2.
50. Vatielli, "Bologna," p. 27; Luin, "Bologna," p. 152. An engraving of the interior of the oratory is reproduced in Capri, *Storia*, 2:197.
51. This inventory (printed in Mischiati, "Bologna," pp. 157–60) lists music given by the Oratorians of Rome to those of Bologna.
52. Ricci, *Bologna*, p. 319ff.
53. A copy of the libretto is in I/Bu: A. V. T I g II, vol. 437.3.
54. Sesini, *Libretti*, p. 27.
55. The largest collection of such librettos is that of I/Bc, catalogued in Sesini, *Libretti*. For a chronological study of theatrical performances at Bologna that includes oratorios, see Ricci, *Bologna*, pp. 319–533.

the Oratorians at Madonna di Galliera, but by a number of other religious societies as well. Thus performances took place in the oratories of the Arciconfraternita di Santa Maria della Morte, the Arciconfraternita de' Santi Sebastiano e Rocco, the Venerabile Compagnia detta de' Fiorentini, the Venerandi Confratelli del Santissimo Sacramento, the Veneranda Compagnia della Carità, the Arciconfraternita della Santissima Trinità, the Veneranda Confratelli di Santa Maria della Cintura, and the Confraternita de' Poveri della Regina de' Cieli. Performances were also given at the oratory of San Domenico and the church of San Petronio. In the church of San Benedetto, staged dramatic works with oratoriolike subjects were performed in connection with the exercises of the society of the Dottrina Cristiana.[56] These works, which are not called oratorios on the title pages of their printed librettos, seem to be survivals of the *sacra rappresentazione*; yet from the mid-eighteenth century on, they have occasionally been referred to as oratorios.[57] Performances of oratorios throughout the year marked a variety of occasions—including the feasts of the church, the taking of religious vows, the visits of dignitaries, and the celebration of such events as a marriage or a baptism. Although more oratorios were performed during Lent than in any other season, apparently more were performed outside of Lent in Bologna than in Rome. The preaching of a sermon between the two parts of an oratorio performed in a sacred context was evidently practiced in Bologna: five of the printed librettos of Maurizio Cazzati's oratorios and one of those of Petronio Franceschini's make special mention of this fact in a note printed before the beginning of the oratorio's second part.[58]

Oratorios were performed in both secular and sacred contexts in such Bolognese academies as the Accademia dei Unanimi, the Accademia degli Anziani, and the Accademia delle Belle Lettere. Likewise in private palaces the contexts of oratorio performances were either sacred or secular. Cazzati's *Il transito di San*

56. An example is G. B. Bassani's *Il trionfo dell'amor divino* (Bologna, 1683). A copy of the libretto is in I/Bc: Lib. 421.

57. They appear as oratorios in the MS list, dating from the mid-eighteenth century, "Indice osia nota degli oratorij posti in musica da diversi autori," in I/Bc: Ms. H/6. In Luin, "Bologna," p. 155, they are also referred to as oratorios.

58. Cazzati: *Celeste aiuto* (Bologna, 1664; I/Bc: Lib. 7433), *Oratorio del diluvio* (Bologna, 1664; I/Bc: Lib. 928), *Il zelante difeso* (Bologna, 1664; I/Bc: Lib. 927), *Il transito di S. Gioseppe* (Bologna, 1665; I/Bc: Lib. 7435) and *Il Sisara* (Bologna, 1667; I/Bc: Lib. 929). Franceschini: *La vittima generosa* (Bologna, 1679; I/Bc: Lib 1765).

Gioseppe ("The Passing of St. Joseph"), for instance, was performed with a sermon at the midpoint in the private oratory of the palace of the marquis Giuseppe Maria Paleotti. Yet performances in private residences in Bologna had at times much the same secular atmosphere—that of social gatherings for the entertainment of the aristocracy—as did those in Rome. A contemporary source describing a performance of Pietro Degli Antoni's *Il Nabal* on 5 April 1682 at the Pepoli palace includes more information about the nonmusical than the musical aspects: the audience included visiting and local nobility, "to whom was given a very abundant refreshment of sweets, candies, fruits, drinks, ices, chocolates, etc. in many dishes, and it was truly most beautiful and well arranged."[59] The same source relates the details of a less orderly affair, the performance of Giovanni Paolo Colonna's *La caduta di Gerusalemme* ("The Fall of Jerusalem") on 21 June 1690. It appears to have taken place in a room attached to San Petronio for the use of the maestro di cappella—at that time Colonna—and was in honor of the visiting cardinal Radiziowski of Poland. "Thursday evening, in the room of Gio. Paolo Colonna, was sung the famous oratorio, *La caduta di Gerusalemme*, after which the ladies danced; and there was a great crowd with refreshments of many dishes of confections and other things, with drinks and ices. The Cardinal Legate [of Bologna, the chief executive of the city,] disliked these dances and ordered the guards to imprison Paolo Colonna in the house where these entertainments had been held."[60] Colonna avoided imprisonment, the report continues, through the influence of a powerful friend. This curious instance of extreme levity at a private oratorio performance is the only one of its kind known to the present author.

As a result of the geographical proximity of Bologna and Modena, their musical cultures were closely related.[61] Although no Congregation of the Oratory was established at Modena, the city followed the lead of Bologna in fostering performances of oratorios, often by Bolognese composers. From the end of the sixteenth century, the Este family dominated the cultural life of the

59. Antonio Ghiselli, "Memorie antiche mss. di Bologna," 43:116 (in I/Bu), translated from Ricci, *Bologna*, p. 353.

60. Ghiselli, "Memorie antiche," 52:340–41, translated in Schnoebelen, "Mass," p. 20.

61. For Modena's musical history and its relationship to that of Bologna, see G. Roncaglia, "Modena," in *MGG*, 9:cols. 396–401; Roncaglia, "Scuola"; and Luin, "Bologna."

city. Modena owes its period of greatest musical vitality in the seventeenth century to Francesco II d'Este (1660–94), who succeeded his father in 1662. For the first twelve years he reigned under the regency of his mother, Laura d'Este; at fourteen years of age, he became in fact duke of Modena, but he delegated most of the administrative duties to others and devoted his time to more pleasurable activities. As one of his first acts in this position, the musically trained boy increased the number of musicians at court from the previous eight to nineteen[62] and thus initiated a twenty-year period of intense musical activity and general splendor at court and throughout the city. Francesco II was also serious enough to distinguish himself by founding the University of Modena and vastly enlarging the Este Library. As a patron of music, he seems to have been more fond of oratorio than of opera; an inventory of his music lists ninety-eight manuscripts of oratorios and only sixty-three operas.[63] In Modena's period of greatest oratorio activity, 1680 to 1691, more than one hundred oratorios were performed there.[64] The most important location of oratorio performances sponsored by Francesco II was the oratory of San Carlo, which belonged to the Congregation of San Carlo; that congregation also operated a college that was important for musical education in the city.[65] Other performances took place in the court church, San Vincenzo, as well as in the churches of San Bartolomeo, San Domenico, and San Eufemia; in the court theater; and in the Teatro della Spelta.[66]

While oratorios from various parts of Italy—particularly from Rome and Venice—were performed at Bologna and Modena, many of the local composers, too, were active in this field. Among the most important were Maurizio Cazzati, Giovanni Paolo Colonna, Antonio Gianettini, Giacomo Antonio Perti, Giovanni Bonocini, and Giovanni Battista Vitali. Also active as composers of oratorios in these cities were Giuseppe Aldrovandini,

62. Roncaglia, "Scuola," p. 74.
63. Luin, *Repertorio*, pp. 421–24.
64. Luin, "Bologna," p. 153. In the same period only twelve opera performances are documented in Tardini, *Modena*, 3:862–63. It seems questionable that Tardini's findings reflect the actual practice, however, as the number of operas in Francesco's library would imply greater opera activity.
65. G. Roncaglia, "Modena," in *MGG*, 9:col. 397; Roncaglia, "Scuola," p. 72. For librettos of oratorios performed at this oratory, see *Raccolta* (vols. 2 and 3 are in I/MOe).
66. Luin, "Bologna," p. 153; Suess, "Vitali," p. 52; and Tardini, *Modena*, 3:862, 1437.

Attilio Ariosti, Giulio Cesare Arresti, Pirro Capacelli d'Albergati, Pietro degl'Antoni, Petronio Franceschini, Benedetto Ferrari, Domenico Gabrielli, Clemente Monari, Evil Merodach Millanta, Antonio Maria Pacchioni, Francesco Passarini, Francesco Antonio Pistocchi, Giacomo Cesare Predieri, Giovanni Antonio Riccieri, Pietro Giuseppe Sandoni, Giuseppe Antonio Silvani, and Angela Teresa Muratori Scanabecchi. Most of these composers are represented in the extremely rich Bologna and Modena libraries and archives by manuscript scores and/or printed librettos of oratorios. The two poets who are represented by more oratorio librettos in the Bologna and Modena libraries than any others are Giacomo Antonio Bergamori and Giovanni Battista Giardini. Other librettists represented are Benedetto Giuseppe Balbi, Valentino Carli, Vaiani de' Borghi, Alessandro Gargieria, the marquis Francesco Sacrati, Giovanni Francesco Savaro (who signed some of his librettos as Archdeacon of Mileto), Tomaso Stanzani, and Giovanni Battista Taroni.

Florence

Most who have written about the oratorio have assumed that the genre was introduced in Florence only near the end of the seventeenth century.[67] Recent research, however, indicates that this assumption is far from accurate.[68] It now appears that sacred dramatic dialogues were cultivated in Florence as early as the second decade of the century, that some of those from the 1620s to the 1640s (known in libretto only) were sufficiently long and dramatically developed to be classified as oratorios, and that works designated as oratorios were performed in Florence by the 1660s, if not somewhat earlier.

It seems strange that Florence, an important cultural center and the birthplace of St. Philip Neri, was not among the first cities to establish a Congregation of the Oratory. Yet it was only in 1632 that two young Florentine priests of noble birth, Pietro Bini and Francesco Cerretani, who were strongly influenced by the Ora-

67. For examples see Pasquetti, *Oratorio*, p. 373; Schering, *Oratorium*, p. 126; and Lustig, "Oratorii," p. 57.

68. I am grateful to Professor John Hill, whose study in progress of the oratorio in Florence is based on recent and extensive research in the archives and libraries of that city, for the valuable suggestions that he contributed to this section on Florence. Professor Hill's research will culminate in a monograph on the oratorio in Florence from its earliest appearances to 1808.

torians while in Rome, returned to Florence with permission to found a community of Oratorians at the small church of San Sebastiano.[69] There they conducted modest oratory services for eight years. In 1640 the community, consisting of eight members by then, transferred to the old church of San Firenze, which was to be the site of the new structures of this continually expanding institution. Not until 1668, however, were the Oratorians able to begin their building program. In the 108 years from 1668 to 1776, they constructed a new church (the present church of the Oratorians, San Firenze, built between 1668 and 1672 and originally intended to be an oratory), the attached residence, and the oratory (built between 1772 and 1776 and used since 1867 as a public building for various purposes).[70]

Little is known about the musical activities of the Florentine community for the first half century of its existence. The letter, cited above, written in the 1660s by the Roman Oratorian Mario Sozzini to the Florentine community implies a Florentine request for information about the musical practices of the Roman Oratorians. A letter from Zanobi Gherardi (d. 1694) of the Florentine community to his fellow Oratorian Filippo Bini is the earliest known indication of the performance of works called oratorios in Florence.[71] Gherardi dates the letter 20 November 1663 and states that he has just received a new oratorio by Melani (no first name is given) on the subject of "Santa Teodora." He also comments on the musicians who perform at the oratory (D. Filippo, Cosimo, D. Nazario, Gianmichele, and Salvetto, the last named of whom writes "most beautiful sinfonie") and adds that an oratorio, *Sant'Agostino*, will be performed on the evening of the feast of that saint. How much earlier than 1663 works called oratorios had been performed in Florence can only be a matter of conjecture until more evidence appears, but Gherardi's letter does not imply that they are new. Florentine recognition of the oratorio as a genre might well antedate this letter by ten years or more, since the Florentine Oratorians, like Oratorians elsewhere, sought to imi-

69. For details of the Florentine community's early history, see Cistellini, "Firenze," and its continuation, Cistellini, "Oratorio."

70. For the history of these structures, with illustrations, see Cistellini, *Momenti*, and Cistellini, *San Firenze*.

71. Gherardi to Bini, 20 November 1663, in I/Fo: D. 11. I gratefully acknowledge the help of Father Antonio Cistellini, Preposito of the Florentine Congregation of the Oratory, who called my attention to this letter.

tate Roman practices.[72] That music played a central role in the oratory services of the Florentine community by 1668 is clearly evident from the last-minute change in the design of the new church, which they considered at the time to be their new oratory; for musical reasons they drastically modified the design by eliminating the dome and adding a flat ceiling because "music, to which the said oratory will be especially dedicated, will have a better effect with a ceiling than with a dome."[73]

Most of the evidence of oratorio activity in Florence is found in the period of Cosimo III de' Medici, grand duke of Tuscany from 1670 to 1723. Extreme to the point of bigotry in his piety and devotion, Cosimo dedicated much of each day to prayer and to visiting churches and monasteries—"providing his people with a rare example of devotion," according to a contemporary report.[74] Although Cosimo personally preferred to have little to do with music or musicians,[75] and is not known to have given financial support to oratorio performances, his religious attitude would seem to have favored the activities of the oratories; a particularly large number of oratorio performances can be documented from about 1690 to 1725.[76] Cosimo's son, Prince Ferdinando de' Medici (1663–1713), was Florence's most munificent patron of music in this period and a great admirer of the works of Alessandro Scarlatti, as is indicated by the considerable correspondence between the two men.[77] Although Ferdinando's special interest was opera, he also encouraged performances of oratorios, particularly those by Scarlatti.[78]

72. Other societies, too, held services in which oratorios might have been performed at an early date. As pointed out in chapter 5, it is possible that some Latin works by Carissimi that could be called oratorios were heard in a Jesuit oratory service in Florence as early as 1642.

73. Translated from Cistellini, *San Firenze*, p. 14. Cistellini bases this writing on documents in the archive of the Florentine Oratorians; although he apparently quotes here from a document in the archive, he does not cite his source.

74. Quotation from Labat, *Voyages*, cited in Acton, *Medici*, p. 262. For a study of Cosimo III's rule and of Florence in his time, see Acton, *Medici*, pp. 116–306.

75. Fabbri, *Scarlatti*, p. 27.

76. For a bibliography of librettos printed in Florence in this period, see Lustig, "Oratorii." Collections of Florentine librettos in addition to those listed by Lustig exist in I/Fr (Misc. 226 and 227), I/Fo, and I/Fn. Four bound volumes (probably originally the property of the Florentine Oratorians) containing librettos of oratorios performed mostly in Florence from the late seventeenth to the late eighteenth century are found in D-brd/Hs: A/19015. Some of these librettos are of particular interest because of the scenic descriptions included, apparently to help the listener visualize the context of the dramatic action. Such descriptions are found in vol. 1, nos. 10, 37; vol. 2, nos. 44, 55, 61; vol. 3, nos. 93–95, 98, 99, 102, 109, 111–14, 116, 118, 119, 121–24, 130, 134. (See also above, n. 40.)

77. Fabbri, *Scarlatti*, pp. 33–98.

78. Ibid., pp. 28, 49–51, 67–68.

The Oratorians at the church of San Firenze appear to have been the most active in presenting oratorios in Florence, but performances also took place at the churches and oratories of many other societies—chief among them being the Compagnia dell'Arcangelo Raffaello detta la Scala, the Compagnia di San Sebastiano, the Compagnia della Purificazione di Maria Vergine e di San Zanobi detta de San Marco, and the Compagnia di San Jacopo detta del Nicchio. The performances at the church of the last-named society are particularly well documented, not only by the extant printed librettos of works they presented, but also by an important diary of the society's activities.[79] In an account of an oratorio performance sponsored by Ferdinando de' Medici on 12 April 1705 at this church, the diarist comments on the large audience and indicates that compline was sung before the beginning of the oratorio.[80] In this context the oratorio appears to have had a quasi-liturgical function, that of an appendage to the Divine Office. A particularly vivid account of the immense crowd that packed the church is found in the diarist's entry regarding a performance on Easter of 1712. This account is quoted here at length, for it sheds considerable light on both the practices surrounding such a performance and the economics of the Florentine oratorio.

On March 27, 1712. Some of our loving brothers having decided to present, in our venerable company of S. Jacopo Apostolo called del Nicchio, a noble oratorio with 4 voices entitled *Il figliuol prodigo* to be sung solemnly the evening of Easter, an invitation was first sent to the Most Serene Prince Gian Gastone, and then to Monsignor Girolamo Archinto, Papal Nuncio, and to Monsignor the Bishop of Fiesole; and the news of such a celebration having spread throughout the city, at 20 hours some of the brothers began to arrive to take their places. In this day the Vespers gathering was put aside, and although the great door of the company [i.e., the church of the company] was kept locked, many people were admitted privately through the exit from the sacristy past the small cross; and the great door of the company having been opened at 22½ hours, there was such a crowd of people that they not only filled the

79. Diary of the Compagnia di San Jacopo detta del Nicchio, in I/Fas: Compagnie religiose sopresse, "Partiti e ricordi della Compagnia del Nicchio." For quotations from this MS diary, see Pasquetti, *Oratorio*, pp. 381, 393–95; U. Kirkendale, *Caldara*, p. 148; and Fabbri, *Scarlatti*, p. 28.

80. Diary of the Compagnia di San Jacopo detta del Nicchio, 12 April 1705, in Fabbri, *Scarlatti*, p. 28; Pasquetti. *Oratorio*, p. 393.

whole company, but also the cloak room and the outer corridor, beyond which it was filled with people right up to the musicians' stage; and many of the nobility had to sit above it. The said stage occupied all the presbytery from one side to the other, right up to the cornice of the benches [choir stalls?]; the stage was made in an oval shape because of the altar, of which it was in front and was movable. The [number of] people continually growing, they had to stand in the sacristy and above it on the balconies at the main altar; in sum there was such a crowd of people that one cannot clearly explain it. It was so big that [though] it had been decided to sing Compline, it was not possible to sing it. Thus at 24 hours the said oratorio was begun with great triumph, the parts of which were distributed to the following performers:

First soprano: Sig. Stefano Frilli, virtuoso musician, who played the part of the Prodigal Son.

Second soprano: Sig. Morasi, Florentine musician as also the above, who played the part of the Brother of the Prodigal.

Contralto: Sig. Domenico Tempesti, excellent Florentine musician, who played the part of the Mother of the Prodigal.

Bass: Rev. Father Ferdinando Paolucci, Servite, favorite musician of Most Serene Prince Ferdinando of Tuscany, who played the part of the Father of the Prodigal.

In sum everything was greeted by general applause; the said voices were accompanied by a great quantity of instruments, as follows: Three harpsichords, two contrabasses, and in place of the 3rd contrabass, a bassoon was played by a German; then three bass viols, the first among which was played by Sig. Dr. . . . Salucci, celebrated player; the theorbo was played by Gio. Filippo Palafuti, our brother; and beside there were 16 violins, including violas, the first of which was played by Sig. Martino Bitti, Genovese, favorite of Most Serene Prince Ferdinando, a most celebrated player and famous throughout the world; and beside the oboe was played by Sig. _____ [Lodovico Erdtman?] and in fact he also was a celebrated performer; since a fine ensemble was created with such a quantity of instruments a smooth sound greeted the ears. When, in the course of the said oratorio Sig. Martino Bitti, the first violinist, as well as the said Sig. [Lodovico Erdtman?], oboe player, played things to arouse admiration, the people responded by crying *viva* in loud voices. . . . The said oratorio was finished; it was set by Giuseppe Maria Orlandini, Florentine, maestro di cappella of Most Serene Prince Gian Gastone, and composer to the same prince; it was dedicated to Most Illustrious Sig.ra Marchessa Teresa Tornaquinci Borboni del Monte, [of the] illustrious and prestigeous family [who therefore paid the composer]; the expense of the stage and wax [candles] for the choir stalls [?] and altar was paid by a collection among the brothers; and especially Most Illustrious Sig.

Canon Verrazzani, Monsignor of the Innocenti, gave 14 lire for the celebration, having been previously sollicited by our treasurer. The remainder of the expense for the singers and players and other attendant expenses of the said oratorio were paid by some loving brothers who had not [previously] agreed to such a burden.[81]

The excellence of the musicians hired for this performance, the enormous crowd that began to gather as early as four hours before the oratorio began, and the enthusiastic reception testify to the importance of oratorio in Florence at this time. The necessity of cancelling not only vespers but compline too, the latter because of the crowded and probably noisy condition of the hall, reveals something of the audience's attitude. They had clearly come for a musical experience, not for prayer or edification, and it is not surprising that such an audience would greet everything "with general applause" and would shout "viva!" in admiration of what they heard.

Little is known about performances of oratorios in the private palaces of Cosimo III's Florence. They were probably infrequent, since printed librettos attesting to their existence are rare. One such libretto is that of *La conversione di sant'Andrea Corsini* with music by Francesco Santini, which was sung in the palace of Marquis Filippo Corsini in 1705.[82] An instance of a performance in an educational institution is that of Cardinal Ottoboni's and A. Scarlatti's *Il regno di Maria Vergine assunta in Cielo*, presented at Florence in 1706,[83] the year following its elaborate performance in the courtyard of the Cancelleria at Rome. The Florentine performance took place in the rooms of the Pages of Honor of Cosimo III—children of the aristocracy, some from foreign countries, to whom the grand duke is said to have given an excellent education and early employment in his service.[84]

81. Diary of the Compagnia di San Jacopo detta del Nicchio, 27 March 1712, in MS in I/Fas: Compagnie religiose soppresse 1246, no. 10, "Ricordi e partiti della Compagnia di S. Jacopo detta del Nicchio," fols. 299v–300r. For this quotation I gratefully acknowledge the help of Professor John Hill, who supplied me with a transcription of the original Italian and an English translation of the entire passage. I have slightly modified his translation for use here. For partial quotations of the original Italian of this passage, see U. Kirkendale, *Caldara*, p. 148; and Pasquetti, *Oratorio*, pp. 395–96. In the above quotation the time designated as "24 hours," when the oratorio began, is sunset. (Cf. above, chapter 2, n. 58.) For another description of an oratorio performance (Benedetto Marcello's *Joaz*, in 1729), translated from the same MS source, see Hill, "Veracini," pp. 264–65.

82. Lustig, "Oratorii," p. 113.

83. For a copy of the libretto, see I/Fr: Musc. 227 (43).

84. Acton, *Medici*, p. 263.

Judging from the names of composers on printed librettos, the principal native Florentines whose oratorios were performed in Florence are Lorenzo Conti, Giuseppe Maria Orlandini, Francesco Maria Veracini, Anton Francesco Piombi, and Giovanni Maria Casini. Chief among the non-Florentines whose oratorios were performed in Florence are A. Scarlatti, Francesco Gasparini, Alessandro Melani, and Giovanni Carlo Clari. According to documents, the following Florentines wrote oratorios in the period before printed librettos: Bonaventura Cerri, Giovanni Battista Benvenuti, and Piero Sanmartini. The leading Florentine librettists were Pier Alessandro Ginori, Giovanni Pietro Berzini, and Cammillo Tacchi.[85]

Venice

The avid pursuit of opera in Venice by the laity and clergy alike provided a favorable atmosphere for the development of the operatically conceived oratorio of the late seventeenth and early eighteenth centuries.[86] The Congregation of the Oratory initiated its activities at Venice in 1661 in the small church of Santa Maria della Consolazione, called Santa Maria della Fava because of its location at the bridge known as Ponte della Fava.[87] The earliest known record of payment for the services of musicians by this community is dated 4 December 1667, when unnamed musicians were paid for performing in the oratory.[88] On the next day the following entry was made in a record of the Oratorians' activities: "Regarding the convenience of the new oratory, yesterday, which

85. The lists in this paragraph, kindly given to me by Professor John Hill, are based on his unpublished research.

86. For a discussion of this atmosphere, see U. Kirkendale, *Caldara*, p. 147.

87. For information regarding the musical activities of the Venetian Oratorians, I gratefully acknowledge the generosity of Dr. Paolo Pancino of Venice, who put at his disposal the unpublished typescript of his study "L'Archivio Musicale di S. Maria della Consolazione detta 'della Fava, già sede della Congragazione di S. Filippo Neri in Venezia"; Pancino's study has been published, with a much abbreviated historical preface, as Pancino, *Venezia*. Prior to Pancino's study the earliest evidence of oratorios performed at Venice dated from the early eighteenth century. (Schering, *Oratorium*, p. 130; and L. Tagliavini, "Oratorium, B," in *MGG*, 10: col. 127.)

Useful for studying the oratorio in Venice will be the catalogue of Venetian librettos compiled by Professor Sven Hansell, which is as yet unpublished and which bears the provisional title, "Texts of Oratorios, Motets and Other Sacred Works of Venice: A Catalogue of Published and Unpublished Librettos, 1675–1875." This catalogue corrects and expands Zorzi, "Venezia."

88. MS in I/Vas: Fondo Congregazione dei Filippini di Venezia, Busta 68 (Giornali di cassa e quaderni, 1662–73), int. 1, p. 56 (1).

was the second Sunday of Advent, the first *oratorio in musica* was performed, certainly with a great crowd, but with various difficulties and much expense."[89] Although the oratory services with music appear to have begun in 1667, it is not known whether this first service with music included an oratorio in the sense of a musical genre; this seems probable, however, if one considers the stage of development of the genre by this time and the Venetians' strong interest in the closely related genre of opera. From 1 January through 18 March 1668, musicians were paid for eleven performances in the oratory, and in the period between 1672 and 1674 the titles—without composers' names—of ten oratorios performed there are listed: *Moisè, Giuditio, Sicera [Sisara], Huomo moribondo, Creation del mondo, Oratorio del Passione, Cuor humano, S. Giovanni Battista, Peccator pentito*, and *Salomone*.[90] Giovanni Legrenzi is frequently listed in the records of Santa Maria della Fava throughout the 1670s. From about 1680 on, the records of this church are more general and provide little information about musical performances there.

In the course of the seventeenth century, the four hospitals of Venice that provided a home and an education for orphaned and unwanted children began to emphasize musical performance in the education of their girls. These institutions—the Ospedale della Pietà, the Ospedale degl'Incurabili, the Ospedale dei Mendicanti, and the Ospedale dei Derelitti ai Santi Giovanni e Paolo (called the Ospedaletto)—were generally transformed into conservatories of music.[91] By the 1660s the musical performances in the chapels of these institutions were important attractions for Venetians and visitors alike. A description of Venice published in 1663 takes special note of the music for mass, vespers, and compline at all four of the hospitals. It states that the girls sang and played various musical instruments for these services throughout the year and that the congregation was especially large during Lent.[92] Since

89. MS in I/Vsmc: "Libro de' Decreti della Congregazione dell'Oratorio di S. Filippo Neri di Vinezia, 1662," p. 6. I gratefully acknowledge the assistance of Padre Mario Cattappan of the church of Santa Maria della Consolazione for placing this volume at my disposal.

90. MS in I/Vas: Fondo Congregazione dei Filippini di Venezia, Busta 68, int. 1, pp. 56 (1), 66; int. 2, entry for 14 February 1673. Busta 63 (Libro Mastro, 1671–74), p. 60. Two of the oratorios listed had titles that are similar to two oratorios by Giovanni Legrenzi, his *La vendita del cuor humano* and *Oratorio del Giudizio*.

91. For details of the conservatories, see Arnold, "Conservatories," and Meyer-Baer, "Conservatories."

92. Sansovino, *Venetia*, p. 90; these comments on music are dated 1659.

oratorios were performed at Santa Maria della Fava in the 1670s, and probably even in the late 1660s, they might be assumed to have been performed at the conservatories in the same period. This assumption is strengthened by what appears to be an official connection between the Oratorians and the Mendicanti that was revealed in a printed libretto of an anonymous moral drama, *Anima pentita*, which was performed in 1667 "by the children of the pious Oratory of St. Philip Neri of the Hospital of the Mendicanti."[93] The earliest clear evidence known to the present author of the performance of oratorios in the conservatories is an anonymous libretto, dated 1683, of a work performed at the Pietà.[94] Other printed librettos of oratories show that they were performed at the conservatories throughout most of the period under consideration in this chapter.[95] It is of special interest that the majority of the oratorios performed at the conservatories were in Latin; these institutions and Crocifisso in Rome were highly exceptional in Italy for their cultivation of the Latin oratorio. One Venetian libretto, in Italian, includes comments about the context of the performance that show that the oratorio, performed at the Incurabili, formed a portion of a service that included a sermon between its two parts.[96] If Venetian oratorios were also performed in the palaces of the nobility in a secular context, which would seem probable, the evidence has not yet come to light.

Among the composers of oratorios active in Venice in this period were Giovanni Legrenzi, Carlo Pallavicino, Carlo Francesco Pollarolo, Antonio Caldara (until 1700), Francesco Gasparini (after 1700), Antonio Lotti, and Antonio Vivaldi. Since comparatively few librettos of oratorios performed in Venice are extant, the relative importance of the librettists represented in them cannot be determined. Among the librettists are Bernardo Sandrinelli, Nicolò Minato (but more important for Vienna than Venice), Francesco Maria Piccioli, G. M. Giannini, P. Pariati, Z. Vallaresso, and J. Cassetti.

93. Cited in Allacci, *Drammaturgia*, col. 90.

94. *La Maddalena che va all'Eremo: Oratorio per musica da recitarsi nel pio Ospitale della Pietà di Venetia* (Venice, 1683; I/Rsc: Carvalhaes, 9470).

95. The dates and numbers of additional Venetian librettos in the Carvalhaes collection of I/Rsc are 1686 (15337), 1690 (4146), 1701 (15421 and 9471), 1702 (12547 and 3740), 1707 (3308), 1709 (183), 1710 (8833). For references to other oratorio performances in the conservatories of Venice, see U. Kirkendale, *Caldara*, pp. 146–47. For a bibliography of oratorios performed at Venice in the seventeenth and eighteenth centuries, see Zorzi, "Venezia"; see also Hansell's catalogue in progress, cited above in n. 87.

96. *La Maddalena penitente* (Venice, 1701), p. 7. (I/Rsc: Carvalhaes, 9471.)

CHAPTER VII

The Later Baroque II:
The Libretto and Music

֍ *The Libretto*

Although incunabula of the oratorio date from around 1620 and
fully developed examples of the genre appear by the 1640s, not
until the 1660s are librettos known to have been printed for the
use of those attending oratorio performances.[1] In comparison
with opera, this is indeed late, for opera librettos were printed
throughout the first half of the seventeenth century—notably in
Florence, Mantua, and Venice.[2] The delay in the printing of oratorio librettos is probably due in part to the Roman origin of the
genre, for the Romans rarely printed librettos of operas and related
entertainments until the second half of the seventeenth century.
Furthermore, the humble social position of the oratorio in the
earliest stage of its development would scarcely have motivated
the printing of librettos. Intended as modest entertainments during
spiritual exercises that were usually of a popular nature, the earliest oratorios functioned in a context quite different from that of
early operas, which were performed in sumptuous palaces for the
aristocracy on festive occasions. The printed oratorio libretto,
increasingly prominent from the 1660s on, is concomitant with
the growing similarity of the functions of oratorio and opera and
with the cultivation of the oratorio in cities other than Rome. The
more the oratorio functioned as an operalike entertainment, the

1. The only librettos known to have been printed prior to this date appeared within the
collected works of Ciampoli and Balducci, both treated above, in chapter 4.
2. For a treatment of the early Baroque libretto in general, see Rolandi, *Libretto*, pp.
23–53.

more appropriate it became to make printed librettos available to the listeners, a large percentage of whom would be opera enthusiasts accustomed to using librettos in the theater.

Numerous designations were applied to oratorios in printed librettos even in this post-1660 period, when the word *oratorio* had already become clearly identified with the genre. The use of the terms *cantata* and *componimento sacro* for oratorios or oratoriolike works performed on Christmas Eve at the Vatican Apostolic Palace has been mentioned above. Latin oratorios performed at Crocifisso between 1678 and 1710 were designated by several terms—including *oratorium*, *melodrama*, *dialogus*, *drama sacrum*, and *drama tragicum*.[3] Oratorios in Italian, too, were designated by a variety of terms: *oratorio* is the one that was most frequently employed, but others are *compositione*, *componimento per musica*, *cantata musicale*, *dialogo*, *dramma* (also *dramma sacro*, *dramma musicale*, and *dramatica musicale*), *tragedia sacra*, and *accademia spirituale*.[4] There appears to have been no generally applicable rationale for the use of these terms, although further research might reveal some distinctions within the works of a given poet.

From the mid-century to the late Baroque, oratorios in two structural parts were characteristic, while those in three parts were highly exceptional.[5] Somewhat less exceptional were oratorios in one part, among which are the "cantatas" performed on Christmas Eve in the Vatican Apostolic Palace. In Palermo one-part oratorios in Italian, usually called *dialogo* on the title pages of their printed librettos, seem to have been preferred; and in Venice one-part

3. For oratorios designated by these terms, see the bibliography of oratorios performed at Crocifisso in Alaleona, *Oratorio*, pp. 351–62.

4. Examples of librettos using these terms are the following: G. Zagi, *La vera scorta al cielo appresa da i documente dalla morte: Compositione fatta in musica* (Bologna, 1671; I/Rsc: G. VIII. 16), music by G. A. Manara; P. F. Carli, *Il trionfo dell'amor divino: Componimento per musica* (Rome, 1687; I/Rli: 172. I. 19 [14]), music by G. Pacieri; anonymous, *Il colosso della constanza: Cantata musicale* (Rome, 1689; I/Rli: 171. J. 19 [3]), music by B. Pasquini; N. G. A. Tagliaferro, *La vittoria illustrata da raggi del sole eucharistico nel martirio di S. Giorgio: Dialogo* (Palermo, 1695; I/Rsc: Carvalhaes, 16154), music by I. Pulci; G. F. Savaro, *Il Caino condannato: Drama* (Bologna, 1669; I/Bc: Lib. 933), music by M. Cazzati; G. Gigli, *La Giuditta: Drama sacro* (Venice, 1700; I/Rsc: G. CS. 3. C. 26), music anonymous; Girolamo Frigimelica Roberti, *Tragedie sacre per musica* (Venice, 1702), a collection of librettos, treated in Leich, *Frigimelica Roberti* pp. 65–94; several anonymous authors, *La Giuditta: Accademia spirituale*, (Bologna, 1668; I/Bc; Lib. 932), music by Cazzati.

5. Examples of three-part oratorios are G. F. Savaro's *Il Caino* (Bologna, 1669; I/Bc: Lib. 933) with music by Cazzati and the anonymous *Oratorio per la Santissima Annunziata* (Rome, 1713) with music by Caldara. For information on the Caldara work, see U. Kirkendale, *Caldara*, pp. 119–20, 153, 337–40.

Latin oratorios were occasionally performed.[6] Brief, spiritual cantatas for two or more voices, using dialogue between characters and sometimes including a *testo*, continued to be heard in oratories throughout the Baroque period. These are usually designated by a term other than *oratorio*, as are Maurizio Cazzati's *Diporti spirituali per camera e per oratorii* (Bologna, 1668) and Giacomo Cesare Predieri's *Cantate morali e spirituali* (Bologna, 1696); a few such works, however, are actually given the term of the larger form, as are Hippolito Ghezzi's *Oratorii sacri a tre voci* (Bologna, 1700) and Pirro Capacelli d'Albergati's *Cantate ed oratorii spirituali* (Bologna, 1714).[7]

The chief tendencies of subject matter and its treatment in oratorio librettos are presented in the following comparison of Spagna's recommendations in his "Discorso intorno à gl'oratori" ("Discourse about Oratorios")[8] with the practice of his time. Termed a "Discorso dogmatico" on the title page of Spagna's *Oratorii* (Rome, 1706) in which it is found, his essay is both historical and didactic in purpose. The essay is based on its author's experience of at least fifty years as an oratorio librettist: Spagna states that one of his oratorios was written and performed in 1656.[9] If taken literally, Spagna would appear to have reformed successfully the oratorio libretto between 1656 and 1706, for by the latter date most of the ideas of his "Discorso," ideas that he

6. For examples of one-part librettos used at Palermo, see N. A. G. Tagliaferro's *La vittoria illustrata* (Palermo, 1695; I/Rsc: Carvalhaes, 16154), music by I. Pulci; the anonymous *L'effetti della penitenza nella conversione di S. Maria Maddalena: Dialogo* (Palermo, 1707; I/Rsc: Carvalhaes, 5295); and the anonymous *Le gare de gli elementi nella morte dell'autor della vita: Oratorio* (Palermo, 1708; I/Rsc: Carvalhaes, 7048). For examples of one-part oratorios performed at Venice, see the two anonymous librettos *Davidis conversio* (Venice, 1690; I/Rsc: Carvalhaes, 4146) and *Manassis captivitas* (Venice, 1693; I/Rsc: Carvalhaes, 9558).

7. For brief treatments of music from these four prints, see Schering, *Oratorium*, pp. 102, 125.

8. Spagna, "Discorso." All subsequent references in this chapter to the "Discorso" will be to the more readily available reprint and German translation in Schering, "Beiträge," pp. 49–64.

9. Schering, "Beiträge," p. 53. Other than this date, virtually nothing is known of Spagna's life until the early eighteenth century, when he served Cardinal Pietro Ottoboni as *maestro di casa*. Spagna calls himself a canon in 1706 and an abbot in 1720. (For his clerical titles, see the title pages of Spagna, *Oratorii*, vol. 2, and Spagna, *Fasti*.) Despite his patron's membership in the Accademia dell'Arcadia, Spagna seems not to have been a member; neither does he identify himself as such in his publications, nor does Crescimbeni, one of the founders of the academy, mention him in his history of Italian poetry, with its brief but important treatment of the oratorio: Crescimbeni, *Historia*, 1:312–14. For a modern reprint and German translation of these pages in Crescimbeni's work, see Schering, "Beiträge," pp. 67–70.

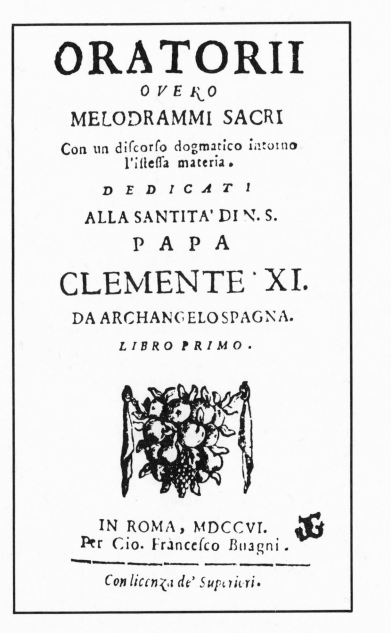

ORATORII

OVERO

MELODRAMMI SACRI

Con un difcorfo dogmatico intorno
l'ifteffa materia.

DEDICATI

ALLA SANTITA' DI N. S.

P A P A

CLEMENTE·XI.

DA ARCHANGELOSPAGNA.

LIBRO PRIMO.

IN ROMA, MDCCVI.
Per Cio. Francefco Buagni.

Con licenza de' Superiori.

FIGURE VII-1. Title page of Archangelo Spagna's *Oratorii*
(Rome, 1706).
(Courtesy of US/Wc.)

implied he had held for the entire fifty-year period, had been generally accepted; in fact, Schering sees Spagna as "the father of the sacred oratorio in the Italian language."[10] Had Spagna published his "Discorso" fifty years earlier, this appellation would have been more deserving; it is impossible to know, however, how many of the ideas in his treatise he actually professed from the 1650s on and how many are merely summaries of early eighteenth-century practice. Nevertheless, his treatise provides a useful frame of reference for understanding the development of the oratorio libretto in the Baroque period.

In the historical sketch of the oratorio with which Spagna begins his "Discorso," he pays considerable attention to Balducci and his extensive use of the narrator's part (in Balducci's *La fede*)—a role that, Spagna says, was probably derived from the Evangelist's part in the recitations of the Passion story sung during Holy Week. The *testo*—sometimes termed *textus, poeta, storico,* or *historicus*—was common in oratorios throughout the second half of the seventeenth century. Spagna disapproves of its use, however, for three reasons: the monotony of the usual concluding formulas that introduce characters in the drama (e.g., "thus he said," or "he exclaimed in these words"); the great amount of time allotted to the *testo* within a work (Spagna puns, "the *testo*, a large head in a small body"—"il testo, una gran testa in picciol corpo"); and the fact that the *testo* had "very few arias and many recitatives."[11] Spagna implies that his *Oratorio di Debora* (which he says was written in 1656 and performed in that year at San Girolamo della Carità) was innovative for the absence of a *testo*;[12] yet other works without a *testo* antedated it, possibly by ten years.[13] Although Spagna consistently rejected the *testo* for all of his librettos, it nevertheless remained characteristic—though often its lines were brief—until about the last decade of the seventeenth century; in the eighteenth century librettists virtually abandoned it. Spagna states that objections to abandoning the *testo* were raised in the seventeenth century on the grounds that the difference between "sacred and profane works"—that is, between oratorios and operas—thus disappears; but he argues that the subject matter,

10. Schering, *Oratorium*, p. 95.
11. Schering, "Beiträge," pp. 51–52.
12. Ibid., p. 53.
13. For instance, the *Oratorio per la Settimana Santa* attributed to L. Rossi and treated above in chapter 4 does not have a *testo*.

not the presence or absence of the *testo*, differentiates the libretto of oratorio from that of opera.[14] Since oratorio is not a scenic genre, however, narrative and descriptive elements must be included in the recitatives of the characters in the drama when a *testo* is not used; furthermore, the printed librettos of some oratorios include scenic descriptions to help the listener visualize the implied scenery and acting (cf. chapter 6, nn. 40, 76).

Abandoning the *testo* is one of Spagna's steps toward accomplishing his aim of making the oratorio "un perfetto melodramma spirituale" rather than a narrative-dramatic genre.[15] A further step is his recommendation that the librettist observe the Aristotelian precepts of restricting the action of the drama to one solar day and of casting the work in three phases: protasis, epitasis, and catastrophe. Turning to the ancients for guidance, he considers the tragedies of Seneca to be ideal models for oratorios because they are pithy and brief and they use few characters.[16] Spagna suggests that the length of an oratorio be restricted to about five hundred lines of poetry, that each of the two parts be limited to about one hour of music, and that no fewer than three and no more than five characters be employed.[17] His recommendation that poets follow ancient precepts and models appears to have had little effect on the oratorio's development in the seventeenth century. Except for the use of a commenting chorus, the influence of antiquity on the oratorio is scarcely in evidence until the eighteenth-century librettos of Zeno and Metastasio (treated in chapter 8), whose oratorios observe the unities of time, action, and place (the last two unities are not mentioned by Spagna). Spagna's recommendations regarding the length of an oratorio and the number of characters to be used, however, are more or less in accord with the normal practice during his lifetime. Most oratorios contain 350 to 450 lines of text and last one and one-half to two hours, with those in the earlier part of the period (Legrenzi, Stradella) tending to be somewhat shorter than those in the later part. Exceptions to the recommended limitations on the number of characters appear to be more frequent in the seventeenth-century *oratorio latino*, which occasionally requires nine to sixteen characters, than in the

14. Schering, "Beiträge," pp. 51–52.
15. Ibid., p. 54.
16. Ibid., pp. 54–55.
17. Ibid., pp. 60–61.

oratorio volgare;[18] after the turn of the century, however, such exceptions are extremely rare.

Turning to the question of the chorus in the oratorio,[19] Spagna says that it was once thought necessary to include parts for solists in the four vocal ranges (SATB) for the performance of the "madrigals," or choruses, that conveyed the moral at the end of the work. Speaking from the viewpoint of the early eighteenth century, however, Spagna says that it is no longer essential to include all those vocal ranges, since the moderns have generally abandoned the choruses for two good reasons: upon hearing a chorus the audience would assume that the action of the work was finished and "tumultuously leave," and not all composers have the ability to write well for chorus. (The librettist would never know, of course, what composer might set his work to music.) Spagna recommends, therefore, that an oratorio be concluded, not by a chorus, but by an "*arietta allegra*, which will disperse the audience with universal approval."[20] Both Spagna's comments about audience behavior and his questioning the ability of composers to write choruses seem to reflect the influence of opera, which even earlier than oratorio had begun to minimize the use of the chorus. It is understandable that opera lovers, who might have constituted the majority at an oratorio performance, would become impatient and walk out during a long, moralizing chorus at the end of an oratorio and that a composer of operas would have had little practice in writing choruses. Although the chorus is little used in oratorios of the late seventeenth and early eighteenth centuries—many oratorios have none at all—it is never completely abolished from the genre. For certain themes the poet would find a chorus of soldiers, Hebrews, or some other group, even an anonymous commenting chorus, to be essential; despite his comments in the "Discorso," Spagna himself includes such choruses in many of his librettos. When choruses are used, however, the librettist tends to restrict them to a few lines of poetry, and the composer usually sets

18. For examples of librettos requiring nine to sixteen characters, see the anonymous *Jericho urbis casus* (Rome, 1683; I/Rli: 170. F. 33 [24]; nine characters); I. B. Durante's *Judith de Holoferne triumphus* (Rome, 1685; I/Rli: 171. J. 19 [25]; ten characters); the anonymous *Davidis conversio* ([Venice], 1690; I/Rsc: Carvalhaes, 4146; twelve characters); the anonymous *Manassis captivitas* (Venice, 1693; I/Rsc: Carvalhaes, 9558; fifteen characters); and F. M. Piccioli's *Il trionfo dell'innocenza* (Venice, 1686; I/Rsc: Carvalhaes, 15336; sixteen characters).

19. Schering, "Beiträge," pp. 60–61.

20. Ibid.

the text so that it can be sung by an ensemble of the soloists who sing the dramatic roles; the requirement of a separate choral group is rare after Carissimi.

Spagna insists that recitatives as well as arias should be rhymed, and he takes to task those poets who are unwilling to spend the time and effort to write rhymed recitatives.[21] In this respect he followed his own advice in his librettos, and many other poets of the seventeenth century also wrote rhymed recitatives. Toward the end of the century, however, the use of rhymed recitative generally declined; it is rarely found in eighteenth-century librettos. In its place, both in Italian and Latin librettos, is a kind of blank verse with a free mixture of lines of seven and eleven syllables, occasional rhymes, and a rhymed couplet at the end of a recitative. Arias are rhymed throughout the Baroque period and tend to use line lengths other than seven and eleven syllables. Commenting on the structures of stanzas intended for arias, Spagna points to the trend toward the da capo aria in his time.[22] Strophic arias were formerly common, he says, but in recent times composers have begun to repeat the words and music of the first stanza after those of the second one; Spagna cautions poets to construct the text of an aria so that its first stanza will make sense when thus repeated. This comment reflects a fairly recent practice at the time of Spagna's writing, for the da capo aria was not generally used in oratorios until about the last decade of the seventeenth century.

The three principal sources of oratorio texts from the mid-seventeenth century to the late Baroque were the Bible, hagiography, and allegorically presented Christian virtues. The Old Testament, so rich in colorful stories of Jewish history and religion, was the primary source of biblical texts. Of the relatively few librettos based on the New Testament, those on the Passion story, without a *testo* and in poetic form, appear to have been the most numerous; these are found mostly in the repertories of Bologna and Modena.[23] Hagiographical texts were set to music with increasing frequency from the mid-seventeenth to the early eighteenth century until they rivaled, and with some composers surpassed, the number of Old Testament texts. Spagna states that he drew the material of his earliest oratorios from the Bible but

21. Ibid., pp. 56–58.
22. Ibid., p. 62.
23. For descriptions of such Passion oratorios, see Dardo, "Ariosti," and Schnitzler, "Perti."

that he turned to hagiography in his search for new subjects. He implies that his oratorio *Il pellegrino nella patria overo il santo Alessio* ("The Pilgrim in His Homeland or St. Alexis"), which he says he wrote in 1663, was innovative for its hagiographical derivation;[24] nevertheless, at least one such work, the *Santa Caterina* attributed to Marco Marazzoli and Luigi Rossi and discussed in chapter 4, appears to have preceded it.

The prominence of hagiographical subjects for oratorios has been attributed to the influence of the Counter-Reformation in general and to that of Jesuit dramas in particular;[25] the latter turned increasingly to hagiographical stories of conversion from about 1590 in an effort to further the process of conversion called for by the Council of Trent. Another possible reason for the prominence of hagiographical oratorios, as well as for the relative paucity of oratorios based on the New Testament, is the poets' fear of being accused of heresy for attempting to portray stories dealing with Christ and the Apostles.[26] Certainly the function of the oratorio as a substitute for opera would prompt poets to seek heroes—comparable to those of the opera stage— whose life stories could be elaborated with impunity; hagiography, already an inextricable mixture of fact and fiction, would provide such heroes. The heroic tendencies of both opera and oratorio, however, may be traced to a basic heroizing tendency in Baroque arts and letters.[27] This tendency is manifested in drama and the visual arts in several ways: in Venetian opera, by the numerous portrayals of great heroes of antiquity;[28] in Jesuit drama, as in oratorio, by the heroic attitudes of the saints and martyrs who are the spiritual counterparts of worldly heroes;[29] and in the visual arts of the Counter-Reformation, by the saints and martyrs who are only slight modifications of the heroic

24. Schering, "Beiträge," p. 54.

25. U. Kirkendale, *Caldara*, pp. 154–55; Müller, *Jesuitendrama*, 1:31.

26. Damerini, "Giuseppe," pp. 63–64. Fear of the accusation of heresy is also responsible for the *protesta* (declaration) found in many oratorio librettos of the period. The *protesta* usually states that references to pagan concepts and gods (Destiny, Fate, Fortune, Pluto, Proserpina, Jove, and others) are only poetic license and that the poet, nevertheless, professes the Roman Catholic faith. For Spagna's *protesta* in his *Oratorii*, see Schering, "Beiträge," p. 67.

27. Weisbach, *Kunst*, p. 24; U. Kirkendale, *Caldara*, pp. 155–56.

28. For brief summaries of numerous characteristic Venetian opera plots of the time, which reveal the emphasis on ancient heroes, see Kretzschmar, "Venetianische," pp. 8–15; on the heroic opera see also Wolff, *Venezianische*, pp. 32–69.

29. Müller, *Jesuitendrama*, 1:608.

figures portrayed by the ancients and by the Renaissance artists who reflected the humanism of their time.[30]

The third principal source of oratorio subjects, Christian virtues, which were presented allegorically, represents a continuation of the mode of thought that produced the dialogues between allegorical characters in the *laude* and the *sacre rappresentazioni* of the Renaissance and early Baroque, including Cavalieri's *Rappresentatione di Anima et di Corpo*. The oratorio with allegorical characters has much in common with Jesuit allegorical dramas and with the Spanish *autos sacramentales* of Pedro Calderón (1600–81).[31] Though seldom used, another source of oratorio texts is the life of a historical figure who, though not a saint, is viewed as a hero for his defense of the Roman Catholic faith. Two examples of works based on such subjects are Giovanni Battista Grappelli's oratorios on episodes in the lives of Thomas More and of Mary Stuart, Queen of Scots.[32]

Since the oratorio originated in Rome within the cultural milieu of the Tridentine reform and the Counter-Reformation, it is not surprising that the librettos reflect several aspects of this milieu other than the heroic. Mysticism, asceticism, gruesomeness, and eroticism have been considered important elements of the literature and art of the Counter-Reformation,[33] and all are reflected in oratorio librettos. The most important of these are the currents of mysticism and asceticism that run through virtually the entire corpus of oratorio librettos; although these elements appear in virtually any type of libretto, they are most evident in works that are based on the lives of mystical and ascetic saints. A characteristic example is the anonymous libretto *S. Editta, vergine e monaca, regina d'Inghilterra* ("St. Edith, Virgin and Nun, Queen of England"), set to music by Stradella.[34] This libretto portrays a queen who rejects her crown in favor of the ascetic life in a convent; she

30. Weisbach, *Kunst*, pp. 24–28.

31. Müller, *Jesuitendrama*, 1:60–62; Schering, *Oratorium*, p. 93.

32. *Il Tomaso Moro, gran cancelliere dell'Inghilterra* (Rome, 1702; I/Rli: 172. I. 19 [5]), music anonymous; *La morte di Maria Estuarda, regina di Scotia* (Rome, 1706; I/Rli: 170. C. 2 [5]), music by G. B. Pioselli. In the early eighteenth century Thomas More had not yet been canonized; thus, *Tomaso Moro* is a historical work, rather than a hagiographical one. Both librettos are treated in Pasquetti, *Oratorio*, pp. 347–53, where he terms this type of libretto the *oratorio civile*.

33. Each element is treated extensively, with illustrations, in Weisbach, *Kunst*, pp. 28–39, 78–202.

34. The libretto is printed in *Raccolta*, vol. 2.

obeys both the counsel of the personage Humility and the mystical inner voices by which God speaks to her heart, and she rejects the worldly arguments of the personages Greatness, Nobility, Sensuality, and Beauty. A more mystical and less ascetic example is the anonymous *San Filippo Neri* (Rome, 1705), set by A. Scarlatti.[35] In this work Faith, Hope, and Charity converse with, and reflect on, the life of St. Philip—who, having rejected riches and the world, yearns for a mystical union with God. The mystical and ascetic spirit of such librettos forms yet another link between the oratorio and the religious literature of Spain in the same period.[36]

Gruesomeness appears less frequently than asceticism and mysticism, but scenes of murder, execution, and martyrdom occasionally stress the horror and bloodiness of the situation, as paintings of the same period often do. An example of this tendency is found in Antonio Ottoboni's libretto *La Giuditta*, set to music by A. Scarlatti. The gruesome point is that at which Judith cuts off the head of Holofernes during his drunken sleep. After her first blow with the sword, her maid comments on the gory scene and describes the blood bubbling from Holofernes's neck; but Judith says she has not yet severed his head from his body; so she strikes a second time, and both women, delighted by their triumph, share in the lurid description, which compares the color of the victim's blood to the purple of royal vestments. Judith then tells her maid to pick up the bloody head with a cloth, for they will take it with them to their people in Bethulia.[37]

The erotic element is important in those oratorios that stress the sensual aspects of female characters and emphasize love scenes of a worldly, and operatic, nature. The oratorio with sensual emphasis has been termed the *oratorio erotico*.[38] Although most previous treatments of this type of libretto restrict it to the *oratorio latino*, it appears to have been equally important in the *oratorio volgare*. Characteristic subjects for such oratorios are those with female leading characters—especially Susanna, Judith, Esther, and Mary Magdalene—and subjects—such as the stories of David and

35. A copy of the printed libretto is in I/Rvat: St. Barb. JJJ. IX. 47 (8).

36. Schering, *Oratorium*, p. 93, includes the suggestion that the religious plays of Lope de Vega (1562–1635) and Pedro Calderón might have been used as models for oratorios.

37. Scarlatti, *Oratorii*, 3:137–39.

38. For comments on the *oratorio erotico*, with printed excerpts from librettos, see Pasquetti, *Oratorio*, pp. 257–71; Schering, *Oratorium*, pp. 84–85; Rolandi, *Libretto*, pp. 162–66; and U. Kirkendale, *Caldara*, pp. 156–57.

Bathsheba, Samson and Delilah, and Adam and Eve—that lend themselves to the exploitation of scenes involving sexual attraction. Recognizing the tendency of some poets to dwell on the sensual and erotic aspects of these stories, Spagna recommends that librettists pass as quickly as possible over episodes of secular love and place the major emphasis on penitence and virtue.[39] If one judge from their librettos, some poets evidently agreed with Spagna, but many clearly did not. In P. Gini's *Davidis amor in Bethsabeam*, for example, the scene of the first meeting of David and Bathsheba develops an ardent dialogue between them that stops just short of the passionate embrace that would be its logical conclusion.[40] The blend of sensuality and religious example in such works may be compared to a similar blend in the period's numerous poems, paintings, and sculptures on similar subjects, such as portrayals of Mary Magdalene.[41]

Understandably enough, humor is rare in oratorios; yet occasionally the musico-poetic conception of one or more characters is essentially comic. Such is the case in at least one passage of G. B. Giardini's libretto *La Susanna*, set by Stradella. In their duet "Chi dama non ama," the two Elders (T, B), lechers lusting after the beautiful Susanna, seem both poetically and musically related to *opera buffa* characters as they comically rationalize their passion for the young woman.[42]

Most oratorio texts of this period employ a strong conflict between good and evil or heaven and the world.[43] In the numerous works based on the lives of martyrs, for instance, the saint is the chief representative of heaven and receives support and counsel from one or more real, allegorical, or angelical characters; representing the world is a tyrant, often a Roman emperor, who seeks the moral downfall of his adversary, and he, too, is supported by one or more characters. If a *testo* is included, his narration is usually neutral, or it reflects the viewpoint of the representatives of heaven; at times, however, the *testo* shows considerable sympathy for a sinner who is being justly punished. The principal theme of a work based on the life of a martyr is the triumph of heavenly love,

39. Schering, "Beiträge," p. 62.
40. The passage is quoted in part and discussed in Pasquetti, *Oratorio*, pp. 269–71.
41. For examples in literature and art, see Weisbach, *Kunst*, pp. 32–34, 139–51.
42. For this passage in a MS score, see I/Moe: Mus. F. 1137, fols. 27, 48.
43. For a treatment of this type of libretto in the oratorios of Caldara, which is also generally applicable to oratorios of the period, see U. Kirkendale, *Caldara*, pp. 157–67.

and when the heroine is a virgin martyr, such as St. Cecilia or St. Catherine of Alexandria,[44] the triumph is also that of chastity. The development of such a plot includes various worldly temptations, moral arguments on both sides, threats of physical violence to the saint, and finally a glorious martyrdom for the saint, whose soul will pass into a state of eternal bliss. Hagiographical oratorios based on the conversion of sinners usually present the conflict between heavenly and worldly influences during the portrayal of the saint's early, sinful life; the saint at first rejects but eventually accepts the moral arguments of the representatives of heaven.[45] Allegorical works sometimes follow a plan similar to that of the saint who is a converted sinner. For instance, in an anonymous libretto set by Legrenzi, *La vendita del core humano* ("The Sale of the Human Heart"),[46] Pleasure and the World compete with an Angel for the Human Heart; the latter accepts the "price" of material rewards offered by Pleasure and the World and gives himself to them, only to find that he is miserable. He later discovers that Christ has paid an even greater price for him by His suffering and death on the cross; the Human Heart then repents and gives himself to Christ. Strong conflicts, often between representatives of the people of God and their adversaries, also develop in the biblical stories. As do the hagiographical works, such biblical oratorios employ one central figure representing God or his people and another representing the adversary, and each receives assistance in his arguments from one or more supporting characters. Typical conflicts are those of Moses versus Pharoah, Judith versus Holofernes, and David and the Hebrews versus Goliath and the Philistines.[47]

44. For characteristic librettos based on the lives of these two saints, see the anonymous *Il martirio di S. Cecilia* (Rome, 1708; I/Rvat: St. Barb. JJJ. IX. 30 [6]), music by A. Scarlatti; and F. F. Accolti's *Il martirio di S. Caterina* (Rome, 1708; I/Rli: 171. J. 19 [12]), music by Caldara. Regarding the latter libretto, see U. Kirkendale, *Caldara*, pp. 116, 166, 329–30.

45. For examples of this type, see Pompeo Figari's *La conversione della Maddalena* (Rome, 1702; I/Rli: 172. I. 19 [13]), music by C. Vinchioni; and the anonymous *La conversione di S. Agostino* (Rome, 1705; I/Rli: 172. J. 15 [2]), music by C. Rotondi.

46. This libretto is known to exist only in the MS score (I/Rvat: Chigi, Q. VI. 89).

47. Examples of oratorios on these subjects are G. B. Giardini's *Il Mosè, legato di Dio e liberatore del popolo ebreo* (Modena, 1686; pr. *Raccolta*, vol. 2), music by G. P. Colonna; the two librettos set by A. Scarlatti on the story of Judith and Holofernes, mentioned on p. 338; and the libretto *Davidis pugna et victoria*, music by A. Scarlatti, mentioned on p. 338.

Librettos based on themes with relatively little conflict—all the characters representing heavenly love—clearly constitute a minority. The dramatic element is less important in such works, and they tend to emphasize narration and reflection. An example is the anonymous *San Filippo Neri*, discussed above, a largely narrative-reflective work in which the three allegorical characters are Christian virtues and the only struggle is that within St. Philip's soul as he strives for Christian perfection. Christmas oratorios, too, tend to use narrative-reflective texts with little or no conflict; that mentioned above (*Cantata da recitarsi*, cf. chapter 6, n. 37) of Francesco Maria Gasparrini set by D. Scarlatti for performance on Christmas Eve, 1714, at the Apostolic Palace employs a chorus of Angels and four other characters—Faith, Charity, Virginity, and the Archangel Gabriel—all with heavenly motivation.

The change that occurred in the design of oratorio librettos from the mid-seventeenth century to the late Baroque is similar to the one that occurred in opera librettos: a change from a mid-century flexible design, offering a variety of possibilities in the styles of successive musical passages, to a late Baroque procedure, consisting of the relatively inflexible alternation of poetic units intended for recitatives and arias. According to the rationalistic conventions of the early eighteenth-century *opera seria* and oratorio, the text of each aria (and its music as well) is conceived as a stylization of the basic affection, or mood, for which the preceding recitative prepares. The recitatives carry the narrative and dramatic elements, but the aria, although at times dramatic, is predominantly lyric. Because of the common practice of stylizing the affections in arias, their texts may be classified in a variety of distinct types, some of which are foreshadowed in the mid-seventeenth century. Thus the simile aria—in which the character compares himself or his mood to such phenomena as a bird in flight, a turtledove moaning or weeping, a ship on a stormy sea, or a raging waterfall—is common in both oratorios and operas. Numerous other types—arias of vengeance, rage, jealousy, military combat, love, and bucolic sentiments—are amply provided in librettos of the late Baroque.

The Music of the Oratorio from the 1660s to the 1680s

The above considerations of social contexts, patrons, composers, and poets focuses on some of the chief centers of oratorio activity in Italy. Thus, there are Roman, Bolognese-Modenese, Florentine, and Venetian "schools" of oratorio composers in the sense that certain composers wrote oratorios primarily for those centers. From the standpoint of musical style, however, the extant oratorios of these composers show far more similarities than differences; there seems to be a single, basic, "pan-Italian" style with only slight local variants.[48] The following consideration of the music of the oratorio from the 1660s to the 1680s will first summarize the general characteristics of the pan-Italian oratorio style, which is much like the style of opera; this will be followed by brief descriptions of three representative oratorios.

General Characteristics

As pointed out above, most oratorios of this period require three to five solo voices to sing the roles, and these voices join together in ensembles of characters and in those few numbers marked *coro* or *madrigale*. An independent choral group is rarely needed. The instrumental requirement of many oratorio scores of the period is restricted to the basso continuo; other scores call for two or three stringed instruments (two violins and, at times, a viola) in addition to the continuo, but the requirement of a larger orchestra is exceptional until the 1680s.

A free mingling of passages in recitative, arioso, and aria styles continues to be characteristic of the oratorio throughout the period under consideration. Within an essentially declamatory section, for instance, the music will often fluctuate from one of these styles to another, particularly when certain words or phrases require special affective or descriptive treatment. It is especially characteristic that the last few measures of a recitative be set in arioso or aria style. Recitative and arioso passages are virtually

48. For the concept of a pan-Italian style of mid-seventeenth-century opera, a style stemming from Rome but with variants in the Venetian and other schools, see Pirrotta, "Cesti," pp. 37–38, and Holmes, "Orontea," p. 108. Abert, *Monteverdi*, p. 240, seems to imply a similar concept by pointing out the Roman derivation of Cavalli's style in his earliest operas.

always accompanied by basso continuo alone. Structures comparable to those of solo cantatas of the period are often found within oratorios. In such structures one character will sing a complex of units in recitative, arioso, and aria styles, which will sometimes be unified by repeated material, such as a brief vocal refrain or an instrumental ritornello. As a result of the flexible approach to the succession of styles in oratorios of this period, the contexts of arias are extremely varied: a given aria may be preceded and/or followed by a recitative or arioso, another aria, or an ensemble—any of which may or may not involve the character who sings the aria. Thus the aria context most characteristic of the early eighteenth century, when an aria is usually preceded and followed by recitatives, is only one of many equally important possibilities.

Sections designated as arias are often quite brief—sometimes no more than ten to fifteen measures long—in the earlier works of this period, but they tend to increase in length toward the end of the period. The longest arias are usually in strophic or modified strophic form with two stanzas of poetry. The most common structure of both strophic and nonstrophic arias is the binary with a modified repetition of the second section—that is, the ABB' form. The B section of this structure is characteristically in a key related to that of A; the B'—which either moves back to, or is entirely in, the home key—is usually an elaboration of B, but sometimes it is nothing more than a transposed restatement of it. Among the other aria structures are the simple binary form (AB or AABB) and numerous modifications of it, the through-composed aria organized as a series of unrelated or only generally related sections (found less frequently than the binary forms), and the occasionally used ABA' and ABA forms; the designation *da capo* is virtually nonexistent. Although strophic variation has been abandoned, the aria unified by a basso ostinato or a modulating quasi ostinato is fairly common. The numerous aria styles include those with smooth bel canto melodic lines, syllabic declamation with more or less consistently short note values, march rhythm and fanfares for a martial style, and dance rhythms. Although melismas are often used to express the text, the elaborate coloratura style, found especially in the rage and vengeance arias of the eighteenth century, is rare. Arias with motto beginnings occur frequently. In such arias the voice states the initial motive or phrase, then rests during a brief instrumental interlude, and then restates the initial motive or phrase and continues without further interruption. Arias accompanied only by basso continuo are the most common, but orchestrally accompanied arias become increasingly prominent during the course of the period. Ensembles tend to employ the various aria forms described above.

The most extended instrumental pieces in oratorios are the introductory sinfonie; these range from brief chordal or imitative pieces to longer ones in several contrasting sections that resemble short church sonatas. The orchestral passages in arias, ensembles, and choruses range from brief phrases and ritornellos between vocal sections to rather elaborate accompaniments; concerto grosso instrumentation, however, such as that used in the work by Stradella described below, is exceptional.

The harmonic style of oratorios in this period is clearly tonal with modulations to closely related keys. The Neapolitan sixth is found occasionally, but chromaticism is generally rare and tends to be restricted to the setting of emotive words and phrases and to the rather limited modulations.

Representative Examples

The oratorios described below are by three outstanding composers, whose oratorios show the essential aspects of the genre in the period from the 1660s to the 1680s. Legrenzi is the earliest of the three; Stradella and Colonna, approximate contemporaries, represent a later generation.

Giovanni Legrenzi. Born in 1626 at Clusone, near Bergamo, Legrenzi probably held his earliest professional position at Bergamo's church of Santa Maria Maggiore.[49] In 1657 he went to Ferrara as maestro di cappella of the Accademia dello Spirito Santo. His earliest operas were first performed at Ferrara in the 1660s. Legrenzi went to Venice sometime after 1665 or 1668,[50] and he remained there until his death in 1690. In Venice he became the director of the conservatory of the Mendicanti in 1672; in the 1670s he was also employed at the Oratorians' church of Santa Maria della Fava. Legrenzi was appointed vice maestro at the church of San Marco in 1681 and maestro di cappella in 1685.

49. For Legrenzi's biography see Fogaccia, *Legrenzi*, pp. 19–57, and C. Sartori, "Legrenzi," in *MGG*, 8:cols. 478–83.
50. Capri, *Storia*, 2:97.

FIGURE VII-2. Giovanni Legrenzi (1626–90).
(Reproduced by permission of I/Bc.)

According to his expressed wish, he was buried in Santa Maria della Fava.

Well known in his time as a composer for theater, church, and chamber, Legrenzi wrote at least seven oratorios:[51] *Erodiade* ("Herodias"), *La morte del cuor penitente* ("The Death of the Penitent Heart"), *Oratorio di Giudizio* ("Oratorio of the Judgment"), *Il Sedecia* ("Zedekiah," or "Sedecias"), *Il Sisara* ("Sisera"), *Gli sponsali d'Ester* ("The Nuptials of Esther"), and *La vendita del core humano* ("The Sale of the Human Heart," possibly the same as *Il prezzo del cuore humano*, "The Price of the Human Heart"). Judging only from their known printed librettos, one would assume that his oratorios were performed between 1665 and 1678 only in cities other than Venice—Ferrara, Bologna, Modena, and Vienna. Yet his official connection with two Venetian institutions where oratorios were performed, Santa Maria della Fava and the Mendicanti, supports a reasonable assumption that his oratorios were also performed in Venice at these institutions, if not at others.[52] Of the seven works listed above, the music of only three—*Morte*, *Sedecia*, and *Vendita*—is known to survive.[53] Five of the seven employ biblical subjects, and two are allegorical.[54] All three works of which the music is known are in two structural parts. *Vendita* requires four voices (SATB); the other two require five (SSATB). In each of the three works a chorus, which is called *madrigale* and which can be sung by an ensemble of the soloists, is placed at the end of each structural part; choruses are otherwise rare. Only *Sedecia* includes a *testo*, and only *Morte* requires instruments (three strings) other than basso continuo.

Il Sedecia, selected for special consideration here, is musically representative of Legrenzi's extant oratorios, and its anonymous libretto is characteristic of the majority of his oratorios for its biblical derivation. The libretto is based on the Old Testament

51. For lists of Legrenzi's oratorios, with discrepancies among them, see Fogaccia, *Legrenzi*, pp. 263–69; C. Sartori, "Legrenzi," in *MGG*, 8:col. 481; and H. Wolff, "Legrenzi," in *Enciclopedia d. mus.*, 2:585–86.

52. Two of his oratorios might have been performed in 1672–74 at Santa Maria della Fava (see chapter 6, n. 90).

53. MS sources: *Morte*, A/Wn: 18890; *Sedecia*, I/Rvat: Chigi Q. VI. 90; and *Vendita*, I/Rvat: Chigi Q. VI. 89. *Vendita*, edited by Albert Seay, is scheduled for publication in *Collegium musicum*, ser. 2 (Madison, Wis.: A-R Editions).

54. Biblical: *Erodiade*, *Giudizio*, *Sedecia*, *Sisara*, and *Ester*; allegorical: *Morte* and *Vendita*.

story of Zedekiah, the last king of Judah.[55] According to biblical accounts, Nebuchadnezzar, the Chaldean king of Babylon, appointed his uncle, Zedekiah, to reign as king in Jerusalem. Zedekiah eventually revolted against Nebuchadnezzar, and the latter, with his Chaldean army, laid siege to Jerusalem for three years. During the siege the prophet Jeremiah warned that Zedekiah's patient submission to the dominion of Nebuchadnezzar was the will of God and that his failure to submit would result in his destruction. Zedekiah rejected this warning, and he and his army escaped by night through a breach in the city wall at the royal garden; the Chaldean army pursued them and captured Zedekiah and his sons. Nebuchadnezzar punished Zedekiah by slaying his sons before his eyes, blinding him, and leading him in chains to prison in Babylon.

In the oratorio, which is written for five voices and basso continuo, the two central figures are Nebuchadnezzar (Nabucco, B), portrayed as an instrument of heavenly vengeance, and Zedekiah (T), a faithless vassal; the latter is supported by his two Sons (SS). The *Testo* (A) is sympathetic to the woes of Zedekiah and his Sons. A chorus of Zedekiah's Soldiers (SSATB) sings only once, at the opening of part I, and a chorus of Chaldean Soldiers (ATB) sings twice. As in all of Legrenzi's oratorios, parts I and II close with moralizing choruses labeled *madrigale*. At the beginning of the oratorio, Zedekiah and his army are fleeing Jerusalem. He and his Sons pause outside the royal garden to bid a lamenting farewell to the city and the kingdom. As they continue their flight, the chorus of Chaldean Soldiers signals the victory over Jerusalem. Nebuchadnezzar resolves to have Zedekiah captured and taken prisoner, and the pursuit begins. The *madrigale* that closes the first part warns that in vain one attempts to flee the anger of heaven. At the beginning of part II, Zedekiah and his Sons pause to rest by a brook in the plain of Jericho. As dawn approaches, the Chaldean Soldiers seize them and bring them before Nebuchadnezzar. The latter gives vent to his rage and sentences the Sons to be slain in Zedekiah's presence. Zedekiah begs that his life be taken in place of theirs, while both Sons wish to die to save their father. When

55. 4 Kings (in Douay Version; 2 Kings in King James Version) 24:17–20 and 25:1–7; Jer. 39:4–7 and 52:1–11; 2 Par. (in Douay Version; 2 Chron. in King James Version) 36:10–21.

Nebuchadnezzar gives the sign, the Sons are killed; he then orders that Zedekiah be blinded. Zedekiah, blind and repentant, laments the folly of his unworthiness and accepts his punishment as the just will of God. The final *madrigale* exhorts mortals to learn and obey the laws of God.

About one-fourth of the work is written in recitative; although the recitatives are largely in simple style with little melodic interest, they occasionally slip briefly into arioso and frequently conclude with a few measures in aria style. Of the ten arias in the oratorio, four are for Zedekiah; two for Nebuchadnezzar; and two for each of Zedekiah's two Sons. Over half of the arias have motto beginnings; half are in predominantly triple meter and half in duple. The lengths range from eighteen to forty-four measures for non-strophic and up to eighty-two measures for strophic arias, with most arias less than thirty measures long. Three arias are strophic with two stanzas of poetry. Modified binary forms prevail, with the ABB' form occurring the most frequently. The ABA' form is used only once, but the ABA form is not used.

The two leading characters, Zedekiah and Nebuchadnezzar, are strikingly contrasted in their arias. Zedekiah is a pitiable soul who understands his errors only too late; Nebuchadnezzar is the powerful and angry king who must strike down the perfidious vassal. The four arias sung by Zedekiah form parts of two long cantatalike scenes. The first of these occurs near the beginning of the oratorio when Zedekiah and his Sons pause in their escape. Zedekiah is already repentant for his inconstancy as he expresses his sorrowful farewell to his royal palace. The scene begins with a recitative, "Addio mia reggia," with dissonances resulting from a dominant chord (implied) over a tonic pedal (Example VII–1a); this recitative is followed by a strophic aria, "Io vi perdo," which has a motto beginning (Example VII–1b) and a text reflecting on the fragility of pomp, an unstable gift of fortune. In the following brief section in aria style and in a succeeding recitative, Zedekiah prepares for the change of affection in the last aria of this scene, "Armatevi 'l petto." In this aria, with a motto beginning (Example VII–1c), he advises his sons to arm their breasts with courage and constancy as shields against the arrows of angry fortune and the blows of destiny. This vigorous aria in martial style is dominated by the dactylic pattern frequently used by Carissimi and others to convey excitement. Zedekiah's other cantatalike scene, one of

Example a:

Farewell, my royal palace, farewell . . .

Example b:

I am losing you and abandoning you . . .

Example c:

Arm your breast with strong courage . . .

intense lamentation, occurs just after he has been blinded. This scene is the last musical unit of the oratorio prior to the final chorus. The scene begins with a pair of short arias ("Nabucco hai vinto" and "Io mortal") marked *adagio*, and it continues with two recitatives separated by a brief passage in aria style. Both of Nebuchadnezzar's arias express his wrath and hint at the characteristic vengeance aria of the early eighteenth century; and both employ an essentially quick-note declamatory style with occasional melismas for the expression of violent affections. The first aria, "Dal mio braccio" (Example VII–2a), occurs early in the oratorio when Nebuchadnezzar learns that Zedekiah and his sons have escaped, and the second, "Sù, svennateli" (Example VII–2b), when Nebuchadnezzar orders that the Sons of Zedekiah be killed.

EXAMPLE VII-2. *Il Sedecia*—Legrenzi (I/Rvat: codex Chigi, Q. VI. 90, fols. 19ʳ, 32ʳ).

Example a:

By my lightninglike arm he will be struck down . . .

Example b:

Come, kill them, the perfidious offspring, worthy victims of my rigor . . .

The ensembles of the oratorio include two duets for the Sons, a trio for the Sons and Zedekiah, two choruses of Soldiers as mentioned above, and the two final *madrigali*. Both the imitative and chordal textures are present in most of the ensembles. The two *madrigali* begin with brief chordal passages and are thereafter essentially contrapuntal.[56]

Alessandro Stradella. Born at Rome in 1644, Stradella studied there probably with Ercole Bernabei and became an outstanding representative of the Roman school.[57] He served some of the most illustrious patrons of Rome—among them Queen Christina of

56. For modern performing editions of the final choruses of parts I and II, see Legrenzi, *Quanto*, and Legrenzi, *Mortali*, respectively.
57. For Stradella's biography see O. Jander, "Stradella," in *MGG*, 12:cols. 1418–22.

Sweden, the Colonna family, Flavio Orsini, and the Pamphilj. In 1677 he left Rome and traveled to Turin by way of Venice and then to Genoa, where he was murdered in 1682. Stradella's numerous adventures in love, one of which led to his murder, have given rise to fanciful myths that served as material from the eighteenth to the twentieth centuries for opera librettos, a play, several novels, a song text, and a poem.[58]

Particularly active as a composer of vocal and instrumental music for theater and chamber, Stradella also wrote church music and at least seven oratorios, six of which are extant: *Ester, liberatrice del popolo ebreo* ("Esther, Liberator of the Hebrew People"), *San Giovanni Battista* ("St. John the Baptist"), *San Giovanni Grisostomo* ("St. John Chrysostom"), *Santa Edita, vergine e monaca, regina d'Inghilterra* ("St. Edith, Virgin and Nun, Queen of England"), *Santa Pelagia* ("St. Pelagia"), and *Susanna*.[59] The only known dates and places of performances of Stradella's oratorios during his lifetime are those of a lost work of unknown title (1667 at Crocifisso in Rome), *San Giovanni Battista* (1675 at the oratory of the church of San Giovanni dei Fiorentini in Rome), and *Susanna* (1681 at the oratory of San Carlo in Modena); the remaining oratorios were probably composed for Roman performances in the 1660s and 1670s.[60] All six of the above-named works are settings of Italian texts—three of which are biblical and three nonbiblical and hagiographical.[61] The six extant oratorios are all in two parts, require five singers, and make sparing use of the chorus (always composed so that it may be sung by an ensemble of the soloists); only one closes with a chorus—the others close with recitatives, arias, or duets.[62] Three of the oratorios use a

58. For a bibliography of these, see Jander, "Stradella," 1:3–4. Giazotto, *Stradella*, the most recent of such writings, is a mixture of fact and fantasy. (Cf. Jander, Review.)

59. For the sources of Stradella's oratorios, see the revised catalogue of his works in Jander, "Stradella," 2:11–13. For a modern edition in progress of all of Stradella's oratorios, see Stradella, *Oratori*; only one volume, *Ester*, has appeared to date. Gianturco, "Oratorios," is a brief study of Stradella's oratorios.

60. For comments on other dates and places of performances of Stradella's oratorios, most of which are speculative and remain to be documented, see Giazotto, *Stradella*, 1:133, 203–14, 240, 242–49, 274, 574, 581; 2:720–28, 779, 780, 806–7. See also Jander, "Stradella," 1:25, 28, 45.

61. Biblical: *Ester, San Giovanni Battista*, and *Susanna*; nonbiblical: *San Giovanni Grisostomo, Santa Edita*, and *Santa Pelagia*.

62. *Ester* and *Susanna* close with choruses. Oratorios closing with recitatives are *Grisostomo* (pt. II) and *Edita* (pt. II). Both parts of *Pelagia* close with arias; and parts closing with duets are *Grisostomo* (pt. I), *Ester* (pt. I), *Edita* (pt. I), and *San Giovanni Battista* (pts. I and II).

testo. The instrumental requirements of the oratorios are basso continuo only (one work), basso continuo with a small instrumental ensemble (four works),[63] and a larger ensemble of strings, in *San Giovanni Battista*, divided into concertino and concerto grosso.

San Giovanni Battista was first performed in a series of fourteen oratorios sponsored by a society of Florentine gentlemen in Rome in celebration of the Holy Year of 1675, mentioned above. (See p. 260.) A work of primary historical and musical importance, it was highly prized by Stradella's contemporaries and successors; it exists in an unusually large number of complete manuscript copies from the seventeenth and eighteenth centuries, and many anthologies of the same period include excerpts from it.[64]

The libretto by Abbate Ansaldi is loosely based on the New Testament story of the imprisonment and death of John the Baptist.[65] The central conflict in the plot is between John (A, for castrato) and Herod (B); the former is supported by the chorus of Disciples (STB, SSATB) who briefly enter twice, and the latter, by the Counselor (T), Herodias (S), the Daughter of Herodias (S),[66] and an anonymous chorus (SSTB)—evidently a *turba* of bystanders at Herod's court—which briefly sings twice. A contrast of personalities equally as strong as that between John and Herod occurs between the indecisive, tortured Herod and the cruel Daughter. Part I of the libretto begins with a pastoral scene in which John bids farewell to the woods in which he has lived in blessed seclusion in union with God. When his disciples learn that he intends to go to Herod's court, they urge him to stay, but he fearlessly asserts that he has been elected by God for this mission. At court, festivities are in progress when John enters and interrupts them; as a messenger of God, he calls for Herod to give up his brother's wife. The angry Herod, urged on by those around him, has John thrown into prison. Part I closes with a duet sung by Herod and the

---

63. Two of the oratorios, *Ester* and *Edita*, do not include instrumental parts in their MS scores but do include the word *ritornello* a number of times, possibly implying that more instruments than the basso continuo are to play.

64. For locations of MSS of *San Giovanni Battista*, see Jander, "Stradella," 2:11–12; for a printed libretto see *Raccolta*, vol. 3. A modern performing edition of the oratorio, with commentary, is Daniels, "Stradella."

65. Matt. 14:3–11; Mark 6:17–28; Luke 3:19–20.

66. The Daughter of Herodias is, of course, the notorious Salome, but in both the oratorio and the biblical accounts she is merely called Herodias's daughter.

FIGURE VII-3. Title page of the libretto for the Modena performance in 1688 of Alessandro Stradella's *San Giovanni Battista*. (*Raccolta*, in I/MOe.)

Daughter, who gloat over John's imprisonment for having scorned the wrath of the throne. Part II opens with Herod's birthday festivities at court, reflected in a dancelike aria—clearly Salome's famous dance—sung by the Daughter. Charmed by her, Herod promises her anything she wishes. John, in prison, reproaches them for their worldly rejoicing; he welcomes the torments of imprisonment. Having been counseled by Herodias, the Daughter asks Herod for the death of John. Anguishing over the decision forced upon him, Herod reluctantly grants her request. John looks forward to his death and the liberation of his soul, which will return to its Creator. In a duet between John and the Daughter, both urge the servants to do their duty and kill him; after his death the Daughter celebrates her victory with an aria of rejoicing, but Herod is anxious and fearful. Part II closes, as did part I, with a duet between Herod and the Daughter; the latter continues to rejoice while Herod is filled with torment. The duet ends with the same question asked by each about his own feelings: "And why, tell me, why?"

Aside from its remarkable dramatic qualities, *San Giovanni Battista* is also historically noteworthy for its instrumentation. It is one of the few extant compositions demonstrating the use of concerto grosso instrumentation prior to Corelli's concertos, and it appears to represent a Roman tradition of such instrumentation for vocal accompaniment that antedates Corelli's concertos by at least fifteen years. The young Corelli, incidentally, was almost certainly a violinist in the orchestra at the first performance of this oratorio.[67] The work is composed for five solo voices (SSATB) and seven string parts, including two for the continuo. The string parts are divided into a concertino of two violins and a bass instrument (probably a violoncello) and a concerto grosso of four unspecified parts—the highest evidently for violin, the two inner parts for violas, and the lowest for violoncello, contrabass, or both. Payment records for the performance of 1675 show that five singers and twenty-seven instrumentalists were paid for performing the work, but the instruments of only eight of the orchestral performers can be identified: two violinists (probably the soloists for the concer-

67. For a study of concerto grosso instrumentation in this period, including that in this oratorio, see Jander, "Concerto"; regarding Corelli's probable presence in the orchestra, see ibid., p. 173. For further comments on the instrumentation and orchestration of this oratorio, see Daniels, "Stradella," 1:58–82.

FIGURE VII-4. A page from a manuscript of Stradella's *San Giovanni Battista* that shows the indication of concerto grosso instrumentation. For this aria, "Soffin pur rabbiosi fremiti," sung by San Giovanni, the indication at the beginning of the score (at the left) reads "Aria Concert[at]a con il Concertino, et Concerto grosso delle viole."
(Reproduced by permission of I/MOe: MS Mus. F 1136, fol. [6ᵛ].)

tino), two violists, two contrabass players, a lutenist, and a harpsi-chordist. The remaining nineteen players would no doubt have been assigned to the concerto grosso.[68] A considerable variety of instrumentation is found in the accompaniment to the fourteen arias of the work. They are accompanied by the basso continuo only (six arias), the concertino only (two), the concerto grosso

68. For prints of the payment record, see Casimiri, "Oratorii," p. 165, and Jander, "Concerto," pp. 174–77.

only (four), and both the concertino and concerto grosso (two). Whenever the concertino is used in an accompaniment, it plays more or less continuously with the voice; the concerto grosso, however, with its heavier sound, is used primarily for punctuation between the phrases of the vocal part and for an aria's introductory and concluding orchestral passages. In the three exceptions to this rule, when the concerto grosso plays together with the voice, Stradella indicates that only one instrument is to be used on each part.[69] The oratorio's introductory sinfonia—in four brief, imitative sections—is written for the concerto grosso only and thus does not utilize the available contrast between the lighter and heavier sounds.[70]

The melodic interest of the recitative and the free, subtle mixtures of recitative, arioso, and aria styles are responsible for much of the musical and dramatic effectiveness of this oratorio. Example VII–3, in which Herod's Counselor begins urging him to initiate a period of rest and festivity at court, illustrates the manner in which these styles are mixed. The passage begins in recitative over a slowly moving bass (mm. 1–4), becomes increasingly arioso in the use of sequences and short melismas (mm. 5–8), returns to recitative over a pedal point (mm. 9–11), and finally (m. 12) moves into a section of nineteen measures in aria style. (Sections of this length in aria style are not labeled *aria* in this work, as they often are in the oratorios of Legrenzi, since Stradella's arias, so labeled, tend to be much longer than this.) Although most passages in recitative or in a mixture of the three styles are fairly short, there are two long dialogues of this type that occur at dramatically intense points: the first takes place when John arrives at court, interrupts the festivities, and confronts Herod;[71] and the second, when Herodias counsels her Daughter and the latter hesitantly conveys to Herod her desire for John's death.[72] Both dialogues are of interest, not only dramatically, but musically as well, for Stradella pays careful attention to the musical expression of the text's details. Particularly effective is the second of the dialogues. When the Daughter first approaches Herod, her recitative (Example VII–4), over a pedal point, includes a long melisma (mm. 3–6) on

69. For more details, and for Stradella's performance indications, see Jander, "Concerto," p. 178, and Daniels, "Stradella," 1:75–82.

70. For descriptions of the introductory sinfonie of Stradella's vocal works, including oratorios, see McCrickard, "Stradella," 1:41–44, 377–81.

71. Daniels, "Stradella," 2:65–69.

72. Ibid., 2:120–24.

EXAMPLE VII-3. *San Giovanni Battista*—Stradella (I/MOe: MS mus. F. 1136, fols. 23^v—24^r; Daniels, "Stradella", 2:45–46).

But then, leaving the heavenly roads, the starry path, he [the blond charioteer] takes sweet rest in the bosom of the sea. You also, sire, who rule the world, take guidance from the king of the stars. You cannot err if heaven serves as an example . . .

the word "lusinghiero" ("flattering"); this is followed by a few measures in aria style (mm. 7–12) with melodic sequence and text repetition over a metrically patterned bass. Later in the same dialogue the brief arioso passage that Herod sings after the Daughter states her wish (Example VII–5) is a remarkable expression of his anguish; it abounds in musical-rhetorical figures—the chromatic shift in the basso continuo at his first "Ahi, troppo, ahi," the descending skip of a minor sixth to a dissonance (an a, over the B-flat pedal) at his next "ahi troppo," and the descending sequential passage (mm. 5–7) as he twice asks for her reason.

Characterization in the arias is an important aspect of this work. The second of John's four arias, "Soffin pur rabbiosi fremiti," shows in both its texts and music the strength and certain triumph of his faith over adversity: the concertino and concerto grosso alternate, and the vocal line moves in a vigorous, quick-note syllabic setting (Example VII–6a) with occasional melismas

EXAMPLE VII-4. *San Giovanni Battista*—Stradella (I/MOe: MS Mus. F. 1136, fols. 90ʳ–90ᵛ; Daniels, "Stradella," 2:120–21).

Glorious ruler, with the flattering invitation of your promises, I would wish my request to seem respectful and not bold . . .

EXAMPLE VII-5. *San Giovanni Battista*—Stradella (I/MOe: MS Mus. F. 1136, fols. 92ʳ–92ᵛ; Daniels, "Stradella," 2: 123).

DAUGHTER—I wish him to die. HEROD—Ah, too much, you wish too much! And for what reason do you ask it?

EXAMPLE VII-6. *San Giovanni Battista*—Stradella (I/MOe: MS Mus.
F. 1136, fols. 7ʳ–7ᵛ, 62ᵛ, 48ʳ–48ᵛ, 100ʳ, 73ᵛ, 30ʳ–
30ᵛ; Daniels, "Stradella," 2:16–17, 92, 71–72, 131,
100, 54–55).

Example a:

Let the furious roaring of the most cruel north wind . . .

Example b:

If you are a welcome pledge of death . . .

Example c:

Thunder

Example d:

These tears and sighs . . .

Example e:

Lovely nymphs of the Jordan . . .

(EXAMPLE VII-6, continued)

Example f:

May not indeed such sweet servitude be broken . . .

for text expression. John's other arias reveal the calm, optimistic serenity of his mysticism in their texts and their bel canto style; one of these, "Se pegno gradito," occasionally hints at the sarabande rhythm (Example VII–6b). Herod's three arias reveal his power, wrath, and thirst for vengeance. Particularly noteworthy is his forceful first aria in fanfare style, "Tuonerà tra mille turbini" (Example VII–6c)—accompanied by both the concertino and concerto grosso, it is the aria he sings in part I in response to John's insults.[73] Of the five arias sung by the Daughter, most are in a light and gay dance style, reflecting her superficial nature; the only exception is her "Queste lagrime," in bel canto style, in which she is in tears as she pleads with Herod for John's death (Example VII–6d). Most of her dancelike arias employ repeated rhythmic patterns, as does "Vaghe Ninfe," the opening aria of part II (Example VII–6e); these arias are usually difficult to identify as particular dance types, but one, "Non fia ver," is a gavotte (Example VII–6f).

Of the fifteen arias in the oratorio, seven use clear motto beginnings, and four, modified motto beginnings. Three arias are unified by a free basso ostinato pattern. The arias range in length from about 40 to over 150 measures. A variety of forms is found in the arias: ABB′ form occurs most frequently, and through-composed forms are next; four of the arias are strophic; and one aria, John's "Io per me," is an ABA′, in which the A and A′ have a strophic-aria relationship. None of the arias is in da capo form. There are two "aria pairs"—that is, instances in which two arias

73. The entire aria is printed in Massenkeil, *Oratorium* (and Massenkeil, *Oratorium-*Eng.), pp. 59–68.

of different affections are sung in immediate succession by the same singer.[74]

The four brief choral sections of the oratorio, which are all in part I, are grouped into two pairs with the choruses of each pair singing similar texts and including some similarities of melodic material. The first pair, both choruses of which begin "Dove, Battista," is sung by the chorus of John's Disciples (STB at their first entrance, SSATB at their second). It is used to frame a section consisting of a recitative and an aria: the recitative is a dialogue between a Disciple and John, and the latter sings the aria. The second pair of choruses, both beginning "S'uccida il reo," is sung by the *Turba* at Herod's court, who demand that John be killed. This pair contrasts with and frames John's gentle bel canto aria (Example VII–6b) in which he welcomes his chains. The choruses were probably intended to be sung by an ensemble of soloists, as was usual in the period; thus Stradella deleted the alto voice, that of John, from three of the choruses, no doubt to limit the dramatic inconsistency of John's taking part in choruses about him or addressed to him.

The ensembles of the oratorio consist of one trio and four duets. The item from this oratorio most frequently found in manuscript anthologies of the seventeenth and eighteenth centuries is the duet "Nel seren," between Herod and the Daughter; this duet is a plaintive number of considerable contrapuntal and affective interest. The longest duets are those of Herod and the Daughter that close the two parts of the oratorio. That at the end of part II, "Che gioire"—"Che martire," is of particular interest because of its simultaneous representation of two contrasting affections—the joy of the Daughter represented by dancelike rhythmic patterns and the anguish of Herod, generally by longer notes (Example VII–7a). A curious aspect of the duet is that its final cadence, which is the final cadence of the oratorio, carefully reflects its text, "E perchè, dimmi, e perchè?" ("And why, tell me, why?"), by closing abruptly on the dominant. The duet is clearly in D major;

74. The aria pairs are "Sorde dive" and "Non fia ver" (Daniels, "Stradella," 2:47–60), and "Tuonerà tra mille turbini" and "Di cieco carcere" (ibid., 2:69–89). Such aria pairs are considered possible forerunners of the da capo aria in Jander, "Stradella," 1:226–35. In Massenkeil, *Oratorium* (and Massenkeil, *Oratorium*-Eng.), pp. 59–73, the second of these pairs is printed; although Massenkeil supplies, in brackets, the indication "da capo al fine" at the end of the second aria, there appears to be no evidence in the sources that the first aria of the pair should be repeated.

yet the final cadence (Example VII–7b), closing on an A-major chord, makes no attempt at finality but seems to be a rhetorical device that seeks the disquieting effect of an unanswered question.[75]

A famous work in its time, *San Giovanni Battista* stands well above the other known oratorios of Stradella and his contemporaries in historical significance, and possibly in musical value as well. Vastly different from Carissimi's *Jephte* of a quarter of a century earlier, *San Giovanni Battista* nevertheless deserves a place beside that work as an outstanding masterpiece of seventeenth-century oratorio literature.

EXAMPLE VII-7. *San Giovanni Battista*—Stradella (I/MOe: MS Mus. F. 1136, fols. 8ʳ and 131ʳ; Daniels, "Stradella," 2:158–59).

Example a:

DAUGHTER—What joy, what happiness . . . HEROD—What suffering, what torment . . .

75. This ending is in all the sources that I know, and it seems clearly intended. For discussions of the ending of this oratorio and of similar endings in other works by Stradella, see Jander, "Stradella," 1:121–22, and Daniels, "Stradella," 1:12–15.

(EXAMPLE VII-7, continued)

Example b:

And why?

Giovanni Paolo Colonna. A Bolognese born in 1637, Colonna received his early musical training in Bologna from his father and from Agostino Filipuzzi (Filipucci), organist at the Oratorians' church of the Madonna di Galliera and maestro di cappella at the church of San Giovanni in Monte. The young Colonna also studied in Rome with Antonio Maria Abbatini, Orazio Benevoli, and Giacomo Carissimi, and he served as organist at Sant'Apollinare under Carissimi. Having returned to Bologna, he was appointed second organist at San Petronio in 1658, first organist in 1661, and maestro di cappella in 1674. While serving at San Petronio, Colonna also functioned as organist at the Madonna di Galliera from 1673 to 1689 and at San Giovanni in Monte in 1689–90. He retained his post at San Petronio until his death in 1695.[76]

Primarily a composer of sacred music, Colonna is known to have composed thirteen oratorios, all performed in Bologna or Modena between 1676 and 1694; the music of only six of his oratorios is extant. His *Il Mosè, legato di Dio e liberator del popolo ebreo* ("Moses, Legate of God and Liberator of the Hebrew People"), with a libretto by Giovanni Battista Giardini, was performed in the oratory of San Carlo at Modena in 1686; it well

76. For details of Colonna's biography, see Schnoebelen, "Mass," pp. 78–106, and R. Paoli, "Colonna," in *MGG*, 2:cols. 1565–66.

FIGURE VII-5. Title page of the libretto for the Modena performance in
1686 of Giovanni Paolo Colonna's *Il Mosè*. (*Raccolta*,
in I/MOe.)

represents the oratorio of the 1680s.[77] The printed libretto of the
oratorio carries the subtitle *Oratorio terzo in ordine alla vita di
detto Mosè* ("The Third Oratorio of the Life of Said Moses"), for
it is part of a series on Moses' life. In the collection of printed

77. MS score: I/MOe: Mus. F. 299. Printed source of libretto: *Raccolta*, vol. 2. I gratefully acknowledge the use of an unpublished study and modern edition of this work made
by Julia Ann Griffin preliminary to her doctoral dissertation in progress, Griffin, "Colonna."

librettos that includes the Colonna work are those of the fourth and fifth oratorios of the series by the same poet, set to music by Giacomo Perti and Bernardo Pasquini, respectively, and performed in Modena.[78]

The libretto is freely based on Exodus 8–12, in which the Egyptians are visited with ten plagues before Pharaoh releases the Hebrews. In the oratorio the number of plagues is reduced to seven. The central conflict is between the people of God and the Egyptians; the former are represented by Moses (A), who is supported by Aaron (S), the Leader of the Hebrew People (B), and a chorus of Hebrews (SAB, SSATB). The Egyptians are represented by the tyrant Pharaoh (B), who is supported by his Counselor (S). Part I includes Moses' explanation of his mission, the lamentations of the Hebrew people, Moses' confrontation with Pharaoh, and the first two plagues: the waters turned to blood and the infestation of Egypt by frogs. Pharaoh promises the release of the Hebrews if the plagues are lifted, but he breaks his promise. Part I closes with an aria of vengeance sung by Moses. In part II the Egyptians are besieged by five more plagues: first a pestilence that kills livestock, then storms, locusts, a thick darkness, and the slaying of the firstborn. Pharaoh laments the plagues and delays further, but he finally yields. Moses then orders the Hebrews to follow him and to praise God for their liberation; the oratorio's final number is the Hebrews' chorus of praise.

In the manuscript source this work is called an *oratorio a 5*. The five soloists required for the roles listed above are S, S, A, B, and B, and the final chorus is for SSATB; thus one of the basses would sing the tenor part in the final chorus. In addition to basso continuo, the score also calls for five unspecified instruments, for which strings would no doubt have been used. The instruments provide brief introductory sinfonie for both parts of the oratorio, accompaniments for three of the arias, and ritornellos for many of the continuo arias.

The recitatives in this oratorio, unlike those in the works from this period discussed above, virtually never slip into arioso or aria style; in fact, arioso style is rarely employed. Particularly prominent characteristics of the recitatives are brief motives and phrases separated by rests, frequent short sixteenth-note groups for unaccented syllables, syncopated patterns, and careful atten-

78. *Raccolta*, vol. 2.

tion to the declamation, expression, and depiction of the text. Example VII–8 is a characteristic recitative, with word painting on "terra" and "cielo," occasional sixteenth notes, and short phrases separated by rests in measures 1–2 and 5–7.

EXAMPLE VII-8. *Il Mosè*—Colonna (I/MOe: codex Mus. F. 299, fols. 15^r–15^v; after a transcription by J. Griffin).

Listen, O king of the earth, the king of heaven wishes the Hebrew people free from your laws, and from your empire. Thus to thee he sends me . . .

The twenty-three arias of the oratorio are mostly in duple meter and are generally brief; although they range from twelve to seventy-seven measures in length, all but four have forty measures or less. Only two arias employ motto beginnings. Seven of the arias are in ABA form, rare in oratorios before the 1690s; these are essentially miniature da capo arias that are completely notated. Only one aria is clearly in the ABB' form; nine are in through-composed forms, several of which have an ABB structure in the text and hint vaguely at this structure in the music. There are no strophic arias in this oratorio, despite the continuing interest in them in the 1680s.[79]

Concerning the distribution of arias among the characters, Pharaoh is given favored treatment with nine arias, two of which are orchestrally accompanied; Moses is next, with five arias, one of which is accompanied; three arias each are allotted to Aaron, the Leader of the People, and the Counselor. Although the arias

79. Just five years earlier, Colonna had used nineteen strophic arias in his *Il transito di San Gioseppe* (1681); yet this structure is absent not only from his *Il Mosè* but also from his *La profezia d'Elisio*, also of 1686.

are mostly syllabic and declamatory in style, they also employ melismas on important words. Some of the melismas are extended to virtuosic coloraturas; an example is the one that closes Pharaoh's accompanied aria, "Stelle ingrate" (Example VII–9), in which he rages against the ungrateful stars and unjust gods. The triple-metered, smooth, bel canto style is rarely used, and in only two arias are there hints of dance style; one of these, "Con doppio tormento," in which Pharaoh laments the woes of his realm, is in binary form, and the first section is in *siciliano* style (Example VII–10).

EXAMPLE VII-9. *Il Mosè*—Colonna (I/MOe: codex Mus. F. 299, fols. 58^r–58^v; after a transcription by J. Griffin).

. . . heaven devoid of rays . . .

EXAMPLE VII-10. *Il Mosè*—Colonna (I/MOe: codex Mus. F. 299, fol. 38^v; after a transcription by J. Griffin).

With double torment, with hard trial . . .

The ensembles consist of a brief duet (SA), labeled "due del choro" (i.e., for two members of the chorus of Hebrews), and three choruses sung by the Hebrews. The first two choruses are brief and identical, "framing" an aria by the Leader of the People.

The third chorus is the finale of the oratorio, in which the Hebrews praise God in a more extended number, characteristic of the final *madrigale* in oratorios of the period, with alternating chordal and imitative textures.

In addition to the structural unity afforded by the two identical "framing" choruses mentioned above, several modified repetitions create an unusual degree of musical unity in this work. The clearest and most striking of these is associated with Pharaoh's recurring lamentation over the series of plagues that have afflicted his empire. The repeated material first occurs as a recitative in part I, in the form shown in Example VII–11a; in part II it occurs twice in the form shown in Example VII–11b, first as part of an aria (the B section of the binary aria "Con doppio tormento"—for the beginning of the A section, see Example VII–10) and then as part of an arioso; and another time it is part of a brief arioso passage, as shown in Example VII–11c. This type of unification is rare in oratorios of the period.

EXAMPLE VII-11. *Il Mosè*—Colonna (I/MOe: codex Mus. F. 299, fols. 26ᵛ, 39ʳ, 48ʳ, 56ᵛ; after a transcription by J. Griffin).

Example a:

Wretched, what will happen? What unknown boldness shakes my land . . .

Examples b and c:

Wretched, what shall I do? Steady, steady, my heart . . .

The Music of the Oratorio from the 1680s to about 1720

In this period, as in the previous one, it seems virtually impossible to identify the style traits of oratorios with certain Italian cities or geographical areas. Although many of the traits of this period have long been identified with the so-called Neapolitan school,[80] it now seems that—both in opera and in oratorio—they appeared as early in other Italian cities, such as Venice and Rome, as in Naples.[81] The concept of a "pan-Italian" style appears to be as useful for understanding late Baroque oratorio styles, which often include pre-Classical elements, as it is for the previous period. After the following survey of the general characteristics of oratorios in this period, four representative examples are described.

General Characteristics

Although many oratorios until about the turn of the century are much like those of the earlier period, new styles and structures, described below, grow increasingly important and, by the first decade of the eighteenth century, become the dominant characteristics of both the Italian and the Latin oratorio. The close relationship between oratorio and opera continues throughout this period, and the two genres share many of the following traits.

The number of voices usually required in oratorios is the same as in the previous period, three to five. The greater variety and number of instruments specified shows an increasing interest in orchestral color. Also more prominent are concerto grosso instrumentation and solo passages for instruments.

The regular alternation of recitatives and arias is characteristic. The recitatives are mostly simple (accompanied by basso continuo only) and employ little arioso style. Accompanied recitatives, usually with either a sustained instrumental part or more vigorous,

---

80. Schering, *Oratorium*, p. 169.

81. Wolff, "Vivaldi," pp. 180–82, calls attention to Vivaldi's anticipation of the pre-Classical works of the Neapolitans Leo, Vinci, and Pergolesi; U. Kirkendale, *Caldara*, p. 277, comments on Caldara's "early *galant*" style in his Roman oratorios after 1710; and Downes, "J. C. Bach," 1:14, after having surveyed the literature on the concept of Neapolitan school as applied to opera, rejects that concept in favor of those of pre-Classical and early Classical opera.

excited orchestral punctuations between vocal phrases, are used for particularly intense moments. Thus the function of accompanied recitative is much like that of *recitativo arioso* in the preceding period; yet the vocal style of accompanied recitative is not usually arioso but closer to that of simple recitative. Scenes comparable to solo cantatas, in which a soloist is given a stylistically varied sequence of items (such as simple and accompanied recitatives followed by a passage in arioso style and then by an aria), are occasionally used to mark actions of extreme importance in the drama; the scene of Judith's decapitation of Holofernes in Vivaldi's *Juditha* (described below) is an example of such a cantatalike section.

Nearly all arias in oratorios are in the da capo form and tend to be longer than in the previous period. The motto beginning is still employed, but with decreasing frequency. Arias are more stylized than previously and more easily classified according to the affections expressed. Among the more prominent aria types are those with elaborate coloratura passages for the expression of rage, vengeance, or jealousy; those based on fanfare motives for martial texts; gay dances—such as the minuet, gavotte, or gigue—for lighthearted and joyful moods; and the sarabande and *siciliano* for the expression of lamentation, nostalgia, and various aspects of love, or for the representation of pastoral scenes. Simile arias often include programmatic imitations, in both the orchestral and the vocal parts, of such phenomena as bird calls, storms, wind, ocean waves, and waterfalls.

Most arias are accompanied by the orchestra. The ritornello, longer than in the previous period, becomes a prominent structural element in the aria and sometimes functions much as it does in the solo concerto of the late Baroque. A contrapuntal relationship between the vocal line and the orchestral parts is common, except in the occasional arias with homophonic, pre-Classical tendencies. Although the most common orchestra is that of three string parts plus basso continuo, some oratorios employ a more varied and colorful instrumentation and orchestration. For instance, the strings can be used in as many as six parts—sometimes muted, played pizzicato, scored for soli and tutti alternations (as in a concerto grosso), and scored in unison with the voice either with or without the basso continuo. Among the instruments specified in oratorios, in addition to the usual strings, are the harpsichord, organ, theorbo, mandolin, recorder, transverse flute, oboe, trumpet, and timpani; some of these are employed soloistically in counterpoint or alternation with the vocal line.

Common characteristics of the arias are the tonal, textural, and rhythmic styles generally associated with the late Baroque: strong functional tonality revealing a fully developed system of modulation, a generally fast harmonic rhythm, and a style of texture better described as linear than chordal, with an active basso continuo accompanying sequentially spun-out melodic lines of asymmetrical phrases. Nevertheless, some oratorios of the period include numbers in the pre-Classical style, with its more nearly homophonic texture, slower harmonic rhythm, and more regular phrase structure; such is the tendency in certain arias of Vivaldi's *Juditha* and, to an even greater extent, in some of Caldara's Roman oratorios.

Compared with arias, ensembles and choruses are relatively rare and tend to use the aria's da capo form. Ensembles are also much like arias in their lengths, variety of types, and vocal and instrumental treatment. Choruses are usually quite brief and written in simple chordal texture; they require the same vocal ranges as the oratorio's soloists—the practice of employing an ensemble of the soloists to sing the choruses was evidently continued.

Independent instrumental numbers are longer and somewhat more numerous in oratorios of this period. The opening sinfonia might resemble a church sonata, a French overture, or an Italian overture. The relatively few instrumental numbers within oratorios usually prepare for a contrasting affection in the following section, describe a scene (such as a battle or a joyous festivity), or prepare for the entrance of a character so striking (e.g., Lucifer, Goliath, or the Voice of God) that he is felt to need description even before he begins to sing.

Representative Examples

Alessandro Scarlatti. Born in Palermo in 1660, Scarlatti was taken to Rome as a boy, probably in 1672.[82] Nothing is known of his early musical training, but the influences of his youth would have been Roman, since he resided at Rome until 1683. Scarlatti's first

82. For Scarlatti's biography see E. Hanley, "Scarlatti," in *MGG*, 11:cols. 482–86, and Pagano-Bianchi, *Scarlatti*, pp. 5–244.

FIGURE VII-6. Alessandro Scarlatti (1668–1725).
(Reproduced by permission of I/Bc.)

opera, an extremely successful work, was performed at Rome in 1679. A year later he was named maestro di cappella to Queen Christina of Sweden, and by at least 1683 he was maestro di cappella at San Girolamo della Carità. In 1683 he went to Naples, where he remained for about twenty years. He served as maestro di cappella of the royal chapel and occupied himself chiefly with opera. After a brief visit in 1702 to the court of Prince Ferdinando de' Medici, with whom he had long corresponded and had hoped to find a position, Scarlatti returned to Rome in 1703. There he entered his most fruitful period of oratorio and chamber cantata production, no doubt because church opposition to the theater in that period at Rome limited his opera activities. In 1706–7 he visited Venice, where he unsuccessfully attempted to establish himself by writing two works, an oratorio and an opera, for performance there.[83] The period from 1708 to 1717 Scarlatti spent in Naples, again as maestro di cappella of the royal chapel. In the years between 1717 and 1722, he was mostly in Rome, where his last operas were performed. He then returned to Naples, where he died in 1725.

Throughout his career Scarlatti retained close contact with the Roman nobility; in addition to Queen Christina, his Roman patrons at various times were the Pamphilj and Colonna families, the cardinal Pietro Ottoboni, the marquis (and later prince) Francesco Maria Ruspoli, Pope Clement XI, and the queen of Poland. Scarlatti has long been considered the founder of the Neapolitan school of opera, which was essentially pre-Classical in its musical style; yet research of the mid-twentieth century has shown him to be in many respects more Roman than Neapolitan and his style to be closer to that of the late Baroque than the pre-Classical period.[84] Best known for his chamber cantatas and operas, Scarlatti is also extremely important for his oratorios; he composed over thirty, at least twenty-three of which are extant.[85] As a composer of oratorios, he must be considered an important part of the Roman scene, for more than two-thirds of his oratorios were composed for Roman patrons.

83. Regarding Scarlatti's presence in Venice, see Fabbri, "Torna," p. 249.
84. E. Hanley, "Scarlatti," in *MGG*, 11:cols. 1498–1501.
85. For lists of Scarlatti's oratorios, with discrepancies among them, see ibid., cols. 1496–97; Poultney, "Scarlatti," pp. 65–69; Bianchi, *Carissimi*, pp. 285–86; and Pagano-Bianchi, *Scarlatti*, pp. 497–510. A modern edition of Scarlatti's oratorios in progress is Scarlatti, *Oratorii*.

Scarlatti's oratorios span the period from 1683 to 1720, and they clearly reflect the development of the oratorio in that period. Their texts are based primarily on hagiography and the Bible. The early oratorios (1683–95), such as *Agar et Ismaele esiliati* ("Hagar and Ishmael Exiled," 1683) and the "Naples" *La Giuditta* ("Judith," 1695),[86] represent the type of libretto and the musical style —including the flexible relationship between recitative, arioso, and aria styles—most characteristic of the late seventeenth century. The early works also include numerous arias in strophic and binary forms, but those in ABA or ABA' forms are rare. Most of the arias are accompanied by basso continuo only, and a few are unified by a ground bass. Beginning with the middle period (1696–1708) the tendencies of the late Baroque oratorio appear; these are increased and clarified in the few late oratorios composed after 1708. Among the middle-period works are the "Cambridge" *La Giuditta* (ca. 1700) and *Il primo omicidio* ("The First Murder," 1707),[87] and among the late works are *Oratorio per la santissima Trinità* ("Oratorio for the Most Holy Trinity," 1715) and *La vergine addolorata* ("The Virgin in Sorrow," 1717). In the middle- and late-period oratorios the da capo aria becomes of central importance, to the virtual exclusion of other aria forms; the ground bass is rarely employed; the regular alternation of recitative and aria becomes the norm; orchestrally accompanied arias become increasingly common; and accompanied recitative, with sustained chords in the strings, is occasionally used. Most of Scarlatti's oratorios in every period either exclude the chorus or include only brief "choral" passages that may be sung by an ensemble of the soloists. One significant exception, however, is his only extant Latin oratorio, *Davidis pugna et victoria* ("The Fight and Victory of David"), performed at Crocifisso in 1700.[88] Using five soloists (SSATB) and a separate double chorus (SATB-SATB) that enters several times, it is a conservative work for that date; it also includes other elements—particularly the *testo*, ground bass arias, and strophic arias—that were outmoded by 1700.

Scarlatti's *Il primo omicidio, oratorio a 6 voci*, performed at Venice in 1707 and again at Rome in 1710, well represents his

86. Printed in Scarlatti, *Oratorii*, vols. 2 and 1, respectively. For discussions of the structures and styles of the early-, middle-, and late-period oratorios, see Poultney, "Scarlatti," chapters 5 and 6, and Poultney, "Transformation," pp. 590–601.

87. Printed in Scarlatti, *Oratorii*, vols. 3 and 4, respectively.

88. Printed in Scarlatti, *Oratorii*, vol. 5.

mature oratorios.[89] The work requires six singers for the roles of Eve (S), Abel and the Voice of Abel after death (S), Cain (A), the Voice of God (A), Adam (T), and the Voice of Lucifer (B). The solo parts are occasionally combined into duets, but there are no other ensembles, nor is there a chorus. The orchestra of strings is in five and six parts, and some numbers include one or two solo violins.

Based on Gen. 4:1–16, the anonymous libretto is in two parts. Its central contrast is that of the jealous, murderous, and subsequently remorseful Cain, advised by Lucifer, in opposition to Cain's God-fearing family and the Voice of God. The oratorio begins with the penitent reflections by Adam and Eve on the episode of original sin, followed by Abel's and then Cain's expression of desire to placate God by a sacrifice. Cain's jealousy is revealed when his sacrifice is found unacceptable, as the Voice of God praises Abel's sacrifice but not Cain's. The Voice of Lucifer counsels Cain to murder Abel, which Cain resolves to do. In part II, while Cain and Abel are resting in the shade of a tree, Cain strikes his brother and thus commits the first murder. Following the biblical story, the Voice of God asks where Abel is, and Cain claims not to know, adding, "Am I my brother's keeper?" Cain is then condemned to wander in exile, and he laments his fate. The Voice of Abel tells his parents of his death and happiness with God. Adam and Eve lament the absence of both their sons, but in their duet-finale they joyfully anticipate the salvation of the world through the blood of Christ.

The focus of attention in the work is on the arias, of which there are twenty-two, as opposed to only five duets and four accompanied recitatives. The central character, Cain, sings a total of six arias; Adam and the Voice of God each sing four; Eve, three; Abel and the Voice of Lucifer, two each; and the Voice of Abel after death, one. Every aria and duet of the oratorio is cast in da capo form. All the arias but three and all the duets but one are orchestrally accompanied. Of the arias and duets about half employ motto beginnings, a large majority are in duple meter, and the average length is about sixty-five measures. The melismatic passages, used to emphasize important words, are seldom more than

89. The above title is that of the MS score. The printed librettos for both performances carry the title *Cain over il primo omicidio, trattenimento sacro per musica, a sei voci* ("Cain, or the First Murder, Sacred Entertainment in Music, for Six Voices"). For a brief historical and analytical treatment of the work, see Fabbri, "Torna."

two or three measures long and are never in elaborate coloratura style. (Characteristic melismatic passages are those in Examples VII–12, VII–13, and VII–14.)

EXAMPLE VII-12. *Il primo omicidio*—A. Scarlatti (Scarlatti, *Oratorii*, 4:25–26).

From the flock I shall choose a pure lamb, the whitest, the most beautiful, to sacrifice . . .

EXAMPLE VII-13. *Il primo omicidio*—A. Scarlatti (Scarlatti, *Oratorii*, 4:42–43).

Supreme God, for my sin, for my sons, have pity . . .

EXAMPLE VII-14. *Il primo omicidio*—A. Scarlatti (Scarlatti, *Oratorii*, 4: 82–83).

Disguise yourself, O my anger, in the clothing of love . . .

Most of the arias and duets express a single affection throughout, but a few employ a distinctly contrasting middle section. The oratorio includes a considerable variety of affections and styles. The *siciliano*, for instance, is employed for Abel's "Dalla mandra" (Example VII–12), in which he reflects on his selection of the whitest and most beautiful of his sheep as a sacrifice to God, and again for Eve's "Madre tenera," her last lament for her sons. As many as nine of the arias are marked *adagio*, *lento*, or *grave*; these contribute to the atmosphere of melancholy that pervades much of the work. Characteristic of the melancholy numbers is Eve's "Sommo Dio" (Example VII–13), her plea for God to have pity on her sons, with its pathetic, chromatic progression on "mio peccato" ("my sin"), its Neapolitan sixth moving to the dominant of C minor on "habbi pietà" ("have pity"), its melisma on "pietà," and its rhythmic movement that approximates that of a sarabande. Vigorous, strongly marked rhythmic patterns and moderate-to-quick tempos characterize several of the arias: Adam's "Mi balena," in which he expresses his anguish at his expulsion from paradise; the Voice of Lucifer's cynical "Poche lagrime"; the Voice of God's castigation of Cain, "Vuo il castigo"; and Cain's jealous, deceptive, and angry "Mascheratevi o miei sedgni" (Example VII–14). Joyous moods are represented in moderate-to-quick tempos in several numbers: Cain's and Abel's "La fraterna amica," the duet of brotherly love (the middle section of which, however, is a contrasting expression of Cain's thirst for vengeance) that closes part I; the Voice of Abel's "No, non piangete," in which he urges his parents not to weep; and Adam and Eve's finale-duet, "Contenti presenti," a joyful gigue anticipating the world's future salvation. Characteristic of the arias and duets is a highly contrapuntal relationship between the vocal and instrumental lines.

The simple recitatives in this work rarely even hint at the arioso style found within recitative passages of so many seventeenth-century oratorios, and only twice are there brief passages in aria style, which, in this period, are best called ariosos.[90] One of these, "Or se braman posar," is sung by Abel just before he is murdered. The accompanied recitatives—of which there are four, all sung by the Voice of God, who also sings some simple recita-

90. For some uses of the term *arioso* in the eighteenth century, see Marpurg, *Singcomposition*, pp. 80–81.

tives—do not differ significantly in vocal style from the simple ones; they are all accompanied by four strings, nearly always playing sustained chords.

The opening instrumental number, *Introduzione all'oratorio*, is much like a miniature concerto for solo violin, with four string parts and basso continuo. It is in three movements (*spirituoso*, *adagio*, and *allegro*), each movement including alternations between the solo violin and the other strings; the final movement is a gigue in binary form. The remaining five instrumental numbers of the oratorio are all quite brief and function either to establish a mood or to imitate an event, such as the number that occurs at the time of the murder and depicts Cain's blows.[91] Concerto style, with one or two solo violins contrasting with the orchestra, is employed in one internal instrumental number and four vocal accompaniments. More favored in this work than the concerto style, however, is another characteristic Baroque texture, strings in unison plus basso continuo; in the nine arias and two duets accompanied in this manner, the unison strings usually form a strongly contrapuntal relationship with the voice(s), and the continuo plays an essentially supporting part.

George Frideric Handel. Among the best-known and greatest oratorio composers in history, Handel (1685–1759) is of primary importance for his English oratorios. Although a more extended treatment of the man and his music will be reserved for volume 2, his small but significant contribution to the Italian oratorio deserves a place here.

Virtually nothing is known of Handel's whereabouts and activity between the performance of his first opera, *Almira* (Hamburg, 1705), and his presence in Rome in 1707.[92] He is thought to have left Hamburg sometime in 1706. The earliest-known documentary evidence of his presence in Italy is a copyist's bill, dated 16 May 1707, for his oratorio *Il trionfo del Tempo e del Disinganno* (later revised and translated as *The Triumph of Time and Truth*), with a text by Cardinal Benedetto Pamphilj.[93] This alle-

91. Scarlatti, *Oratorii*, 4:110–11.

92. For a summary of what is known of Handel's Italian period, with bibliographical references and newly discovered details of his Roman sojourn, see U. Kirkendale, "Ruspoli."

93. For facsimiles of the copyist's bill, see Montalto, *Mecenate*, p. 325, and Zanetti, "Haendel," pl. 4.

FIGURE VII-7. George Frideric Handel (1685–1759). Portrait by Sir James Thornhill.
(Reproduced by permission of the Fitzwilliam Museum, Cambridge.)

gorical oratorio in two parts includes four soloists (Beauty, S; Pleasure, S; Disillusionment or Truth, A; and Time, T) and no chorus; the work was probably first performed during Lent of 1707.[94] Of significance for Handel's development as a choral composer, and thus as the future composer of English oratorios in which the chorus is a prominent element, are his settings of the psalms "Dixit Dominus," "Laudate pueri," and "Nisi Dominus" —all composed in Italy in 1707.[95]

On Easter Sunday, 8 April 1708, Handel's second and last oratorio in Italian, *La Resurrezione*, was first performed in Rome at the Bonelli palace, the residence of the marquis Francesco Maria Ruspoli.[96] The spectacular decorations for the stage and hall and the unusually large orchestra led by Corelli, mentioned above (pp. 264–65), indicate that this performance must have been a particularly gala affair. *La Resurrezione* was indeed worthy of the occasion, for it is not only among Handel's best works of his Italian period but also an outstanding example of the early eighteenth-century *oratorio volgare*.[97]

The libretto of *La Resurrezione*, by Carlo Sigismondo Capece, is in two parts and consists of two simultaneous plots. The characters of the principal plot are Mary Magdalene (S), Mary the wife of Cleophas (called simply Cleophas, A), and St. John (T)—all of whom figure in the biblical accounts of the Resurrection. Their dialogue reveals the events from Good Friday to Easter Sunday. In part I they lament the Crucifixion until near the conclusion, when the affection changes to the joyful anticipation of the Resurrection. In part II both Marys visit Jesus' tomb, find that he is risen, and go to seek him; John describes the reaction of Jesus' mother when her

94. U. Kirkendale, "Ruspoli," p. 224, n. 13. Handel revised it for performance in London, first in 1737 (still in Italian) and then in 1757, as the *Triumph of Time and Truth*, with an English text. For an edition of the first and second versions, see Handel, *Werke*, vol. 24; for the English version see Handel, *Werke*, vol. 20.

95. U. Kirkendale, "Ruspoli," pp. 224–25.

96. Handel lived in this palace for at least seven weeks prior to the performance and was probably spending much of his time there on *La Resurrezione*. According to U. Kirkendale, "Ruspoli," p. 233, the work was probably not written in a hurry, as is stated in Flower, *Handel*, p. 70.

97. The edition in Handel, *Werke*, vol. 39, is based on the autograph MS score in GB/Lcm; another MS score, with annotations in the composer's hand, has been discovered at D-brd/MÜs. In the latter score, which appears to be that used for the first performance, the order of the first few numbers is rearranged, some of the numbers are modified, and overtures precede both parts of the oratorio. For details see Ewerhart, "Resurrezione." Hicks, "Resurrezione," summarizes the history of and recent discoveries about the work and provides a synopsis of the libretto and a brief musical description.

son visits her after the Resurrection, and Mary Magdalene tells of her encounter with the risen Jesus in the garden. Throughout the libretto the image of Jesus as a sun occurs frequently; his Resurrection is portrayed as a sunrise. The subsidiary plot, in strong contrast to the principal one, involves a dramatic conflict between its two characters, an Angel (S) and Lucifer (B). These representatives of heaven and hell appear at the beginning of part I and again shortly after the beginning of part II. Lucifer at first maintains that by Jesus's death he has conquered the forces of heaven, but the radiant Angel demands that the gates of dark hell be opened to eternal light. In part II Lucifer, finally weakened and conquered by heavenly power, plunges into the abyss.

A striking aspect of this work, in comparison with other Roman oratorios of its time, is the exceptional variety of its orchestration, including the large orchestra and various combinations of solo instruments. The overture uses concerto grosso instrumentation with a concertino of solo violin and viola da gamba, and a large orchestra of trumpets and oboes in pairs, three violin parts, viola, violoncello, and basso continuo.[98] Concerto grosso instrumentation is also used to accompany two arias, Mary Magdalene's "Per me già di morire" and "Se impassibile immortale." Several other aria accompaniments for strings, which bear the marks *solo* and *tutti* in alternation, create a concerto grosso effect. The Angel's first aria—"Disseratevi oh porte d'averno," intended to reflect the awful power of heaven—is scored for strings, oboes, and trumpets, the last named effectively contributing to the number's brilliance. Several arias are accompanied by basso continuo and unison violins. Two arias, Mary Magdalene's "Hò un non sò che nel cor" (Example VII–15) and Cleophas's "Augeletti rusceletti," both expressing lighthearted affections, are scored for violins in unison with the voice, with the basso continuo entering only when the voice rests. A particularly somber sonority used to evoke the mood of "deadly night" is found in Mary Magdalene's accompanied recitative, "Notte, notte funesta," in which sustained chords are played by two recorders and a viola da gamba without continuo; her following aria on the subject of sleep, "Ferma l'ali," uses nearly as quiet a combination—two recorders, muted violins,

98. The overture, not printed in Handel, *Werke*, vol. 39, is in the MS at D-brd/MÜs and is described in Ewerhart, "Resurrezione," pp. 130–31. The overture is a modified version of that used for *Il trionfo* (printed in Handel, *Werke*, vol. 24).

EXAMPLE VII-15. *La Resurrezione*—Handel (Handel, *Werke*, 39:38).

Magdalene, and all violins in unison.

Ho yn non sò che nel cor; che in-ve-ce di do - lor

[B. c. tace until ritornello.]

I have something in my heart, which instead of sadness . . .

a viola da gamba, and violoni, the last named written mostly in pedal point. John's simile aria, "Così la tortorella," which compares the Virgin Mary's mixture of sorrow and hope following Jesus' death to that of the turtledove whose mate leaves and then returns, is a *siciliano* in its A part, delicately accompanied by solo transverse flute, viola da gamba, and theorbo; the basso continuo is absent, but there are occasional descending runs by the *bassi* (violoncellos) and violins in octaves.

The simple recitatives rarely include arioso style, although significant words will evoke word painting or an affective setting that occasionally approaches that style. Particularly striking in regard to textual expression is Lucifer's final recitative, "Ahi, abborito nome," in which he acknowledges defeat and, as he flees from both heaven and earth, expresses his plunge into the deep abyss of hell in a descending passage of two octaves (Example VII–16). Of the three accompanied recitatives those by Lucifer

EXAMPLE VII-16. *La Resurrezione*—Handel (Handel, *Werke*, 39:59).

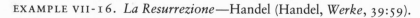

Lucifer

tor-no a pre-ci-pi - tar   nel sen pro-fon-do.

. . . I return to fall into the extreme depth [of the darkest abyss].

and the Angel are in an agitated style, with a large orchestra punctuating between phrases, but that by Mary Magdalene, mentioned above, is given a sustained accompaniment.

Of the twenty arias in the oratorio, five are allotted to Mary Magdalene; four each, to Cleophas, John, and the Angel; and only three, to Lucifer. Eighteen of the arias are in da capo form, eight employ motto beginnings, and four are accompanied by continuo only. Although fairly extended melismas occur in several of the arias, the most elaborate coloratura piece is the Angel's "Disseratevi oh porte d'averno," mentioned above for its brilliant orchestration; the longest of its coloratura passages is illustrated in Example VII–17. Several of the arias are dances. These include the

EXAMPLE VII-17. *La Resurrezione*—Handel (Handel, *Werke* 39:8).

Open, O gates of Avernus!

siciliano "Così la tortorella"; the Angel's sarabande, "D'amor fu consiglio"; the Angel's minuet, "Risorga il mondo"; and Mary Magdalene's gavotte, "Se impassible immortale." Another gavotte sung by Mary Magdalene, "Hò un non sò che nel cor," mentioned above for its unison accompaniment (Example VII–15), is of interest for its origin and subsequent reuse; it appears to have been borrowed, at least in part, from the *Gavotta* of Corelli's chamber sonata Op. 5, No. 10. Handel used the aria again, slightly changed but with the same text, in his opera *Agrippina*, first performed at Venice in 1709.[99] Other arias that Handel modified for use in *Agrippina* are Lucifer's "Caddi è ver" ("Cade il mondo" in the opera) and his "O voi dell'Erebo," ("Col raggio placido" in the opera).[100] The melody of "O voi dell'Erebo" is derived from a passage in Reinhard Keiser's opera *Octavia*.[101]

99. For a comparison of the beginnings of the Corelli and Handel pieces, see Schering, "Entlehnungen," p. 247. For the same aria in *Agrippina*, see Handel, *Werke*, 57:43–44. This aria was performed by the same singer, Margherita Durastante, in the premieres of both the oratorio and the subsequent opera. Ruspoli was rebuked by Pope Clement XI for having employed a female singer, Durastante, for the oratorio, in defiance of the pope's ban on women participating in public performance. (U. Kirkendale, "Ruspoli," pp. 236–37.)

100. For numbers in *La Resurrezione* that Handel borrowed much later for use in the oratorios *Esther* (1732 version), *Alexander Balus*, and *Joshua*, see Dean, *Oratorios*, pp. 207, 645–46.

101. For a comparison of the Handel and Keiser versions, see Taylor, *Indebtedness*, pp. 170–71.

The only ensembles in the oratorio are two duets and two choruses, the latter used to close the oratorio's two parts. The duet of Mary Magdalene and Cleophas, "Dolci chiodi," is best described as a modified strophic piece: Cleophas sings the first strophe; Mary Magdalene, the next; and then they join in singing a modified repetition of the second strophe. In the quite brief duet between the Angel and Lucifer, "Duro è il cimento"—"Impedirlo saprò," the characters express contrasting affections: Lucifer, singing in short notes, is convinced he will impede the events of the Resurrection, but the Angel, in longer notes and a smoother line, is equally convinced that Lucier will fail. Both of the choruses, for SATB, could be performed by an ensemble of the soloists; both are in da capo form, employ an alternation of vocal solo and ensemble passages, and are more chordal than contrapuntal.[102]

Antonio Vivaldi. Born at Venice in 1678, Vivaldi probably received his early musical education from his father, a violinist, and possibly from Legrenzi as well. Vivaldi was also trained for the priesthood and was ordained a priest in 1703; in the same year, however, he was excused from active duty as a priest for reasons of ill health. He subsequently began to teach violin at the Ospedale della Pietà, where in 1716 he was appointed *maestro de' concerti*. He continued to serve the Pietà for most of his life, with numerous interruptions to perform and conduct in other Italian cities and elsewhere in Europe. He met his death on one of these journeys, at Vienna, in 1741.[103]

Best known in his time as well as today for his concertos, Vivaldi was also a composer of about forty-eight operas and at least three oratorios—*Moyses Deus Pharaonis* (1714), *Juditha triumphans* (1716), and *L'adorazione dei tre Re Magi al Bambino Gesù* (1722). The first two oratorios, which in their use of Latin texts are characteristic of oratorios sung in the Venetian conservatories, were performed at the Pietà by the girls of that institution.[104] The music of only one of the oratorios, *Juditha*, is known to have survived.

The title page of this oratorio's printed libretto reads, *Juditha*

102. The final chorus in the MS at D-brd/MÜs is expanded beyond the length of that in Handel, *Werke*, vol. 39. (Ewerhart, "Resurrezione," pp. 132–33.)

103. For a survey of Vivaldi's life and works, see Kolneder, *Vivaldi*.

104. Ibid., pp. 194–95.

FIGURE VII-8. Antonio Vivaldi (1678–1741).
(Hawkins, *History*, 5:230.)

triumphans devicta Holofernis barbarie: sacrum militare orato-
rium hisce belli temporibus a psalentium virginum choro in Templo
Pietatis canendum ("Judith Triumphant, Conqueror of the Barbaric Holofernes: A Sacred Military Oratorio Performed in Times
of War by the Chorus of Virgin Singers, to be Sung in the Church
of the Pietà," Venice, 1716).[105] The libretto by Giacomo Cassetti
is based on Judith 10–13 (Apocrypha), but a note in the printed
libretto explains that the characters are allegorical: Judith symbol-

105. For a facsimile of the title page, see Rinaldi, *Vivaldi*, pl. XXIII; for discussions of
the oratorio, see ibid., pp. 308–14, and Kolneder, *Vivaldi*, pp. 195–99. For a facsimile of
the MS score in I/Tn, on which the present discussion is based, see Vivaldi, *Juditha*. A
scholarly modern edition is lacking.

izes Venice; Holofernes, the Sultan; Abra, Faith; Bethulia, the Church; and Ozias, the Christians.[106] Both the title-page description of this work as a "military oratorio performed in times of war" and the allegorical interpretation of the characters may be readily explained. Venice had been at war with Turkey for several years, and the sultan of Turkey was thus her prime enemy. In 1716 the Venetians successfully defended their Ionian island of Corfù (Kerkira) against the Turks; this victory may have been the occasion for the composition and performance of Vivaldi's *Juditha*.[107]

As is characteristic of Latin oratorios in this period, the structure and style of the libretto and music of *Juditha* are similar to those of Italian oratorios. The libretto—cast in the usual two parts—does not employ a *testo*, requires five soloists, and follows many of the conventions of the contemporary *opera seria*. The dramatic conflict occurs between Judith (A) as a representative of the people of God and Holofernes (A) as the hostile tyrant. Judith is supported by her handmaid Abra (S), the high priest Ozias (A), and a chorus of the People of Bethulia (SATB), which enters twice. Holofernes is supported by his aide Vagans (S) and a chorus of Soldiers (SATB), which enters three times. Part I is set entirely in the camp of Holofernes, the general serving under Nebuchadnezzar, whose forces were laying siege to the Jewish city of Bethulia. Judith, a beautiful widow from Bethulia, accompanied by Abra, enters Holofernes's camp to beg for peace. Struck by Judith's charms (emphasized throughout the work), Holofernes asks her to dine with him and commands Vagans to have a banquet prepared in his tent. At the close of part I, a chorus of the People of Bethulia is heard (marked "pianissimo sempre" and "le voci in lontano"— "always soft" and "the voices in the distance") praying for Judith's success. Part II begins in Bethulia with a prediction by Ozias of Holofernes's death. The scene changes to the banquet in Holofernes's tent, where he declares his burning passion for Judith in an episode that would qualify the work as an *oratorio erotico* but for Judith's steadfast rejection of his advances and her religious and philosophical replies. Finally drunk with wine, Holofernes falls asleep. While Abra guards the entrance, Judith asks God for strength and draws Holofernes's sword from its scabbard; again invoking the name of God, she cuts off his head. Abra puts the

106. Rinaldi, *Vivaldi*, p. 309.
107. Jervis, *Corfù*, pp. viii, 138–42; Giazotto, *Vivaldi*, pp. 60, 152.

head in a sack, and they escape from the camp. In Bethulia, Ozias is observing the beauty of the sunrise when he sees in the distance Judith returning triumphant. He and the people of Bethulia rejoice in Judith's victory.

Although most of the libretto may be interpreted on either the biblical or the allegorical level, the latter occasionally dominates. The relationship between Judith (Venice) and Abra (Faith), for instance, is convincing only on the allegorical level when, near the end of part I, Abra says that she will be Judith's leader ("pro te dux erit") and will draw the lots of Judith's fate ("Tibi traho sors et fatum"); these assertions seem to contradict her position as a servant, but not as Faith. Shortly thereafter Judith declares, "Beloved Abra, bereaved wife, like a turtledove I sigh and breathe in you" ("Abra amata, sposa orbata, turtur gemo et spiro in te")—a declaration more convincing when made by Venice to Faith than by a mistress to her handmaid. The first clear reference in the poetry to the allegory occurs in Ozias's accompanied recitative, introducing the final chorus, in which he refers to Venice as a "new Judith" and calls upon the "maidens of Zion" (the girls of the Pietà?) to exult in Judith's victory. The final chorus, "Salve invicta Judith formosa" ("Hail, O lovely, invincible Judith"), also clarifies the allegory, as it closes with only slightly veiled references to the Turks (the barbarous Thracian), Venice (Queen of the Sea), and the Adriatic Sea (Adria):

Debellato sic barbaro Trace	With the barbarous Thracian thus defeated,
triumphatrix sit Maris Regia,	may the Queen of the Sea triumph,
et placata sic ira divina	and with heaven's rage thus appeased,
Adria vivat et regnet pace.	may Adria live and reign in peace.

The arias of the oratorio are distributed according to the relative importance of the characters: Judith, six; Holofernes and Abra, five each; Vagans, four; and Ozias, two. All but two of the arias have the da capo form, and about half of the arias are in dance style; these include Vagans' "O servi volate" (Example VII–18a), Judith's *siciliano* "Vivat in pace" (Example VII–18b), and Abra's gigue "Si filgida per te" (Example VII–18c). In their opening measures the dancelike arias often approximate a pre-Classical style in their simple homophonic texture, slow harmonic rhythm, and symmetrical phrase structure; but their spun out

EXAMPLE VII-18. *Juditha triumphans*—Vivaldi (Vivaldi, *Juditha*, pp. 79, 120, 157).

Example a:

O servants, fly [and prepare a table] for my lord . . .

Example b:

Long live in peace, and may genuine peace reign.

Example c:

If for you the bright torch of heaven is propitious . . .

continuations, with characteristically Baroque melodic figures, exclude them from classification as clear examples of *galant* style.[108]

Of frequent occurrence in the arias is the style reminiscent of Vivaldi's concertos; this is particularly prominent in allegro arias in which the ritornello employs rapid violin figuration and a consistently active and clearly patterned bass, resulting in a strong rhythmic drive. For example, Holofernes's simile aria "Agitata infido flatu," a highly effective piece depicting the flight of a bird, begins with a ritornello in concerto style (Example VII–19a); the vocal part is then simply added to the material of the ritornello (Example VII–19b). Other ritornellos in concerto style are those

108. Wolff, "Vivaldi," pp. 180–82, describes Vivaldi's operas, which are in much the same style as *Juditha*, as forerunners of the Neapolitan, or pre-Classical, operas of Leo, Vinci, and Pergolesi.

of Holofernes's aria "Nil arma, nil bella" (Example VII–20) and Abra's "Quamvis Abra ferro" (Example VII–21). The use of the ritornello as a structural element in such arias as these is similar to its use in Vivaldi's solo concertos.[109]

Although coloratura passages are of frequent occurrence throughout the oratorio, they are especially prominent in the arias of the strongly rhythmic, concerto type. Particularly effective for their frequent and extended coloratura passages are Holofernes's "Agitata infido flatu," mentioned above, and the aria "Armate face et anguibus," sung by the enraged Vagans after discovering the bloody scene of the decapitated Holofernes.

EXAMPLE VII-19. *Juditha triumphans*—Vivaldi (Vivaldi, *Juditha*, pp. 51–52).

Example a:

Example b:

Tossed by a treacherous wind, long wandering in her flight, [the sad swallow flies weeping].

109. Kolneder, *Vivaldi*, p. 197; for a discussion of similarities between Vivaldi's solo concerto form and his arias, see Kolneder, "Aria-Concerto."

EXAMPLE VII-20. *Juditha triumphans*—Vivaldi (Vivaldi, *Juditha*, p. 11).

EXAMPLE VII-21. *Juditha triumphans*—Vivaldi (Vivaldi, *Juditha*, p. 65).

Vivaldi is well known for his interest in variety of instrumental color in his concertos, and this interest is also exhibited in *Juditha*. A complete list of the instruments specified in the score, though never used all at once, shows that a large and colorful orchestra was available: two recorders, two oboes, *salmoè*, two *clareni*, two trumpets, timpani, mandolin, four theorbos, viola d'amore, viole da gamba (ATB, one each), the usual strings (two violin parts, viola, and violone), two harpsichords, and organ; not specified but implied are at least two bassoons; and the violone part was probably performed by the violoncello as well as by the double bass.[110] The instrumental colors selected from this varied palette are changed from aria to aria. Particularly attractive for the colors of their accompaniments are several of Judith's arias, one of which is "Quanto magis generosa," her plea with Holofernes for mercy for her people, which is accompanied by the viola d'amore treated soloistically, two muted violins, and no basso continuo except at

110. Regarding the orchestration of *Juditha* and the instrumental terminology (especially *salmoè* for "shawm" and *clareni* for "clarinets"), see Kolneder, *Vivaldi*, pp. 198–99; and Selfridge-Field, *Venetian*, pp. 256–58.

the final cadence of the da capo aria's A part; another is "Transit aetas, volant anni," her rejection of Holofernes's compliments by her comments on the transitory nature of physical beauty as "the years fly by," accompanied by a "flying" mandolin solo in sixteenth-note figures and a pizzicato bass. One of Holofernes's arias is given a particularly unusual and charming effect in its accompaniment: his "Nole o cara," in which he begs Judith not to spurn his desires, is accompanied only by solo oboe and organ, the latter completely notated. The texture includes frequent dialogue between the oboe, the organ's right-hand part, and the vocal line.

Of the three accompanied recitatives in the oratorio, two are allotted to Judith and one to Ozias; all three occur near the end of part II. Judith's accompanied recitatives form parts of a cantatalike monologue—sung during Holofernes's drunken sleep—that leads up to and includes his assassination. The cantatalike section begins with a recitative accompanied by a five-part ensemble of violas, "Summe astrorum Creator," in which Judith asks God for help in the deed she is about to attempt; then, in the aria "In somno profundo," she compares Holofernes's deep sleep to the peace of one who rests in God; and finally, in the accompanied recitative, "Impii, indigni tiranni," she accomplishes the assassination. The only other accompanied recitative is Ozias's "Ita decreto aeterno," in which he calls on the virgins of Zion ("Eja virginis Syon") to praise the triumphant Judith; this recitative introduces the oratorio's final chorus.

Juditha includes no ensembles, with the exception of the five choruses, all for SATB. Since neither a tenor nor a bass is among the solo parts of the oratorio, these voices, at least, must have been added for the choruses. The soprano and alto parts could have been performed, according to the custom of the time, by the oratorio's soloists. The choral texture is almost entirely chordal. The first and last choruses of the oratorio are accompanied by a particularly strong orchestral sound that includes two trumpets, two oboes, strings, and timpani; the orchestration gives the opening and closing numbers a decidedly martial aspect.

Antonio Caldara. Born in Venice in 1671, Caldara spent his youth there;[111] as a boy he sang in the chapel at San Marco and probably

111. For Caldara's biography see U. Kirkendale, *Caldara*, pp. 21–102; for a discussion of his birthdate, often said to be 1670, see ibid., p. 21.

studied with Legrenzi. Little is known of his early employment in Venice, although from 1689 to 1700 he was active there as a composer and violoncellist. From 1700 to 1707, Caldara held the position of maestro di cappella at the ducal court in Mantua, and he also visited Venice, Florence, and Rome for performances of his music. In 1708 he was present when his works were performed in Rome, Barcelona, and Venice, and in the following year he settled in Rome as the maestro di cappella for the marquis Ruspoli. He left Rome in 1716 to assume the position of vicemaestro di cappella at the Italianate court of Emperor Charles VI in Vienna; he retained this position until his death in 1736.

Widely recognized by his contemporaries as one of Europe's greatest composers, Caldara was particularly active in opera and oratorio. Both for the high musical quality and for the considerable number of his oratorios (forty-two, of which forty-one are extant), Caldara must be considered one of the major oratorio composers of his time.[112] His first five oratorios were performed before or around 1700 in Venice and Mantua—some of them, at the Oratorians' church in Venice, Santa Maria della Fava. Two oratorios, dated between 1700 and 1707, were composed for performances in Venice and Rome. Most of the following ten were composed for Rome between 1708 and 1715, and most of the last twenty-five were composed for Vienna.

The oratorios of Caldara's Venetian, Mantuan, and Roman periods are relevant to the present chapter.[113] Both in their texts and in their music, these works clearly reflect the state of the oratorio during Caldara's time. The majority employ hagiographical librettos with contrasts between the forces of the world and those of heaven; in only a few works are all the characters on heaven's side.[114] Prominent in the librettos is the influence of contemporary opera, for they include heroic and erotic elements and theatrical scenes involving disguise, lovers' parting, fury, sleep, or the heroine's gazing into a mirror as she reveals her vanity.

Caldara's first six extant oratorios are examples of what has been called his "late Venetian, dramatic, luxuriant style."[115] Char-

112. For full information on the sources of Caldara's oratorios, see ibid., pp. 112–42.

113. Caldara's Viennese works are treated below, in chapter 8.

114. For a tabular classification of the types of librettos that Caldara used, see U. Kirkendale, *Caldara*, pp. 166–67.

115. ". . . spätvenezianischen, dramatischen Prachtstil": ibid., p. 254. For a discussion of this term and a summary of the style of these works, see ibid., pp. 254–57.

Caldara M:ᵈⁱ
Capella di S.M.
Imperiale Apos

FIGURE VII-9. Antonio Caldara (1671–1736).
    (Reproduced by permission of I/Bc.)

acteristic of these works is a heavy orchestral sonority in the sinfonias, ritornellos, and orchestrally accompanied arias. The orchestra employs four to five string parts, with emphasis on the lower strings, and it sometimes uses concerto grosso instrumentation. The vocal parts consist of SATB, SSAB, or SSATB, although ensembles and choruses are rare. The arias are predominantly in da capo form, even in Caldara's earliest extant oratorio, *Maddalena ai piedi di Cristo* (shortly after 1690), and they frequently use folklike melodies and dances. About one-half of the arias are accompanied by the full orchestra; the others, by continuo alone. The continuo part is active and linear, and it often employs an ostinato pattern. The vocal style is clearly dramatic, with its flexible use of dramatically conceived melismas and arioso passages within simple recitatives and with its emphasis on characterization.

The ten oratorios of Caldara's Roman period, composed mostly for his patron Ruspoli, have been divided into two styles: 1708–10, works in Caldara's "Venetian-early *galant* mixed style"; and 1712–15, those in his "polished early *galant* style."[116] The first of these periods is transitional and includes only two oratorios, *Il martirio di Santa Caterina* (1708) and *Oratorio per Santa Francesca Romana* (1710); the later period includes eight works, of which *Santa Flavia Domitilla* (1713), discussed below, is a clearly representative example.

In the "polished early *galant*" oratorios the style is lighter, simpler, smoother, and more elegant than in the earlier works; this style places less emphasis on musical and dramatic contrast. The orchestra tends to be smaller, to emphasize the upper register, and to consist of only two violin parts and continuo, with the violoncello the only low, stringed instrument specified. The continuo, conceived less as a linear part than in the earlier works, often employs triadic lines and rarely uses an ostinato. The vocal parts emphasize the upper ranges, with the bass voice usually omitted; four of the works employ only SSAA. The arias are in da capo form, but their style differs considerably from those of the earlier works: dance rhythms are more prominent, but the folklike styles are abandoned in favor of the courtly minuet and gavotte; periodic

116. For these terms, "venezianisch-frühgalanter Mischstil" and "geglätteter frühgalanter Stil," and for discussions of the oratorios to which they have been applied, see ibid., pp. 257–76, 277–317. Gallico, "Caldara," is a study of one work in the "Mischstil," *Santa Francesca Romana*.

phrase structure and the repetition of the rhythmic patterns of measures and phrases are more prominent; tonal plateaus are more extended; aria accompaniments are simpler, with violins and voice often in unison or in parallel motion; and arias in which the vocal line is accompanied by violins alone (without the continuo), rare in the earliest period, are now common. Characterization and dramatic continuity are less important; coloratura passages in arias tend to be more strongly influenced by idiomatic instrumental writing; and simple recitatives rarely include melismatic or arioso style.

Santa Flavia Domitilla received its first performance in the oratory of the Chiesa Nuova at Rome in 1713.[117] Its anonymous libretto is based on the life of a first-century saint, the niece of Emperors Titus and Domitian. Flavia Domitilla (S)—under the influence of Nereo (A) and Achilleo (S), the Christian officers of her household—embraces Christianity; she decides to reject the world and her betrothed, Aureliano (T), and to consecrate her virginity to God. Part I of the oratorio includes Domitilla's conversion and her rejection of Aureliano, who does not know why she has rejected him. In part II Aureliano learns that his rival for Domitilla is Jesus. Enraged that Domitilla and her servants are Christians, he orders that Nereo and Achilleo be put to death and that Domitilla be imprisoned to await her end. At the conclusion of the oratorio, the three Christians joyfully anticipate their martyrdom.[118] While the conflict between the forces of heaven and the world is essential to the libretto, it is not as harsh a conflict as one might expect. Domitilla's conversion, accomplished by the fourth number of the oratorio, is facile, *galant*; she does not reveal a deep inner struggle to make her decision, the kind of struggle that requires approximately one-half of the oratorio in many works of the period that treat the theme of conversion. Reflections on the joys of Christian love seem more important in the libretto than the dramatic conflict.

The majority of the twenty arias in *Flavia* are in da capo form and reflect the early *galant* tendencies described above.[119] Domi-

117. U. Kirkendale, *Caldara*, pp. 118–19. The MS source of this oratorio is in A/Wn: Cod. 18142.
118. For a more extensive summary of the libretto, see U. Kirkendale, *Caldara*, pp. 334–35.
119. For a discussion (with music examples) of the music of Flavia, to which the present one may be considered supplementary, see ibid., pp. 280–89.

tilla's first aria, "A te dono," which she sings soon after her conversion, well illustrates the style; it is a charming minuet with considerable regularity of phrase structure, unison violins doubling the vocal line, and a solo violoncello playing a sparse, harmonically conceived accompaniment.[120] Another clear example of the early *galant* style is Domitilla's second aria, "Quando piange l'aurora" (Example VII–22), characterized by regular phrase structure, repeated rhythmic patterns in dance style, and a light accompaniment, in which the first and second violins double the voice at the

EXAMPLE VII-22. *Santa Flavia Domitilla*—Caldara (A/Wn: codex 18142, fol. 29^v).

When the nascent dawn weeps it is the harbinger of welcome light.

unison and third, respectively, while the continuo rests. In this aria, as in the other two with similar accompaniments (Achilleo's "Mira il giglio" and Domitilla's "Fa quanto sai"), the continuo enters only to support the violins during ritornellos or when the voice rests.[121] More than half of the numbers in the oratorio are influenced by dance style, and some of these are specific dances—such as the minuet (see above), the gigue (Aureliano's "Pria le fiamme"), the gavotte (Domitilla's "L'onestà nella bellezza"), and the *siciliano* (Domitilla and Aureliano's duet "Lo sà il mio core"). Four of the twenty-four numbers in the oratorio are accompanied by continuo only; the others employ two violin parts or unison violins and continuo. One aria, Domitilla's "Per amar quel ben," is exceptional for its marking, "Aria con violoni di concertino e concerto grosso." In the manuscript score for this number, the

120. For a long music example for this aria, see ibid., pp. 284–85.
121. Concerning a similar procedure in Handel's *Resurrezione*, see p. 345.

violin parts are notated on two staves and include tutti, soli, and solo indications for the alternation of the groups.

The ensembles of the oratorio, four duets, are similar in style to the arias, but two of them are non–da capo numbers. Of special interest are the several brief passages of duet recitative, with simultaneous declamation, by Achilleo and Nereo.

The orchestra never exceeds two written violin parts and basso continuo. In addition to the aria accompaniments and ritornellos mentioned above, the orchestra plays introductory numbers for the oratorio's two parts. The sinfonia at the beginning of part I consists of a slow introduction followed by a fugal allegro, with a characteristic *galant* subject and with solo and tutti alternations. Part II begins with a chordal *Introdutione* of only seven measures.

Conclusion

Theatrical influences were of primary importance in the oratorio from the 1660s to about 1720. Whether performed in an ostensibly religious or a purely secular context, the oratorio gradually changed its function. No longer used primarily as a means of drawing a crowd into an oratory to attend a spiritual exercise, no longer an integral part of an essentially devotional and didactic experience in a place of prayer, the oratorio became the central and often the only feature of an evening's program. Functioning primarily as a poetic-musical entertainment to be performed and enjoyed, like opera, for its own sake, oratorio grew ever closer to opera in its libretto and music (but not in staging or action) and often substituted for opera while the theaters were closed. The libretto gradually abandoned the *testo*, became increasingly dramatic, and reflected tendencies of religious literature, spoken drama, and the visual arts of the period, as well as those of opera. The changes in both the libretto and the music of opera from the mid-seventeenth to the early eighteenth century are clearly reflected in both the Italian and the Latin oratorio.

The operatic tendency of oratorio in this period has been seen by some as a sign of its decadence, and the genre has been harshly judged for having lost so much of its former devotional value.[122]

122. Alaleona, *Oratorio*, pp. 17, 189–95; Pasquetti, *Oratorio*, pp. 370–72, 398. For more positive evaluations of the oratorio in this period, see Schering, *Oratorium*, p. 169; and Damerini, "Oratorio."

Such a judgment, based on a consideration of the oratorio in relation to its service to the church, adopts the viewpoint of the most idealistic of the Oratorians, struggling to retain the devotional emphasis in their oratories. Indeed, the fervent period of the Counter-Reformation had passed; the role of music in the oratories—increasingly like concert halls—could not but reflect the relaxation in Italian religious life, which was also seen in such phenomena as the revival of the Christmas Eve festivities at the Vatican Apostolic Palace. In this milieu, and considering the close relationship between oratorio and opera, the two genres are best evaluated with much the same poetic, dramatic, and musical criteria. When thus evaluated, the oratorio of this period can by no means be considered decadent. Its strengths and weaknesses of structure and style in music and poetry are largely those of opera, and in both genres men of genius—Stradella, Scarlatti, and Handel, among others—succeeded in creating great masterpieces while working within the established conventions.

PART III *The Italian Oratorio*
Outside Italy

CHAPTER VIII *Vienna*

After the oratorio had become a recognized genre in Italy, it began to be exported, as Italian opera had been, to areas outside Italy. The exportation of Italian oratorio was primarily to Roman Catholic centers, of which Vienna and Paris are undoubtedly among the most significant for the cultivation of this genre. Yet so little research has been done on the Baroque oratorio in Spain, Portugal, and the Catholic regions of Austria (except Vienna), southern Germany, and eastern Europe, that it is virtually impossible to determine whether there were other Catholic centers that might also have been significant for oratorio composition and performance. Brief dialogue motets probably were performed in these areas as elsewhere in the early Baroque, but the extent to which there may have been an early Baroque development of longer, sacred dramatic dialogues is not known. For instance, one wonders whether the *Rapraesentatio harmonica conceptionis et nativitatis S. Joannis Baptistae* ("Harmonic Representation of the Conception and Birth of St. John the Baptist") by Daniel Bollius, the court organist at Mainz from 1626 until his death in 1638, is an isolated, exceptional work or whether there were others like it. This work, the manuscript of which is now lost, was composed in the 1620s, or perhaps a bit earlier; it has been called "the first oratorio in the Italian style on German soil."[1] It was in two acts and six scenes, and it included five *symphoniae* to be performed between the scenes. As an extended, sacred dramatic composition, it is of considerable interest for the early history of the oratorio,

---

1. Grottron, *Mainz*, p. 47. The MSS of this work and of Bollius's short, sacred dramatic dialogues, formerly in the Breslau Stadtbibliothek, have been missing since the end of World War II. The music in these MSS is described, with examples, ibid., pp. 46–47; Moser, *Evangelium*, pp. 54–59; and Winterfeld, *Gabrieli*, 2:205–9.

although extant information does not clearly indicate whether or not the work was intended to be staged.

The Oratorio and Sepolcro in Vienna[2]

The history of the oratorio in Baroque Vienna can be best understood when treated together with a closely related genre, the *sepolcro*. The Viennese oratorio, normally in Italian, was unstaged and was textually, structurally, and stylistically much like the oratorio of Italy. The *sepolcro*, also normally in Italian, was similar to the oratorio except that it was usually composed in one structural part, was limited to the theme of the Passion and Crucifixion of Christ, and was intended to be performed with scenery, costumes, and action. The most important, and at times the only, feature of the scenery was a model of the holy sepulchre of Christ, whence the name of the genre.

Social Context, Patrons, Composers, Poets[3]

In the mid-sixteenth century, when the Jesuits were first established in Vienna, this city and much of Austria were strongly Protestant. By the end of the century, however, the diligent educational activities of the Jesuits and the strong Roman Catholic support of the Hapsburg court had combined to return Vienna and Austria at least nominally to Roman Catholicism. In the seventeenth century this Counter-Reformation process continued to gain momentum and penetrated deeply into Austrian cultural life. Jesuit educational institutions became ever stronger and more numerous, and many new monasteries and convents, representing a variety of religious orders, came into being. The Hapsburg emperors of the seventeenth century were militant defenders of the Roman Catholic faith. Ferdinand II (1619–37) sought to crush Protestantism by

2. Among the most useful writings on the Baroque oratorio and *sepolcro* in Vienna are Gruber, *Sepolcro*; Renker, "Sepolcro"; Schering, *Oratorium*, pp. 130–37, 162–68, 195–212; Schnitzler, "Draghi"; Vogl, "Oratorium"; and Wellesz, "Opern." A book by Rudolf Schnitzler on Viennese sacred dramatic music of the Baroque era is in progress. Virtually all the MS scores and printed librettos of Viennese oratorios and *sepolcri* mentioned in this chapter are in A/Wn.

3. Among the numerous studies of the cultural life of Austria and Vienna in the Baroque era, the following are particularly useful: Ginhart, *Kunstgeschichte*, pp. 86–178; Hadamowsky, *Barocktheater*; Hempel, *Art*; Landau, *Literatur*; Mayer, *Österreich*; Weilen, "Theater"; and Weilen, *Theatergeschichte*.

force and virtually succeeded in doing so within the Hapsburg hereditary lands. Ferdinand III (1637–57) and Leopold I (1658–1705) were also strong in their opposition to non-Catholics —Leopold expelled the Jews from Vienna in 1670. The politico-religious and military struggles of the Hapsburg empire in the Baroque era included the Thirty Years War; constant trouble with the Bohemian, Hungarian, Slovene, and Transylvanian areas of the empire; and the war with the Turks, in which the latter invaded Austria and besieged Vienna for two months in 1683 before help came from the Polish king. Despite these external struggles, however, the Hapsburg emperors fostered an intense and sumptuous cultural life in the city of Vienna and at their court. This cultural life was predominantly Italian in both its secular and sacred aspects, the latter of which was also strongly Jesuit.

Of special importance in Vienna were the Jesuit school dramas —with music, dancing, and elaborate staging—intended to provide rhetorical exercise for the participating students and edifying entertainment for the audience. In 1655 a large theater built by Ferdinand III for the performance of Jesuit dramas opened at the University of Vienna. According to a contemporary account, the lavishly decorated hall, which would accommodate an audience of three thousand, included a gallery at the rear for the musicians; the elaborate stage machinery offered numerous staging possibilities, including that of quick changes of as many as twelve or thirteen different scenes.[4] The dramas were virtually always in Latin, but beginning in 1665 some Viennese Jesuit dramas began to include comic *intermedia* in German or in a combination of the two languages. By the late seventeenth century the musical and spoken portions of the dramas were of approximately equal length and importance, and the dramas included the same types of musical numbers as were found in operas of the time: sinfonie, ritornellos, dances, choruses, vocal ensembles, arias, and both simple and accompanied recitatives. A characteristic example is the *Pia et fortis mulier*, with music by Johann Kaspar Kerll, performed in 1677 in honor of Leopold I and his new bride Eleonore of Pfalz-Neuburg. The five-act work begins with a musical prologue in eight sections; a chorus concludes each of the first four acts; a

4. The description of the theater, from the codex Testarello in A/Wn, is quoted in Weilen, "Theater," p. 340.

partially musical epilogue of praise for the emperor and his new wife follows the last act; and musical insertions appear within each of the acts.[5] The subject matter of many of the dramas—being based on biblical, hagiographical, or allegorical material—is the same as that of oratorios, although some dramas derive from secular history or mythology. Viennese Jesuit dramas based on the Passion story were at times acted before a scene of the holy sepulchre of Christ;[6] they thus paralleled the *sepolcro*.

The importation of Italian musicians to German courts became increasingly popular throughout the seventeenth century; the Viennese court strongly supported Italian opera and oratorio, but Italian influence at this court went much further than music. Numerous links with Italy were created by marriage in the sixteenth and seventeenth centuries: the second wife of Ferdinand II and the third wife of Ferdinand III, for instance, were both from Mantua and were both named Eleonora Gonzaga, and the second wife of Leopold I was Anna Claudia Felicitas of Tyrol, the granddaughter of Cosimo II de' Medici. Such family ties with Italy, combined with the strongly Italianate Counter-Reformation, produced a profound effect on Viennese art, architecture, literature, and music. For the numerous new churches and monasteries that were built in Vienna during the seventeenth century and for the modernization of older ones, Italian architects, painters, and craftsmen were strongly preferred. In the field of language and literature, Italian grew increasingly important at the Viennese court.[7] In 1657 Ferdinand III established an Italian literary academy, which later included among its members Leopold I, Anna Claudia Felicitas, and the librettists Nicolò Minato and Francesco Sbarra. By 1675 Italian had become firmly established as the preferred language of the court and intelligentsia: in that year the Tuscan ambassador and scholar Lorenzo Magalotti, who had only recently arrived in Vienna from Florence, was evidently struggling with German; he wrote that he could read the language fairly well but could scarcely speak it for lack of practice, since all educated

5. For a study of the music of this and other Viennese Jesuit dramas of the late seventeenth and early eighteenth centuries—dramas that include music by Johann Bernhard Staudt, Johann Michael Zacher, Ferdinand Tobias Richter, and Johann Jakob Stupan von Ehrenstein—see Kramer, "Jesuitendrama."

6. Gruber, *Sepolcro*, p. 26.

7. For the importance of the Italian language and literature in Vienna, see Landau, *Literatur*, and Campanini, *Precursore*, pp. 63–72.

persons spoke fluent Italian.[8] In the early eighteenth century Italian literature continued to play a prominent role at the Hapsburg court; the use of the Italian language was even further stimulated by political developments, for in this period the Hapsburgs increased their domination of northern Italy.

The earliest performance of an Italian opera at the Viennese court took place on the birthday of Ferdinand II in 1625, when his Mantuan wife sponsored a performance in his honor of a *dramma per musica*, which included *commedia dell'arte* characters.[9] This performance initiates a period of increasing interest for the remainder of the century in the celebration of birthdays, name days, and other festive occasions by performances of Italian operas, ballets, dramatic cantatas, and works in related genres.[10] About twenty-five secular dramatic works were performed during the thirty-eight years of the combined reigns of Ferdinand II and Ferdinand III, but more than three hundred, during the forty-seven-year reign of Leopold I, the most important Hapsburg patron of music in the seventeenth century.

Educated by the Jesuits, Leopold I was intended for the priesthood when the death of his older brother Ferdinand IV in 1654 changed his future from clergyman to emperor. Like most of the Hapsburg emperors in the Baroque era, Leopold was a trained musician; his studies included both musical performance and composition, activities that he continued for most of his life.[11] Among his compositions are at least eight sacred dramatic works; during his reign more than one hundred such works were performed at court—always in Lent as substitutes for opera, which was not performed in that season.

Leopold's priestly education and the generally pervasive Counter-Reformation spirit in Vienna no doubt account for the pronounced religiosity of the court during his reign. Lenten observances were particularly elaborate. During Holy Week, the most solemn period of the Lenten observances, the emperor and

8. Landau, *Literatur*, p. 15.

9. Hadamowsky, *Barocktheater*, pp. 11–12.

10. For lists of secular and sacred dramatic works performed at the Viennese court in the Baroque era, see ibid., pp. 69–115; Köchel, *Fux*, pp. 483–572; and Weilen, *Theatergeschichte*, pp. 5–117.

11. Regarding the musical activities of Ferdinand III, Leopold I, Joseph I, and Charles VI, see Adler, *Kaiser*, 1:i–xxiii; for selections from the emperors' church music see ibid., vol. 1; for selections from their operas, oratorios, *sepolcri*, and instrumental works, see ibid., vol. 2. (Some of the selections given by Adler, however, are misattributed.)

FIGURE VIII-1. The Hapsburg emperor Leopold I, who reigned from 1658 to
1705. An engraving of 1674 by Bartholomäus Kilian after a
drawing by Sebastian van Dryweghen.
(Reproduced by permission of the Bild-Archiv of A/Wn.)

his court participated in processions and liturgical services in the court chapels, at the church of the Discalsed Augustinians, at the Jesuit college, and elsewhere in Vienna. Among the observances were visits to the holy sepulchres that were erected in various churches in Vienna and the traditional Maundy Thursday service in which the emperor washed the feet of twelve old and poor men of Vienna, and the empress, the feet of twelve old and poor women—after which the imperial couple served them at tables.

Although the oratorio in Italy was rarely given in a liturgical context, a sacred dramatic work at the Viennese court of Leopold I usually constituted an integral part of a Lenten service that combined liturgical and extraliturgical elements. Contemporary accounts indicate, for instance, that a sacred dramatic work could be presented after compline or be substituted for either compline or a litany; that at some point during the service at which the composition was to be performed a priest engaged especially for the Lenten season would preach a sermon in Italian; and that the performance would usually close in a liturgical manner with a benediction, a litany, the *Stabat Mater*, or a responsory.[12]

Most of the performances of sacred dramatic compositions sponsored by Leopold took place in the main court chapel, the Hofburgkapelle. This gothic structure (see Figure VIII–2) underwent a number of modifications during the sixteenth and seventeenth centuries; of special interest are the changes made during the reign of Ferdinand III, which included the construction of galleries and "oratories." The latter, still present in the existing structure, are relatively small rooms for the private devotions of the imperial family; they are accessible directly from the imperial quarters and include windows or balconies that open into the Hofburgkapelle. Thus the imperial family could hear and see performances of oratorios and *sepolcri* from the oratories, but the

12. In the period of Charles VI (and probably earlier as well), the position of the sermon, which lasted no longer than fifteen minutes, was between the two structural parts of an oratorio, according to a letter by Apostolo Zeno. (Apostolo Zeno to Pier Caterino Zeno, 1 May 1728, in Zeno, *Lettere, 4:243, letter 739*). For contemporary references to the Lenten observances of the Viennese court and the semiliturgical contexts of the performances of sacred dramatic works, see Schnitzler, "Draghi," pp. 280–85 (excerpts from the 1678–99 issues of *Il corriere ordinario: avisi italiani, ordinarii e straordinarii* [Vienna: Giovanni van Ghelen]), and pp. 296–97 (excerpts from the MS by Kilian Reinhardt, "Rubriche generali per le funzioni ecclesiastiche musicali di tutto l'anno" [Vienna, 1727], in A/Wn: Suppl. mus. 2503).

'Das Te Deum Laudamus in der Hoff Capellen.

1. Ihre Majn: der Kayser. 2. Ihre Mayn: die Kayserin 3. Ihre Durchl: Drhl: die Ertzhertoginen. 4. Bischoff Zür Neustatt. 5. Obr: Erb Caplän. 6. Obr: Erb Marschall. 7. Obr: Erb Panner 8. Angesetzter Hatschiern Hauptmann. 9. Angesetzter Trabanten Hauptmann 10. Obr: Erb Mundtschenck 11. Obr: Erb Truchsäß. 12. Obr: Erb Cammerer. 13. Obr: Erb Vorschneider. 14. Der St: O: Herold 15. Obr: Erb Hoffmaister. 16. Obr: Erb Stallmaister. 17. Obr: Erb Jägermaister. 18 Obr: Erb Falckhenmaister. 19. Obr: Erb Stabelmaister. 20. Der N:O: Land Marschall. 21. Die gesambte N:O: Stände. 22. Die Kay: Hatschiern, ü: Trabanten Esliardi.

J. C. Hackhofer delin. | J. A. Pfeffel et C. Engelbrecht. fe.

FIGURE VIII-2. Interior of the Hofburgkapelle in Vienna. From a drawing by J. C. Hackhofer, engraved by J. A. Peffel and C. Engelbrecht, printed in *Erb-Huldigung . . . Joseph dem Ersten* (Vienna, 1705), following p. 38.
(Reproduced by permission of the Bild-Archiv of A/Wn.)

oratories were not themselves the locations of such performances. (In Figure VIII–2, showing the interior of the Hofburgkapelle on a festive occasion—not the performance of an oratorio—two oratories are visible on the left. The highest one is vacant, but in the lower one are the empress and grand duchesses; the ladies of the court occupy a gallery at the same level in the extreme left of the picture.)

With the exception of Leopold, the chief patron of sacred dramatic music in Vienna was his stepmother, Eleonora, the widow of Ferdinand III. Eleonora maintained her own court, separate from Leopold's, from the death of her husband in 1657 until her own death in 1686. The sacred dramatic works that she sponsored took place during Lent in her private chapel. Although the great majority of oratorios and *sepolcri* were given in the imperial palace, a few were given at other locations in Vienna.[13]

During the reigns of Leopold's sons, Joseph I (1705–11) and Charles VI (1711–40), music continued to play a prominent role in the cultural life of the court. Like Leopold, both emperors were performers and composers, and both fostered Italian music, particularly opera and oratorio.

The earliest composer of sacred dramatic music at the Viennese court may have been Giovanni Valentini, who was also a poet. His libretto *Santi risorti nel giorno della passione di Christo* ("The Holy Revived Ones on the Day of the Passion of Christ," Vienna, 1643), dedicated to Ferdinand III, seems textually related to the *sepolcro*, although nothing is known of its manner of performance, and the music is lost.[14] Another libretto by Valentini for which the music is lost, his *Dialogo: La vita di santo Agapito* ("Dialogue: The Life of St. Agapetus," Vienna, 1643),[15] is clearly that of an early oratorio in one structural part. It is a dramatic libretto of over four hundred poetic lines. The libretto includes six solo personages; choruses of Soldiers, Christians, and Angels; and a final nondramatic chorus that refers to the empress Maria Agapita, for whose birthday the work was written and performed. Although no evidence of continuing sacred dramatic composition

13. For example, A. Draghi's *Le cinque vergini prudenti* was performed in 1694 at the church of the monastery of St. Joseph (Schnitzler, "Draghi," p. 390); regarding a performance in another Viennese church, see below, n. 23.

14. For a detailed discussion of this work and its relationship to the *sepolcro*, see Gruber, *Sepolcro*, pp. 26–36.

15. In A/Wn: 41.T.27.MS.

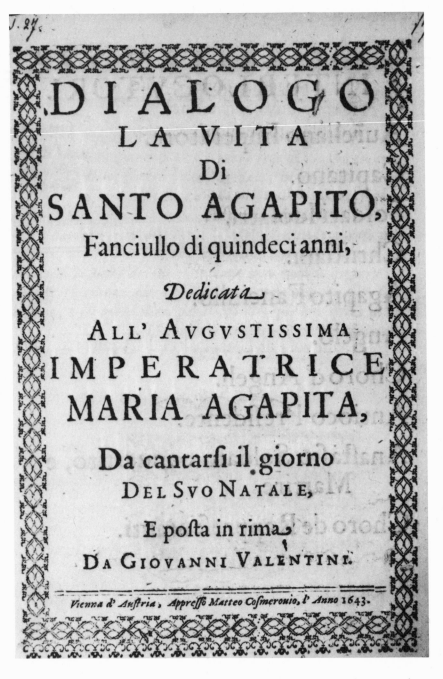

FIGURE VIII-3. Title page of Giovanni Valentini's oratorio libretto of 1643.
(Courtesy of A/Wn.)

in the 1640s and 1650s has appeared, it would seem reasonable to assume that other sacred dramatic works were produced in those decades, if one consider the oratorio activity at that time in Italy and the keen interest in Italian music at the Viennese court.[16] The earliest extant music of a Viennese sacred dramatic work is *Il sagrifizio d'Abramo* ("The Sacrifice of Abraham," 1660) by Leopold I, who continued to compose an occasional sacred dramatic work until at least 1683. Two of his *sepolcri* are highly exceptional for Vienna because they use German texts: *Die Erlösung des menschlichen Geschlechts* ("The Redemption of the Human Race," 1679) and *Sig des Leydens Christi über die Sinnligkeit* ("The Victory of the Suffering of Christ over Sensuality," 1682). Other composers of sacred dramatic works that date mostly from the 1660s and 1690s are Giuseppe Tricarico, Antonio Bertali, Marc'Antonio Cesti, Antonio Draghi, Giovanni Battista Pederzuoli, Giovanni Felice Sances, and Pietro Andrea Ziani. With the notable exception of the extremely prolific Draghi, whose works will be given special attention below, each of these men is known to have composed from one to six sacred dramatic works. Composers representing the Viennese oratorio from the 1690s to the 1730s are Ferdinand Tobias Richter, Carlo Agostino Badia, Marc'Antonio Ziani, Giovanni and Antonio Bononcini, Francesco Bartolomeo Conti, Johann Joseph Fux, Antonio Caldara, Ignazio Conti, Giuseppe Porsile, and Georg Reutter, Jr. Of these composers Fux and Caldara are the outstanding representatives of the late Baroque Viennese oratorio.

The principal librettist of both operas and sacred dramatic works at the Viennese court in the seventeenth century was Nicolò Minato. Born in Bergamo in the 1630s, Minato was an opera librettist in Venice by the 1650s. In 1669 he went to Vienna as imperial court poet, a position that he retained until his death in 1697 or 1698. During his Viennese period he wrote more than 170 secular and approximately 40 sacred librettos, most of which were set to music by Draghi. The latter was also a librettist, as well as a composer, and wrote the texts of at least four sacred dramatic works. Among the librettists of eighteenth-century Vienna were

16. An anonymous oratorio, *Il secondo Adamo disformato nel riformare il primo* (1649), is cited in Köchel, *Fux*, p. 487; Köchel does not indicate the source of his information, however, and I have been unable to verify this performance. Köchel possibly misread 1699 for 1649, since an oratorio by Draghi with that title was performed in 1699.

Pietro Pariati, Giovanni Claudio Pasquini, Silvio Stampiglia, Apostolo Zeno, and Pietro Metastasio. The works of the last two, which are treated later in this chapter, are of primary significance in the history of the oratorio.

Oratorio and Sepolcro: *Distinctions and Terminology*

The chief distinctions between the oratorio and the *sepolcro* were pointed out early in this chapter. The two genres, however, were not consistently identified by these terms. By far the most common use of the term *oratorio* was for works virtually identical to those known by the same term in Italy: they are normally in two structural parts (virtually never in more than two, but occasionally in one part), with an Italian sacred text, and are intended to be performed without staging, costumes, or action. Although Viennese oratorios in the seventeenth century were usually so named, in the eighteenth century they were often called *componimento sacro* or *azione sacra*, the latter having been used by Zeno for all of his oratorio librettos and by Metastasio for some of his. In the seventeenth century oratorios were normally performed at the Viennese court on any day in Lent except during Holy Week, when *sepolcri* were usually given instead.

The term *sepolcro* was used in the seventeenth century to designate a work of the type briefly described early in this chapter —the essential features of which are a single structural part, a text on the theme of the Passion of Christ, and an intended performance with scenery, costumes, and action. Yet other terms—chief among them *azione sacra*, *azione sepolcrale*, and *rappresentazione sacra*—were more frequently applied to *sepolcri* in the seventeenth century; the term *rappresentazione sacra* is of particular importance, since it was used for all but four of Draghi's twenty-six *sepolcri*.[17] Highly exceptional is Leopold I's use of the term *oratorio* for his first sacred dramatic composition, *Il sagrificio d'Abramo*, a work in one structural part that was intended for performance before a model of the holy sepulchre.

The tradition of performing sacred music for ceremonies taking place before a model of, or scenery depicting, the holy sepulchre is not strictly Viennese but has medieval antecedents throughout

17. Despite the relatively infrequent use of the term *sepolcro* for these sacred dramatic works in the Baroque era, the term is so firmly established in musicological literature and is so convenient and descriptive a label that it is retained here.

western Europe in the liturgical drama, the office of the *Depositio*, the Forty Hours devotion, and the office of the *Elevatio*.[18] The *Depositio* was a semidramatic ceremony that symbolized the burial of Christ by the placement of a cross, a consecrated Host, or both (*Depositio crucis, Despositio Hostiae,* or *Depositio crucis et Hostiae*) in a model of the holy sepulchre; this ceremony followed the Mass of the Presanctified and the Adoration of the Cross on Good Friday. The Forty Hours devotion was an extended vigil before the model of the sepulchre containing the cross or Host; the devotion began on Good Friday evening and lasted for the forty hours of Christ's Crucifixion and entombment. In the *Elevatio* ceremony the elements that had been placed in the tomb on Good Friday were removed on Easter morning to symbolize the Resurrection. Although the *Elevatio* survived only until the sixteenth century, the Forty Hours devotion was still being observed in the mid-twentieth century; vestiges of the *Depositio* remained until then, too, in the Maundy Thursday ceremony of carrying the reserved Host to its "altar of repose." In the Renaissance the Forty Hours devotion began to be held at other times during the year in addition to Lent, and the consecrated Host replaced the sepulchre as the focal point of the decor. For Good Friday observances of this devotion, however, the sepulchre continued to form a part of the decor.

Particularly in Italy, seventeenth-century decorations for the Forty Hours devotions became increasingly ornate and began to resemble elaborate stage sets, with the Host in a monstrance occupying the position of primary importance; in such decorations, at times called *teatri sacri*, not only the holy sepulchre but also other scenes of redemption would be included when the observance took place at the end of Lent.[19] Elaborate scenery for the veneration of the sepulchre of Christ through spectacle and music was evidently not restricted to churches. In 1627 the archi-

18. For information about these ceremonies, see Young, *Drama*, 1:112–77; Young, *Easter Sepulchre*; Brooks, "Sepulchre"; Brooks, "Sepulchrum"; Santi, *Quarant'ore*; and Gruber, *Sepolcro*.

19. For a study, with illustrations, of sixteenth- and seventeenth-century Roman decorations for the Forty Hours devotion, see Weil, "Forty Hours." I gratefully acknowledge the help of Professor Mark Weil, who called my attention to the visual aspect of the Forty Hours devotion and its connection with the Viennese *sepolcro*, as well as to the reference, below, to Joseph Furttenbach. For descriptions of a Forty Hours service at Florence in the private chapel of the archduchess of Austria and duchess of Tuscany that began on Good Friday in 1619 and featured elaborate scenery and music, see Solerti, *Musica*, p. 144, and Solerti, *Melodramma*, 2:335–45.

tect Joseph Furttenbach published a description of an elaborate stage set for the holy sepulchre, which he saw on Good Friday in the Pitti Palace at Florence; the stage set was the work of the Medici stage designer Giulio Parigi.[20] Furttenbach speaks of the scene as "a beautiful *prospectiva* or holy sepulchre," the facade of which was ornamented with clouds on which angels who performed lovely music were seated; the perspective of the scene was very deep, and in the distance one could see the city of Jerusalem. On the right side of the stage was the *castrum doloris*, or sepulchre of the Lord, which was eight spans long and six spans high; it was draped in black and heavily laden with diamonds and a gold crown, which brilliantly sparkled in the bright stage lights. During the course of the ceremony for which the scene was designed, the grand duke of Tuscany, the knights of St. Stephen, and numerous Florentine nobility paid visits to the sepulchre. Nothing is known about the music for this event, and little is known about that for the *Depositio*, the Forty Hours, and the *Elevatio* services; yet in their visual and semidramatic elements they contribute to the establishment of the tradition from which the Viennese *sepolcro* developed.

In the seventeenth century, *sepolcri* are known to have been performed at the Viennese court only on Maundy Thursday and Good Friday; there tends to be a correspondence between the places and the degree of elaboration of the performances on those two days. On Maundy Thursday a *sepolcro* was performed in the chapel of the empress dowager Eleonora virtually every year from the 1660s until her death in 1686; for these performances the scenery, limited to a model of the holy sepulchre, was apparently simple. On Good Friday, however, a *sepolcro* would be performed in the Hofburgkapelle, and an elaborately painted background, illustrating the theme of the libretto, would be used in addition to the holy sepulchre.[21] Among the extant designs of these backgrounds by court stage designer Ludovico Ottaviano Burnacini is that depicting the sacrifice of Abraham on a mountain (see Figure VIII–4), for Draghi's *Il sagrificio non impedito* ("The Unimpeded

20. Furttenbach, *Itinerarium*, pp. 81–83; Furttenbach's description is quoted and discussed in Tintelnot, *Barocktheater*, pp. 271–72 and n. 346.

21. For a discussion of the scenery and costumes used for *sepolcro* performances, with plates showing sketches of scenic designs, see Schnitzler, "Draghi," pp. 63–100; on the manner of staging *sepolcri*, see Biach-Schiffmann, *Burnacini*, pp. 68–69, and Haas, "Orchesterteilung," pp. 9–10.

FIGURE VIII-4. Watercolor sketch by Ludovico Ottaviano Burnacini of his scenic design for Antonio Draghi's *sepolcro* entitled *Il sagrificio non impedito* (1692). The scene shows the sacrifice of Abraham at the top of the mountain.
(Reproduced by permission of the Theatersammlung of A/Wn: Min. 29/36.)

Sacrifice"); that depicting Calvary, for Draghi's *Il prezzo dell'humana redentione* ("The Price of Human Redemption"); and a composite scene of a glory with angels, the burning bush that was seen by Moses, and a portion of hell with frightened demons, for Draghi's *La Passione di Christo*.[22] According to the stage directions in the printed librettos, a curtain would open at the beginning of the performance to reveal the holy sepulchre and scenery, and in the course of the *sepolcro* the members of the cast would perform actions—such as weeping, carrying a cross, lifting a veil, kneeling, or bringing flowers—appropriate to the circumstances of the drama. The *sepolcro*'s visual elaboration, its function as the music for the most solemn days at the close of the Lenten period, and its elaborate musical scoring (treated below) all point to the genre's undoubtedly greater significance than the oratorio at the Viennese court.

In the early eighteenth century—after the period of Minato and Draghi—action, costumes, and scenic backgrounds were gradually discontinued. The tradition of erecting holy sepulchres in the various chapels lingered on, but sacred dramatic compositions in two structural parts began to be presented in semistaged or unstaged performances at the sepulchre. As late as 1714, however, there is evidence of a scenic performance of a sacred dramatic work, possibly by Antonio Lotti, in the Augustinerkirche in Vienna.[23] Among the terms used in the eighteenth century for such works are *oratorio per il santissimo sepolcro*, *componimento sacro cantato al santissimo sepolcro*, and *componimento sacro per musica applicato al santissimo sepolcro*. At least three of Fux's oratorios and eight of Caldara's were intended for performance at a replica of the holy sepulchre.

Oratorio and Sepolcro Librettos, 1660–1720

Oratorio librettos of the Viennese repertory are similar to those of Italy, as described in chapter 7, with certain exceptions.[24] Allego-

22. For reproductions of Burnacini's designs for the backgrounds of these three works by Draghi, see Schnitzler, "Draghi," pls. V–VII.

23. For information regarding this performance, see Wiener Diarium, 17 March 1714, in Hugo Zelzer's "Historische Bemerkungen," Fux, *Werke*, ser. 4, vol. 1, p. ix, n. 29. The manner in which sacred dramatic works were performed at the holy sepulchres in the early eighteenth-century transitional period is the subject of a study in progress by Dr. Gernot Gruber of the Musicological Institute of the University of Vienna.

24. For a discussion of the librettos of Draghi's sacred dramatic works, which appear to be characteristic of Viennese librettos in his period, see Schnitzler, "Draghi," pp. 138–89.

rical personages are considerably more prominent in the oratorios of Vienna than in those of Italy. Such characters as Faith, Hope, Love, Divine Providence, Sin, and Death frequently appear, either together with real personages or in purely allegorical works. In two oratorio librettos written by Ignazio Savioni and set by Draghi in 1674, for instance, all the personages except the angels are allegorical. His *Il cuore appassionato: Oratorio per li dolori di Maria Vergine* ("The Passionate Heart: Oratorio for the Sorrows of the Virgin Mary") includes as personages the Heart of Mary, Love, Angel, Thought, Author (i.e., *testo*), and a chorus of Thoughts; and his *La potenza della croce* ("The Power of the Cross") includes the personages Author, Angel, Nature, and Fire in addition to a chorus of the Three Elements and a chorus of Angels. Also appearing occasionally as personages, and more characteristically than in oratorios of Italy, are God the Father, Jesus Christ, and the Holy Spirit. Another distinction between the oratorio of Vienna and that of Italy is in the treatment of female personages; while they are often prominent in Viennese oratorios, the erotic element seems to be less emphasized than in Italy.

Sepolcro librettos, as pointed out above, are based on the theme of the Passion and Crucifixion of Christ. Their primary emphasis is on the period after the Crucifixion, and they combine lamentation with interpretation of the Passion and Crucifixion. Numerous allusions to events of the Old and New Testaments are usually made in the course of the *sepolcro*. Old Testament events are compared with the Crucifixion, and episodes from the life of Christ are drawn upon to summarize the essential meaning of his life, climaxed by the Crucifixion and Resurrection. There is a strong tendency for *sepolcri* to be descriptive (although they never use a *testo*), doctrinal, and reflective, rather than to present a chronological sequence of events. *Sepolcri* normally include six to ten personages—thus more than do oratorios—and allegorical characters tend to be even more prominent in *sepolcri* than in Viennese oratorios. Among those using only allegorical characters is the anonymous libretto set by Marc'Antonio Cesti, *Natura et quatuor elementa dolentia ad sepulchrum Christi* ("Nature and the Four Elements Sorrowful at the Sepulchre of Christ"),[25] which is unusual for its use of the Latin language; the personages are

25. The MS is D-ddr/Bds: Mus. ms. 30305. I gratefully acknowledge the help of Professor David Burrows, who called my attention to this work.

Nature and the four elements—Earth, Air, Fire, and Water. Allegorical librettos by Minato are *L'eternità soggetta al tempo* ("Eternity Subject to Time"), set by Draghi in 1683, which includes ten characters (Penitent Man, Time, Eternity, Winter, Spring, Summer, Autumn, Day, Night, and Three Hours of Darkness in the Daytime), and *La virtù della croce* ("The Virtue of the Cross"), set by Draghi in 1687, which uses six personages (Love of God, Faith in Christ, Hope, Fear, Conversion, and Angelic Consolation).

Oratorios and *sepolcri* were nearly always sung in Italian in Vienna, and the audience was normally supplied with printed copies of the libretto without a German translation. In the later seventeenth and early eighteenth centuries, however, some copies of the libretto for a given performance were printed in Italian and others, in German. That the works were sung in Italian, however, is clear, not only from the musical manuscripts, but also from the title pages of the German translations, which often include such phrases as "Waelsch-gesungener vorgestellt," or "in waelscher Sprache gesungen," with the term *waelsch* (or sometimes *welsch* or *welisch*) referring to a foreign language—in this case Italian.[26] The appearance of these German translations would seem to imply a change in the audiences for oratorios and *sepolcri* in this period, although no information has as yet come to light on this point.

The Librettos of Zeno and Metastasio: 1719–1740

Zeno.[27] Apostolo Zeno (1668–1750), from an old Venetian family, revealed his literary inclinations at an early age, and he was sent for his education to the seminary of the Somaschians in the Castello district of Venice. Having developed interests in the history of Italian and Latin literature and in fostering high literary standards in his own time, he was among the founders of the Accademia degli Animosi in 1691. This academy received the distinction of affiliation with the famous Roman Accademia dell'Arcadia in 1698, when it was declared a Colonia dell'Arcadia. Zeno

---

26. For examples of German translations of librettos by Minato and others, see the following libretto collections in A/Wn: 406–741–B.M.Adl.; 406–742–B.M.Adl.; and 406–743–B.M.Adl.

27. For Zeno's biography see Negri, *Zeno*. For studies of Zeno's oratorio librettos, see Fehr, *Zeno*, pp. 103–13; Michieli, "Poesie"; Pasquetti, *Oratorio*, pp. 406–13; and Schering, *Oratorium*, pp. 162–65.

FIGURE VIII-5. Apostolo Zeno (1668–1750).
(Reproduced by permission of the Bärenreiter Bild-Archiv, Kassel.)

published numerous scholarly contributions in the history of literature; in 1710 he was among the founders of the *Giornale de' letterati d'Italia*. In striking contrast to his scholarly work and his espousal of high standards in literature, however, in 1695 he embarked upon a long career as a librettist for opera. At first he followed what he himself considered the literarily disreputable conventions of the contemporary Venetian opera libretto, but later he sought to improve the libretto's literary quality. From 1705 on, Zeno frequently collaborated with Pietro Pariati (1665–1733) on opera librettos.[28] By 1718, the year in which the emperor Charles VI invited him to accept the position of poet and historian of the Viennese court, Zeno had become a noted opera librettist and one of Italy's most distinguished scholars. After he accepted Charles VI's invitation, he was required to write librettos for both operas and oratorios presented at court. In 1729 Zeno retired and returned to Venice, and Metastasio became his successor. Zeno continued to write oratorio librettos for Vienna after his retirement. Between 1719 and 1737 he completed seventeen oratorios, all for Vienna and all but six of which were first set to music by Caldara. Zeno's final oratorio libretto was left incomplete in 1740, when the death of Charles VI severed his relationship with Vienna.

Since the mid-eighteenth century, writers on the history of opera have generally referred to Zeno as a reformer of the opera libretto.[29] This traditional view of his work has been questioned, however, as it tends to overemphasize the extent of changes in the libretto of his time and his role in those changes.[30] Neither Zeno nor his immediate contemporaries considered his effort for, and partial achievement of, a literarily more respectable opera libretto to constitute a thoroughgoing reform. If his librettos represent a reform, it is a limited one: while they are more serious, rationalistic, and carefully constructed than the librettos of his predecessors, they nevertheless retain, in Zeno's words, "a great many improbable things,"[31] some of which are dramatic weaknesses

28. On Pariati's life and works see Campanini, *Precursore*.

29. For specific references to eighteenth-century writings in which he is so considered, see Freeman, "Zeno," pp. 333–34, n. 39. For a survey of eighteenth-century literary criticism dealing with the works of Zeno and Metastasio, see Giazotto, *Poesia*; and for a twentieth-century study of Zeno as a reformer of the libretto, see Fehr, *Zeno*.

30. Freeman, "Zeno."

31. Zeno to Giuseppe Gravisi, 3 November 1730, translated from Zeno, *Lettere*, 4:278, letter 756. For the context of this quotation in translation, see Freeman, "Zeno," p. 334.

that Zeno considered to be in the very nature of opera of his time. He retained these improbabilities as a necessary compromise with opera conventions, for he earned his living by writing opera librettos. Zeno's librettos for oratorios, like those for operas, represent a reform in only a limited sense. In this genre, too, he compromised by accepting the oratorio's essential structural conventions as he found them; yet he sought to improve the oratorio libretto by removing "certain abuses, which were more conspicuous."[32] The changes he introduced were important for the future of the genre.

According to his correspondence of the 1730s and 1740s, Zeno much preferred his librettos for oratorio to those for opera. In 1733, for instance, he wrote, "I am thinking of gathering together all my sacred dramatic poems and publishing them in a volume in order to satisfy no less my friends than my own devotion. I shall not do that with my secular ones, which I should like rather to abolish than to reproduce."[33] Nevertheless, in 1744 Gaspare Gozzi published an edition of all of Zeno's dramatic works, both secular and sacred, without the cooperation, and with only the sufferance, of their author. With regard to the publication, Zeno wrote to a friend in 1744, "You will say that I am a cruel and inhumane father towards these [secular librettos], which, after all, are part of me; they, however, now appear to me abortions, not to say monsters, which awaken in me rather repentance than affection."[34] Zeno had long felt this embarrassment and regret for earning his living by writing opera librettos.[35] His strong preference for the oratorios is no doubt based in part upon his satisfaction in working with sacred subjects—for he seems to have been deeply religious—and in part upon his evaluation of them as literary and dramatic achievements superior to his operas.

Although Zeno's oratorio librettos were published individually for the performances in Vienna, all but one of them appeared in the volume mentioned in the letter of 1733 cited above: *Poesie sacre drammatiche di Apostolo Zeno, Istorico e Poeta Caesareo, cantate nella imperial cappella di Vienna* ("Sacred Dramatic Poetry of Apostolo Zeno, Caesarean Historian and Poet, Sung in the Imperial Chapel of Vienna," Venice, 1735). This volume contains

32. Zeno to Giusto Fontanini, 30 April 1734, translated from Zeno, *Lettere*, 5:10, letter 838.
33. Zeno to Fontanini, 6 November 1733, ibid., 4:382, letter 810.
34. Zeno to Gioseffantonio Pinzi, 27 February 1744, ibid., 6:288, letter 1226.
35. Regarding this point, see Freeman, "Zeno," pp. 329–30.

the sixteen oratorio librettos that Zeno had completed by the time of its publication. The terminology for these works and the title of the volume were problems for Zeno. In a letter of 1734, he says that he was extremely busy "revising and correcting my *Oratorios* sung in Vienna."[36] Yet in the same letter, and in a slightly later one,[37] he indicates his reluctance to use the term *oratorio* on the title page, and he considers using the title *Drammi sacri* because of the dramatic emphasis of the works. Ultimately he decided to avoid the term *oratorio*, which does not appear at all in the volume; while the librettos are collectively called *poesie sacre drammatiche*, each work is subtitled *azione sacra*, the term normally used for them in Vienna.

The *Poesie sacre drammatiche* is dedicated to the imperial couple, Charles VI and Elisabeth Christina. The dedication consists of four paragraphs, the third of which is quoted almost in its entirety below, since it includes Zeno's clearest statement regarding his intentions in writing these librettos:

Since I was, therefore, obliged to occupy myself with writing about sacred subjects, two serious considerations soon came to mind: one, that in this genre of poetry [the subjects] would not have to be worked out by me, for the marvels of God operate in both laws, nor would I have to be guided by any other compass than that of the Divine Scripture; the other, that one would have to satisfy You with such compositions in that area in which, more than any other, You are sensitive. Fixed, then, with all my spirit on these two all important goals, I sought to restrict to the best method the art of weaving and working out this dramatic poetry; for since it is not intended for acting, but is organized only for singing, those who cultivate it have believed that it is not subject to rules. Therefore they have introduced discourse not only by merely ideal personages, but the sacred Text itself, and even the adorable Divine Persons; in addition to which, I do not know to what advantage, certain profane expressions were put into their mouths, certain wretched little comparisons, and even musical *ariette*. Therefore, since it appeared to me to be necessary and praiseworthy to remove such abuses and to handle such sublime subjects with more dignity and skill, I restricted them little by little, in accordance with the precepts of unity of action and of time, and for the most part, even of place, and I finally succeeded in arranging and extending them so that they might be not only suitable for singing but even for acting, so

36. Zeno to Fontanini, 10 April 1734, translated from Zeno, *Lettere*, 4:462, letter 832.
37. Zeno to Fontanini, 30 April 1734, ibid., 5:9, letter 837.

POESIE
SACRE
DRAMMATICHE
D I
APOSTOLO ZENO
Iſtorico e Poeta Ceſareo,

CANTATE NELLA IMPERIAL CAPPELLA
DI VIENNA.

IN VENEZIA,
PRESSO CRISTOFORO ZANE,
MDCCXXXV.

CON LICENZA DE' SUPERIORI, E PRIVILEGIO.

FIGURE VIII-6. Title page of Zeno's *Poesie sacre* (Venice, 1735), which contains his oratorio librettos.
(Courtesy of I/Rvat.)

that if they were given a greater extension and the suitable distribution, which was not permitted because of the restriction of the time in which they had to be sung, they could be reasonably called sacred musical Tragedies. Furthermore, I was careful to make the persons speak, in particular the Patriarchs, the Prophets, and the Apostles, in the style of the Scriptures, and with the sentiments of the Fathers and Doctors of the Church, considering that the less my interference, the more [a sense of] compunction and offence would be aroused in the souls of the listeners, and principally in Yours, by the sanctity of the expressions and by the sublimity of the thoughts.[38]

The essential points of this statement of purpose may be summarized as follows: (1) the restriction of the subject matter to biblical material; (2) the avoidance of divine personages, presumably the persons of the Trinity; (3) the restriction of the work by the three unities; (4) the creation, not only of musical librettos, but also of sacred dramas that might be spoken and acted; and (5) the approximation of the style of the scriptures, particularly in the lines of the patriarchs, prophets, and apostles.[39]

For the most part, Zeno accomplished his purpose as set forth in the above statement. Reacting against the hagiographical and allegorical works of the seventeenth century, he used only biblical subjects, all but four from the Old Testament.[40] He also drew on the writings of the church fathers for interpretations of the biblical material, and in two cases he acknowledged some dependence upon other dramas: for *Gioaz*, he says, "The famous Racine has been an excellent guide for me, in his Tragedy entitled *Atalia*,"[41] and for *Sedecia*, "An excellent Tragedy was written and published in the year 1737 by P. Giovanni Granelli, of the Company of Jesus, which was read by me with particular attention and was also imitated in a few places."[42] All of Zeno's librettos are heavily documented by marginal notes referring to passages in the Bible or in the writings of the church fathers on which specific poetic lines

38. Translated from Zeno, *Poesie*, fols. [6–8].

39. The third and fourth of these points are somewhat reminiscent of recommendations by the Roman Spagna in his "Discorso" of 1706. It is not known whether Zeno arrived at these conclusions independently or knew of Spagna's work.

40. Based on the Old Testament are *Sisara* (1719), *Tobia* (1720), *Naaman* (1721), *Giuseppe* (1722), *David* (1724), *Le profezie evangeliche d'Isaia* (1725), *Gioaz* (1726), *Gionata* (1728), *Nabot* (1729), *Daniello* (1731), *David umiliato* (1731), *Sedecia* (1732), and *Ezechia* (1737). The New Testament texts are *Il Battista* (1727), *Gerusalemme convertita* (1733), *San Pietro in Cesarea* (1734), and *Gesù presentato nel Tempio* (1735).

41. Translated from Zeno, *Poesie*, p. 190.

42. Ibid., p. 376.

are based. Before Zeno such documentation for oratorio librettos is occasionally found in Italy, but more often in Vienna. His scrupulosity and his struggles to make the poetry of his librettos correspond to the precise meaning of the scriptures as taught by the church are reflected in his letters of the 1730s.[43] Before mailing the libretto of *La Gerusalemme convertita* ("Jerusalem Converted") to Vienna to be set to music, for instance, he subjected it "to the approval of two eminent Theologians, not wanting to trust myself, nor should I, in the divine sciences."[44] Zeno's attempt to approximate the style of the scriptures leads him to write close poetic paraphrases of biblical passages—at times to the detriment of the poetry and the drama, particularly at points where he documents by chapter and verse.[45] No divine personage appears in any of Zeno's librettos, and only once, in *La Gerusalemme convertita*, does he use an allegorical personage: Jerusalem, according to the list of personages, "represents those Jews who are converted to the Faith of Jesus Christ." All the librettos are restricted by the unities of time and action, and all but one, *David umiliato* ("David Humiliated"), by unity of place.[46] Zeno's interest in increasing the dramatic aspects of the oratorio librettos is clear, not only from his dedication of the *Poesie sacre drammatiche*, but also from his comments in letters. In 1734, for instance, he wrote, "I have given to this sort of composition [the oratorio] a form, I believe, more regular than that which it previously had, having taken away certain abuses, which were more conspicuous, and I have modified my [librettos] to the point that they can be acted, as in fact some have been in some religious communities and with happy success."[47] Zeno's oratorio librettos are considerably longer than those of his predecessors and contemporaries, and they include many more lines of recitative and proportionally fewer lines of aria.[48] Yet he apparently never considered abolishing the aria from

43. Zeno to Marco Foscarini, 14 February 1732, in Zeno, *Lettere*, 4:355, letter 796; Zeno to Gravisi, 13 July 1733, ibid., 4:364, letter 801; Zeno to Gravisi, 18 December 1733, ibid., 4:400–401, letter 816.

44. Zeno to Gravisi, 13 July 1733, ibid., 4:364, letter 801.

45. On this point see Michieli, "Poesie," pp. 24–25.

46. The place is stated at the beginning of every libretto but one (*La Gerusalemme convertita*) in Zeno, *Poesie*.

47. Zeno to Fontanini, 30 April 1734, translated from Zeno, *Lettere*, 5:10, letter 838.

48. Zeno's librettos average about 700 poetic lines and include an average of eighteen arias and/or small ensembles; in the first two decades of the eighteenth century, the characteristic oratorios in Italy and Vienna range from about 370 to 550 lines and include about twenty-five to thirty arias and/or small ensembles.

his librettos, although he himself recognized that to make these works "good tragedies" he would need "to express them in more verses and to free them from the necessity of music."[49]

In many respects Zeno's oratorio librettos are similar to those of his immediate predecessors and contemporaries in Vienna. All the works are in two structural parts. Most of the librettos have five or six characters, but a few have seven. The chorus is used rarely and conventionally: either functioning within the dramatic action or as a commentator, it regularly concludes each structural part, and it occasionally appears with a dramatic function within a part. The versification is similar to that of his contemporaries' oratorios, and the arias are, of course, nearly always intended for da capo settings.

Zeno was not a great poet, for his verse often seems ungraceful and unconvincing and his long recitatives, introduced to improve the literary and dramatic elements of the libretto, often seem dramatically weak and thus unjustified.[50] Nevertheless, his oratorio librettos are significant for having provided a foundation for the superior work of his successor, Metastasio. The influence of Zeno's oratorio librettos was not purely local; in 1760 they were published in a German translation,[51] and they were occasionally set to music, in either Italian or German, throughout the eighteenth century and even in the nineteenth. The latest known setting is Michele Costa's *Naaman*, composed for performance in Birmingham in 1864.[52]

Metastasio.[53] Pietro Trapassi (1698–1782), born in Rome to a family of modest means, was fortunate to have had as his godfather a munificent patron of the arts, Cardinal Pietro Ottoboni, who made it possible for him to attend school in his early years. Having developed by his eleventh year a remarkable ability in the improvisation of poetry, the boy attracted the attention of another patron,

---

49. Zeno to Gravisi, 3 November 1730, translated from Zeno, *Lettere*, 4:279, letter 756.

50. For a critique of Zeno's oratorios as poetry and drama, see Michieli, "Poesie," pp. 14–32.

51. Zeno, *Poesie*-Ger.

52. For a list of settings of Zeno's oratorio librettos, see Fehr, *Zeno*, pp. 141–42.

53. For a basic bibliography of writings on Metastasio's life and works, see Metastasio, *Opere*, 5:827–37. Particularly useful are Apollonio, *Metastasio*; Bruno Brunelli, "Pietro Metastasio," in Metastasio, *Opere*, 1:xi–xlix; and Russo, "Metastasio." Regarding the oratorio librettos, see Pasquetti, *Oratorio*, pp. 414–516, and Schering, *Oratorium*, pp. 165–68.

FIGURE VIII-7. Pietro Metastasio (1698–1782).
(Reproduced by permission of the Bärenreiter Bild-Archiv,
Kassel.)

the legal scholar and litterateur Gian Vincenzo Gravina, who obtained permission from the boy's parents to take him into his home and raise him as his son. Gravina was one of the founders of the Accademia dell'Arcadia and a great admirer of ancient classical literature. He provided the youth with a foundation in that literature and in philosophy, and he hellenized the name Trapassi to Metastasio, a change that was then adopted by the Trapassi family as well. In 1714 Metastasio received the tonsure and the title *abate*, perhaps because of the current opinion that the clerical state increased the dignity necessary for one aspiring to a literary career. His first volume of poems appeared in 1717 and included the tragedy *Giustino*, written at fourteen years of age. Metastasio's patron and teacher Gravina died in 1718; later the same year the young poet was honored by acceptance into the Accademia dell'Arcadia. Friction developed between the new Arcadian and his colleagues, however, and this, as well as an unhappy love affair, prompted him to move to Naples. There he was befriended by the prima donna Marianna Benti Bulgarelli, called "La Romanina," who introduced him to her circle of friends—mostly actors and musicians—which included Nicola Porpora, who instructed him for a time in singing and composition. Induced by this Neapolitan milieu to write for opera, Metastasio completed his first opera libretto, *Didone abbandonata*, in 1723; with a musical setting by Domenico Sarro, the work was a success at its first performance in 1724. In 1727 Metastasio moved back to Rome, where he wrote his first oratorio libretto; a work for Christmas called a *componimento sacro*, it was performed in a setting by Giovanni Costanzo at the Cancelleria, the palace of Cardinal Pietro Ottoboni. (The staging of the introduction of this work was discussed in chapter 6.) In 1729 Metastasio was invited to become Zeno's successor as the Hapsburg court poet. He accepted the position and in 1730 arrived in Vienna, where he was to live for the rest of his life. His most active period in Vienna was his first decade there, a time of splendor at the imperial court. His dramatic work decreased thereafter, during the reign of the empress Maria Theresa (1740–80), for court life tended to be less festive because of war and a faltering economy; furthermore, in the mid-century the court shifted its dramatic interest increasingly to French *opèra comique*.

Metastasio has often been linked with Zeno as a reformer of the libretto, since he substantially adopted Zeno's conception of the libretto. What has been said above regarding the limited nature of Zeno's opera and oratorio reform, however, may also be applied to Metastasio's works in these genres.[54] Despite the similarities in basic conception between the librettos of these two poets, the differences between their librettos are striking because of Metastasio's superior poetic gift and skill. Unlike Zeno, Metastasio appears never to have felt the necessity to apologize for his activity as a librettist.

Metastasio's seven Viennese oratorio librettos were written between 1730 and 1740, mostly for performance during Holy Week at the Hofburgkapelle.[55] Like Zeno he referred to his librettos as oratorios in his correspondence but chose other designations, *componimento sacro* and *azione sacra*, for their first published versions.[56] All but one of his Viennese oratorios have biblical subjects, five from the Old Testament and one from the New; the remaining work, contrary to Zeno's practice, is based on hagiography.[57] Metastasio followed Zeno in fully documenting his librettos but differed considerably in his use of source material. While Zeno's close poetic paraphrases of biblical and other sources often seem forced, Metastasio gives the impression of having fully assimilated the source material and of expressing it in a new and convincing manner entirely suitable to its poetic context. It is of interest to note, in regard to their use of sources, the opposite attitudes taken by Zeno and Metastasio toward Racine's *Athalie*. Although Zeno cites Racine's work as "an excellent guide" for his *Gioaz* (see above), Metastasio, in a letter of 1735 written just after the completion of *Gioas, Re di Guida* ("Joash, King of Judah") asserts his independence of the French poet: "Monsieur Racine has treated this subject excellently under the name of *Athalia*. My greatest obligation has been not to duplicate [his work] in any way; in this I have succeeded."[58] Metastasio employs four to six characters in

54. Regarding Metastasio's strong ties with librettos of the past and the limited nature of the reform revealed in his opera librettos, see Abert, "Reformdrama."

55. Metastasio's librettos were printed individually for use at performances, and they have also appeared in numerous collected editions of his works published from the eighteenth century to the present. The most recent critical edition of his works is Metastasio, *Opere*, edited by Bruno Brunelli, vol. 2 of which includes the oratorios.

56. All the sacred works are called *azioni sacre*, however, in Metastasio, *Opere*.

57. The Old Testament librettos are *La morte d'Abel* (1732), *Giuseppe riconosciuto* (1733), *Betulia liberata* (1734), *Gioas Re di Giuda* (1735), *Isacco figura del Redentore* (1740); the New Testament libretto is *La Passione di Gesù Cristo* (1730), and the hagiographical one is *Sant'Elena al Calvario* (1731).

58. Metastasio to Leopoldo Trapassi, 5 March 1735, translated from Metastasio, *Opere*, 3:126, letter 94.

his librettos, which is slightly fewer than the number used by Zeno; he follows the latter in avoiding both allegorical and divine personages, except for angels, who have significant roles in two of the librettos, *La morte d'Abel* ("The Death of Abel") and *Isacco figura del Redentore* ("Isaac, Figure of the Redeemer"). Metastasio's oratorios, all in the standard two structural parts, tend to be slightly shorter than Zeno's and to have slightly fewer arias, but the proportion of aria to recitative lines is about the same. Following the trend of the period, Metastasio uses the chorus sparingly; it occurs at the end of each structural part in every work but rarely within a part.

Among the strengths of Metastasio's librettos are the excellent characterization, the skillful and subtle rendering of a wide variety of affections, the wealth of musically stimulating imagery, and the sheer musicality of the poetry's sonorous element. Particularly convincing for their psychological penetration are the roles of Peter, in *La Passione di Giesù*, a man spiritually tormented by his denial of Jesus and by the latter's Crucifixion; Judith, in *Betulia liberata*, a heroic figure from the very moment of her first appearance; and Eve, in *Abel*, a mother who tries to understand her embittered son, Cain, and whose deep, human suffering is convincingly revealed as the drama unfolds. Also especially well expressed are the emotional relationships among the mother, father, and children in *Abel* (i.e., among Adam, Eve, Cain, and Abel) and in *Isacco* (among Abraham, Sarah, and Isaac). For specific examples of Metastasio's poetry at its best in the oratorios, Ranieri de' Calsabigi is an excellent guide. Among the eighteenth century's more perceptive literary critics, Calsabigi expressed his great admiration for Metastasio in his "Dissertazione" written as a preface to an edition of Metastasio's works that appeared in Paris in 1755; thus the "Dissertazione" was written before Calsabigi's reversal of opinion about the structural aspects of opera and his collaboration with Gluck for purposes of opera reform. In his "Dissertazione" Calsabigi cites six of Metastasio's oratorio arias as among his truly great poems; these arias are "Te solo adoro" and "Lodi al gran Dio che oppresse" in *Betulia*, "Ovunque il guardo io giro" in *Passione*, "Qual diverrà quel fiume" and "Non sa che sia pietà" in *Abel*, and "Se a ciascun interno affanno" in *Giuseppe riconosciuto* ("Joseph Recognized").[59] Calsabigi further praises, and partially analyzes, three of Metastasio's oratorio librettos—*Gioas, Giu-*

59. Calsabigi, "Dissertazione," pp. clxxix–clxxxii.

seppe, and *Isacco*; he calls them "perfect Tragedies, which will serve henceforth as models for those who want to use their talent for that kind of composition."[60] These are, indeed, Metastasio's most clearly and consistently dramatic oratorios. The dramatic action develops, as it does in opera, during the relatively long recitatives, which, unlike those of Zeno, tend to be justified by their dramatic and poetic qualities. Much of the action takes place outside the confines of the librettos; when this occurs the action is narrated by the personages—a technique used to overcome the poet's restriction of the works by unity of place. In Metastasio's *Passione*, John, Mary Magdalene, and Joseph of Arimathea answer Peter's questions about Jesus' Crucifixion, and the story is conveyed in their dialogue; the libretto is almost entirely narrative and reflective in style. Only slightly more dramatic than *Passione* is *Sant'Elena a Calvario* ("Saint Helena at Calvary"). Both of the last-mentioned works were originally performed at the holy sepulcre in the Hofburgkapelle. On the title page of the libretto published for the first performance, *Sant'Elena* is designated *componimento sacro per musica applicato al santissimo sepolcro e cantato nell' augustissima cappella . . . di Carlo VI* ("Sacred Composition for Music, Applied to the Most Holy Sepulchre and Sung in the Most August Chapel . . . of Charles VI"); the first edition of *Passione* bore a similar designation.

Metastasio's oratorio librettos were far more popular than those of any other poet of the period. First set to music by composers of the Viennese court (Caldara, two oratorios; G. Reutter, Jr., three; Porsile and L. A. Predieri, one each), they continued to be set by numerous composers throughout the eighteenth and nineteenth centuries.[61] *Betulia*, the one most frequently set, was also the one that Metastasio, in a letter written shortly after its completion, considered his best oratorio.[62]

The Music of the Viennese Oratorio and Sepolcro

So thoroughly Italianate was music at the Viennese court in the second half of the seventeenth century that the stylistic features

---

60. Translated from ibid., p. cxxxv.

61. According to Brunelli's lists of settings in Metastasio, *Opere*, 2:1322–25, the librettos were set by the following numbers of composers in the eighteenth and nineteenth centuries: *Betulia*, 33; *Isacco*, 27; *Giuseppe*, 25; *Gioas*, 24; *Abel*, 22; *Passione*, 19; *Sant'Elena*, 14.

62. Metastasio to Giuseppe Bettinelli, 10 April 1734, in Metastasio, *Opere*, 3:108, letter 77.

distinguishing Viennese oratorios from those of Italy are few. In general, both secular and sacred dramatic music in Vienna was conservative, and the chief differences between Italian and Viennese oratorios resulted from this conservatism.[63] Thus the general characteristics of the Italian oratorio from the 1660s to the 1680s, as described in chapter 7, apply to the Viennese oratorio as late as the 1690s—that is, through the entire creative life of Draghi and his generation.

A noteworthy musical distinction between the Viennese oratorio and *sepolcro* in the seventeenth century is that of their instrumental scoring. Although oratorios are normally scored for continuo only or for continuo plus a small ensemble of strings (usually two violins), the *sepolcri* tend to employ more instruments and darker sonorities. Characteristic of *sepolcri* is an ensemble of four or five viols, in SATB ranges, at times together with two or more violins. Such scoring is represented, for instance, in all the extant *sepolcri* by Leopold I: *Il sagrifizio d'Abramo* (1660), *Il lutto dell' universo* ("The Mourning of the Universe," 1668), *Die Erlösung des menschlichen Geschlechts* (1679), and *Sig des Leydens Christi* (1682). Only one of Leopold's oratorios, *Il figliuol prodigo* ("The Prodigal Son," 1663), uses a comparable instrumental ensemble. Of Bertali's two sacred dramatic works, the *sepolcro* entitled *Maria Maddalena* (1663) uses the heavy scoring associated with the genre (two violins, five viols, two *cornetti muti*, and continuo), but his oratorio *La strage de gl'innocenti* ("The Massacre of the Innocents," 1665) calls for the smaller ensemble characteristic of the oratorio (two violins, a bass stringed instrument, and continuo).[64] This distinction in scoring between the two sacred dramatic genres is also clear in the works of Draghi: of his nine oratorios for which scores are extant, six are scored for continuo only and three for small ensembles (two violins, three violins, and two viols, respectively) plus continuo; of his twenty *sepolcri*, however, at least seventeen use the heavy scoring characteristic of that genre.[65]

63. Regarding the conservatism of Viennese secular and sacred dramatic music, see Wellesz, "Opern," pp. 11, 36, 93, 115, 128, 138.

64. For a study of these Bertali works, see La Roche, "Bertali." Olsen, "Bertali," is an edition of Bertali's *Strage*; and Bartels, "Instrumentalstücke," provides information on the instrumental numbers in his oratorios.

65. For the vocal and instrumental scoring of Draghi's sacred dramatic works, see Schnitzler, "Draghi," pp. 200–202, table 17.

Beginning in the mid-1690s with the sacred dramatic works of Badia and others of his generation, the da capo aria begins to predominate, as do other elements of late Baroque style and structure.[66] Nevertheless, musical conservatism continues in the Viennese oratorios of the early eighteenth century, and as late as the 1730s the oratorio in Vienna shows few of the pre-Classical elements that had been rapidly gaining ground in Italy since the second decade of the century. The chief indication of this conservatism is a strong interest in contrapuntal texture.

It is of particular interest that Caldara's oratorios became much more contrapuntal when he began his tenure as vice maestro di cappella in 1716 at the Viennese court. Fux had been the maestro di cappella of the court for only about one year when Caldara arrived, but he had served the court as a composer since 1698. The contrapuntal style of which Fux was a master appears to have been much admired by Charles VI; Caldara evidently wanted his oratorios to conform to the emperor's taste.[67] For Lent of 1717, Caldara prepared two oratorios, his first works in this genre intended for the Viennese court; one of these is a revision of an earlier work, *Santa Ferma*, and the other is *Cristo condannato* ("Christ Condemned"). The original version of the former dates from 1713 in Rome, the period in which Caldara's works began to show strong pre-Classical, or "early *galant*," tendencies. For the Viennese version Caldara enlarged the orchestra and introduced more counterpoint—imitation and fugal expositions, virtually absent from the original version, are common in the ritornelli of the Viennese revision.[68] In *Santa Ferma* and *Cristo condannato*, as well as in Caldara's subsequent oratorios for Vienna, single- and double-fugue expositions in sinfonie and ritornelli seem to be used as frequently as in the oratorios of Fux.[69] Yet Caldara did not

---

66. For surveys of the oratorios of two representative Viennese composers in this period, see Stollbrock, "Reuter jun.," pp. 298–304; and Köchel, *Fux*, pp. 175–86.

67. U. Kirkendale, *Caldara*, p. 318.

68. For a brief comparison of the two versions, see ibid., p. 317.

69. For characteristic examples of such passages in Caldara's Viennese oratorios, see the following double-fugue expositions. In *Cristo condannato*: opening Sinfonia, andante movement; and aria by the wife of Pilot, "Rimorso più non sento." In *La Passione*: Introduzione, andante movement; and aria by Joseph, "All'idea di' tuoi perigli." Single-fugue expositions or partial expositions are found as follows. In *Cristo condannato*: aria by the Leader of the People, "Dove certi son"; and aria by Pilate, "E' un pensier." In *Il Re del dolore*: Introduzione, andante movement; aria by Penitent Soul, "Più di quante"; aria by the angel Gabriel, "Con la sua morte"; aria by Sacred Text, "Chi ravvisa l'innocenza"; and duet by Divine Justice and Divine Love, "Per aprir del ciel."

entirely avoid the new style in his oratorios, as Fux appears to have done, but he employed it sparingly.[70] Thus it is not surprising that in 1776 the aged Metastasio, who had lived in Naples as a young man and had studied music briefly with Porpora, and who evidently preferred the newer style to that of the late Baroque, remembered Caldara as "an eminent master of counterpoint but a composer exceedingly deficient in expression and in his attention to what pleases."[71]

Representative Examples

Antonio Draghi.[72] Little is known of the early life of Draghi before his appearance in Vienna. He was born in Rimini in 1635; his name appears in a list of opera singers in Venice in 1657; and he began his services at the court of Vienna in 1658. His position at the Viennese court seems always to have been that of a musician, but his earliest known work is a libretto, *L'Almonte*, first performed in 1661 with music by G. Tricarico. His first musical composition, *Achille in Sciro*, with a libretto by Cavaliere Ximemes, was first performed in 1663. By 1668 Draghi had become vice maestro di cappella at the court of the empress dowager Eleonora; in the following year he was appointed maestro di cappella at her court. By 1674 Leopold I had appointed Draghi the director of dramatic music at the imperial court, a position that he held simultaneously with that at Eleonora's court. In 1682 Draghi left the service of Eleonora to accept an appointment to the highest musical position in Vienna, that of maestro di cappella at the court of Leopold I, which he held until his death in 1700.

Primarily a composer of dramatic music, Draghi produced at least one new dramatic work each year from 1666 to the end of his life. During this period he dominated the field of dramatic music at the Viennese court and composed over 170 secular and at least 41

70. In Caldara's *Passione*, for example, three numbers in a simple, homophonic style comparable to that common in his later Roman works are the arias sung by Magdalene, "Vorrei dirti il mio dolore" and "Ai passi erranti," and the duet for Magdalene and Peter, "Vi sento, oh Dio."

71. Metastasio to Antonio Eximeno, 22 August 1776, translated from Metastasio, *Opere*, 5:402, letter 2254.

72. For studies of Draghi's sacred dramatic works, see Neuhaus, "Draghi," and Schnitzler, "Draghi." The latter includes extended musical excerpts in appendix D, pp. 298–341. I gratefully acknowledge the assistance of Professor Rudolf Schnitzler, who made available unpublished materials and information that facilitated the preparation of this section of the chapter.

sacred dramatic works—15 oratorios and 26 *sepolcri*.[73] Printed librettos are extant for all forty-one of the sacred dramatic works, but scores are extant for only nine of the oratorios and twenty of the *sepolcri*.[74] Draghi's oratorios and *sepolcri* are characteristic of those of Vienna in his time. Of the fifteen oratorios for which librettos are extant, all but three are in two structural parts (the exceptions are in one part), and all but two include a role for the *testo*. Choruses are rare in Draghi's sacred dramatic works; final ensembles are characteristic, but in only five instances—all in oratorios—is the final number designated a chorus. Draghi's *Oratorio di S. Agata* (1675) is exceptional, for the chorus appears frequently throughout the work. As in the oratorios of Italy in this period, there tends to be a free intermingling of passages in aria, arioso, and recitative styles. The majority of the arias are strophic and are in some type of binary form, with the ABB' type the most prominent; relatively few are in ternary form, and of these the da capo aria is rare: most ternary arias use a modified repetition of the opening section. Characteristic of Draghi's sacred dramatic works is the repetition, for purposes of structural unity, of an ensemble, an aria, or a brief arialike section after intervening new material. As pointed out above, Draghi's *sepolcri* use more instruments than his oratorios—a characteristic typical of seventeenth-century sacred dramatic music in Vienna; six of Draghi's nine extant oratorio scores employ basso continuo only.

Draghi's oratorio *Jephte*,[75] performed at the Hofburgkapelle during Lent of 1687, is in most respects characteristic of the Viennese oratorio of its time. The anonymous libretto, probably by Giuseppe Apolloni,[76] is based on an Old Testament story (Judg. 11:28–38) used frequently for oratorios in the Baroque era. Part I of this libretto begins with an introduction by the *Testo* (B), after which Amon (B) threatens to wage war against Israel. The frightened Israelites, represented by the First and Second Sons of Gilead

73. The classification of Draghi's sacred dramatic works followed here is that of Schnitzler, "Draghi," pp. 64–66, except for a simplification of terminology: the works termed *sepolcro* and *rappresentazione sacra* in Schnitzler's study are here grouped together under the general designation *sepolcro*.

74. For a list of sources, see ibid., pp. 123–25, table 9. For a catalogue of the sacred dramatic music of Draghi, see ibid., pp. 342–97. For an additional anonymous oratorio score by Draghi, see ibid., Addendum, p. 412.

75. A score in MS is in A/Wn: 18,884; a printed libretto is in I/Vnm: Misc. 2482 (35).

76. The attribution is found in Weilen, *Theatergeschichte*, no. 344; Köchel, *Fux*, no. 274; Neuhaus, "Draghi," no. 162; and Schnitzler, "Draghi," p. 134.

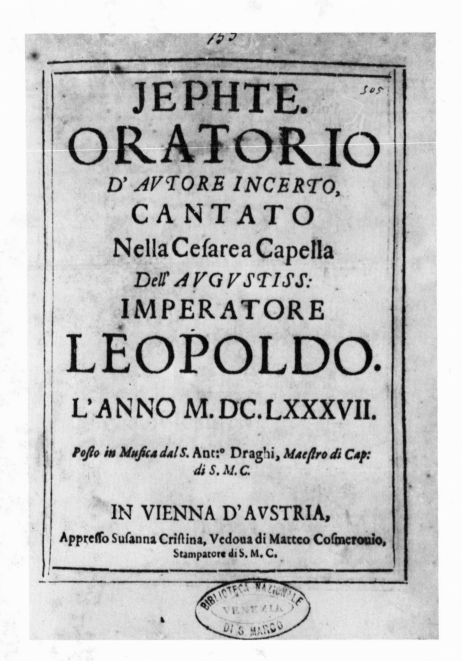

FIGURE VIII-8. Title page of the libretto for the performance in 1687 of Draghi's *Jephte*.
(Courtesy of A/Wn.)

FIGURE VIII-9. Beginning of Draghi's *Jephte*.
(Reproduced by permission of A/Wn: 18884, fol. 1^r.)

(S and T, respectively), go to visit Jephthah (A), whom the Gilead-ites have forced to live in exile for years because of his illegitimate birth. They see his brave leadership in battle as their only hope, and they beg for his pity, his pardon, and his help. At first resisting their pleas, Jephthah finally agrees to lead them. Before going into battle, however, he vows that if he is victorious, whomever he first sees on his return he will sacrifice on the new day to the Lord. The battle begins at the end of part I with a militant crowd chorus by the Ammonites (SSATB). By the beginning of part II, the Ammon-ites have been defeated; the lament of Ammon wounded and dying, constitutes some of the best poetry and music of the orato-rio. (Draghi did not set to music all the recitative of the lament, and, following a common practice of the time, the printer of the libretto designated for the reader which lines were not set.) As Jephthah returns from battle, his Daughter (S) rushes joyfully to be the first to meet him. Noticing her father's anguished expres-sion, she asks the reason, and, in the long section of recitative dialogue that follows, Jephthah tells her that he has made a vow to God. Overcome with emotion, however, he cannot continue and does not reveal the nature of the vow. His daughter suspects the truth, and the First Son of Gilead confirms her suspicions. She accepts her fate: she will die happily, for the vow derives from God and must be just. She consoles her father as she willingly ap-proaches death; yet she laments the necessity of leaving him. The final chorus of Gileadites (only partially scored in the manuscript source but probably for SSATB, as is the closing chorus of part I) admonishes the audience to be cautious in making vows, for one must fulfill one's promises to God.

This oratorio is characteristic of its time in every respect except its small number of arias and ensembles and its long pas-sages of recitative, particularly in part II. The work consists of about 350 lines of poetry but only eight arias, three small en-sembles (two of which are actually complexes of solos and en-sembles), and two choruses, one at the end of each structural part. Five of the arias are strophic, with two stanzas of poetry; five are in binary form (including four of the strophic arias)—all but one of these using extended binary, ABB'; three are freely sectional; none is in ternary form. The trio, "Ti commova il nostro pianto," is a dialogue between the Sons of Gilead and Jephthah in the form ABCB; A and C are duets in which the Sons tenderly plead for

Jephthah's pity, and B is Jephthah's brief, sympathetic refrain in aria style—the three voices never sing together. Of the other two ensembles, the first, "Poichè il Ciel," is a brief through-composed duet of the Sons of Gilead; the second—"A me sola tocca," a lament in the form ABCAD—is a dialogue between Jephthah and his Daughter. This dialogue consists of a complex of stylistically varied sections: the two A sections are the first and second stanzas of an aria for Jephthah's daughter; B, a brief passage in aria style for Jephthah; C, a brief arioso passage for his Daughter; and D, a section in aria style for both singers. This type of complex, with mixed styles and with ensemble and solo passages, is characteristic of Draghi's sacred dramatic music in general. Also characteristic is the mixture of aria, arioso, and recitative styles such as that found in the *Testo*'s introduction to part II and in Amon's lament (see below). The oratorio's manuscript source includes no instrumental parts other than the continuo and specifies no continuo instruments.

The most effective music of the oratorio is allotted to the principal characters—Jephthah, his Daughter, and Ammon—and the last named has the work's most difficult music. Because of the nature of the subject matter and the libretto, the chief affections expressed in the oratorio's numbers are those of militarism and deep pathos. Ammon's aria "Non più tregua" (Example VIII–1) is characteristic of the several martial arias, with its quick runs and its transferring of material between the vocal and continuo lines in measures 2–3, 7–10, and 11–13. Near the beginning of part II of the oratorio, Ammon sings a long lament, much like a brief solo cantata, that is a complex of units: beginning with a brief passage in aria style, "Spalancatevi negri abissi," the lament continues in recitative style and concludes with the aria "Ma già stanco." The lament's opening (Example VIII–2a, p. 405) is remarkable for its descending leap of a minor ninth and total descent of a thirteenth in the first phrase and its descent of a tenth in the second phrase to depict the idea of the deep, dark abysses expressed in the text. The lament is melodically unified by the similarity between the initial phrases of the opening unit in aria style and the closing aria (compare the beginnings of Examples VIII–2a and b); the closing aria, however, is in duple meter rather than triple and does not span such a wide range as the earlier unit since its text does not require it. The only light moment of the entire oratorio is

EXAMPLE VIII-I. *Jephte*—Draghi (A/Wn: codex 18884, fols. 17ᵛ–18ʳ).

No more truce, to arms! My phalanx, do not delay, attack, conquer whoever fancies striking me down!

the Daughter's aria in dance style, "Miei spirti brillate" (Example
VIII–3, page 406), sung as she greets her father upon his return
from battle. This mood is short-lived, however, and is replaced by
the deeply pathetic one that reaches its point of greatest intensity
in the lament of Jephthah and his Daughter, the solo-duet complex
mentioned above. In this number the Daughter's aria "A me sola
tocca" (Example VIII–4a), which forms the first and fourth units
of the ABCAD form, is a sarabande with long melismas on the
accented syllables of "piangere" ("weep") and "s'io ti lascio" ("if
I leave you"). The duet that concludes the complex, "Ah ch'io
sento" (Example VIII–4b), is a highly chromatic expression of the
torment felt by both Jephthah and his Daughter. Of the two
choruses in the work, that at the end of part I (the only one
completely scored in the manuscript) is an expression of battle and
vengeance, with a chordal beginning and ending and a longer,
agitated, and imitative central section.

EXAMPLE VIII-2. *Jephte*—Draghi (A/Wn: codex 18884, fols. 24[v], 26[r]).

Example a:

Open wide, black abysses, hide me in the depths, that the world may not see my shame.

Example b:

But already I am tired, I fall, I am growing weak; and already more than one wound is breaking through to my life.

EXAMPLE VIII-3. *Jephte*—Draghi (A/Wn: codex 18884, fol. 27ᵛ).

My spirits sparkle with a joyous soul . . .

EXAMPLE VIII-4. *Jephte*–Draghi (A/Wn: codex 18884, fol. 38ᵛ).

Example a:

It is for me alone to weep, if I leave you, O father; . . .

Example b:

Ah! I feel from the torment . . .

Johann Joseph Fux.[77] One of the few Austrian oratorio composers active in the Viennese court in the Baroque era, Fux (ca. 1660–1741) was born in Hirtenfeld, in the rural district of Steiermark. Little is known of his youth, but in the dedication of his *Gradus ad Parnassum* (Vienna, 1725), Fux indicates that the imperial house supported his musical education. In 1680 he matriculated at the Jesuit university in Graz, where he was also a student at the Ferdinandeum. Having left Graz probably before 1684, he may have studied for a time in Italy. By 1696 he had settled in Vienna and had become the organist at the Schottenkirche. In 1698 he was named imperial court composer, and from 1705 to 1715 he was also employed at Vienna's cathedral, the Stephanskirche, initially as second Kapellmeister and later as Essentialkapellmeister. In 1713 he was appointed vice maestro di cappella at the imperial court; in 1715 he succeeded Marc'Antonio Ziani as the court's maestro di cappella, a position that he held until his death.

Fux was primarily a church-music composer; he is known to have composed approximately seventy masses, ten requiems, and numerous motets and other sacred works. In this music, as also in his famous instruction book *Gradus ad Parnassum*, he reveals himself as a late Baroque traditionalist, a highly skilled contrapuntist, and a great admirer of Palestrina. Nevertheless, in most of his sacred works and especially in his approximately eighteen Italian operas and ten extant Italian oratorios, he fuses recent musical styles and structures with his essentially traditional, contrapuntal approach.

Between 1702 and 1728 Fux is known to have composed fifteen oratorios or *sepolcri*, most of which were intended for performance in the Hofburgkapelle.[78] About half of the fifteen works are based on the Passion story; they would be particularly appropriate for performance on Good Friday at the holy sepulchre. The others are based on stories from the Old or New Testament or from hagiography; one is purely allegorical. Although the librettos

77. For studies of Fux's life and works, see Köchel, *Fux*; Meer, *Fux*; and A. Liess, "Fux," in *MGG*, 4:cols. 1159–75. The only oratorio by Fux that is now available in a modern edition is *La fede sacrilega* in Fux, *Werke*, ser. 4, vol.1

78. MSS of ten of Fux's sacred dramatic works are in A/Wn. For oratorios and *sepolcri* in addition to those listed in A. Liess, "Fux," in *MGG*, 4:col. 1165, see those listed in Fux, *Werke*, ser. 4, vol. 1, p. viii, n. 24. The distinction between an oratorio and a *sepolcro* in this period depends upon the intended manner of performance; it is not yet possible to determine which of Fux's sacred dramatic works should be classified in each of these categories.

FIGURE VIII-10. Johann Joseph Fux (ca. 1660–1741). Painting by Nicolas Buck (1717).
(Reproduced by permission of the Gesellschaft der Musikfreunde, Vienna.)

of several of Fux's sacred dramatic works are anonymous, at least six are by Pietro Pariati, who had come to Vienna in 1714 as court poet after having collaborated with Zeno since 1705 on opera librettos in Venice.[79] Claudio Pasquini is also among the librettists of Fux's sacred dramatic works.

In general, the formal structures in Fux's sacred dramatic works are similar to those in Italian oratorios: most of the works are in two structural parts; virtually all the arias, duets, and trios are in da capo form; the chorus is regularly used at the end of a structural part and only occasionally elsewhere; and the few accompanied recitatives are found at dramatically important points. The most significant musical trait that distinguishes Fux's oratorios from those characteristic of Italy in this period is his strong preference for contrapuntal texture and his apparent avoidance of pre-Classical style, even in arias with dance rhythms. His emphasis on counterpoint appears to be a continuation of the musical conservatism of the Viennese court. Fux was a master of fugal technique, as is clear from his sacred music and theoretical writing. Despite this mastery and the predominantly contrapuntal texture in the sacred dramatic works, however, only a few numbers in each work are clearly fugal. The introductory sinfonia will often include a fugal movement, and the opening ritornellos of one or two arias will also be fugal; prominent in such instances is the double-fugue exposition, in which two subjects are presented simultaneously, usually in invertible counterpoint. In a fugal aria, one of these subjects will usually be taken up by the voice at the end of the opening ritornello, and much of the thematic material of the aria will derive from the ritornello.[80] These arias using fugal technique are among the most fascinating numbers of Fux's sacred dramatic works. While the fugal numbers are rarely in dance rhythm, the more numerous nonfugal numbers use a variety of dance styles—including those of the minuet, sarabande, *siciliano*, and gigue. The

79. Although the Zeno-Pariati collaboration on opera librettos continued after Zeno went to Vienna in 1718, the two poets appear not to have collaborated on oratorio librettos.

80. A few representative examples of the fugal numbers in Fux's sacred dramatic works, in addition to those in *La fede* discussed below, are the following (all are in MSS at A/Wn). In *Il disfacimento di Sisara* (1717): the third movement (presto) of the orchestral introduzione, Debora's aria "Tu vedrai fatta," and Jabin's aria "Sù si tolga a miei nemici" (all three with double-fugue expositions); in *La cena del Signore* (1720): the second movement (allegro) of the orchestral sinfonia (double-fugue exposition), and Jesus's aria "L'impossibil del mistero" (double-fugue exposition); in *La deposizione della croce* (1728): Magdalene's aria "Caro mio Dio" (double-fugue exposition).

same variety of affections—including those of militarism, vengeance, rage, joy, and lamentation—is expressed in the arias of Fux's works as in those of his Italian contemporaries. When the texts are clearly intended for simile arias, Fux's settings draw upon the stock of descriptive techniques that had become common practice in the late Baroque. The choruses in Fux's sacred dramatic works combine chordal and imitative styles but are rarely fugues; they are sometimes brief, chordal utterances of a crowd and at other times extended, highly expressive pieces of a madrigalesque quality.

Fux's third oratorio, the earliest one fully extant, is *La fede sacrilega nella morte del precursor San Giovanni Battista* ("Sacrilegious Faith in the Death of the Precursor, St. John the Baptist"). This work, which dates from 1714, probably received its first performance in the Hofburgkapelle on the Friday before Palm Sunday of that year.[81] The libretto by Pietro Pariati is based on the New Testament story of John the Baptist;[82] Köchel considers this libretto to be "perhaps the best that Fux set to music."[83] The chief personage of the libretto is Herod (A), who is portrayed as a tragic figure torn between his desires for tolerance and benevolent justice toward John the Baptist (T) on the one hand and his diametrically opposed desire to be faithful to his own word on the other. His faithfulness to his sworn word, which leads to the beheading of John, is the "sacrilegious faith" of the oratorio's title. The time of the libretto is the celebration of Herod's birthday, a celebration that is, however, interrupted by John's condemnation of Herod's adulterous marriage to his brother's wife, Herodias (S). Throughout the oratorio Herodias and her daughter, Oletria (S), apply all possible pressure to lead Herod to imprison and execute John. The women are joined in their efforts at times by Aronte (B), who is in the service of Herod. By the end of part I John has been imprisoned. During Herod's birthday celebration in part II, Oletria dances for him—to an orchestral "sonatina" and a congratulatory chorus—and Herod promises her any reward she wishes. Counseled by her mother, Oletria asks for the head of the Baptist. After initially resisting, Herod finally yields and commands that John be exe-

81. Fux, *Werke*, ser. 4, vol. 1, p. ix. For historical and analytical remarks about this work, see the introduction by Hugo Zelzer and Leopold Ergens ibid., pp. vii–xvii; see also Köchel, *Fux*, p. 178.
82. Matt. 14:3–11; Mark 6:17–28; Luke 3:19–20.
83. Translated from Köchel, *Fux*, p. 178.

cuted. In Herod's final utterance, the accompanied recitative "O sacrilega fede," he painfully expresses his remorse for having been faithful to his word. In the oratorio's last aria, "Sommo Iddio," John prays that Herod not be punished but that he repent. The chorus (SSATB) appears briefly in the dramatic roles of a chorus of the People and a chorus of Ministers, and it sings a reflection on the drama's meaning at the close of each of the oratorio's structural parts.

The contrapuntal style that plays so prominent a role in Fux's oratorios in general is characteristic of *La fede sacrilega*. In the introductory sinfonia (a French overture), after an andante opening section in chordal style, there follows a fugal allegro on two subjects presented simultaneously (Example VIII–5). The first aria of the oratorio, Aronte's "Se del sole," also begins with a double-fugue exposition in the opening ritornello (Example VIII–6a); one fugue subject of the ritornello is reminiscent of one of those in the sinfonia (compare Example VIII–5 with VIII–6a: Vln. I, mm. 1–2). The initial subject of the ritornello is taken up

EXAMPLE VIII-5. *La fede sacrilega*—Fux (Fux, *Werke*, ser. 4, vol. 1, p. 2).

by the voice for the motto beginning, while the violins play the second subject (Example VIII–6b); these subjects provide the material for the orchestra, and often for the voice as well, throughout both the A and the B parts of this consistently contrapuntal aria. Another number with an introductory double-fugue ritornello is John's aria "Chi a l'infermo," the opening measures of which are shown in Example VIII–7. In this aria, too, most of the orchestral, and some of the vocal, lines are derived from the fugue subjects. Although these are the only fugal arias of the oratorio, nearly all the arias are essentially contrapuntal. Exceptional for its pre-Classical elements, homophonic texture and slow harmonic rhythm, is Herod's aria "Fra due nembi," although even there the

EXAMPLE VIII-6. *La fede sacrilega*—Fux (Fux, *Werke*, ser. 4, vol. 1, pp. 29–31).

Example a:

Example b:

If from the sun a loving ray . . .

EXAMPLE VIII-7. *La fede sacrilega*—Fux (Fux, *Werke*, ser. 4, vol. 1, p. 170).

normally stepwise motion of the continuo part stems from a characteristically late Baroque contrapuntal conception.

La fede sacrilega includes eighteen arias (four each for every character but Aronte, who sings two), one duet, one trio, and one accompanied recitative. All the arias are in da capo form, and over half use motto beginnings. Ten of the arias are accompanied by the orchestra, and two are accompanied by continuo only; six use the orchestra only in ritornellos and at other times use continuo accompaniment. A light, gay dance style is characteristic of four of the arias: Herod's "Mi contento che il perdono," and "A delitti Astra," Herodias's "L'odio non parla in me," and Oletria's "E' indegno del trono." The last named of these, a simple aria with continuo acompaniment followed by an orchestral ritornello, is extremely effective in its context, both in terms of characterization and mood: Oletria, who has just finished dancing and has shocked Herod by naming her gruesome reward, continues her attitude of dancelike gaiety, despite Herod's reaction, as she playfully admonishes him to keep his word if he is to be worthy of the throne and laughs at him in sixteenth-note melismas on the final syllables of the phrases "chi fede non *ha*" and "giustizia non *fa*." Three of the dancelike numbers, Herod's "Fra due nembi" and John's "Terger puote le machie" and "Sommo Iddio," are in slower tempo, triple meter, and sarabande rhythmic style. All three of these express serious affections basic to the personalities of the two characters: the first, among the best numbers of the oratorio, is a simile aria in which Herod compares his struggle to that of a ship tossed between two contrary winds (the troubled waters are orchestrally depicted by sixteenth-note figures); the other two arias admirably reveal John's strong faith and sense of morality. Four of the arias, all in quick tempos, in which Oletria and Herodias try to convince Herod of the necessity of punishing John, seem clearly related to one another in their initial melodic ideas: Examples VIII–8a, b, and d—all sung by Oletria—conclude with a descending leap of a perfect fifth followed by a rest, which contributes musical consistency to her characterization. Examples VIII–8b and c, sung by Oletria and Herodias, respectively, are somewhat similar in their melodic outlines; they are the beginnings of arias that are separated only by a brief recitative, and their evident musical similarity is paralleled by the agreement in the ideas of the mother and daughter as expressed in the two arias'

EXAMPLE VIII-8. *La fede sacrilega*—Fux (Fux, *Werke*, ser. 4, vol. 1, pp. 42, 81, 88, 141).

Example a:

You deny us the vengeance . . .

Example b:

It is not always clemency . . .

Example c:

Ingrate, I shall go under another star . . .

Example d:

The impious heads of the rebellious . . .

texts. Occurring at the dramatic high point of the oratorio are two of its most effective numbers, Herodias's aria "Mesto amor" followed immediately by Herod's accompanied recitative, "O sacrilega fede." This aria by Herodias, immediately following Herod's command that John be executed, is her expression of vengeance accomplished. The number includes elaborate theorbo solos, alternating allegro and adagio sections, and extended coloratura passages on the words "vendicarmi" and "L'armi." Herod's accompanied recitative, expressing his anguish at his decision, is melodically simple but harmonically chromatic and highly effective.

The two ensembles of the oratorio, a trio in part I and a duet in part II, both include an opposition in their texts between John and his antagonist(s). In the trio, in da capo form, the parts of Herodias and Oletria begin in imitation, but John's melodic lines are distinct from theirs; soon, however, all three voices share the same material. In the duet, structured as if it were the A part of a da capo form, both voices have similar melodic material most of the time. The final choruses of parts I and II are similar in that both begin with a relatively long polyphonic section and close with a generally chordal section. The final chorus of part I retains the term *madrigale*, in use since the mid-seventeenth century for final choruses in oratorios. The internal choruses of the oratorio (in part I, one chorus; in part II, one chorus plus two choral exclamations of two measures each) are essentially in chordal style and are comparable to crowd choruses in operas of the time.

The instruments normally called for in *La fede sacrilega* are the usual strings and continuo (two violin parts, one viola part, and a continuo of cello, bassoon, violone, and organ). Additional instruments required at times are the chalumeaux (used in both solo and ensemble passages in Herodias's aria, "L'odio non parla in me") and the theorbo (as mentioned above). The only instrumental numbers are the sinfonia, or French overture, preceding part I and the binary "sonatina" that begins Oletria's dance and introduces the internal chorus of part II.

CHAPTER IX

Paris

Social and Musical Background

The political and cultural contacts between Italy and the French royal court in the seventeenth century were by no means as close nor as numerous as those between Italy and the Viennese imperial court, and the French were slow to adopt many aspects of the Italian Baroque. Nevertheless, Italian Baroque influences were gradually assimilated into French cultural life.[1] At the beginning of the seventeenth century, an important Franco-Italian link was created by the marriage of Henry IV of France to Maria de' Medici. The celebrations for the wedding, which took place at Florence in 1600, included performances of two operas, Peri's *Euridice* and Caccini's *Rapimento di Cefalo*. Four years later the queen invited Caccini to visit Paris; during his month-long stay, he appears to have exerted some influence on French song.[2] French composers did not adopt recitative, however, until much later: they had not yet done so in 1639, according to the French violist André Maugars, who in that year was greatly impressed with the recitative in the oratorios performed at Crocifisso in Rome.[3]

After the death of Henry IV in 1610, the queen mother became the regent for Louis XIII (b. 1601). Many of her political policies were determined by her Florentine adviser Concino Concini, who became the marshal d'Ancre and whose power was

1. For a summary of the influences of Italian Baroque painting as seen in the works of Simon Vouet, François Perrier, and Jacques Blanchard, among others, see Blunt, *Art*, pp. 167–73, 176–78. For Italian influences on French music, see Anthony, *French*, pp. 45–51; Liuzzi, *Musicisti*, pp. 141–254; and Prunières, *Opéra*.
2. Liuzzi, *Musicisti*, pp. 146–48; and Prunières, *Opéra*, pp. xxxii–xxxiii.
3. See above, p. 121.

continually augmented until his murder in 1617. In the subsequent period, that of Cardinal Richelieu's position as prime minister (1624–42), the Italian Giulio Mazzarini (in France called Jules Mazarin), who had served the Barbarini in Rome, became Richelieu's protégé in matters of French government. In 1641 Mazarin was appointed a cardinal, and in 1643, after the deaths of Richelieu (1642) and Louis XIII (1643), he was declared the prime minister.

It was during Mazarin's period as prime minister (1643–61) that Italian Baroque style began to exert a strong influence on French music. Mazarin's hospitality to Antonio Barberini when the latter fled from Rome to Paris in 1645 and his invitation for Francesco Buti and Luigi Rossi (among others in the service of Antonio Barberini) to go to Paris were directly responsible for the first Italian opera written specifically for Paris, Buti and Rossi's *Orfeo* (1647). Among the other Italian operas performed at Paris around the middle of the century were *La finta pazza* (1645) by Francesco Sacrati, *Le Nozze di Peleo e di Teti* (1654) by Carlo Caprioli ("Carlo del Violino"), and three of Francesco Cavalli's operas—*Egisto* (1646), *Serse* (1660), and *Ercole amante* (1662). Although no performances of oratorios have been documented in France during the same period, it is clear from French copies of Carissimi's oratorios that some of them were known in France by 1649, as indicated above (p. 225). Printed music that included a continuo part, common with Italian music publishers since early in the century, first appeared in France in the mid-century; among the earliest examples are Constantijn Huygens's *Pathodia sacra et profana* (Paris, 1647) and Henry Du Mont's *Cantica sacra* (Paris, 1652).[4]

The death of Mazarin in 1661 initiated the period of Louis XIV's personal reign (1661–1715), a period of utmost importance for the development of French music. In 1661 the king appointed the Italian Jean-Baptiste Lully (1632–87) as *surintendant de la musique de la chambre*, and in the following year he appointed him *maître de la musique de la famille royale*; both were positions of considerable responsibility and authority. French opera began in 1671, the date of *Pomone*, with a libretto by Pierre Perrin and music by Robert Cambert; the genre became firmly established in 1673, when Lully, who had just gained a monoply on operatic

    4. Concerning the reluctance of French musicians to use the basso continuo, see Anthony, *French*, p. 158, and Launay, *Anthologie*, pp. x–xi. See also Huygens, *Pathodia*.

performances, began to produce an opera every year. The most prominent type of sacred music performed at the royal chapel of Louis XIV and elsewhere in Paris in the late seventeenth and early eighteenth centuries was the *grand motet*—a long work for double chorus, soloists, and orchestra.[5] Such motets were composed first by Henry Du Mont, Pierre Robert, and Lully, and later by Marc-Antoine Charpentier and Michel-Richard Delalande. The *grand motet* reveals Italian influence in its use of polychoral, concertato, and recitative styles; yet its recitatives, like those of French opera, have a peculiarly French quality in their rhythmic and melodic organization. Contributing to the image of brilliant majesty with which Louis XIV wished to be identified, these *grands motets* served to ornament the Low Mass, for the king preferred a musically elaborate, but liturgically minimal, service.[6] The use of such extended motets at Mass established a precedent in Paris for church performances of the Latin oratorios of Charpentier and others; these oratorios, as is indicated below, at times functioned as motets.

There are few sacred dramatic compositions in France before Charpentier that one may regard either as oratorio antecedents or as oratorios. Guillaume Bouzignac's dialogues in Latin from the first half of the seventeenth century relate to the development of the oratorio in only a general way: their texts include the narrative and dramatic elements of the oratorio, but their musical settings, though highly dramatic, do not use the basso continuo and are thus closer to late Renaissance dialogues than to those characteristic of the Baroque era.[7] The poet Pierre Perrin wrote several texts for Latin dramatic dialogues, most of which were published in his *Cantica pro capella regis* (Paris, 1665).[8] Some additional Latin dialogues—essentially reflective ones—form part of his manuscript of musical texts that was presented around 1668 to Louis XIV's

5. The durations of the *grands motets* printed in Lully, *Oeuvres: Motets*, vols. 1–2, range from about seven to about fifty minutes.

6. Regarding sacred music under Louis XIV, see Brenet, *Louis XIV*.

7. For discussions of Bouzignac's dialogues, with music examples, see Quittard, "Bouzignac," pp. 380–95, 404–17; and Quittard, *Du Mont*, pp. 142–50. According to information recently published by Albert Cohen, the names of several lost oratoriolike works by René Ouvrard appear in his correspondence of the 1660s and 1670s: *Une Guerre en Musique* (the war of the Maccabees), *Histoire du Publicain et du Pharisien, Histoire en Musique de Jericho*, and *Histoire de Joseph*. Cf. A. Cohen, "Ouvrard-Nicaise," pp. 359–60.

8. Quittard, *Du Mont*, pp. 153–54.

minister of finance, Jean-Baptiste Colbert.[9] One of Perrin's dramatic dialogues, *In Elevatione dialogus: Anima et Peccator* ("For the Elevation: A Soul and a Sinner"), was set to music by Thomas Gobert (d. 1672) and was published in Gobert's *Cantica a sacelli regii musicis in sacrificio missae decantata* (after 1661), which also includes two other dramatic dialogues.[10] Among the most interesting dialogues of the period prior to or contemporary with the earliest of Charpentier's oratorios are those of Henry Du Mont (1610–84), some of which were published in his *Motets à deux voix avec la basse-continue* (Paris, 1668);[11] a setting of Perrin's dialogue text, *Anima et Peccator*, is the second dialogue of the book. The most extensive and effective of Du Mont's dialogues is his *Dialogus de Anima*,[12] which formed a part of the collection of Sébastien de Brossard; the latter wrote in the catalogue of his collection that this work "is a very excellent species of oratorio, or dialogue, between God, a Fisherman, and an Angel, and at the end of it there is a very beautiful chorus for five voices, CATTB, with two violins and an essential organ."[13] Because of its dramatic text, expressive recitative style,[14] and approximately fifteen-minute duration, this work is comparable to such Latin oratorios of mid-century Rome as those of Marazzoli and D. Mazzocchi and to the shorter ones of Carissimi. The date of Du Mont's work has been estimated at 1670–80,[15] which is about the time of Charpentier's earliest oratorios.

Marc-Antoine Charpentier and the Latin Oratorio[16]

Few specifics are known of Charpentier's life before the early 1670s. He is thought to have been born in Paris in 1634, 1636, or

9. F/Pn: MS français 2208. For a brief discussion of this MS, see Quittard, *Du Mont*, pp. 151–52. All the texts in this MS will be published in Auld, *Perrin*. I gratefully acknowledge the help of Dr. Louis E. Auld, who allowed me to see the MS of his forthcoming book and who supplied the approximate date for Perrin's MS.

10. Quittard, *Du Mont*, p. 154.

11. For a discussion of Du Mont's dramatic dialogues, see ibid., pp. 161–74.

12. MS in F/Pn: Vm¹ 1303. (In Ecorcheville, *Catalogue*, the work is mistakenly numbered Vm¹ 1302.)

13. Translated from Brossard, "Catalogue," p. 483.

14. For an extended excerpt from this dialogue, see "Supplement musical," in Quittard, *Du Mont*, pp. 17–24.

15. Ibid., p. 166.

16. Among the most useful writings on Charpentier's oratorios are: Barber, "Oratorios"; Hitchcock, "Oratorios" (art.); Hitchcock, "Oratorios" (diss.); Nef, "Char-

perhaps some years later.[17] He studied composition with Carissimi in Rome for several years, a period that at least partly fell between 1662 and 1667.[18] By 1672 he had returned to Paris, for that is the date of a performance of Molière's comedy *La Comtesse d'Escarbagnas*, which included music by Charpentier. This performance began a long association with Molière's theater company, called the Troupe de Guénégaud after Molière's death (1673) and the Comédie-Française after 1680.[19] Charpentier's association with this company lasted at least until the mid-1680s, during which period he also held several other positions. Beginning about 1672 he served as the maître de musique for Marie de Lorraine, duchesse de Guise (1615–88), a position that he probably retained until this patron's death. For the musical establishment of Mademoiselle de Guise, among the most imposing private ones in Paris, Charpentier composed both secular and sacred works, including at least four oratorios. In the period from 1679 to 1681, he composed and probably directed the sacred music for the private services of the young Dauphin (b. 1661). In the early 1680s he became a composer and the maître de musique at the Jesuit church of Saint-Louis and at the Jesuit Collège Louis-le-Grand (Collège de Clermont).[20] For the Jesuits' church, one of Paris's more important musical centers, Charpentier composed numerous sacred works; some of his oratorios may have been performed there. He composed music for the sacred dramas that were presented by the students at the college, although this institution seems not to have fostered the performance of oratorios. The peak of Charpentier's career was the post that he held from 1698 until his death in 1704, that of maître de musique at the Saint-Chapelle du Palais. Charpentier was a prolific composer who wrote both secular and sacred music, but the large majority of his works are sacred. He is particularly significant as the earliest-known French composer of a large number of oratorios. All settings of Latin texts, his oratorios clearly reflect the influence of Carissimi.

---

pentier"; and Nielsen, "Charpentier." For modern editions of Charpentier's oratorios, see CS, vol. 3; Charpentier, *Judicium*; and Hitchcock, "Oratorios" (diss.), vol. 3.

17. For information and bibliography regarding Charpentier's birthdate, see Hitchcock's preface to Charpentier, *Judicium*, p. v; Hitchcock, "Comédie-Française," p. 256, n. 3; and D. Launay, "Charpentier, Marc-Antoine," in *MGG*, 2: col. 1107.

18. Hitchcock, "Comédie-Française," p. 256, n. 3.

19. For a study of Charpentier's contributions to this theater company, see Hitchcock, "Comédie-Française."

20. For a study of Charpentier's work at this college, see Lowe, *Charpentier*.

Like the Latin works of Carissimi, those of Charpentier raise some difficult questions of terminology and classification. Charpentier designated none of his works by the term *oratorio*, and in fact that term was virtually never used in seventeenth-century France.[21] One might expect Claude François Ménestrier, in his book entitled *Des Représentations en musique ancienne et modernes* (Paris, 1681), to have used the term in his discussion of the oratorios sponsored by the Oratorians of Rome, but instead he speaks only of *musique dramatique*, as he does in his references to the sacred dramatic works of Charpentier.[22] Among Charpentier's designations for his works that are similar in varying degrees to the genre commonly identified by the term *oratorio* in Italy are *motet*, *canticum*, *historia*, *dialogus*, and *méditation*. Some of his works of this type bear no designation of a genre but only titles and/or indications of the feasts of the church calendar for which they are appropriate. Nevertheless, since a number of Charpentier's Latin works are like oratorios and since they clearly derive from Italy—in particular from Carissimi—it seems reasonable to apply the Italian term *oratorio* to them and to assess their historical position at least partially in terms of Italian music.

Research on Charpentier's Latin dramatic works is still in progress,[23] and any attempt (including the following one) to determine precisely which of them might best be classified as oratorios must be considered provisional. Thirty-four of them have been called oratorios in previous musicological writings;[24] yet a number of these are much shorter than are compositions normally called oratorios by seventeenth-century composers of Italy—even in the mid-century, the earliest period of that term's use for a musical genre. In the interest of approximating seven-

21. For a discussion of the rare use of the term *oratorio* in France, see Smither, "Carissimi," pp. 59–60.

22. [Ménestrier], *Représentations*, pp. 191–92.

23. H. Wiley Hitchcock is continuing his work on the classification of Charpentier's works.

24. The classification presented in Hitchcock, "Oratorios" (diss.), 1:70–71, and in Hitchcock, "Oratorios" (art.), pp. 64–65, is the most recent to have appeared in print. For earlier classifications, see Gastoué, "Charpentier," p. 158; Ecorcheville, *Catalogue*, 4:8; Crussard, *Charpentier*, pp. 111–13; and Brenet, "Charpentier," p. 75. A new catalogue by H. Wiley Hitchcock of the works of Charpentier is in progress. I am grateful to Professor Hitchcock for making available to me the portion of his unpublished catalogue that lists Charpentier's oratoriolike works. In the new catalogue most of the works previously classified by Professor Hitchcock as oratorios are grouped under the heading "Dramatic motets ('oratorios')."

teenth-century usage, it would seem appropriate to apply the term *oratorio* only to the longer of Charpentier's Latin dramatic dialogues and to classify the others as dramatic motets. If the criteria used above (see pp. 223–24) for the classification of the Latin dialogues by Carissimi are applied to those by Charpentier, twenty-two of the latter's dialogues would be termed oratorios. For the purpose of the present discussion, it is useful to consider these twenty-two works as forming three groups, according to their approximate durations:[25]

GROUP 1

H 392 *Judith sive Bethulia liberata* ("Judith or Bethulia Liberated") H-Or 1

H 398 *Caecilia virgo et martyr octo vocibus* ("Cecilia, Virgin and Martyr, for Eight Voices") H-Or 6

H 404 *Mors Saulis et Jonathae* ("The Death of Saul and Jonathan") H-Or 11

H 418 *In nativitatem Domini canticum* ("Canticum for the Nativity of the Lord") H-Or 15

H 423 *Judicium Salomonis* ("The Judgment of Solomon") H-Or 24

GROUP 2

H 397 *Historia Esther* ("The Story of Esther") H-Or 5

H 400 *Filius prodigus* ("The Prodigal Son") H-Or 8

H 402 *Extremum Dei judicium* ("The Last Judgment of God") H-Or 10

H 403 *Sacrificium Abrahae* ("The Sacrifice of Abraham") H-Or 18

H 412 *Caedes sanctorum innocentium* ("The Slaughter of the Holy Innocents") H-Or 22

H 413 *Nuptiae sacrae* ("Sacred Nuptials") H-Or 23

H 414 *Caecilia virgo et martyr* H-Or 12

H 416 *Caecilia virgo et martyr* H-Or 14

H 421 *Dialogus inter angelos et pastores Judeae in nativitatem Domini* ("Dialogue between the Angel and the Shepherds of Judea, for the Nativity of the Lord") H-Or 25

H 426 *Dialogus inter Christum et peccatores* ("Dialogue between Christ and the Sinners") H-Or 28

25. In this list the "H" numbers in the first column are those of Professor Hitchcock's new, unpublished catalogue. Following the title of each work is the number, designated "H-Or," given to the work in Hitchcock, "Oratorios" (diss.), 1:70–71, and Hitchcock, "Oratorios" (art.), pp. 64–65. The grouping of the works in my list, made according to their approximate durations, is based on my estimates. The estimates correspond approximately to the lengths in measure numbers given in Hitchcock, "Oratorios" (diss.), 1:70–71.

H 399 *Pestis Mediolanensis* ("The Plague of Milan") H-Or 7

H 405 *Josue* ("Joshua") H-Or 16

H 406 *In resurrectione Domini Nostri Jesu Christi canticum* ("Canticum for the Resurrection of Our Lord Jesus Christ") H-Or 26

H 407 *In circumcisione Domini: Dialogus inter angelum et pastores* ("For the Circumcision of the Lord: Dialogue between the Angel and the Shepherds") H-Or 19

H 409 *Elevation* H-Or 20

H 415 *In nativitatem Domini Nostri Jesu Christi canticum* ("Canticum for the Nativity of Our Lord Jesus Christ") H-Or 13

H 425 *Le Reniement de Saint-Pierre* ("The Denial of St. Peter") H-Or 27

The five dialogues in Group 1 of this list are the longest; they range from approximately thirty to forty minutes, and in this respect they are the ones most like works called oratorios in Italy. The dialogues in Group 2 are shorter, between twenty and thirty minutes in length, and those in Group 3 are still shorter, between ten and twenty minutes. If the works in these three groups are to be classified as oratorios, they must be considered exceptional ones for their period because of their brevity (particularly those of Group 3), the one-part structural division of the majority of them,[26] and their Latin language—in late seventeenth-century usage the term *oratorio* normally referred to a composition of one to two hours in length, in two structural parts, and in the Italian language. (Latin was still used but was not the norm.) Furthermore, the works in this list do not reflect the normal operatic conception of the oratorio of their own period, as exemplified in the oratorios of such composers as Legrenzi, Stradella, Colonna, and A. Scarlatti (whose early period coincides with that of the works in the above list); rather, these works by Charpentier are closer in general conception (although not in the details of musical style) to the mid-century Latin oratorios of Carissimi, D. Mazzocchi, Marazzoli, F. Foggia, and Graziani. Thus the most appropriate frame of reference for understanding many of the features of the works in the above list is that of the Latin oratorio of mid-century Rome, and it is in the mid-century Roman sense that the present author applies the term *oratorio* to them.

26. Only nine of the twenty-two works have two structural parts: Group 1: H 392, 398, 404, and 423; Group 2: H 400, 414, 416, and 421; Group 3: H 405.

Few specifics are known about the exact places and dates of the performances of Charpentier's oratorios. Although they may have been performed at Lenten concerts in churches, there is evidence that they functioned at times as motets in a liturgical context[27]—as some of Carissimi's Latin oratorios may well have done. Charpentier's *Judicium Salomonis*, a work about thirty-five minutes in length, for example, was performed as a motet at a mass celebrated for a special event. The work entitled simply *Elevation*, with a text on the subject of the Eucharist, was clearly intended to be performed during the canon of a mass. The Christmas oratorios (H 415, 418, and 421) have texts closely related to the Gospel for midnight mass. In fact, all but three of Charpentier's oratorios are settings of texts appropriate for certain feast days; the exceptions are *Saulis et Jonathae, Dialogus inter Christum et peccatores*, and *Josue*.

The texts of Charpentier's oratorios,[28] all anonymous, are similar to those of Carissimi's in several respects: most are based on biblical stories, the techniques of elaborating the biblical material are similar; and the nonbiblical insertions, largely in prose, employ similar rhetorical devices through which the prose at times approaches the condition of poetry. Among the texts based on the Bible, three use the same subjects as Carissimi's oratorios; these three are *Extremum Dei Judicium, Sacrificium Abrahae*, and *Judicium Salomonis*. Among the oratorios based on biblical stories that frequently served as the bases of oratorios throughout the Baroque era are *Judith, Historia Esther, Filius prodigus, Mors Saulis et Jonathae*, and *Josue*. Representing the hagiographical oratorio are three works based on the life of St. Cecilia (H 398, 414, and 416). In the biblical oratorios the Vulgate text is seldom quoted verbatim but is elaborated in a variety of ways: modified word order, paraphrase in prose, and nonbiblical insertions in prose and occasionally in poetry. The two biblical texts that are closest to the Vulgate are *Judith* and *Esther*; characteristic of those that use the biblical material only as a skeleton for the drama are *Filius prodigus, Extremum Dei judicium*, and *Caedes sanctorum innocentium*.

27. For discussions of the functions of Charpentier's oratorios, see Hitchcock, "Oratorios" (diss.), 1:99–108, and Hitchcock, "Oratorios" (art.), pp. 45–46.
28. All the texts, together with some music examples, are given in Hitchcock, "Oratorios" (diss.), vol. 2.

If Charpentier's oratorios are conservative and reflect the mid-century in their general conception, they are by no means so in their musical style. While in some respects they reveal Carissimi's stylistic influence, it is blended with Italian and French styles characteristic of Charpentier's own generation. The recitatives occasionally employ the triadic and sequential melodic patterns prominent in Carissimi's music, but they share with Lully's recitatives their tendency to include a greater variety of note values, a wider range of pitch, and a greater number of large intervals than do the recitatives of either Carissimi or later seventeenth-century Italians. The general tendency in the second half of the seventeenth century to intermingle sections in recitative, arioso, and aria styles is present in Charpentier's oratorios, both within passages that are primarily recitative and within arias.

The largely prose texts of Charpentier's oratorios, like those of Carissimi's, include relatively few passages that lend themselves to musical setting as arias. A typical aria in Charpentier's oratorios uses one of two types of texts: either a prose text at a point where an affective plateau that the composer wishes to emphasize has been reached, or a text that is poetic or at least clearly structured. These two types have been termed *affective* and *poetic* arias, respectively.[29] The structure of an affective aria is usually an ABA, ABA', ABACA, or some other adaptation of the *rondeau* scheme. The text of the A section will usually consist of a sentence expressing the affection basic to the entire aria. While the A section is always in aria style, the contrasting sections may be in aria, arioso, or recitative styles. The poetic arias are characteristically dances, usually minuets, and are in binary form with both sections repeated. Ensembles using solo voices include ensemble recitatives, ensembles functioning as choruses in the works calling for only a few voices, and dramatic ensembles. The last named are of particular interest, for in them the composer reveals his skill in characterization by maintaining the individuality of each personage; an excellent example is the quarrel between the two women in *Judicium Salomonis*.

In both Carissimi's oratorios and those of Charpentier, the longest works are those making the most extensive use of the chorus. In Charpentier's oratorios the chorus is used far more than in contemporary Italian oratorios. At times the chorus func-

29. Hitchcock, "Oratorios" (art.), p. 49.

tions in the role of the narrator, or *historicus*, although that role is also given to soloists and ensembles as it is in Carissimi's oratorios. Other functions of the chorus are to represent a crowd within the drama, to comment on the action, or to present a concluding, moralistic summary. In the shorter works these functions tend to be taken over by ensembles of soloists. While the choruses in Charpentier's oratorios are comparable to those in Carissimi's in regard to their extent and function, they are not comparable in style, for Charpentier's choruses are clearly products of their own time: in their harmonic resources and concertato combinations with instruments, they reflect the influence of the French *grand motet* of the second half of the seventeenth century. Although in Carissimi's oratorios chordal style prevails, in those of Charpentier it is balanced by counterpoint, usually imitative, that is more intricate than that of most Italian or French choral music in Charpentier's own time. Among the other choral resources of these oratorios are polychoral antiphony and the alternation of choral passages with those of soloists, small vocal ensembles, or instrumental groups, such as a trio of two woodwinds and continuo.

A feature of Charpentier's oratorios that is unusual in comparison with either Carissimi's or with those of composers in Charpentier's own generation is the emphasis upon instrumental music. Even in the shorter works the instruments, usually a trio-sonata ensemble of two violins and continuo, tend to be used more than in most seventeenth-century oratorios. In some of the works, an orchestra of four strings is used in addition to the trio-sonata group; three of the oratorios (H 398, 399, and 405) call for a double orchestra of two string sections with four parts each. To the strings are sometimes added pairs of flutes, oboes, bassoons, and trumpets.[30] The instrumental music of the oratorios consists not only of ritornellos and accompaniment for the voices, but it also includes some remarkable programmatic numbers—" 'night symphonies,' 'awakening symphonies,' 'enchantment symphonies,' fanfares, marches, and *bruits de guerre*."[31]

30. For a tabular summary of the instrumentation, see Hitchcock, "Oratorios" (diss.), 1:312.
31. Hitchcock, "Oratorios" (art.), p. 55.

Judicium Salomonis[32]

The only one of Charpentier's oratorios that can be precisely dated, *Judicium* bears the inscription on some of the separate manuscript parts, "motet pour la messe rouge du Palais en 1702."[33] The "red mass" for which the oratorio served as a motet was that celebrated in the *grand salle* of the Palais de Justice every year on 11 November for the convening of Parlement. The red robes of the assembly gave this mass its name, and the judicial nature of the Parlement made the subject matter of this oratorio particularly appropriate.

The text of *Judicium*, in two structural parts, is based primarily on 3 Kings 3:1–28 (in the Vulgate; 1 Chron. 3:1–28, in the King James version) but includes fragments from various other biblical sources, particularly from Psalm 117. The occasion for which the work was composed conditioned not only the biblical story to be used, that of Solomon's judgment concerning which of two women was the real mother of the child in question, but also other aspects of the text. All of part I, for instance, is devoted to the praise and glory of King Solomon (no doubt a veiled reference to Louis XIV) and the piety and happiness of his realm. Part I emphasizes narration, description, praise, and rejoicing more than drama. In the manner of Carissimi, Charpentier gives the narrative lines a variety of settings (B, T, SATB, and TTB). King Solomon (T) and his People (SATB) go up to the heights of Gibeon to sacrifice burnt offerings to the Lord, and there they praise and glorify him in music. In part II God (B) appears to Solomon in a dream; Solomon asks for "wisdom and knowledge to judge Thy People and to distinguish between good and evil," a request that God grants him. Upon his return from Gibeon, Solomon is confronted with the task of judging which of the two Women (S, S) is the mother of a child. He applies his test—ordering that the child be divided in half—and thus determines which is the true mother. The final chorus (no. 20),[34] clearly written for the occasion, directly addresses the assemblage ("Vos autem purpurati proceres" —"Likewise, ye empurpled leaders") to whom judicial powers

32. Printed in Charpentier, *Judicium.*
33. For this quotation and other historical information about this work, see Hitchcock's preface to Charpentier, *Judicium,* pp. vii–viii.
34. Numbers refer to the editorial numbers for sections given in Charpentier, *Judicium.*

have been given from God and whose judgment will therefore "shine forth as the noonday."

The five choruses of *Judicium* constitute its most striking musical feature. Most of them are extended multisectional numbers mixing contrapuntal and chordal writing and including instruments used in both *colla parte* and concertato style. In part I the narrative choruses and those of the People of Solomon are particularly notable both for their exuberant expressions of praise and for their descriptions of the instruments used. These descriptions are found in the first chorus (no. 3), "Tunc laetata est" (in the section "Sacerdotes in tubis," see Example IX-1), and also in the chorus (no. 6) "Ideo cunctis unanimiter laetantibus et tubis et citharis psallentibus" ("Therefore as they were all rejoicing together, with trumpets and harps resounding"). Among the choruses of interest for their fugal or freely imitative sections are "Et rex similiter" (no. 4), "Ideo cunctis" (no. 6, in the section "et voces a

EXAMPLE IX-1. *Judicium Salomonis*—Charpentier (Charpentier, *Judicium*, pp. 14—15).

The priests with trumpets and the Levites with instruments of music sang praises; . . .

sublimi flectentibus"), and "Et facto mane" (no. 12, in the section "Comedentibus autem," see Example IX–2). Of interest as an element of structural unity is the repetition of part of the oratorio's first chorus (no. 3, final section, "Confitemini Domino") at the end of part I.

The majority of the solo passages are in an expressive style of recitative. The oratorio includes only one aria—Solomon's prayer in Gibeon, "Benedictus es, Domine" (no. 5, see Example IX–3). This is an "affective aria" (according to the above aria classifica-

EXAMPLE IX-2. *Judicium Salomonis*—Charpentier (Charpentier, *Judicium*, p. 83).

And as he [Solomon] was eating and drinking [joyfully with them . . .].

Blessed art thou, O Lord God of Israel, and highly to be praised.

tion) in ABA form, in which the text of the A section is a brief sentence ("Blessed art thou, O Lord God of Israel, and highly to be praised"), and that of the B section is a reflection on the meaning of the sacrifices being offered to God. Highly effective for its solo passages is the dialogue between God and Solomon during the latter's dream: Solomon's long speech to God, "Dominus Deus meus" (no. 10, see Example IX–4), is the oratorio's only accompanied recitative, and God's reply, "Quia non petisti" (no. 11), is a long section in arioso style.

EXAMPLE IX-4. *Judicium Salomonis*—Charpentier (Charpentier, *Judicium*, p. 65).

(EXAMPLE IX-4, continued)

tu re - gna - re fe - ci - sti ser - vum tu - um.

O Lord God, thou hast made thy servant king.

The dramatic high point of the oratorio, the judgment scene in part II, is a varied complex of duet and solo passages with the following structure:

	Styles
Conflict between the Mothers:	
A False Mother (solo) "Non est ita"	
A′ True Mother (solo) "Non est ita"	Aria
B Both Mothers (duet) "Non est ita"	
Solomon's summary:	
C Solomon (solo) "Haec dicit"	Recitative
Conflict between the Mothers resumed:	
A	
A′ As above	Aria
B	
Solomon's test:	
D Solomon (solo) "Adferte mihi"	Recitative
Revelation of the true Mother:	
E Both Mothers (duet) "Ah, domine mi"	Arioso, aria
Solomon's judgment:	
F Solomon (solo) "Date huic infantem"	Aria

In the AA′B sections each Mother first presents her case (sections A and A′), and then, singing simultaneously (section B), they argue. Solomon summarizes their statements (C), but in the intensity of their anger, they begin again (AA'B, as above). Solomon then applies his test (D), which reveals the True Mother (E), and in a brief section in aria style, the king announces his judgment (F).

The instruments of *Judicium* are divided into two groups, the concertant and continuo; the former consists of two flutes, oboe, bassoon, and four strings, and the continuo consists of basses de violon (violoncellos) and organ. The only two independent instrumental numbers are the preludes to parts I and II. That for part I is an essentially homophonic number in a rounded binary form without repeat signs. The prelude to part II is programmatic, for it functions as an introduction to a night scene, that of Solomon's dream: all the strings are muted, and the flutes are used, but the oboes and bassoon are excluded. This "night music" opens and closes in chordal style and includes a middle section that is slightly more active and contrapuntal, with gently moving quarter notes in slurred pairs.

Parisian Oratorios after Charpentier

Charpentier's considerable interest in oratorio composition seems not to have been shared by contemporary or immediately succeeding Parisian composers. As pointed out above, his contemporaries composed some sacred dramatic dialogues, but few of these are extended and dramatically developed enough to be considered oratorios—Du Mont's *Dialogus de Anima* is an exception. The situation appears not to have changed in the early eighteenth century. In fact, the four compositions mentioned in the remainder of this chapter are the only known Parisian oratorios, other than Charpentier's *Judicium Salomonis*, from the first half of the eighteenth century.[35]

Although the word *oratorio* appears virtually never to have been used in seventeenth-century France, it was occasionally used there in the early eighteenth century. Sébastien de Brossard, in his *Dictionaire de musique* (Paris, 1703), recognizes the oratorio as a genre and describes it as follows:

35. An additional work, César-François-Nicolas Clérambault's *Idylle pour la paix* (1739) is similar to an oratorio in some respects and is called an oratorio in Foster, "Oratorio." I gratefully acknowledge the assistance of Professor Donald F. Foster, who kindly made available to me the results of his study, Foster, "Oratorio," prior to its publication. Most of this section is based on his study, which should be consulted for more details.

Oratorio. It is a species of *spiritual opera*, or a web of *dialogues*, *recitatives*, *duets*, *trios*, *ritornellos*, *large choruses*, etc., of which the subject is taken either from Scripture or the story of some saint. Or else it is an allegory on some one of the mysteries of the religion, or some moral point, etc. Its music ought to be enriched by all the finest and the most choice that the art has. The words are almost always Latin and usually taken from the Holy Scripture. There are many of which the words are in Italian, and one could write them in French. Nothing is more common at Rome, above all during Lent, than these kinds of *oratorio*. One by Sieur Lochon, in which there are great beauties, has just been presented to the public—it is for four voices and two violins.[36]

This is Brossard's entire entry under the term *oratorio*. Although he refers to the genre as a "spiritual opera," the context implies that he considers the similarity between opera and oratorio to include only style and structure—he makes no mention of staging. It is curious that Brossard does not call attention to his older contemporary Charpentier, even though his description of the oratorio, with its emphasis on Latin texts and biblical material, would fit Charpentier's oratorios. The only work that Brossard does mention is Jacques-François Lochon's *Oratorio à quatre voix et 2. dessus de violons ajoutez, pour la naissance de l'enfant Jesus, entre l'ange & les pasteurs* ("Oratorio for Four Voices and 2 Added Treble Violins, for the Birth of the Infant Christ, between the Angel and the Shepherds"), published in a book of motets[37] two years before the appearance of Brossard's *Dictionaire*. Lochon's work, a relatively brief and lighthearted dialogue in Latin between the Angel (S) and the Shepherds (ATB), is by no means as impressive musically as are most of Charpentier's oratorios. Lochon's is the only work called an oratorio that is known to have been printed in eighteenth-century France. Its appearance in a book of motets would seem to imply that it was intended to function as a motet during a mass, probably midnight mass, as did some of Charpentier's oratorios.

A work close in spirit and style to those of Charpentier is *L'Histoire de la femme adultère* by Louis-Nicolas Clérambault (1676–1749), with a prose text based on John 8:1–11.[38] Extant

36. Brossard, *Dictionaire*, "Oratorio." (No pagination.)
37. The oratorio is on pp. 60–92 of *Motets en musique par Monsieur Lochon . . . Et un oratorio à six parties, piece particuliere. Livre premier.* Paris: Christoph Ballard, 1701.
38. Printed in Clérambault, *Histoire.*

only in an unfinished state is the *Oratorio sopra l'immaculata conceptione della B. Vergine* by Sébastien de Brossard.[39] Its complete text, in Latin verse, is extant, but in the musical manuscript (the composer's rough copy) less than half of the text has been set. This is by far the longest of the three oratorios just mentioned: the works by Locon and Clérambault are comparable in length (ten to twenty minutes) to Group 3 of Charpentier's oratorios, but that by Brossard, if the entire text were set, would appear to last about one hour. Musically these three oratorios have several elements in common: the instrumental passages use a trio-sonata setting, the choruses are for ATB or SATB and are at times stylistically similar to those of *grands motets*, and all three works are clearly influenced by Italian music (Brossard's oratorio, for instance, includes some arias with motto beginnings). The only other known oratorio from the first half of the eighteenth century in Paris is an anonymous *Oratoire St. François de Borgia à grand choeur sur la mort d'Esabelle reine d'Espagne*;[40] a work of about an hour in duration with a text in French, it is reminiscent of the style of Lully in both its vocal and its instrumental sections.

39. F/Pn: MS Vm¹ 1629.
40. F/V: MS mus. 57.

℘ Bibliography

This bibliography lists all the sources referred to by short title in the main body of the book and also a few that are not referred to but may prove useful to the reader. Materials fully identified in the main body, mostly encyclopedia articles and primary sources, are omitted.

Abert, *Monteverdi*
    Abert, Anna Amalie. *Claudio Monteverdi und das musikalische Drama.* Lippstadt: Kistner & Siegel, 1954.
Abert, "Reformdrama"
    ———. "Zum metastasianischen Reformdrama." In *Kongress-Bericht Lüneburg 1950, Gesellschaft für Musikforschung*, edited by Hans Albrecht, Helmuth Osthoff, and Walter Wiora, pp. 138–39. Kassel: Bärenreiter, n. d.
Acton, *Medici*
    Acton, Harold. *The Last Medici.* London: Faber & Faber, 1932.
Ademollo, *Roma*
    Ademollo, Alessandro. *I teatri di Roma nel secolo decimosettimo.* Rome: L. Pasqualicci, 1888.
Adler, *Kaiser*
    Adler, Guido, ed. *Muskalische Werke der Kaiser Ferdinand III., Leopold I. und Joseph I.* 2 vols. Vienna: Artaria, 1892–93.
Alaleona, "Laudi"
    Alaleona, Domenico. "Le laudi spirituali italiane nei secoli XVI e XVII e i loro rapporto coi canti profani." *Rivista musicale italiana* 16 (1909): 1–54.
Alaleona, *Oratorio*
    ———. *Storia dell'oratorio musicale in Italia.* Milan: Fratelli Bocca, 1945. Reprint, with different pagination, of *Studi su la storia dell'oratorio musicale in Italia.* 1908.
Allacci, *Drammaturgia*
    Allacci, Lione. *Drammaturgia di Lione Allacci, accresciuta e continuata fino all'anno MDCCLV.* 1755. Reprint. Turin: Bottega d'Erasmo, 1966.
Analecta hymnica
    Dreves, Guido Maria; Blume, Clemens; and Bannister, Henry Marriott, eds. *Analecta hymnica medii aevi.* 55 vols. Leipzig: Fues's Verlag, R. Reisland, 1886; Leipzig: O. R. Reisland, 1890–1922.
Anthony, *French*
    Anthony, James R. *French Baroque Music from Beaujoyeulx to Rameau.* New York: W. W. Norton, 1974.

Apel, *Chant*
　　Apel, Willi. *Gregorian Chant*. Bloomington, Ind.: Indiana University Press, 1958.
Apollonio, *Metastasio*
　　Apollonio, Mario. *Metastasio*. Milan: Athena, 1930.
Armellini, *Chiese*
　　Armellini, Mariano. *Le chiese di Roma dal secolo IV al XIX*. 2 vols. 3d ed. Rome: Edizioni R. O. R. E. di Nicola Ruffolo, 1942.
Arnold, "Conservatories"
　　Arnold, Denis. "Orphans and Ladies: The Venetian Conservatories (1680–1790)." *Proceedings of the Royal Musical Association* 89 (1962–63): 31–47.
Auld, *Perrin*
　　Auld, Louis E. *The "Lyric Art" of Pierre Perrin, Founder of French Opera. The Union of Poetry and Music in Theory and Practice: 1643–1671. Including "Recueil de Paroles de Musique de Mr Perrin (Bibliothèque Nationale ms 2208)."* Brooklyn, N.Y.: Institute for Mediaeval Music, forthcoming.
Baini, *Palestrina*
　　Baini, Giuseppe. *Memorie storico-critiche della vita e delle opere di Giovanni Pierluigi da Palestrina*. 2 vols. Rome: Società Tipografica, 1828.
Balducci, *Rime*
　　Balducci, Francesco. *Le rime*. 2 vols. Rome: F. Moneta, 1645–46.
Bangert, *Society*
　　Bangert, William V., S. J. *A History of the Society of Jesus*. St. Louis: Institute of Jesuit Sources, 1972.
Barber, "Oratorios"
　　Barber, Clarence. "Les Oratorios de Marc-Antoine Charpentier." *Recherches sur la musique française classique* 3 (1963): 91–125.
Baronio, *Annales*
　　Baronio, Caesere. *Annales ecclesiastici*. 19 vols. Lucca: Leonardo Venturini, 1738–46.
Baronio, *Annali*
　　———. *Annali ecclesiastici*. Drawn from [the *Annales*] of Cardinal Baronio by Odorico Rinaldi Trivigiano. 3 vols. Rome: Vitale Mascardi, 1641–43.
Bartels, "Instrumentalstücke"
　　Bartels, Isolde. "Die Instrumentalstücke in Oper und Oratorium des frühvenezianischen Zeit." Ph.D. dissertation, University of Vienna, 1970.
Bartholomaeis, *Laude*
　　Bartholomaeis, Vincenzo de. *Laude drammatiche e rappresentazioni sacre*. 3 vols. Florence: Felice Le Monnier, 1943.
Bartholomaeis, *Origini*
　　———. *Origini della poesia drammatica italiana*. Nuova biblioteca italiana, vol. 7. 2d ed. Turin: Società Editrice Internationale, 1952.
Batiffol, *Bréviaire*
　　Batiffol, Pierre. *Histoire du Bréviaire romain*. Bibliothèque d'histoire religieuse. 3d ed. Paris: Alph. Picard & Fils, Auguste Picard, successeur, 1911.
Beat, "Carissimi"
　　Beat, Janet E. "Two Problems in Carissimi's Oratorio *Jephte*." *Music Review* 34 (1973): 339–45.
Becherini, *Catalogo*
　　Becherini, Bianca. *Catalogo dei manoscritti musicali della Biblioteca Nazionale di Firenze*. Kassel: Bärenreiter, 1959.

Becherini, "Rappresentazioni"
_____. "La musica nelle 'Sacre rappresentazioni' fiorentine." *Rivista musicale italiana* 53 (1951): 193–241.

Belcari, *Rappresentazioni*
Belcari, Feo. *Le rappresentazioni di Feo Belcari ed altri di lui poesie.* Florence: Ignazio Moutier, 1833.

Beveridge, "Carissimi"
Beveridge, Lowell P. "Giacomo Carissimi (1605–1674): A Study of His Life and His Music with Latin Texts in the Light of the Institutions Which He Served and through the Perspectives of Liturgical, Literary, and Musical Theory and Practice." Ph.D. dissertation, Harvard University, 1944.

Bevignani, *Arciconfraternita*
Bevignani, Augusto. *L'Arciconfraternita di S. Maria dell'Orazione e Morte in Roma e le sue rappresentazioni sacre.* Rome: R. Società Romana di Storia Patria, 1910. Offprint from *Archivio della R. Società Romana di Storia Patria*, vol. 33.

Biach-Schiffmann, *Burnacini*
Biach-Schiffmann, Flora. *Giovanni und Lodovico Burnacini: Theater und Feste am Wiener Hofe.* Arbeiten des I. Kunsthistorischen Instituts der Universität Wien Lehrkanzel Strzygowski, vol. 43. Vienna and Berlin: Krystall, 1931.

Bianchi, *Carissimi*
Bianchi, Lino. *Carissimi, Stradella, Scarlatti, e l'oratorio musicale.* Rome: De Santis, 1969.

Bitter, *Oratorium*
Bitter, C[arl] H[ermann]. *Beiträge zur Geschichte des Oratoriums.* Berlin: R. Oppenheim, 1872.

Bjurström, "Theater"
Bjurström, Per. "Baroque Theater and the Jesuits." In *Baroque Art: The Jesuit Contribution*, edited by Rudolf Wittkower and Irma B. Jaffe, pp. 99–110. New York: Fordham University Press, 1972.

Blume, *Monodische*
Blume, Friedrich. *Das monodische Prinzip in der Protestantischen Kirchenmusik.* Leipzig: Breitkopf & Härtel, 1925.

Blunt, *Art*
Blunt, Anthony. *Art and Architecture in France, 1500 to 1700.* The Pelican History of Art, vol. Z4. London: Penguin Books, 1953.

Böhme, *Geschichte*
Böhme, Franz Magnus. *Die Geschichte des Oratoriums für Musikfreunde kurz und fasslich dargestellt.* 1887. Reprint. Walluf bei Wiesbaden: M. Sändig, 1973.

Böhme, *Oratorium*
_____. *Das Oratorium: Eine historische Studie.* Leipzig: J. J. Weber, 1861.

Borrelli, *Costituzioni*
Borrelli, Mario. *Le Costituzioni dell'Oratorio napoletano.* Naples: Congregazione dell'Oratorio, 1968.

Brambach, *Historia*
Brambach, Wilhelm. *Die verloren geglaubte Historia de Sancta Afra Martyre und das Salve Regina des Hermanus Contractus.* Karlsruhe: Ch. Th. Groos, 1892.

Brenet, "Carissimi"
Bobillier, Marie [Brenet, Michel]. "Les 'oratorios' de Carissimi." *Rivista musicale italiana* 4 (1897): 460–83.

Brenet, "Charpentier"
———. "Marc-Antoine Charpentier." *La Tribune de Saint-Gervais: Bulletin mensuel de la Schola Cantorum* 6 (1900): 65–76.

Brenet, *Louis XIV*
———. *La musique sacrée sous Louis XIV: Conférence prononcée 12 janvier 1899 dans le grand Amphithéâtre de l'Institut Catholique.* Paris: Bureau d'édition de la Schola cantorum, 1899.

Brinckmann, "Disegni"
Brinckmann, Albert Erich. "I disegni." In *Filippo Juvarra*, edited by the Comitato per le Onoranze a Filippo Juvarra, vol. 1, pp. 113–77. Milan: Oberdan, 1937.

Broderick, *Jesuits*
Broderick, James. *The Origin of the Jesuits.* 1940. Reprint. New York: Longmans, Green, [1949].

Brooks, "Sepulchre"
Brooks, Neil Conwell. "The Sepulchre of Christ in Art and Liturgy with Special Reference to the Liturgic Drama." *University of Illinois Studies in Language and Literature* 7 (1921): 139–248.

Brooks, "Sepulchrum"
———. "The 'Sepulchrum Christi' and Its Ceremonies in Late Medieval and Modern Times." *Journal of English and Germanic Philology* 27 (1928): 147–61.

Brossard, "Catalogue"
Paris. Bibliothèque nationale. MS, Rés Vm^8 21. "Catalogue des livres de musique théorique et pratique, vocalle et instrumentale, tant imprimée que manuscript, qui sont dans le cabinet du Sr. Sébastien Brossard, Chanoine de Meaux, et dont il supplie très humblement sa Majesté d'accepter dans sa Bibliothèque. Fait et escrit en l'année 1724."

Brossard, *Dictionaire*
Brossard, Sébastian. *Dictionaire de musique.* Paris: C. Ballard, 1703. Reprint. Amsterdam: Antiqua, 1964.

Brosses, *Lettres*
Brosses, Charles de. *Lettres familières écrites d'Italie à quelques amis en 1739 et 1740.* 2 vols. Paris: Poulet-Malassis et De Broise, 1858.

Bukofzer, *Baroque*
Bukofzer, Manfred F. *Music in the Baroque Era.* New York: W. W. Norton, 1947.

Burney, *History*
Burney, Charles. *A General History of Music.* 4 bks. 1789. Reprint (4 bks. in 2 vols.). London: G. T. Foulis, 1935.

Calabrese, *Melodramma*
Calabrese, Giuseppe. *Origini del melodramma sacro in Roma.* Gravina: L. Attolini, [1907].

Calsabigi, "Dissertazione"
Calsabigi, Ranieri de'. "Dissertazione di Ranieri Calsabigi, dell'Accademia di Cortona, su le poesie drammatiche del signore abate Pietro Metastasio." Introduction to *Poesie del signor abate Pietro Metastasio*, by Pietro Metastasio. 9 vols. Paris: La Vedova Quillau, 1755.

Calouri, *Rossi*
Calouri, Eleanor. *Luigi Rossi.* The Wellesley Edition: Cantata Index Series, No. 3a–b. Wellesley, Mass.: Wellesley College, 1965.

Cambridge
 Clark, George N. et al., eds. *New Cambridge Modern History.* Cambridge: At the University Press, 1958–. Vol. 1, *The Renaissance: 1493–1520,* edited by George R. Potter, 1961. Vol. 2, *The Reformation: 1520–1559,* edited by Geoffrey R. Elton, 1958.
Cametti, "Carissimi"
 Cametti, Alberto. "Primo contributo per una biografia di Giacomo Carissimi." *Rivista musicale italiana* 24 (1917): 379–417.   •
Campanini, *Precursore*
 Campanini, Naborre. *Un precursore del Metastasio: [Pietro Pariati].* Reggio-Emilia: Luigi Bondavalli, 1883.
Campbell, *Jesuits*
 Campbell, Thomas J. *The Jesuits (1534–1921): A History of the Society of Jesus from Its Formation to the Present Time.* London: Encyclopedia Press, [1921].
Capecelatro, *Neri*
 Capecelatro, Alfonso. *La vita di S. Filippo Neri.* 3 bks. in 2 vols. 4th ed. Tournai: Desclée, Lefebure, 1901.
Capponi, "Marazzoli"
 Capponi, Piero. "Marco Marazzoli e l'oratorio 'Cristo e i Farisei.'" In *La scuola romana: G. Carissimi, A. Cesti, M. Marazzoli,* Accademia musicale chigiana, Settimana musicale senese, no. 10, pp. 101–6. Siena: Ticci, 1953.
Capri, *Storia*
 Capri, Antonio. *Storia della musica dalle antiche civiltà orientali alla musica elettronica.* 3 vols. to date. [Milan]: Francesco Vallardi, 1969–.
Carissimi, *Jephte*-B
 Carissimi, Giacomo. *Jephte (Jephthah): Oratorio.* Edited by Janet Beat. Borough Green, Sevenoaks, Kent: Novello, 1974.
Carissimi, *Jephte*-C
 ———. *Jephte.* Edited by Fiora Contino. Harmoniae musarum, no. CMC–107. Macomb, Ill.: Roger Dean, 1976.
Carissimi, *Jephte*-W
 ———. *Historia di Jephte a 6 voc. et organo.* Edited by Gottfried Wolters. Basso continuo realization by Mathias Siedel. Wölfenbüttel: Möseler, 1969.
Carissimi, *Jephthah*-P
 ———. *Jephthah: An Oratorio.* Edited and the pianoforte accompaniment arranged by Ernst Pauer. English adaptation by the Rev. John Troutbeck. New York: H. W. Gray (Novello), n. d.
Carissimi, *Jonah*
 ———. *Jonah.* Edited by Jack Pilgrim. London: Oxford University Press, 1972.
Carreras, *Oratorio*
 Carreras y Bulbena, Josè Rafael. *El oratorio musical desde su origen hasta nuestros dias.* Barcelona: Ronda de la Universidad, 1906.
Casimiri, "Disciplina"
 Casimiri, Raffaele. "'Disciplina musicae' e 'mastri di capella' dopo il Concilio di Trento nei maggiori istituti ecclesiastici di Roma." *Note d'archivio per la storia musicale* 12 (1935): 1–26, 73–81; 15 (1938): 1–14; 16 (1939): 1–9; 19 (1942): 102–29, 159–68; 20 (1943): 1–17.
Casimiri, "Òasi"
 ———. "Òasi filippini. . . . " *Bollettino ceciliano* 30 (1935): 120–28.

Casimiri, "Oratorii"
———. "Oratorii del Masini, Bernabei, Melani, Di Pio, Pasquini e Stradella."
Note d'archivio per la storia musicale 13 (1936): 157–69.
Casimiri, "Vittoria"
———. " 'Il Vittoria': Nuovi documenti per una biografia sincera di Tommaso
Ludovico Victoria." Note d'archivio per la storia musicale 11 (1934): 111–
97.
Cavalieri, Rappresentatione-Facs.
Cavalieri, Emilio de'. Rappresentatione di anima et di corpo. Novamente posta
in musica dal sig. Emilio del Cavalliere, per recitar cantando. Data in luce da
Alessandro Guidotti, Bolognese. 1600. Facsimile reprint. Edited by
Francesco Mantica, with an introduction by Domenico Alaleona. Primo
fioriture del melodramma italiano, vol. 1. Rome: Casa Editrice Claudio
Monteverdi, 1912.
———. Rappresentatione di anima et di corpo. Facsimile reprint. Farnborough,
Hants, England: Gregg Press, 1967.
Cavalieri, Rappresentazione-G
———. Rappresentazione di anima e di corpo. Realization, elaboration, and
instrumentation by Emilia Gubitosi. Reduction for voice and piano. Milan:
Ricordi, 1956.
Cavalieri, Rappresentazione-T
———. Rappresentazione di anima e di corpo. Edited by Giovanni Tebaldini.
Reduction for voice and piano by Corrado Barbieri. Preface by Domenico
Alaleona. Turin: Soc. Tipografico Editrice Nazionale, [1914].
CDMI
I classici della musica italiana: Raccolta nazionale. Directed by Gabriele d'An-
nunzio. 36 vols. Milan: Società Anonima Notari, 1919–21. Vol. 5, Oratorii
per canto e pianoforte, by Giacomo Carissimi, edited by [F.] Balilla Pratella,
1919. Vol. 10, Rappresentazione di anima et di corpo, per canto e
pianoforte, by Emilio del Cavaliere, edited by Francesco Malipiero, 1919.
Celani, "Cantori"
Celani, E. "I cantori della Cappella Pontificia nei secoli 16–18." Rivista
musicale italiana 14 (1907): 83–104, 752–90.
Charpentier, Judicium
Charpentier, Marc-Antoine. Judicium Salomonis. Edited by H. Wiley Hitch-
cock. Recent Researches in the Music of the Baroque Era, vol. 1. New Ha-
ven, Conn.: A-R Editions, 1964.
Chastel, Art
Chastel, André. Italian Art. Translated by Peter and Linda Murray. New York:
Thomas Yoseloff, 1963.
Chauvin, "Ratti"
Chauvin, Regina. "Six Gospel Dialogues for the Offertory by Lorenzo Ratti."
Studien zur italienisch-deutschen Musikgeschichte 7, Analecta musicologica
9 (1970): 64–77.
Chrysander, "Carissimi"
Chrysander, Friedrich. "Die Oratorien von Carissimi." Leipziger allgemeine
musikalische Zeitung 11 (1876): cols. 67–69, 81–83, 113–15, 129–32,
145–47.
Chrysander, "Jephta"
———. "Das Oratorium Jephta von Carissimi." Leipziger allgemeine
musikalische Zeitung 13 (1878): cols. 337–39, 353–55, 369–71, 385–88.

Cioni, *Bibliografia*
Cioni, Alfredo. *Bibliografia delle sacre rappresentazioni*. Florence: Sansoni Antiquariato, 1961.
Cistellini, "Firenze"
Cistellini, Antonio. "Una pagina di storia religiosa a Firenze nel secolo XVII." *Archivio storico italiano* 125 (1967): 186–245.
Cistellini, *Momenti*
———. *Momenti gaudiosi e dolorosi della storia di San Firenze*. Florence: Robuffo, 1967.
Cistellini, "Oratorio"
———. "I primordi dell'Oratorio filippino in Firenze." *Archivio storico italiano* 126 (1968): 191–285.
Cistellini, *San Firenze*
[———.] *San Firenze dopo tre secoli e un'alluvione*. Florence: Robuffo, 1969.
Clérambault, *Histoire*
Clérambault, Louis-Nicolas. *L'Histoire de la femme adultère*. Edited by Donald H. Foster. Harmoniae musarum, no. CMC–104. Macomb, Ill.: Roger Dean, 1974.
Cohen, A., "Ouvrard-Nicaise"
Cohen, Albert. "The Ouvrard-Nicaise Correspondence (1663–93): A Glimpse into Attitudes of the French Baroque," *Music and Letters* 56 (1975): 356–63.
Cohen, G., *Mis en scène*
Cohen, Gustav. *Histoire de mis en scène dans le théâtre religieux française du moyen age*. Rev. ed. Paris: Honoré Champion, 1926.
Comelli, *Bologna*
C[omelli], G[iovanni] B[attista]. *L'Oratorio in Bologna: Note storiche per ricordo del terzo solenne centenario della morte S. Filippo Neri, anno MDCCCXCV*. Bologna: Mareggiani, 1895.
ConM
Musikgeschichtliche Abteilung des Deutschen Historischen Instituts in Rom, ed. *Concentus musicus*. Cologne: Arno Volk Verlag Hans Gerig, 1973–. Vol. 3, *Sacrae concertationes*, by Domenico Mazzocchi, edited by Wolfgang Witzenmann, 1975.
Coppola, *Poesia*
Coppola, Domenico. *La poesia religiosa del secolo XV*. Biblioteca dell' "Archivium Romanicum," ser. 1, vol. 68. Florence: Leo S. Olschki, 1963.
Coppola, *Rappresentazioni*
———, ed. *Sacre rappresentazioni del sec. XIV*. Biblioteca dell' "Archivium Romanicum," ser. 1, vol. 56. Florence: Leo S. Olschki, 1959.
Crescimbeni, *Historia*
Crescimbeni, Giovan Mario. *L'historia della volgar poesia*. 6 vols. 3d ed. Venice: Lorenzo Basegio, 1730–31.
Crussard, *Charpentier*
Crussard, Claude. *Un musicien français oublié: Marc-Antoine Charpentier 1634–1704*. Paris: Floury, 1945.
CS
Concerts spirituels (série ancienne): Documents pour servir à l'histoire de la musique religieuse de concert. Paris: Bureau d'édition de la Schola cantorum, [19–?]. Vol. 3, *Histoires sacrées*, by Marc-Antoine Charpentier, edited by Charles Bordes, n.d.

Culley, *German*

   Culley, Thomas D., S. J. *A Study of the Musicians Connected with the German College in Rome during the 17th Century and of Their Activities in Northern Europe*. Sources and Studies for the History of the Jesuits, vol. 2, Jesuits and Music, vol. 1. St. Louis, Mo.: Jesuit Historical Institute, St. Louis University, 1970.

Culley, "Influence"

   ————. "The Influence of the German College in Rome on Music in German-Speaking Countries during the Sixteenth and Seventeenth Centuries." *Studien zur italienisch-deutschen Musikgeschichte 6, Analecta musicologica* 7 (1969): 1–35.

D'Accone, "Chapels"

   D'Accone, Frank A. "The Musical Chapels at the Florentine Cathedral and Baptistry during the First Half of the 16th Century." *Journal of the American Musicological Society* 24 (1971): 1–50.

Damerini, "Bononcini"

   Damerini, Adelmo. "Le due 'Maddalene' di Giovanni Bononcini." *Collectanea historiae musicae* 2 (1957): 115–25.

Damerini, "Giuseppe"

   ————. "La morte di San Giuseppe." In *G. Pergolesi (1710– 36)*, Accademia musicale chigiana, Settimana musicale senese, [no. 4], pp. 63–70. Siena: Ticci, 1942.

Damerini, "Oratorio"

   ————. "L'oratorio musicale nel seicento dopo Carissimi." *Rivista musicale italiana* 55 (1953): 149–63.

Damilano, *Ancina*

   Damilano, Piero. *Giovenale Ancina: Musicista filippino (1545–1604)*. Florence: Leo S. Olschki, 1956.

D'Ancona, *Origini*

   D'Ancona, Alessandro. *Origini del teatro italiano*. 2 vols. 2d ed. Turin: Ermano Loescher, 1891.

Daniel-Rops, *Catholic*

   Petiot, Jules Charles Henri [Daniel-Rops, Henri]. *History of the Church of Christ*. 10 vols. London: J. M. Dent & Sons, 1961–67. Vol. 5, *The Catholic Reformation*, translated by John Warrington, 1962.

Daniels, "Stradella"

   Daniels, David W. "Alessandro Stradella's Oratorio *San Giovanni Battista*: A Modern Edition and Commentary." 2 vols. Ph.D. dissertation, State University of Iowa, 1963.

Dardo, "Ariosti"

   Dardo, Gianluigi. "'La Passione' di Attilio Ariosti." *Chigiana: Rassegna annuale di studi musicologici* 23 (n.s. 3, 1966): 59–87.

Dardo, "Felice Anerio"

   ————. "Felice Anerio e la Congregazione dell'Oratorio." *Chigiana: Rassegna annuale di studi musicologici* 21 (n.s. 1, 1964): 3–18.

Dean, *Oratorios*

   Dean, Winton. *Handel's Dramatic Oratorios and Masques*. London: Oxford University Press, 1959.

Della Valle, "Musica"

   Della Valle, Pietro. "Della musica dell'età nostra che non è punto inferiore, anzi migliore di quella dell'età passata." In *Le origini del melodramma: Testimonianze dei contemporanei*, edited by Angelo Solerti, pp. 148–79. Turin: Fratelli Bocca, 1903.

Dent, "Laudi"
  Dent, Edward J. "The Laudi Spirituali in the XVIth and XVIIth Centuries."
    Proceedings of the Musical Association 43 (1916–17): 63–92.
Dickens, *Counter Reformation*
  Dickens, Arthur Geoffrey. *The Counter Reformation*. London: Thames and
    Hudson, 1968.
Dietz, "Stradella"
  Dietz, Hanns-Bertold. "Musikalische Struktur und Architektur im Werke Ales-
    sandro Stradellas." *Studien zur italienisch-deutschen Musikgeschichte* 7,
    Analecta musicologica 9 (1970): 78–93.
Dizionario biografico
  Dizionario biografico degli italiani. 18 vols. to date. Rome: Istituto della Encic-
    lopedia Italiana, 1960–.
Downes, "J. C. Bach"
  Downes, Edward O. D. "The Operas of Johann Christian Bach as a Reflection
    of the Dominant Trends in Opera Seria 1750–1780." 3 vols. Ph.D. disserta-
    tion, Harvard University, 1958.
DT
  Chrysander, Friedrich, ed. *Denkmäler der Tonkunst*. 6 vols. Bergedorf bei
    Hamburg: H. Weissenborn, Expedition der Denkmäler, 1869–71. Vol. 2,
    *Giacomo Carissimi's Werke, Abteilung 1: Oratorien (Jephthe, Judicium
    Salomonis, Baltazar, Jonas)*, 1869.
Ecorcheville, *Catalogue*
  Ecorcheville, Jules. *Catalogue du fonds de musique de la Bibliothèque
    Nationale*. Publications annexes de la Société Internationale de Musique. 8
    vols. Paris: Terquem, 1910–14.
Einstein, *Madrigal*
  Einstein, Alfred. *The Italian Madrigal*. 3 vols. 1949. Reprint, with the texts of
    the madrigals in vol. 3 edited and translated by Antonio Illiano and Howard
    E. Smither. Princeton, N.J.: Princeton University Press, 1971.
Eisley, *Savioni*
  Eisley, Irving. *Mario Savioni*. The Wellesley Edition, Cantata Index Series, no.
    2. [Wellesley, Mass.]: Wellesley College, 1964.
Elwert, "Barocklyrik"
  Elwert, W. Theodor. "Zur Charakteristik der italienischen Barocklyrik."
    Romanistisches Jahrbuch 3 (1950): 421–98.
Elwert, *Poesia*
  ———. *La poesia lirica italiana del seicento: Studio sullo stile barocco*. Flor-
    ence: Leo S. Olschki, [1967].
Enciclopedia d. mus.
  Enciclopedia della musica. 4 vols. Milan: Ricordi, 1963.
Enciclopedia d. spet.
  D'Amico, Silvio, ed. *Enciclopedia dello spettacolo*. 10 vols., 1 supp. Rome: Le
    Maschere, 1954–62.
Erythraeus, *Pinacotheca*
  Rossi, Giovanni Vittoria. [Erythraeus, Ianus Nicius]. *Pinacotheca tertia im-
    aginum virorum aliqua ingenii & eruditionis fama illustrium*. Cologne:
    Iodocum Kalcovium & Socios, 1648.
Ewerhart, "Händel-Handschriften"
  Ewerhart, Rudolf. "Die Händel-Handschriften der Santini-Bibliothek in Müns-
    ter." *Händel-Jahrbuch* 6 (1960): 111–61.

Ewerhart, "Resurrezione"
———. "New Sources for Handel's 'La Resurrezione.'" *Music and Letters* 41 (1960): 127–35.

Fabbri, *Scarlatti*
Fabbri, Mario. *Alessandro Scarlatti e il Principe Ferdinando de' Medici*. Historiae musicae cultores biblioteca, vol. 16. Florence: Leo S. Olschki, 1961.

Fabbri, "Torna"
———. "Torna alla luce la partitura autografa dell'oratorio 'Il primo omicidio' di Alessandro Scarlatti." *Chigiana: Rassegna annuale di studi musicologici* 23 (n.s. 3, 1961): 245–64.

Fehr, *Zeno*
Fehr, Max. *Apostolo Zeno (1668–1750) und seine Reform des Operntextes*. Zurich: A. Tschopp, 1912.

Felder, *Reimofficien*
Felder, Hilarin. *Die liturgischen Reimofficien auf die Heiligen Franciscus und Antonius gedichtet und componiert durch Fr. Julian von Speier*. Fribourg, Switzerland: Universitaets-Buchhandlung (B. Veith). 1901.

Fellerer, "Council"
Fellerer, Karl G. "Church Music and the Council of Trent." *The Musical Quarterly* 39 (1953): 576–94.

Flower, *Handel*
Flower, Newman. *George Frideric Handel: His Personality and His Times*. Rev. ed. London: Cassell, 1959.

Fogaccia, *Legrenzi*
Fogaccia, Piero. *Giovanni Legrenzi*. Bergamo: Orobiche, [1954].

Foster, "Oratorio"
Foster, Donald F. "The Oratorio in Paris in the 18th Century." *Acta musicologica* 47 (1975): 67–133.

Frati, "Giunte"
Frati, Lodovico. "Giunte agli 'Inizii di antiche poesie italiane religiose e morali' a cura di Annibale Tenneroni." *Archivium romanicum* 1 (1917): 441–80; 2 (1918): 185–207, 325–43; 3 (1919): 62–94.

Freeman, "Zeno"
Freeman, Robert. "Apostolo Zeno's Reform of the Libretto." *Journal of the American Musicological Society* 21 (1968): 321–41.

Frutaz, *Piante*
Frutaz, Amato Pietro, ed. *Le piante di Roma*. 3 vols. Rome: Istituto di Studi Romani, 1962.

Furttenbach, *Itinerarium*
Furttenbach, Joseph. *Newes itinerarium Italie*. Ulm: Jonam Saurn, 1627.

Fux, *Werke*
Fux, Johann Joseph. *Sämtliche Werke*. Edited by the Johann-Joseph-Fux-Gesellschaft, Graz. Ser. 4, *Oratorien*. Kassel: Bärenreiter, 1959–.

Gallico, "Caldara"
Gallico, Claudio. "'Santa Francesca Romana' di Caldara." *Chigiana: Rassegna annuali di studi musicologici* 26–27 (n.s. 6–7, 1971): 415–30.

Gasbarri, *Oratorio fil.*
Gasbarri, Carlo. *L'oratorio filippino (1552–1952)*. Rome: Istituto di Studi Romani, 1957.

Gasbarri, *Oratorio rom.*
———. *L'oratorio romano dal cinquecento al novecento*. Rome: n.p., 1962.

Gasbarri, *Spirito*
———. *Lo spirito dell'Oratorio di S. Filippo Neri.* Brescia: Morcelliana,
1949.
Gasbarri, *La visita*
Lazzarini, Andrea, and Gasbarri, Carlo. *La spettacolarità del "Gaudium"; La
visita delle sette chiese.* Rome: Fratelli Palombi, 1947.
Gastoué, "Charpentier"
Gastoué, Amadée. "Notes sur les manuscrits et sur quelques oeuvres de M.-A.
Charpentier." In *Mélanges de musicologie offerts à M. Lionel de la Lauren-
cie*, Publications de la Société Française de Musicologie, ser. 2, vols. 3–4, pp.
153–64. Paris: E. Droz, 1933.
Ghisi, "Carissimi"
Ghisi, Frederico. "The Oratorios of Giacomo Carissimi in the Hamburg
Staatsbibliothek." In *Kongress-Bericht, Gesellschaft für Musikforschung,
Lüneburg, 1950*, edited by Hans Albrecht, Helmuth Osthoff, and Walter
Wiora, pp. 103–7. Kassel: Bärenreiter, n.d.
Ghislanzoni, "Oratori"
Ghislanzoni, Alberto. "Tre oratori e tre cantate morali di Luigi Rossi ritrovati
nella Biblioteca Vaticana." *Revue belge de musicologie* 9 (1955): 3–11.
Ghislanzoni, *Rossi*
———. *Luigi Rossi.* Milan: Fratelli Bocca, 1954.
Gianturco, "Oratorios"
Gianturco, Carolyn. "The Oratorios of Alessandro Stradella." *Proceedings of
the Royal Musical Association*, in press.
Giazotto, *Poesia*
Giazotto, Remo. *Poesia melodrammatica e pensiero critico nel settecento.* Mi-
lan: Fratelli Bocca, 1952.
Giazotto, *Stradella*
———. *Vita di Alessandro Stradella.* 2 vols. Milan: Curci, 1962.
Giazotto, *Vivaldi*
Giazotto, Remo. *Antonio Vivaldi.* Turin: Edizioni RAI Radiotelevisione
Italiana, 1973.
Ginhart, *Kunstgeschichte*
Ginhart, Karl. *Wiener Kunstgeschichte.* Vienna: Paul Neff, 1948.
Gnerghi, *Teatro*
Gnerghi, Gualtiero. *Il teatro gesuitico ne' suoi primordi a Roma.* Rome:
Officina Poligrafica, 1907.
Goldschmidt, *Oper*
Goldschmidt, Hugo. *Studien zur Geschichte der italienischen Oper im 17. Jah-
rhundert.* 2 vols. Leipzig: Breitkopf & Härtel, 1901–4.
Grace, "Marazzoli"
Grace, Michael D. "Marco Marazzoli and the Development of the Latin
Oratorio." Ph.D. dissertation, Yale University, 1974.
Grandi, *Croce*
Grandi, Marcello de. *Benedetto Croce e il seicento.* Milan: C. Marzorati,
[1962].
Griffin, "Colonna"
Griffin, Julia Ann. "Giovanni Paolo Colonna: His Oratorios and Late
Seventeenth-Century Oratorio Style in Bologna and Modena." Ph.D. disser-
tation, University of North Carolina at Chapel Hill, in progress.
Grottron, *Mainz*
Grottron, Adam. *Mainzer Musikgeschichte von 1500 bis 1800.* Beiträge der
Stadt Mainz, vol. 18. Mainz: Stadtbibliothek, 1959.

Grout, *Opera*
> Grout, Donald J. *A Short History of Opera.* 2d ed. New York: Columbia University Press, 1965.

Grove-5
> Blom, Eric, ed. *Grove's Dictionary of Music and Musicians.* 9 vols. and 1 supp. 5th ed. London: Macmillan; New York: St. Martin's Press, 1954–61.

Gruber, *Sepolcro*
> Gruber, Gernot. *Das Wiener Sepolcro und Johann Joseph Fux: I. Teil.* Graz: Johann-Joseph-Fux-Gesselschaft, Institut der Universität Graz, 1972.

Guibert, *Jesuits*
> Guibert, Joseph de, S. J. *The Jesuits, Their Spiritual Doctrine ana Practice: A Historical Study.* Translated by William J. Young, S. J. Edited by George E. Ganss, S. J. [St. Louis]: Institute of Jesuit Sources; Chicago: Loyola University Press, 1964.

Haas, "Orchesterteilung"
> Haas, Robert. "Dreifache Orchesterteilung im Wiener Sepolcro." In *Festschrift Adolf Koczirz zum 60. Geburtstag,* edited by Robert Haas and Joseph Zuth, pp. 8–10. Vienna: E. Strache, [1930].

Haberl, "Anerio"
> Haberl, Franz X. "Giovanni Francesco Anerio." *Kirchenmusikalisches Jahrbuch* 1 (1886): 51–65.

Hadamowsky, *Barocktheater*
> Hadamowsky, Franz. *Barocktheater am Wiener Kaiserhof, mit einem Spielplan (1625–1740).* Vienna: A. Sexl, 1955. Offprint from the *Jahrbuch der Gesellschaft für Wiener Theaterforschung, 1951–52.*

Hager, *S. Maria*
> Hager, Helmut. *S. Maria dell'Orazione e Morte.* Le chiese di Roma illustrate, vol. 79. Rome: Edizioni "Roma," Marietti, 1964.

Hale, *Renaissance*
> Hale, John Rigby. *Renaissance Europe: Individual and Society, 1480–1520.* History of Europe, edited by J. H. Plumb. New York: Harper & Row, 1971.

HAM
> Davison, Archibald T., and Apel, Willi, eds. *Historical Anthology of Music.* 2 vols. Cambridge, Mass.: Harvard University Press, 1947–59.

Handel, *Werke*
> Händel, Georg Friedrich. *Werke.* Edited by Friedrich Chrysander, 96 vols. and 6 supps. Vol. 49 not published. Leipzig: Ausgabe der Deutschen Händel-Gesellschaft, 1858–1902.

Hansell, "Ottoboni"
> Hansell, Sven Hostrup. "Orchestral Practice at the Court of Cardinal Pietro Ottoboni." *Journal of the American Musicological Society* 19 (1966): 398–403.

Harney, *Jesuits*
> Harney, Martin Patrick. *The Jesuits in History: The Society of Jesus through Four Centuries.* New York: America Press, 1941.

Haskell, *Patrons*
> Haskell, Francis. *Patrons and Painters: A Study in the Relations between Italian Art and Society in the Age of the Baroque.* London: Chatto & Windus, 1963.

Hawkins, *History*
> Hawkins, John. *A General History of the Science and Practice of Music.* 5 vols. London: T. Payne, 1776.

Hempel, *Art*
    Hempel, Eberhard. *Baroque Art and Architecture in Central Europe: Germany, Austria, Switzerland, Hungary, Czechoslovakia, Poland.* The Pelican History of Art, edited by Nikolaus Pevsner, vol. Z22. Harmondsworth, Middlesex: Penguin Books, 1965.
Hicks, "Resurrezione"
    Hicks, Anthony Charles. "Handel's *La Resurrezione.*" *Musical Times* 110 (1969): 145–48.
Hill, "Veracini"
    Hill, John Walter. "Veracini in Italy." *Music and Letters* 56 (1975): 257–76.
Hitchcock, "Comédie-Française"
    Hitchcock, H. Wiley. "Marc-Antoine Charpentier and the Comédie-Française." *Journal of the American Musicological Society* 14 (1971): 255–381.
Hitchcock, "Oratorios" (art.)
    ————. "The Latin Oratorios of Marc-Antoine Charpentier." *The Musical Quarterly* 41 (1955): 41–65.
Hitchcock, "Oratorios" (diss.)
    ————. "The Latin Oratorios of Marc-Antoine Charpentier." 3 vols. Ph.D. dissertation. University of Michigan, 1954.
HMT
    Eggebrecht, Hans Heinrich, ed. *Handwörterbuch der musikalischen Terminologie.* Wiesbaden: Franz Steiner, [1972–].
Hobbs, "Anerio"
    Hobbs, Wayne C. "Giovanni Francesco Anerio's *Teatro armonico spirituale di madrigali:* A Contribution to the Early History of the Oratorio." 2 vols. Ph.D. dissertation, Tulane University, 1971.
Holmes, "Orontea"
    Holmes, William C. "Giacinto Andrea Cicognini's and Antonio Cesti's *Orontea* (1649)." In *New Looks at Italian Opera: Essays in Honor of Donald J. Grout,* edited by William A. Austin, pp. 108–32. Ithaca, N.Y.: Cornell University Press, 1968.
Huelsen, *Chiese*
    Huelsen, Christian. *Le chiese di Roma nel medio evo: Cataloghi ed appunti.* Florence: Leo S. Olschki, 1927.
Huygens, *Pathodia*
    Huygens, Constantijn. *Pathodia sacra et profana unae voci basso continuo comitante.* Edited by Frits Noske, with the collaboration of Noelle Barker. Amsterdam: North-Holland Publishing Co.; Kassel: Bärenreiter, 1957.
IISM-3
    Istituto Italiano per la Storia della Musica, presso L'Accademia Nazionale di Storia della Musica. *Monumenti 3:* [*Giacomo Carissimi: Oratorios and Related Works*]. Vol. 1 edited by Carlo Dall'Argine, Federico Ghisi, and Roberto Lupi. Later vols. edited by Lino Bianchi. Rome: n. p., 1951–.
IMAMI
    Istituzioni e monumenti dell'arte musicale italiana. 7 vols. Milan: Ricordi, 1931–41. Vol. 5, *L'oratorio dei Filippini e la scuola musicale di Napoli,* edited by Guido Pannain, 1934.
Jacopone, *Laudi*
    Jacopone da Todi. *Laudi, trattato e detti.* Edited by Franca Ageno. Florence: Felice Le Monnier, 1953.

Jamison, *Italy*

Jamison, Evelyn M.; Ady, Cecilia M.; Vernon, Katherine D.; and Terry, C. Sanford. *Italy Mediaeval and Modern: A History*. Oxford: Clarendon Press, 1917.

Jander, "Concerto"

Jander, Owen. "Concerto Grosso Instrumentation in Rome in the 1660's and 1670's." *Journal of the American Musicological Society* 21 (1968): 168–80.

Jander, "Stradella"

————. "Alessandro Stradella and His Minor Dramatic Works." 2 vols. Ph.D. dissertation, Harvard University, 1962.

Jander, Review

————. Review of Giazotto, *Stradella*. *Journal of the American Musicological Society* 17 (1964): 222–24.

Janelle, *Catholic Reformation*

Janelle, Pierre. *The Catholic Reformation*. Milwaukee: Bruce Publishing Co., 1949.

Jeppesen, *Laude*

Jeppesen, Knud, ed. *Die mehrstimmige italienische Laude um 1500: Das 2. Laudenbuch des Ottaviano dei Petrucci (1507) in Verbindung mit einer Auswahl mehrstimmiger Lauden aus dem 1. Laudenbuch Petrucci's (1508) und aus verschiedenen gleichzeitigen Manuskripten*. Leipzig: Breitkopf & Härtel, 1935.

Jervis, *Corfù*

Jervis, Henry Jervis-White. *History of the Island of Corfù, and of the Republic of the Ionian Islands*. 1852. Reprint. Chicago: Argonaut, 1970.

Kade, *Passionskomposition*

Kade. Otto. *Die ältere Passionskomposition bis zum Jahre 1631*. 1893. Reprint. Hildesheim: Georg Olms, 1971.

Kidd, *Counter-Reformation*

Kidd, Beresford J. *The Counter-Reformation*. London: Society for Promoting Christian Knowledge, 1933.

Kircher, *Musurgia*

Kircher, Athanasius. *Musurgia universalis: Sive ars magna consoni et dissoni in X. libros digesta*. 2 vols. in 1. Rome: Haerides F. Corbelletti, 1650.

Kirkendale, U., *Caldara*

Kirkendale, Ursula. *Antonio Caldara: Sein Leben und seine venezianisch-römischen Oratorien*. Wiener Musikwissenschaftliche Beiträge, vol. 6. Graz: Hermann Böhlaus Nachf., 1966.

Kirkendale, U., "Ruspoli"

————. "The Ruspoli Documents on Handel." *Journal of the American Musicological Society* 20 (1967): 222–73.

Kirkendale, W., "Cavalieri"

Kirkendale, Warren. "Emilio de' Cavalieri, a Roman Gentleman at the Florentine Court." *Quadrivium* 12 (1971): 9–21.

Köchel, *Fux*

Köchel, Ludwig Ritter von. *Johann Josef Fux: Hofcompositor und Hofkapellmeister der Kaiser Leopold I., Josef I. und Karl VI. von 1698 bis 1740*. Vienna: Alfred Hölder (Beck'sche Universitäts-Buchhandlung), 1872.

Kolneder, "Aria-Concerto"

Kolneder, Walter. "Vivaldi's Aria-Concerto." *Deutsches Jahrbuch der Musikwissenschaft* 9 (1964): 17–27.

Kolneder, *Vivaldi*
    _____. *Antonio Vivaldi: His Life and Work*. Translated by Bill Hopkins. Los
    Angeles and Berkeley: University of California Press, 1970.
Kramer, "Jesuitendrama"
    Kramer, Waltraute. "Die Musik im Wiener Jesuitendrama von 1677–1711."
    Ph.D. dissertation, University of Vienna, 1961.
Kretzschmar, "Venetianische"
    Kretzschmar, Hermann. "Die venetianische Oper und die Werke Cavalli's und
    Cesti's." *Vierteljahrsschrift für Musikwissenschaft* 12 (1892): 1–76.
Kroyer, "Dialog"
    Kroyer, Theodor. "Dialog und Echo in der alten Chormusik." *Jahrbuch der
    Musikbibliothek Peters* 16 (1909): 13–32.
Labat, *Voyages*
    Labat, [Jean Baptiste]. *Voyages du P. Labat de l'Ordre des FF. Precheurs en
    Espagne et en Italie*. 8 vols. in 4. Amsterdam: Aux dépens de la Compagnie,
    1731.
Landau, *Literatur*
    Landau, Marcus. *Die italienische Literatur am österreichischen Hofe*. Vienna:
    Carl Gerold's Sohn, 1879.
Lang, *Handel*
    Lang, Paul Henry. *George Frideric Handel*. New York: W. W. Norton, 1966.
Lang, *Western*
    _____. *Music in Western Civilization*. New York: W. W. Norton, 1941.
La Roche, "Bertali"
    La Roche, Charles. "Antonio Bertali als Opern- und Oratorienkomponist."
    Ph.D. dissertation, University of Vienna, 1919.
Lassels, *Voyage*
    Lassels, Richard. *The Voyage of Italy, or a Compleat Journey through Italy*.
    Paris: [Vincent du Moutier], 1670.
Lasso, *Werke*
    Lasso, Orlando di. *Sämtliche Werke*. Edited by Franz Xavier Haberl and Adolf
    Sandberger. 21 vols. Leipzig: Breitkopf & Härtel, 1894–1926.
Lasso, *Werke*-N
    Lasso, Orlando di. *Sämtliche Werke*. New series. Edited by the Académie
    Royale de Belgique and the Bayerische Akademie der Wissenschaften. Kas-
    sel: Bärenreiter, 1956–.
Laude spirituali
    *Laude spirituali di Feo Belcari, di Lorenzo de' Medici, di Francesco D'Albizzo,
    di Castellano Castellani, e di altri, comprese nelle quattro più antiche rac-
    colte*. Florence: Molini e Cecchi, 1863.
Launay, *Anthologie*
    Launay, Denise, ed. *Anthologie du motet latin polyphonique en France
    (1609–1661)*. Publications de la Société Française de Musicologie, ser. 1,
    vol. 17. Paris: Heugel et Cie., 1963.
Lazarini, *Oratorii*
    Lazarini, Sebastiano. *Sacra melodia di oratorii musicali*. Rome: Bartolomeo
    Lupardi, 1678.
Legrenzi, *Mortali*
    Legrenzi, Giovanni. *Mortali apprendete (madrigale)*. Edited by Jill Tyler. Mas-
    terworks of Yesterday, series A, edited by Albert Seay. Colorado Springs,
    Colo.: Colorado College Music Press, 1960.

Legrenzi, *Quanto*

———. *Quanto delirio (madrigale)*. Edited by Jill Tyler. Masterworks of Yesterday, series A, edited by Albert Seay. Colorado Springs, Colo.: Colorado College Music Press, 1961.

Leich, *Frigimelica Roberti*

Leich, Karl. *Girolamo Frigimelica Robertis Libretti (1694–1708): Ein Beitrag insbesondere zur Geschichte des Opernlibrettos in Venedig*. Schriften über Musik, vol. 26. Munich: Emil Katzbichler, 1972.

Liess, "Musikerlisten"

Liess, Andreas. "Materialien zur römischen Musikgeschichte des Seicento: Musikerlisten des Oratorio San Marcello 1664–1725." *Acta musicologica* 29 (1957): 137–71.

Liess, "Oratorienlibretti"

———. "Die Sammlung der Oratorienlibretti (1679–1725) und der restliche Musikbestand des Fondo San Marcello in der Biblioteca Vaticana in Rom." *Acta musicologica* 31 (1959): 63–80.

Liuzzi, *Lauda*

Liuzzi, Ferdinando. *La lauda e i primordi della melodia italiana*. 2 vols. [Rome]: La Libreria della Stato, [1935].

Liuzzi, *Musicisti*

———. *I musicisti italiani in Francia*. L'opera del genio italiano all'estero, series 2. Rome: Edizioni d'Arte Danesi, 1946. Vol. 1, *Dalle origini al secolo XVII*.

Lockwood, *Counter-Reformation*

Lockwood, Lewis. *The Counter-Reformation and the Masses of Vincenzo Ruffo*. Studi di musica veneta, vol. 2. [Vienna]: Universal Edition, [1970].

Lockwood, "Ruffo"

———. "Vincenzo Ruffo and the Musical Reform after the Council of Trent." *The Musical Quarterly* 43 (1957): 342–71.

Lorenz, *Scarlatti*

Lorenz, Alfred. *Alessandro Scarlattis Jugendoper*. 2 vols. Augsburg: Benno Filser, 1927.

Loschelder, "Carissimi"

Loschelder, Josef. "Neue Beiträge zu einer Biographie Giacomo Carissimis." *Archiv für Musikforschung* 5 (1940): 220–29.

Lowe, *Charpentier*

Lowe, Robert W. *Marc-Antoine Charpentier et l'opera de collège*. Paris: G.-P. Maisonneuve & Larose, 1966.

Luin, "Bologna"

Luin, Elizabeth J. "La musica sacra alla fine del secolo XVII a Bologna e Modena." *Musica d'oggi: Rassegna di vita e di coltura musicale* 14 (1932): 151–57.

Luin, *Repertorio*

———. *Repertorio dei libri musicali di S. A. S. Francesco II d'Este nell'Archivio di Stato di Modena*. Florence: Leo S. Olschki, 1936. Offprint from *Bibliografia*, vol. 38.

Lully, *Oeuvres*

Lully, Jean-Baptiste. *Oeuvres complètes*. Edited under the direction of Henry Prunières. 10 vols. Paris: Éditions de la Revue Musicale, 1930–39.

Lustig, "Oratorii"

Lustig, Renzo. "Saggio bibliografico degli oratorii stampati a Firenze dal 1690 al 1725." *Note d'archivio per la storia musicale* 14 (1937): 57–64, 109–16, 244–50.

McGhee, "Quem quaeritis"

    McGhee, Timothy J. "The Liturgical Placements of the *Quem quaritis* Dialogue." *Journal of the American Musicological Society* 29 (1976): 1–29.

McCrickard, "Stradella"

    McCrickard, Eleanor F. "Alessandro Stradella's Instrumental Music: A Critical Edition with Historical and Analytical Commentary." 2 vols. Ph.D. dissertation, University of North Carolina at Chapel Hill, 1971.

Maggi-Maupin-Losi, *Roma*

    Maggi, Giovanni. *Roma al tempo di Urbano VIII. La pianta di Roma Maggi-Maupin-Losi del 1625, riprodotta da uno dei due esemplari completi finora conosciuti.* Edited by the Vatican Library, with an introduction by Francesco Ehrle, S. J. Le piante maggiori di Roma del sec. XVI e XVII, riprodotta in fototipia a cura della Biblioteca Vaticana, no. 4. Rome: Danesi, 1915.

    Maggini, Emilio. *Lucca: Biblioteca del Seminario. Catalogo delle musiche stampate e manoscritte del fondo antico.* Biblioteca musicale: Collana di cataloghi e bibliografie, edited by Claudio Sartori, vol. 3. Milan: Istituto Editoriale Italian, 1965.

Mâle, *L'Art*

    Mâle, Émile. *L'Art religieux après le Concile de Trente: Étude sur l'iconographie de la fin du XVIe siècle, du XVIIe siècle; Italie, France, Espagne, Flandres.* Paris: Armand Colin, 1932.

Marbach, *Carmina*

    Marbach, Karl, ed. *Carmina scriptuarum silicet antiphonas et responsoria ex Sancto Scripturae fonte in libros liturgicos Sanctae Ecclesiae Romanae.* 1907. Reprint. Hildesheim: Georg Olms, 1963.

Marciano, *Oratorio*

    Marciano, Giovanni. *Memori historiche della Congregatione dell'Oratorio.* 5 vols. Naples: De Bonis, Stampatore Arcivescovale, 1693–1702.

Marpurg, *Singcomposition*

    Marpurg, Friedrich Wilhelm. *Anleitung zur Singcomposition.* Berlin: Gottlieb August Lange, 1758.

Marx, "Ottoboni"

    Marx, Hans Joachim. "Die Musik am Hofe Pietro Kardinal Ottobonis unter Arcangelo Corelli." *Studien zur italienisch-deutschen Musikgeschichte* 5, *Analecta musicologica* 5 (1968): 104–77.

Massenkeil, "Oratorische"

    Massenkeil, Günther. "Die oratorische Kunst in den lateinischen Historien und Oratorien Giacomo Carissimis." Ph.D. dissertation, Johannes Gutenberg-Universität, Mainz, 1952.

Massenkeil, *Oratorium*

    ———. *Das Oratorium.* Das Musikwerk, no. 37. Cologne: Arno Volk Verlag Hans Gerig, 1970.

Massenkeil, *Oratorium*-Eng.

    ———. *The Oratorio.* Translated by A. C. Howie. Anthology of Music, no. 37. Cologne: Arno Volk Verlag Hans Gerig, 1970.

Massenkeil, "Wiederholungsfiguren"

    ———. "Die Wiederholungsfiguren in den Oratorien Giacomo Carissimis." *Archiv für Musikwissenschaft* 13 (1956): 42–60.

Mattheson, *Ehren-Pforte*

    Mattheson, Johann. *Grundlage einer Ehren-Pforte, woran der tüchtigsten Capellmeister, Componisten, Musikgelehrten, Tonkünstler u. Leben, Werke,*

Verdienste u. erscheinen sollen. Hamburg, 1740. Edited by Max Schneider. Berlin: Kommissionsverlag von Leo Liepmannssohn, 1910.

Maugars, *Response*
Maugars, André. *Response faite à un curieux sur le sentiment de la musique d'Italie, escrit à Rome le premier octobre 1639.* [N.p., n.d.]

Mayer, *Österreich*
Mayer, Franz Martin. *Geschichte Österreichs mit besonderer Rücksicht auf das Kulturleben.* 2 vols. 3d ed. Vienna: Wilhelm Braumüller, 1909.

Meer, *Fux*
Meer, John Henry van der. *Johann Josef Fux als Opernkomponist.* 3 vols. Bilthoven: A. B. Creyghton, 1961.

[Menestrier], *Représentations*
[Menestrier, Claude François]. *Des Représentations en musique anciennes et modernes.* Paris: René Guignard, 1681.

Metastasio, *Opere*
Metastasio, Pietro. *Tutte le opere.* Edited by Bruno Brunelli. 5 vols. Milan: Arnoldo Mondatori, 1943–54.

Metastasio, *Poesie*
————. *Poesie del signor abate Pietro Metastasio.* 9 vols. Paris: La Vedova Quillau, 1755.

Meyer, "Offizium"
Meyer, Kathi. "Das Offizium und seine Beziehung zum Oratorium." *Archiv für Musikwissenschaft* 3 (1921): 371–404.

Meyer-Baer, "Conservatories"
Meyer-Baer, Kathi. "Communications: [The Conservatories of Venice]." *Journal of the American Musicological Society* 24 (1971): 139–40.

Meyer-Baer, "Office"
————. "From the Office of the Hours to the Musical Oratorio." *Music Review* 32 (1971): 156–75.

MGG
Blume, Friedrich, ed. *Die Musik in Geschichte und Gegenwart.* 14 vols. and 1 supp. to date. Kassel: Bärenreiter, 1949–.

Michieli, "Poesie"
Michieli, Armando. "*Le Poesie sacre drammatiche* di Apostolo Zeno." *Giornale storico della letteratura italiana* 95 (1930): 1–33.

Mirolo, *Marino*
Mirolo, James V. *The Poet of the Marvelous: Giambattista Marino.* New York: Columbia University Press, 1963.

Mischiati, "Bologna"
Mischiati, Oscar. "Per la storia dell'Oratorio a Bologna: Tre inventari del 1620, 1622 e 1682." *Collectanea historiae musicae* 3 (1963): 131–70.

Mitjana, *Upsala*
Mitjana, Rafael, and Davidsson, Ake, eds. *Catalogue critique et descriptif des imprimés de musique des XVIe et XVIIe siècles conservés à la Bibliothèque de l'Université Royale d'Upsala.* 3 vols. Upsala: Almquist & Wiksell, 1911–51.

Montalto, *Mecenate*
Montalto, Lina. *Un mecenate in Roma barocca: Il cardinale Benedetto Pamphilj (1653–1730).* Florence: Sansoni, 1955.

Monteverdi, *Opere*
Monteverdi, Claudio. *Tutte le opere.* Edited by G. Francesco Malipiero. 16 vols. Asolo: G. Francesco Malipiero; Vienna: Universal Edition, 1926–42.

Monti, "Bibliografia"
Monti, Gennaro Maria. "Bibliografia della laude." *La bibliofilia: Rivista di storia del libro e delle arti grafiche di bibliografia ed erudizione* 21 (1919–20): 241–57; 22 (1920–21): 288–99; 23 (1921–22): 260–67; 24 (1922–23): 29–40; 25 (1923–24): 71–75, 256–65; 27 (1925–26): 38–46. Reprinted as *Bibliografia della laude con introduzione e appendice*. Florence: Leo S. Olschki, 1925.

Monti, *Confraternite*
————. *Le confraternite medievali dell'alta e media Italia*. Storici antiche e moderni. 2 vols. Venice: "La nuova Italia" Editrice, 1927.

Morichini, *Istituti*
Morichini, Carlo-Luigi. *Degli istituti di carità per la sussistenza e l'educazione dei poveri e dei prigionieri in Roma*. Rev. ed. (3 vols. in 1). Rome: Camerale, 1870.

Mortoft, *Travels*
Mortoft, Francis. *Francis Mortoft: His Book, Being His Travels through France and Italy, 1658–1659*. Edited by Malcolm Letts. 1925. Reprint. London: Krauss, 1967.

Moser, *Evangelium*
Moser, Hans Joachim. *Die mehrstimmige Vertonung des Evangeliums*. Veröffentlichungen der Staatlichen Akademie für Kirchen- und Schulmusik Berlin, vol. 1. 2d ed. 1931. Reprint. Hildesheim: Georg Olms, 1968.

Müller, *Jesuitendrama*
Müller, Johannes, S. J. *Das Jesuitendrama in den Ländern deutscher Zunge vom Anfang (1555) bis zum Hochbarock (1655)*. 2 vols. Augsburg: Benno Filser, 1930.

Müller-Blattau, "Carissimi"
Müller-Blattau, Wendelin. "Untersuchungen zur Kompositionstechnik in den Oratorien Giacomo Carissimis." *Die Musikforschung* 16(1963): 209–23.

Murata, "Operas"
Murata, Margaret Kimiko. "Operas for the Papal Court with Texts by Giulio Rospigliosi." 2 vols. Ph.D. dissertation, University of Chicago, 1975.

Nef, "Charpentier"
Nef, Karl. "Das Petrus-Oratorium von Marc-Antoine Charpentier und die Passion." *Jahrbuch der Musikbibliothek Peters* 37 (1930): 24–31.

Negri, *Zeno*
Negri, Francesco. *La vita di Apostolo Zeno*. Venice: Alvisopoli, 1816.

Neuhaus, "Draghi"
Neuhaus, Max. "Antonio Draghi." *Studien zur Musikwissenschaft* 1 (1913): 104–92.

Nielsen, "Charpentier"
Nielsen, Bodil Ellerup. "Les grands oratorios bibliques de Marc-Antoine Charpentier." In *Dansk aarbog for musikforskning 1966–67*, edited by Nils Schiørring and Søren Sørensen, pp. 29–61.

Olsen, "Bertali"
Olsen, Sharon Stevenson. "Antonio Bertali's 'La strage degl'innocenti': An Edition with Commentary." M.A. thesis, University of Missouri at Columbia, 1972.

Oxford
Hartnoll, Phyllis, ed. *The Oxford Companion to the Theatre*. 3d ed. London: Oxford University Press, 1967.

Ozolins, "Pasquini"
Ozolins, Egils. "The Oratorios of Bernardo Pasquini." Ph.D. dissertation, University of California at Los Angeles, in progress.

Pagano-Bianchi, *Scarlatti*
    Pagano, Roberto, and Bianchi, Lino. *Alessandro Scarlatti*. Turin: Edizioni RAI Radiotelevisione Italiana, 1972.
Palisca, "Alterati"
    Palisca, Claude V. "The Alterati of Florence, Pioneers in the Theory of Dramatic Music." In *New Looks at Italian Opera: Essays in Honor of Donald J. Grout*, edited by William A. Austin, pp. 9–38. Ithaca, N.Y.: Cornell University Press, 1968.
Palisca, *Baroque*
    ———. *Baroque Music*. Englewood Cliffs, N.J.: Prentice-Hall, 1968.
Palisca, "Camerata"
    ———. "The 'Camarata fiorentina': A Reappraisal." *Studi musicali* 1 (1972): 203–36.
Palisca, "Cavalieri"
    ———. "Musical Asides in the Diplomatic Correspondence of Emilio de' Cavalieri." *The Musical Quarterly* 49 (1963): 339–55.
Pancino, *Venezia*
    Pancino, Paolo, comp. *Venezia: S. Maria della Consolazione detta "Della Fava," già sede della Congregazione di S. Filippo Neri. Catalogo del fondo musicale*. Biblioteca musicale: Collana di cataloghi e bibliografie, edited by Claudio Sartori, vol. 6. Milan: Istituto Editoriale Italiano, 1969.
Parrish, *Treasury*
    Parrish, Carl, ed. *A Treasury of Early Music*. New York: W. W. Norton, 1958.
Parry, *Seventeenth*
    Hadow, W. H., ed. *The Oxford History of Music*. 7 vols. 2d ed. London: Oxford University Press, 1929–34. Vol. 3, *The Music of the Seventeenth Century*, by C. Hubert H. Parry, Oxford Clarendon Press, 1902.
Pascher, *Stundengebet*
    Pascher, Joseph. *Das Stundengebet der römischen Kirche*. Munich: Karl Zink, 1954.
Pasquetti, *Oratorio*
    Pasquetti, Guido. *L'oratorio musicale in Italia*. 2d ed. Florence: Successori Le Monnier, 1914.
Pastor, *Popes*
    Pastor, Ludwig, Freiherr von. *The History of the Popes from the Close of the Middle Ages*. Translated from the German. Edited by Frederic I. Antrobus, Ralph F. Kerr, Ernest Graf, and E. F. Peeler. 40 vols. London: Routledge & Kegan Paul; St. Louis: B. Herder, 1938–61.
Pirchegger, *Österreich*
    Pirchegger, Hans, ed. *Mayer-Kaindl Geschichte und Kulturleben Österreichs von 1493 bis 1792: Auf Grundlage der "Geschichte Österreichs" von Franz Martin Mayer und Raimund Kaindl*. 5th ed. Vienna: Wilhelm Braumüller, 1960.
Pirrotta, "Camerata"
    Pirrotta, Nino. "Temperaments and Tendencies in the Florentine Camerata." *The Musical Quarterly* 40 (1954): 169–89.
Pirotta, "Cesti"
    ———. "Tre capitoli su Cesti." In *La scuola romana: G. Carissimi, A. Cesti, M. Marazzoli*, Accademia musicale chigiana, Settimana musicale senese, no. 10, pp. 27–79. Siena: Ticci, 1953.

Policastro, "Catania"
Policastro, Guglielmo. "La cappella musicale del duomo e l'oratorio sacro in Cantania nel '600." *Rivista musicale italiana* 52 (1950): 1–24.

Ponnelle, *Néri*
Ponnelle, Louis, and Bordet, Louis. *Saint Philippe Néri et la société romaine de son temps (1515–1595).* Paris: Bloud & Gay, 1929.

Ponnelle, *Neri*-Eng.
———. *St. Philip Neri and the Roman Society of His Times (1515–1595).* Translated by Ralph Francis Kerr. London: Sheed & Ward, 1932.

Ponnelle, *Neri*-It.
———. *San Filippo Neri e la società romana del suo tempo (1515–1595).* Translated by Tito Casini. Florence: Edizioni Cardinal Ferrari, Libreria Editrice Fiorentina Depositaria, 1931.

Portoghesi, *Borromini*
Portoghesi, Paolo. *The Rome of Borromini: Architecture as Language.* Translated by Barbara Luigia La Penta. New York: G. Braziller, [1968].

Poultney, "Scarlatti"
Poultney, David G. "The Oratorios of Alessandro Scarlatti: Their Lineage, Milieu, and Style." Ph.D. dissertation, University of Michigan, 1968.

Poultney, "Transformation"
———. "Alessandro Scarlatti and the Transformation of Oratorio." *The Musical Quarterly* 59 (1973): 584–601.

Pratella, "Carissimi"
Pratella, F. Balilla. "Giacomo Carissimi et i suoi oratorii." *Rivista musicale italiana* 27 (1920): 1–30.

Preussner, *Uffenbach*
Preussner, Eberhard. *Die musikalischen Reisen des Herrn von Uffenbach: Aus einem Reisetagebuch des Johann Friedrich A. von Uffenbach aus Frankfurt a M. 1712–1716.* Kassel: Bärenreiter, 1949.

Prizer, "Animuccia"
Prizer, William F. "Giovanni Animuccia's *Primo libro delle laudi* (Rome, 1563) and the Beginnings of the Oratorian *Lauda*," in progress.

Procacci, *History*
Procacci, Giuliano. *History of the Italian People.* Translated by Anthony Paul. London: Weidenfeld and Nicolson, 1968.

Processo
Incisa della Rocchetta, Giovanni; Vian, Nello; and Gasbarri, Carlo, eds. *Il primo processo per San Filippo Neri nel codice vaticano latino 3798 e in altri esemplari dell'Archivio dell'Oratorio di Roma.* 4 vols. Studi e testi, vols. 191, 196, 205, and 224. Vatican City: Biblioteca Apostolica Vaticana, 1957–63.

Prunières, "Barberini"
Prunières, Henry. "Les musiciens du Cardinal Antonio Barberini." In *Mélanges de musicologie offerts à M. Lionel de la Laurencie.* Publications de la Société française de musicologie, series 2, vols. 3–4, pp. 117–22. Paris. E. Droz, 1933.

Prunières, *Opéra*
———. *L'Opéra italien en France avant Lulli.* Paris: Librairie Ancienne Honoré Champion, Édouard Champion, 1913.

Quittard, "Bouzignac"
Quittard, Henri. "Un musicien oublié du XVIIe siècle français: G. Bouzignac." *Sammelbände der internationalen Musikgesellschaft* 4 (1905): 356–417.

Quittard, *Du Mont*

———. *Un musicien en France au XVIIe siècle: Henry Du Mont (1610–1684)*. Paris: Société du Mercure de France, 1906.

Raccolta
Raccolta d'oratorii per musica fatti cantare in diversi tempi dall'altezza serenissima di Francesco II, Duca di Modona, Reggio &c. nell'Oratorio di S. Carlo di Modona. 3 vols. Modena: Eredi Soliani, 1689.

Raguenet, *Comparison*
Raguenet, François. *A Comparison between the French and Italian Musick and Operas.* [Translated by J. E. Galliard?] 1709. Reprint. London: Gregg, 1968.

Raugel, *Oratorio*
Raugel, Félix. *L'Oratorio: Forms, écoles et oeuvres musicales.* Paris: Larousse, 1948.

Razzi, *Laudi*
Razzi, Serafino. *Libro primo delle laudi spirituali.* 1563. Reprint. Bibliotheca musica bononiensis, directed by Giuseppe Vecchi, sec. 4, no. 37. Bologna: Forni, 1969.

Reese, *Renaissance*
Reese, Gustave. *Music in the Renaissance.* Rev. ed. New York: W. W. Norton, 1959.

Renker, "Sepolcro"
Renker, Gustav. "Das Wiener Sepolcro." Ph.D. dissertation, University of Vienna, 1913.

Ricci, *Bologna*
Ricci, Corrado. *I teatri di Bologna nei secoli XVII e XVIII: Storia aneddotica.* Bologna: Successori Monti, 1888.

Riemann
Riemann, Hugo. *Riemann Musik Lexikon.* Edited by Wilibald Gurlitt. 3 vols. 12th ed. Mainz: B. Schott's Söhne; New York: Schott Music Corp., 1959–67.

Rinaldi, *Vivaldi*
Rinaldi, Mario. *Antonio Vivaldi.* Milan: Istituto d'Alta Cultura, 1943.

RISM
International Musicological Society and the International Association of Music Libraries. *Répertoire international des sources musicales.* Munich-Duisberg: G. Henle; Kassel: Bärenreiter, 1960–. Series BI, vol. 1, *Recueils imprimés XVIe–XVIIe siècles,* edited by François Lesure, 1960. Series AI, vol. 1, *Einzeldrucke vor 1800,* edited by Karlheinz Schlager, 1971.

Rolandi, *Libretto*
Rolandi, Ulderico. *Il libretto per musica attraverso i tempi.* Rome: Edizioni dell'Ateneo, 1951.

Romita, *Ius*
Romita, Fiorenza. *Ius musicae liturgicae: Dissertatio historica-iuridica.* Turin: Officina Libraria Marietti, 1936.

Roncaglia, *Modena*
Roncaglia, Gino. *La cappella musicale del duomo di Modena.* Historia musicae cultores biblioteca, vol. 5. Florence: Leo S. Olschki, 1957.

Roncaglia, "Scuola"
———. "La scuola musicale modonese." In *Musicisti della scuola emiliana,* Accademia Musicale Chigiana, edited by Adelmo Damerini and Gino Roncaglia, pp. 69–82. Siena: Ticci, 1956.

Rose, "Agazzari"
Rose, Gloria. "Agazzari and the Improvising Orchestra." *Journal of the American Musicological Society* 18 (1965): 382–93.
Rose, "Carissimi"
———. "The Cantatas of Giacomo Carissimi." *The Musical Quarterly* 48 (1962): 204–15.
Rose, "Madrigals"
———. "Polyphonic Italian Madrigals of the Seventeenth Century." *Music and Letters* 47 (1966): 153–59.
Rose, "Portrait"
———. "A Portrait Called Carissimi." *Music and Letters* 51 (1970): 400–403.
Rossi, *Effigie*
Rossi, Giovanni Giacomo de. *Effigie, insignia . . . summorum pontificium et S. R. E. cardinalium.* [Rome, 16—.]
Rotondi, "Opera"
Rotondi, Joseph Emilio. "Literary and Musical Aspects of Roman Opera, 1600–1650." Ph.D. dissertation, University of Pennsylvania, 1959.
Russo, "Metastasio"
Russo, Luigi. "Pietro Metastasio." *Annali della R. Scuola Normale Superiore di Pisa: Filosofia e filologia* 27 (1915): 1–260.
Sandberger, "Christine"
Sandberger, Adolf. "Beziehungen der Königen Christine von Schweden zur italienischen Oper und Musik, insbesondere zu M. A. Cesti. Mit einem Anhang über Cestis innsbrucker Aufenthalt." *Bulletin de la Société "Union Musicologique"* 5 (1925): 121–73.
Sansovino, *Venetia*
Sansovino, Francesco. *Venetia città nobilissima, et singolare, descritta in XIIII libri. . . . Con aggiunta di tutte le cose notabili della stessa città, fatte, & occorse dall'anno 1580 fino al presente 1663 da D. Giustiniano Martinioni.* Venice: Steffano Curti, 1663.
Santi, *Quarant'ore*
Santi, Angelo de. *L'orazione delle quarant'ore e i tempi di calamità e di guerra.* Rome: "Civiltà Cattolica," 1919.
Sartori, *Carissimi*
Sartori, Claudio. *Giacomo Carissimi: Catalogo delle opere attribuite.* Milan: Instituto Finanziario per l'Arte, Finarte, 1975.
Saville, *Clari*
Saville, Eugenia. *Giovanni Carlo Maria Clari, Musician of Tuscany.* In progress.
Scarlatti, *Oratorii*
Scarlatti, Alessandro. *Gli oratorii.* 5 vols. to date. Edited by Lino Bianchi. Rome: De Santis 1964–.
Schering, *Beispielen*
Schering, Arnold, ed. *Geschichte der Musik in Beispielen.* Leipzig: Breitkopf & Härtel, 1931.
Schering, "Beiträge"
———. "Neue Beiträge zur Geschichte des italienischen Oratoriums im 17. Jahrhundert." *Sammelbände der internationalen Musikgesellschaft* 8 (1906–7): 43–70.

Schering, "Entlehnungen"
———. "Zum Tema: Händel's Entlehnungen." *Zeitschrift der Internationalen Musikgesellschaft* 9 (1907–10):244–47.
Schering, *Oratorium*
———. *Geschichte des Oratoriums*. Kleine Handbücher der Musikgeschichte nach Gattungen, vol. 3. 1911. Reprint. Hildesheim: Georg Olms, 1966.
Schnitzler, "Draghi"
Schnitzler, Rudolf. "The Sacred Dramatic Music of Antonio Draghi." Ph.D. dissertation, University of North Carolina at Chapel Hill, 1971.
Schnitzler, "Perti"
———. "The Passion-Oratorios of Giacomo Antonio Perti." M.F.A. thesis, Ohio University, 1967.
Schnoebelen, "Mass"
Schnoebelen, Anne [Sister Mary Nicole]. "The Concerted Mass at San Petronio in Bologna, ca. 1660–1730: A Documentary and Analytical Study." Ph.D. dissertation, University of Illinois, 1966.
Schrade, *Monteverdi*
Schrade, Leo. *Monteverdi: Creator of Modern Music*. New York: W. W. Norton, 1950.
Selfridge-Field, *Venetian*
Selfridge-Field, Eleanor. *Venetian Instrumental Music from Gabrieli to Vivaldi*. New York: Praeger, 1975.
Sesini, *Libretti*
Gaspari, Gaetano, ed. *Catalogo della Biblioteca del Liceo Musicale di Bologna*. 5 vols. Bologna: Libreria Romagnoli dall' Acqua and Cooperativa Tipografica Azzoguidi, 1890–1943. Vol. 5, *Libretti d'opera in musica*, edited by Ugo Sesini, 1943.
Shedlock, "Maugars"
Shedlock, J. S. "André Maugars." In *Studies in Music, by Various Authors, Reprinted from "The Musician,"* edited by Robin Grey, pp. 215–32. London: Simkin, Marshall, Hamilton, Kent, 1901.
Smither, "Carissimi"
Smither, Howard E. "Carissimi's Latin Oratorios: Their Terminology, Functions, and Position in Oratorio History." *Studien zur italienisch-deutschen Musikgeschichte, Analecta musicologica*, in press (11? [1976?]: 53–78).
Smither, "Dialogue"
———. "The Latin Dramatic Dialogue and the Nascent Oratorio." *Journal of the American Musicological Society* 20 (1967): 403–33.
Smither, "Laude"
———. "Narrative and Dramatic Elements in the Laude Filippine, 1563–1600." *Acta musicologica* 41 (1969): 186–99.
Smither, "Micheli"
———. "Romano Micheli's 'Dialogus Annuntiationis' (1625): A Twenty-Voice Canon with Thirty 'Obblighi.'" *Studien zur italienisch-deutschen Musikgeschichte 5, Analecta musicologica* 5 (1968): 34–91.
Smither, "Oratorio"
———. "What Is an Oratorio in Mid-Seventeenth-Century Italy?" In *Report of the Eleventh Congress, Copenhagen, 1972*, International Musicological Society, edited by Hendrik Glahn, Søren Sørensen, and Peter Ryom, 2: 657–63. 2 vols. Copenhagen: Wilhelm Hansen, 1974.

Smither, "Report"

———. "The Baroque Oratorio: A Report on Research Since 1945." *Acta musicologica* 48 (1976): 50–76.

Smolden, "Drama"

Smolden, William L. "Liturgical Drama." In *New Oxford History of Music*, edited by J. A. Westrup, Gerald Abraham, E. J. Dent, Anselm Hughes, and Egon Wellesz. Rev. ed. London: Oxford University Press, 1954–. Vol. 2, *Early Medieval Music up to 1300*, edited by Anselm Hughes, 1955, pp. 175–219.

Soldati, *Mamertino*

Soldati, Benedetto. *Il Collegio Mamertino e le origini del teatro gesuitico.* Turin: Ermano Loescher, 1908.

Solerti, "Cavalieri"

Solerti, Angelo. "Laura Guidiccioni Lucchesini ed Emilio de' Cavalieri." *Rivista musicale italiana* 9 (1902): 797–829.

Solerti, "Della Valle"

———. "Lettere inedite sulla musica di Pietro Della Valle a G. B. Doni ed una veglia drammatica-musicale del medesimo." *Rivista musicale italiana* 12 (1905): 271–338.

Solerti, *Melodramma*

———. *Gli albori del melodramma.* 3 vols. Milan: Remo Sandron, [1904].

Solerti, *Musica*

———, ed. *Musica, ballo e drammatica alla corte medicea dal 1600 al 1637: Notizie tratte da un diario con appendice di testi inediti e rari.* Florence: R. Bemporad & Figlio, 1905.

Solerti, *Origini*

———, ed. *Le origini del melodramma: Testimonianze dei contemporanei.* Turin: Fratelli Bocca, 1903.

Sommervogel, *Bibliothèque*

Sommervogel, Carlos, ed. *Bibliothèque de la Compagnie de Jesus.* 12 vols. Brussels: Oscar Schepens, 1890–1960.

Spagna, "Discorso"

Spagna, Archangelo. "Discorso intorno a gl'oratori." In *Oratorii overo melodrammi sacri.* 2 vols. Rome: Gio. Francesco Buagni, 1706.

Spagna, *Fasti*

———. *I fasti sacri.* Rome: Domenico Antonio Ercole, 1720.

Spagna, *Oratorii*

———. *Oratorii overo melodrammi sacri.* 2 vols. Rome: Gio. Francesco Buagni, 1706.

Spitz, *Renaissance*

Spitz, Lewis W. *The Renaissance and Reformation Movements.* Chicago: Rand McNally, 1971.

Statuti

Statuti della ven. Arciconfraternita del SS. Crocifisso in San Marcello di Roma. [Urbino: Venerabile Cappella del SS.mo Sagramento, per Antonio Fantauzzi, 1731.]

Steude, "Markuspassion"

Steude, Wolfram. "Die Markuspassion in der Leipziger Passionen-Handschrift des Johann Zacharias Grundig." *Deutsches Jahrbuch der Musikwissenschaft für 1969* 14 (1970; vol. 61 of *Jahrbuch der Musikbibliothek Peters*): 96–116.

Stollbrock, "Reuter jun."
  Stollbrock, L. "Leben und Wirken des k. k. Hofkapellmeisters und Hofkompositors Johann Georg Reuter jun." *Vierteljahrsschrift für Musikwissenschaft* 8 (1892): 289–306.
Stradella, *Oratori*
  Stradella, Alessandro. *Gli oratori*. Edited by Lino Bianchi. 1 vol. to date. [Rome]: Istituto Italiano per la Storia della Musica, presso L'Accademia Nazionale di Santa Cecilia, 1969–.
Suess, "Vitali"
  Suess, John G. "Giovanni Battista Vitali and the Sonata da Chiesa." Ph.D. dissertation, Yale University, 1962.
Symonds, *Reaction*
  Symonds, John A. *Renaissance in Italy: The Catholic Reaction*. New ed. 2 vols. London: Smith, Elder, 1906.
Tacchi-Venturi, *Compagnia*
  Tacchi-Venturi, Pietro, and Scaduto, Mario. *Storia della Compagnia di Gesù in Italia, narrata col sussidio di fonti inedite*. 2d ed. 3 vols. to date. Rome: Civiltà Cattolica, 1950–.
Tardini, *Modena*
  Tardini, Vincenzo. *I teatri di Modena: Contributo alla storia del teatro in Italia*. 3 vols. Modena: Forghieri, Pellequi, 1899–1902.
Taylor, *Indebtedness*
  Taylor, Sedley. *The Indebtedness of Handel to Works by Other Composers: A Presentation of Evidence*. Cambridge: Cambridge University Press, 1906.
Tempesta, *Roma*
  Tempesta, Antonio. *Roma al tempo di Clemente VIII: La pianta di Roma di Antonio Tempesta del 1593 ... con introduzione di Francesco Ehrle*. Le piante maggiori di Roma dei sec. XVI e XVII, riprodotte in fototipia a cura della Biblioteca Vaticana, no. 3. Facsimile. Vatican City: Biblioteca Apostolica Vaticana, 1932.
Tenneroni, *Inizii*
  Tenneroni, Annibale, ed. *Inizii di antiche poesie italiane religiose e morali con prospetto dei codici che le contengono e introduzione alle "laudi spirituali."* Florence: Leo S. Olschki, 1909.
Terry, *Rite*
  Terry, Richard R. *The Music of the Roman Rite: A Manual for Choirmasters in English-Speaking Countries*. London: Burns, Oates, & Washbourne, 1931.
Testi, *Seicento*
  Testi, Flavio. *La musica italiana nel seicento*. Storia della musica italiana da Sant'Ambrogio a noi, vols. [3–4]. Milan: Bramante, 1970–72.
Thoinan, *Maugars*
  Thoinan, Ernest. *Maugars . . . : Sa biographie suivi de sa "Response faite à un curieux sur le sentiment de la musique d'Italie."* 1865. Reprint. London: H. Baron, 1965.
Tintelnot, *Barocktheater*
  Tintelnot, Hans. *Barocktheater und barocke Kunst: Die Entwicklungsgeschichte der Fest- und Theater-Dekoration in ihrem Verhältnis zur barocken Kunst*. Berlin: Gebr. Mann, 1939.
Torchi, *Arte*
  Torchi, Luigi, ed. *L'arte musicale in Italia: Publicazione nazionale delle più importanti opere musicali italiane del secolo XIV al XVIII*. 7 vols. Milan: Ricordi, [1897–1908?]. Vol. 5, *Compositioni ad una e più voci, secolo XVII*, n. d.

Totti, *Roma*

Totti, Pompilio. *Ritratto di Roma moderna*. Rome: Mascardi, 1638.

Trevelyan, *History*

Trevelyan, Janet P. *A Short History of the Italian People from the Barbarian Invasions to the Present Day*. Rev. ed. London: G. Allen & Unwin, 1956.

Trevor, *Neri*

Trevor, Meriol. *Apostle of Rome: A Life of Philip Neri, 1515–1595*. London: Macmillan, 1966.

Tronsarelli, *Drammi*

Tronsarelli, Ottavio. *Drammi musicali*. Rome: Francesco Corbeletti, 1632.

Vasi, *Magnificenze*

Vasi, Giuseppe. *Delle magnificenze di Roma antica e moderna*. 10 pts. in 5 vols. Rome: Chracas, et al. (publisher varies), 1747–61.

Vatielli, "Bologna"

Vatielli, Francesco. "L'Oratorio a Bologna negli ultimi decenni del seicento." *Note d'archivio per la storia musicale* 15 (1938): 26–35, 77–87.

Vattasso, "Rappresentazioni"

Vattasso, Marco. "Le rappresentazioni sacre al Colosseo nei secoli XV e XVI secondo nuovi documenti tratti dall'archivio dell'Arciconfraternita di S. Lucia del Gonfalone." In *Per la storia del dramma sacro in Italia*, by Marco Vattasso, pp. 71–89. Studi e testi, vol. 10. Rome: Tipografia Vaticana, 1903.

Viale Ferrero, *Juvarra*

Viale Ferrero, Mercedes. *Filippo Juvarra: Scenografico e architetto teatrale*. Turin: Edizioni d'Arte Fratelli Pozzo, 1970.

Visconti, *Controriforma*

Visconti, Alessandro. *L'Italia nell'epoca della controriforma dal 1516 al 1713*. Storia d'Italia, vol. 6. Milan: Arnoldo Mondatori, 1958.

Vivaldi, *Juditha*

Vivaldi, Antonio. *Juditha triumphans: Sacrum militare oratorium*. Facsimile. Siena: Accademia Musicale Chigiana, 1948.

Vogl, "Oratorium"

Vogl, Hertha. "Zur Geschichte des Oratoriums in Wien von 1725 bis 1740." *Studien zur Musikwissenschaft* 14 (1927): 241–64.

Wagner, *Einführung*

Wagner, Peter. *Einführung in die gregorianischen Melodien*. Vol. 1, *Ursprung und Entwicklung der liturgischen Gesangsformen*, 3d ed., 1911. Vol. 2, *Neumenkunde*, 2d. ed, 1912. Vol. 3, *Gregorianische Formenlehre*, 1921. Reprint. 3 vols. Hildesheim: Georg Olms, 1962.

Wangemann, *Oratorium*

Wangemann, Otto. *Geschichte des Oratoriums von den ersten Anfängen bis zur Gegenwart*. 2d ed. Demmin: A. Frantz, 1882.

Ward, *Time*

Ward, Francis Alan Burnett. *Handbook of the Collection Illustrating Time Measurement*. Ministry of Education. Science Museum. 2 vols. London: Her Majesty's Stationery Office, 1958.

Warner, "Ottoboni"

Warner, Frederick E. "The Ottoboni Theatre." *The Ohio State Theatre Collection Bulletin* 11 (1964): 37–45.

Wasielewski, "Musikbericht"

Wasielewski, Wilhelm Joseph von. "Ein französischer Musikbericht aus der ersten Hälfte des 17. Jahrh." *Monatshefte für Musikgeschichte* 10 (1878): 1–9, 17–23.

Weil, "Forty Hours"
  Weil, Mark. "The Devotion of the Forty Hours and Roman Baroque Illusions."
    Journal of the Warburg and Courtald Institutes 37 (1974): 218–58.
Weilen, "Theater"
  Weilen, Alexander von. "Das Theater." In *Geschichte der Stadt Wien*, by Alter-
    tumsverein zu Wien, edited by Heinrich Ziermann, Albert Starzer, and
    Anton Mayer, vol. 6, pp. 333–456. Vienna: Adolf Holzhausen, 1897–1918.
Weilen, *Theatergeschichte*
  _____. *Zur Wiener Theatergeschichte: Die vom Jahre 1629 bis zum Jahre
    1740 am Wiener Hofe zur Aufführung gelangten Werke theatralischen
    Characters und Oratorien*. Schriften des österreichische Vereins für Bib-
    liothekswesen. Vienna: Alfred Hölder K. u. K. Hof- und Universitäts-
    Buchhändler, 1901.
Weinmann, *Konzil*
  Weinmann, Karl. *Das Konzil von Trient und die Kirchenmusik*. Leipzig: Breit-
    kopf & Härtel, 1919.
Weisbach, *Kunst*
  Weisbach, Werner. *Der Barock als Kunst der Gegenreformation*. Berlin: P. Cas-
    sirer, 1921.
Wellesz, "Opern"
  Wellesz, Egon. "Die Opern und Oratorien in Wien von 1660–1708." *Studien
    zur Musikwissenschaft* 6 (1919): 5–138.
Wessely-Kropik, *Colista*
  Wessely-Kropic, Helene. *Lelio Colista, ein römischer Meister vor Corelli:
    Leben und Umwelt*. Österreische Akademie der Wissenschaften,
    Philosophisch-Historische Klasse, Sitzungsbericht, vol. 237, Abhandlung 4.
    Veröffentlichungen der Kommission für Musikforschung, edited by Erich
    Schenk, bk. 3. Vienna: Hermann Böhlaus, 1961.
Wilkins, *Literature*
  Wilkins, Ernest Hatch. *A History of Italian Literature*. Cambridge, Mass.:
    Harvard University Press, 1954.
Willaert, *Concile*
  Fliche, Augustin; Martin, Victor; Duroselle, J. B.; and Garry Eugéne, eds. *His-
    toire de l'Eglise depuis les origines jusqu'à nos jours*. [Paris]: Bloud & Gay,
    1934–. Vol. 18, *Après le concile de Trente: La Restauration catholique,
    1563–1648*, by Léopold Willaert, 1960.
Williams, "Anerio"
  Williams, Nyal Zeno. "The Masses of Giovanni Francesco Anerio: A Histori-
    cal and Analytical Study with a Supplementary Critical Edition." 2 vols.
    Ph.D. dissertation, University of North Carolina at Chapel Hill, 1971.
Winter, "Studien"
  Winter, Carl. "Studien zur Frühgeschichte des lateinischen Oratoriums." *Kir-
    chenmusikalisches Jahrbuch* 42 (1958): 64–76.
Winterfeld, *Gabrieli*
  Winterfeld, Carl von. *Johannes Gabrieli und sein Zeitalter*. 3 vols. Berlin:
    Schlesinger'schen Buch- und Musikhandlung, 1834.
Wittkower, *Art*
  Wittkower, Rudolf. *Art and Architecture in Italy 1600 to 1750*. The Pelican
    History of Art. 3d rev. ed. [Harmondsworth, Middlesex]: Penguin Books,
    1973.

Wittkower, *Baroque*
  Wittkower, Rudolf, and Jaffe, Irma B., eds. *Baroque Art: The Jesuit Contribution*. New York: Fordham University Press, 1972.
Witzenmann, "Marazzoli"
  Witzenmann, Wolfgang. "Autographe Marco Marazzolis in der Biblioteca Vaticana (I)." *Studien zur italienisch-deutschen Musikgeschichte 6, Analecta musicologica* 7 (1969): 38–86.
Witzenmann, *Mazzocchi*
  _____. *Domenico Mazzocchi, 1592–1665: Dokumente und Interpretationen*. Analecta musicologica, vol. 8. Cologne: Böhlau, 1970.
Wolff, *Venezianische*
  _____. *Die Venezianische Oper in der zweiten Hälfte des 17. Jahrhunderts*. Theater und Drama, vol. 7. Berlin: Otto Elsner, 1937.
Wolff, "Vivaldi"
  _____. "Vivaldi und der Stil der italienischen Oper." *Acta musicologica* 40 (1968): 179–86.
Young, *Drama*
  Young, Karl. *The Drama of the Medieval Church*. 2 vols. Oxford: Clarendon Press, 1933.
Young, *Easter Sepulchre*
  _____. *The Dramatic Associations of the Easter Sepulchre*. University of Wisconsin Studies in Language and Literature, no. 10. Madison: n. p., 1920.
Zanetti, "Haendel"
  Zanetti, Emilia. "Haendel in Italia." *L'approdo musicale* 12 (1960): 3–73.
Zeno, *Lettere*
  Zeno, Apostolo. *Lettere di Apostolo Zeno, citadino veneziano, Istorico e Poeta Cesareo*. 6 vols. 2d ed. Venice: Francesco Sansoni, 1785.
Zeno, *Poesie*
  _____. *Poesie sacre drammatiche di Apostolo Zeno, Istorico e Poeta Cesareo, cantate nella imperial cappella di Vienna*. Venice: Cristoforo Zane, 1735.
Zeno, *Poesie*-Ger.
  _____. *Des Herrn Apostolo Zeno weil. K. K. Hofpoeten Schaubüne bibl. Begebenheit in XVII Schauspielen*. Translated by P. Obladen. Augsburg; n.p., 1760.
Ziino, "Della Valle"
  Ziino, Agostino. "Pietro Della Valle e la 'musica erudita': Nuovi documenti." *Studien zur italienisch-deutschen Musikgeschichte 4, Analecta musicologica* 4 (1967): 97–111.
Zorzi, "Venezia"
  Zorzi, Maria Antonietta. "Saggio di bibliografia sugli oratori sacri eseguiti a Venezia." *Accademie e biblioteche d'Italia* 4 (1930): 226–46, 394–403, 529–43; 5 (1931): 79–96, 493–508; 6 (1932): 256–69; 7 (1933): 316–41.

❧ Index

This index includes persons, places, institutions, terms, concepts, and works (musical, literary, architectural, and others in the visual arts). Page numbers in boldface type refer to pages that include music examples; numbers in italics refer to pages that include illustrations. The names of composers and librettists are placed in parentheses after the titles of their works, as follows: (composer/librettist), (composer and composer), (composer only), (—/librettist only).

churches associated with oratories: Chiesa Nuova, 45, 46, 47–48, 53, 79–80, 90, 123–24, 153, 154, 155, 159–64, 167, 187, 195, 210–11, 219, 259–60, 359; Madonna di Galliera, 91, 279, 327; Pantheon, the, 38, 159–60; San Firenze, 284, 286; San Giovanni dei Fiorentini, 44, 46, 48, 50, 260, 315; San Girolamo della Carità, 41–42, 43, 44, 47–49, 56, 121–24, 148, 159–60, 174n, 210–11, 259, 296, 337; San Marcello, 38, 208, 209, 214; San Sebastiano, 284; Santa Maria della Consolazione, 289–91, 308, 310, 356; Santa Maria della Fava, 289–91, 308, 310, 356; Santa Maria della Rotonda, 38, 159–60; Santa Maria dell'Orazione e Morte, 159–60; 164–65; Santa Maria in Vallicella (see churches associated with oratories, Chiesa Nuova); Santi Barbara e Ippolite, 279

Ciampoli, Giovanni, 147, 155–56, 164, 168–69, 205, 292n

Cifra, Antonio, 101–2, 110–13

Le cinque vergini prudenti (Draghi), 373n

Clama ne cesses (Carissimi), 223

Clari, Giovanni Carlo, 289

Clement VII (pope), 30–32, 209

Clement VIII (pope), 61, 73, 77

Clement IX (pope), 150. See also Rospigliosi, Giulio

Clement XI (pope), 260–61, 264, 274, 337, 347n

Clementine College, 261, 263

Clérambault, César-François-Nicolas, 432n

Clérambault, Louis-Nicolas, 433–34

Cola, Gregorio, 276

Colbert, Jean-Baptiste, 419

"Col fausto augurio" (Marazzoli), 194

Collège Louis-le-Grand, 420

Collegio Romano. See Roman College

Colombani, Quirino, 276

Colonia dell'Arcadia. See Accademia degli Animosi

Colonna, Giovanni Paolo, 220, 281–82, 304n, 308, 327, 328, 329, 330–32, 423

Colonna family, 315, 337

Il colosso della constanza (Pasquini), 293n

Combattimento di Tancredi e Clorinda (Monteverdi), 158–59

commedia dell'arte, 369

componimento sacro, 269, 275, 293, 376, 392–93

Componimento sacro per la festività del SS. Natale (Costanzi/Metastasio), 269, 272–73, 392

La Comtesse d'Escarbagnas (Charpentier/Molière), 420

Concerti morali e spirituali (Savioni), 165

concerto grosso instrumentation, 308, 318–20, 333, 345, 358

Concilio de'Farisei (D. Mazzocchi), 248

Concini, Concino, 416–17

confraternities: musical practices of, 22–24, 27–28; ceremonies of, 209–10; Arciconfraternita della Pietà dei Fiorentini, 44; Arciconfraternita della Santissima Trinità, 280; Arciconfraternita de' Santi Sebastiano e Rocco, 280; Archiconfraternita di Santa Lucia del Gonfalone, 27–28; Arciconfraternita di Santa Maria della Morte, 280; Compagnia della Purificazione di Maria Vergine e di San Zanobi detta de San Marco, 286; Compagnia dell'Arcangelo Raffaello detta la Scala, 286; Compagnia di San Jacopo detta del Nicchio, 286; Compagnia di San Sebastiano, 286; Confraternita della Santissima Trinità dei Pellegrini, 41; Confraternita de' Poveri della Regina de' Cieli, 280; Dottrina Cristiana, society of, 280; San Girolamo della Carità, 148, 195; Santa Maria dell'Orazione e Morte, 164–65; Venerabile Compagnia della Pietà della Natione Fiorentina, 260; Venerabile Compagnia detta de' Fiorentini, 280; Veneranda Compagnia della Carità, 280; Veneranda Confratelli di Santa Maria della Cintura, 280; Venerandi Confratelli del Santissimo Sacramento, 280

Congregation of San Carlo, 282, 299

Congregation of the Oratory (Bologna), 157n, 279–80, 299; inventories of, 90–91, 96–97, 123n, 186n, 191n, 279

Congregation of the Oratory (Florence), 259, 284–89

Congregation of the Oratory (Rome): composers and librettists with, 5, 55–56, 79–91, 119, 121–22, 150, 155–56, 169, 174, 205; and oratorio antecedents, 9, 24, 57–76, 87–91; beginnings of, 29, 42–53; social context of, 29–57; character of, 34, 47–48, 154; spiritual exercises of, 47–53, 77, 160–61, 163–64, 167; influence of on other oratories, 90, 278–79, 283–85; buildings for, 153–55; decrees of, 160–61; musical expansion of, 161–64. See also Neri, Philip

Congregation of the Oratory (Venice), 289–91

Contarini, Gaspero, 33

Conti, Francesco Bartolomeo, 375

Conti, Ignazio, 375

Lanciani, Flavio Carlo, 277
Landi, Stefano, 148, 157, 210
Lasso, Orlando di, 20, 24–25
lauda, 27, 56, 301; as oratorio antecedent, 12, 19, 22–24, 57–61, 62, **63–69**, 70, 71, 72–75; books for Roman Oratory, 39, 42, 57–75; books for Roman Oratory listed, 58–59; and Anerio, 124, 127, 129
"Laudate pueri" (Handel), 344
Laude, libro primo (printed by Petrucci), 24
Laude, libro secondo (printed by Petrucci), 24
Laudi, trattato e detti (Jacopone), 23–24, 57
Laurelli, Domenico, 277
Laurentino, Francisco, 277
Lazarini, Sebastiano, 277
Legrenzi, Giovanni, 290–91, 297, 304, 308, *309*, 310–14, 318, 348, 356, 423
Lent, Fridays of, 162, 259; and Latin oratorio, 209–11, 214, 219, 249, 251
Leo X (pope), 31
Leo XIII (pope), 61
Leopold I (Hapsburg emperor): as patron, 367–69, 370, 371–73, 398; as composer, 376, 396
libretto, oratorio, 179, 299, 305; origins of, 13–15; in later Baroque, 292–305. *See also* text, oratorio
Libro delle laudi spirituali (anon., 1589), 59–60, 70
Libro primo delle laudi spirituali (Razzi), 24n, 74
Licenza di Giesù da Maria (Arresti), 279
Life of Saint Mary Magdalene (anon.), 157
liturgical drama, 12, 20, 26–27, 377
Liuzzi, Fernando, 23
Lochon, Jacques-François, 433–34
Lope de Vega, 302n
Lotti, Antonio, 291, 380
Lotti, Giovanni, 148, 203, 205
Louis XII (king of France), 30
Louis XIII (king of France), 416–17
Louis XIV (king of France), 417–20
Lübeck: *Abendmusiken*, 12
Lucifer (Carissimi), 225n
Lulier, Giovanni Lorenzo, 277
Lully, Jean-Baptiste, 417–18, 425, 434
Lutheranism. *See* Germany, Protestant
Il lutto dell'universo (Leopold I), 396

M

Macque, Giovanni, de, 195
Madalena errante (D. Mazzocchi), 174
Maddalena ai piedi di Cristo (Caldara), 358
La Maddalena che va all'Eremo (anon.), 291n

La Maddalena penitente, 291n
madrigal, 12–13, 158; for an oratory, 6, 165–67; and *lauda*, 70, 72
madrigale (chorus), 197, 306, 311–12, 314, 332, 415
Madrigali à cinque voci et altri varij concerti (D. Mazzocchi), 158, **171–72**
Madrigali e canzonette spirituali (Bonini), 90–91
Magalotti, Lorenzo, 368
Mainz, 365
Mamertine College, 28
Manara, G. A., 293n
Manni, Agostino, 51, 60, 61, 89, 121; and Cavalieri, 83, 86n, 87
Maphae I, S.R.E. Card. Barberini nunc Urbani PP. VIII. poemata (D. Mazzocchi/M. Barberini), 147n
Marazzoli, Marco, 148, 194; Italian oratorios of, 168, 182, 187, *188*, 189, **190**, 191, **192**, 253; and *Oratorio di Santa Caterina*, 191, 300; Latin oratorios of, 250–51, 252, **253**, 254, 257, 419, 423
Marenzio, Luca, 73, 119, 126, 210
Maria Agapita (Hapsburg empress), 373
Maria Grazia, Sister, 261
Maria Maddalena (Bertali), 396
"Maria Magdalena et altera Maria" (Päminger), 25
Maria Theresa (Hapsburg empress), 392
Marie de Lorraine, duchesse de Guise, 420
Marino, Giovan Battista, 155–56, 168, 174, 179, 205, 228, 277
Mariotgi (singer), 266
Martini, Francesco, 90, 124
Il martirio de'santi Abundio prete (D. Mazzocchi), 168n
Il martirio di Santa Caterina (Caldara), 358
Il martirio di Sant'Eustachio (—/Pradalini), 276
Martyres (Carissimi), 224–25, 226n, 240n
Masini, Antonio, 260, 276
Mass, 19
Massenkeil, Günther, 229n
Massucci, Teodoro, 166
Mattheson, Johann, 8–9
Maugars, André, 210–13, 220, 251, 416
Mazarin, Jules (Mazzarini, Giulio), 148, 195, 417
Mazzei, Cesare, 205
Mazzocchi, Domenico, 147, 152, 158, 164, 166, 206; biography of, 168; Italian oratorios of, 168–69, *170*, **171**, 172, **173**, 174; use of instruments, 171–72; use of word painting, 171–72; Latin oratorios of, 247–48, **249**, 250–51, 254, 257, 419, 423

A NOTE ABOUT THE AUTHOR

*Howard E. Smither is professor of music at
The University of North Carolina at
Chapel Hill and a contributor to* Acta
musicologica, Analecta musicologica, Journal
of the American Musicological Society, The
Journal of Music Theory, The Musical
Quarterly, Notes, *and* Grove's Dictionary of
Music and Musicians, *6th edition.*

A NOTE ABOUT THE BOOK

Text set in Photocomposition Sabon

*Composition by The University of North
Carolina Press*

*Printed on sixty-pound 1854 paper by S. D.
Warren Company, Boston, Massachusetts*

*Cover stock, Columbia Bayside Vellum 3927,
and spine stock, Columbia Milbank Vellum
4487, by Columbia Mills, Incorporated,
Syracuse, New York*

*Printing and binding by Kingsport Press,
Kingsport, Tennessee*

*Designed by Joyce Kachergis, assisted by
Dariel Mayer*

*Published by The University of North
Carolina Press*

ENDPAPERS After a 1625 map of Rome (Maggi-Maupin-Losi, *Roma*).

Legend: 1. Church of San Giovanni dei Fiorentini.
2. Oratory known as Oratorio dei Fiorentini, Oratorio della
Pietà, and Sant'Orsola della Pietà.
3. Church of Santa Maria in Vallicella (Chiesa Nuova).